fish

To Florence and Sidney,
in the hope that
they will eat lots of fish

fish

SOPHIE GRIGSON
AND
WILLIAM BLACK

With photographs by
Georgia Glynn Smith

HEADLINE

Photographs © Georgia Glynn Smith
Fish portraits © Anna Koska

First published in 1998
by HEADLINE BOOK PUBLISHING

First published in paperback in 2000
by HEADLINE BOOK PUBLISHING

10 9 8 7 6

ISBN 0 7472 7677 3

Jacket design by Head Design

Interior design by Design/Section, Frome, Somerset

Home economist: Kit Chan

Printed and bound in Great Britain by
Butler & Tanner Ltd, Frome and London

HEADLINE BOOK PUBLISHING
A division of Hodder Headline Group
338 Euston Road
London NW1 3BH

www.headline.co.uk
www.hodderheadline.com

Sophie's Acknowledgements

First and foremost I'd like to thank my mother for teaching me to love fish at an early stage in my life and for showing me the beauty of the fish stall at the Wednesday market in Montoire. And, secondly, I'd like to thank William for renewing my delight in eating good fish and teaching me to distinguish the best from the second-rate. He despairs sometimes when I fail to recognise a particular species, but overall he's done a good job with this pupil.

This is the fifth book I've worked on with our editor, the lovely Heather Holden-Brown, whose patience and understanding are remarkable. I'd also like to thank Liz Allen, Doug Young, Susan Fleming and others at Headline for having confidence in this project, Deborah Savage for her editorial work on the recipes and Graham Webb for his design work. At home, I must give due to those who make our working lives possible – to Sue and Jennine, especially. Michele King and Wendy Malpass have retyped endless recipes without a murmur. Annabel Hartog (now Briggs), Ros Wilson and again Wendy Malpass have all helped me to test recipes, sharing the joys of a really good dish and not being too censorious over my failures. All of the above, and William, have proved enthusiastic tasters, full of comment and welcome suggestions.

William's Acknowledgements

My thanks to all those who have put up with endless questions, taught me, and supplied fish over the years. To Tony and Mark Allan and Ron Truss at Cutty's, not only for teaching me what a margin is but for their excellent fish and their ability to deliver it when asked; to Nick Howell at British Cured Pilchards for fish and valuable information from the south west; to Richard Cooke at Severn and Wye for his expertise on eels and salmon; to John Shelton at J. Bennett's Ltd for helping me brush up on my exotics; to Taha Sirag in Massawa for introducing me to the Red Sea; to Heine Dil in Holland for his help on freshwater fish; to Joannes Johannesen on the Faroe Islands for introducing me to the world of rotting fish; and to Alan Davidson for his help over the years and his overwhelming influence.

This book has been accumulating in my brain for many years. It was helped along its way by Joel Kissin at Conran Restaurants, but very special thanks must go to Heather Holden-Brown at Headline, who showed faith in the idea and has been a wonderful support through thick and thin. An enormous thank you also to Susan Fleming, who has managed to hone and tidy up my rambling text, and to Doug Young for his help and encouragement throughout.

Thanks also to Wendy, ably assisted by Holly, for organising and proofreading as well as recipe testing, to Anna Koska for her fine drawings, to Georgia Glynn Smith for her photographs, to Kit Chan for making the food look so enticing and to the Clerk and Superintendent of Billingsgate Market.

Lastly from me, an enormous thank you to Sophie for too, too many things to mention, but above all for her incredible ability to create recipes that people can recreate and which taste wonderful. No thanks to our lovely children for keeping her awake at night . . .

CONTENTS

Introduction

At about the time that Sophie was developing a passion for earrings, I was just beginning to develop one for fish. During the summer of 1979 I worked on an Irish oyster farm: easy, enjoyable work, made even easier by a ready supply of succulent oysters and Murphy's stout. When I started I was a complete fish dunce; indeed I was the one member of my family who resolutely refused to eat any fish at all. I had never seen, let alone eaten, an oyster, and had nearly jumped overboard when, many years earlier, we caught some flippingly fresh mackerel while sailing in Torbay.

My job was to sell the oysters in London, so off I set, giving samples here and there, gradually building up a regular network of chefs and merchants to supply. We built a storage tank to keep the oysters fresh, and soon started bringing salmon, the odd turbot, lobsters and huge creaking crawfish in with the oysters, which pleased the chefs enormously, for fish in those days was treated with a remarkable lack of interest by the few London merchants who supplied it.

One particular chef, Pierre Koffmann, who had opened his restaurant in Chelsea, La Tante Claire, a few years earlier, not only began to teach me the basics of buying fish but even cooked little bits of this and that when he saw me drooling over some of the dishes he created. Pierre is a very special sort of chef, multi-starred and immensely talented but still to be found, day in, day out, working in the kitchen rather than in a TV studio. He has a brilliant sense of taste. He once cooked a dish for my birthday that brought together two of my favourite fish – turbot and sea urchins – and created a meal so memorable that even I, with a notoriously fuzzy memory, can remember the look, the taste and even the texture over ten years later. I learned more about cooking by watching him than from anyone else until I met Sophie. Critically, I learned even more about produce, for the key to all successful cooking lies, as I quickly discovered, in the quality of the ingredients that you use, and never more so than when working with fish. Fish is fine but fragile food, an extremely good source of digestible protein, and it must be eaten when extremely fresh. Tired old fish, sad eyed and smelly, will never taste good however you cook it.

Initially I was surprised by just how little time it takes to cook fish. Sometimes seconds will do, and you seldom need to spend more than a few minutes when cooking a fillet of fish. Yes, precision is vital to avoid overcooking, but quite honestly there is no great mystery to it. With time and experience you develop a sixth sense and can almost 'feel' when it is ready.

Another great plus about eating fish is that it's actually good for you, a fact which is, by the way, firmly in the realm of science rather than opinion. People who eat a lot of fish *do* tend to live longer. The Japanese, among the world's greatest fish eaters, have one of the lowest death rates from heart disease. Interestingly, this is now beginning to rise as the younger generation eat more meat. Ideally, we should all eat fish at least twice a week, particularly fish such as mackerel or herring, which are rich in what are called Omega-3 fatty acids (more of which later on).

So, here is a food that is conveniently easy and quick to cook, which should surely appeal to everyone. And it does, in principle, but there's still a touch of reticence and ignorance out there. This is something that I well understand. My very first trip to a fish market was frankly embarrassing. When asking for some whiting, I was told by a sharp-tongued merchant, 'You're looking at them, mate!'

What this book aims to do is demystify fish, make it accessible, and maybe tempt you into being experimental. For things have changed a lot recently. Fish are now flown in from many obscure parts of the world to keep the markets full and fairly happy throughout the year, for if markets had to rely on fish caught in home waters many would find it hard to function, so difficult can supplies be at times.

Many of you will know that Sophie's mother, the late and great Jane Grigson, wrote a now classic work in the Seventies, which in later versions was called *The Fish Book*. Although, sadly, I never met Jane, I hope she would approve of what we are trying to do. Our intention is to produce a book to complement, rather than replace, her wonderful, erudite work. In combining my buying knowledge with Sophie's practical and approachable recipes, we hope that we have crafted a book that will serve for years to come. When Jane was writing in the Seventies, Patagonian toothfish and orange roughy were virtually unknown; even snappers were a rarity then, but these days they are easier to buy than turbot.

I have to admit to being exceedingly puritanical about eating fish. Dover sole should,

I believe, only be eaten grilled, and tuna always cooked rare. I deplore fussy, over-rich sauces with fish and have a special dislike for quirky, irrelevant ingredients (e.g. vanilla). Sophie is far more catholic in her tastes, and we have had some lively discussions over the recipes in this book. Every one has been tested and tried, and I have more than once been astonished at how fish that I have written off as being virtually inedible have become, in Sophie's hands, quite delicious. Marlin is the classic case. I have never liked it and would still never eat it cooked, but Sophie's Hawaiian Poke (page 165) works amazingly well. And it's also incredibly easy to make.

I suspect that many of you will say, it's all very well but if you tell us that we should only eat spankingly fresh fish, then where on earth are we to buy it? That, I admit, is not an easy problem to solve, but in this book we have devoted space to information on buying, and hope that it will not be in vain. Things *are* slowly improving. Britain has, perhaps a little late in the day, come to food with the passion of the recent convert. Fishmongers, for long written off as doomed, have smartened up and often have excellent fish on offer. Supermarkets, where many of us buy our fish these days, are well aware of the criticism about the poor quality of much of their fish on display and continue to improve their standards. We may not be a nation of overt complainers, fonder of a bit of covert

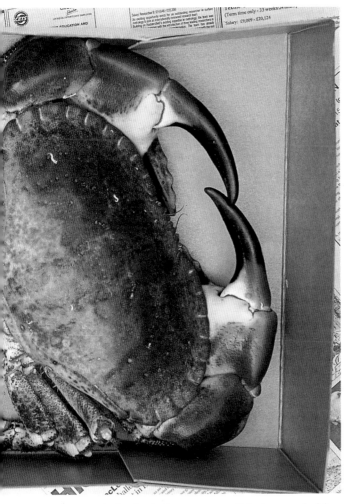

moaning, but don't be shy; if you see horrible fish on display, complain away until things improve. Cultivate your suppliers. Work with them. Find out what is around and possible rather than out of season and impossible.

However, no amount of moaning will bring fish back into the sea. This is more a question of good management, a theme very close to my heart. I have been working with fish for nearly twenty years now, not a long time by any means but quite long enough to notice a marked change – for the worse – in the size and quantity of fish available. Fish have been caught in a remarkably irresponsible way the world over, and continue to be so. Several fisheries have been fished to exhaustion and suddenly the ghastly possibility that if this all goes on we'll have virtually no fish left in the sea has begun to be openly discussed.

I hope and believe that good sense will prevail. Fish, the world's last great wild food resource, have to be caught sustainably or we'll all be deprived of one of the greatest sources of natural protein. Apart of course from farmed fish, they are hunted and caught by increasingly sophisticated boats with expensive and powerful machinery. At times too powerful. I recently looked at a very small but remarkably well managed fishery practically within spitting distance of London. Just off the Essex coast, a small stock of spring-spawning herring – unusual at this latitude, where most are autumn spawning – is fished with a remarkable degree of local co-operation between the buyers, the fishers and MAFF (Ministry of Agriculture, Fisheries and Food). This Thames herring fishery exists entirely within the six-mile limit, so is under local, rather than EU, auspices, and each year a few small boats set drift nets to catch the herring as they come inshore to spawn. The choice of fishing method is entirely theirs. The Ministry calls in the fishermen to discuss the year's quota and explains to them how they arrive at the TAC (Total Allowable Catch) for that season. Everyone is well aware that technologically the fishery is relatively unsophisticated, but its value is greater than the price at which the fish are sold. Families have lived off this fishery for generations, and intend to do so for many more. A few years back, trawlers were allowed on to the fishing grounds and wreaked havoc. And so they could today. A really powerful boat could fish in one day what the whole fleet fishes in a season. But what would that achieve? Nothing – rapidly. Perhaps this will be the way that fishing will develop in the future, where Essex fishermen will have a say over their fisheries, Basques over theirs, and so on.

What we will also begin to see is the increased use of selective fishing methods. It is basic common sense not to catch immature fish – the fishery's future if you like – and using nets with wide mesh or trawls with panels that enable younger fish to escape will ultimately help to keep the fishery in good condition. Leaving a fishery alone isn't always the answer either. What can happen in this case is that, with a limited food supply, as the population increases beyond a certain level the fish become smaller and scrawnier, so a fine balance has to be struck between too high and too low a level of fishing.

This is often an area of constant dispute between fishers and scientists, who, it has to be said, have made some massive blunders in the past. In this context good practice means constant consultation between all parties; agreement by consensus rather than diktat wherever possible, which has proved to be virtually impossible under the cumbersome bureaucratic system we have in the EU. Fishers often feel utterly remote from, and almost invariably hostile to, any decision that comes from Brussels.

Good practice should also avoid the ludicrous levels of discard – estimated to be as high as 40 million tonnes each year – where fish, marine mammals, turtles and even sea birds are thrown back into the sea dead because they are either over quota, unsellable, caught illegally or simply too small. Many fisheries are what are known as target fisheries: where fishers look for one species, which in the case of shoaling fish is quite easy to manage. But as soon as other species get mixed into the nets and trawls – what is called the by-catch – problems can occur if the level is too high.

The great hope in many people's eyes is fish farming, or aquaculture, which will inevitably supply increasing amounts of fish in the future. Here too, good sense will, I hope, eventually prevail over bad practice, for many fish farms are run in a far from ideal way. It isn't good practice, for example, to routinely dose salmon or prawns with antibiotics, since bacteria develop resistance. It isn't good practice to use organophosphates to control sea lice, or to blithely develop mangrove swamp areas as prawn farms when those mangroves provide vital nursery grounds for young fish. But, again, it is not all doom and gloom. The problems *can* be solved and, as we consumers have become increasingly inquisitive about the quality of the food that we eat, we will, I sincerely hope, be able to make sensible, informed decisions about what food – what fish in this case – we can afford in the very broadest sense of the word . . .

William Black

PART ONE

FISH AND FISHING

First Catch Your Fish . . .

Scattered around the coasts of Denmark and Ireland are a number of intriguing sites where mound upon mound of discarded ancient shells have been found by archaeologists. It seems that our Neolithic ancestors had a taste for shellfish, and more particularly the native oyster, *Ostrea edulis*. We may take this as an indication of impeccable good taste, but it is thought that this sea-front larder was instrumental in man's transition from hunter to farmer. I like this idea.

These mounds, known as shell middens, have provoked an intense debate among archaeologists. There are some who go for the wretched, miserable ancestor theory, which roughly proposes that things were so grim that they – the ancestors, that is – were driven to eating mountains of oysters. Others go for the happier, more idyllic notion that all they really wanted was to settle down and become civilised, and were merely helped on their way by the presence of oysters to eat.

The problem with shellfish is that they are, in nutritional terms, too insubstantial to sustain hard-working hunting people in the serious business of survival. This very practical consideration explains why, for instance, the Inuit (Eskimos) did not traditionally eat a lot of fish, and would not do so today if they hadn't given up their nomadic way of life. A morning's hunting for seal could bring meat, fat, skin and bone, which were of far greater nutritional and practical use than a measly cod.

Our own ancestors took another route. Farming the land increased the food available, and oysters and fish, both trapped in rock-pools and caught from primitive boats, helped provide a fairly easy calorie or two.

As boat-building became more refined, hand-lining and drift-netting were used more frequently and we even have records stretching right back to the fourteenth century of the beginning of one of the fishing industry's most intractable problems: the conflict between the trawlers and drift netters. In 1376 some aggrieved fishermen complained to King Edward III that their livelihood was threatened by the appearance of a 'subtly contrived instrument' called the 'wondyrchoun', a net that was pulled through the water and was even then thought to destroy too many young fish.

Our appetite for fish really took off in the Middle Ages when the Church decreed that good Christians should eat fish on Fridays and fast days. Christianity attached great importance to the effect that food had on the body and soul. Fish, being basically cold-blooded, were thought to be cooling, and as such they became the proper food to induce reflection and spirituality. Meat, from warm-blooded animals, was thought to induce lasciviousness.

But the demand from willing Christians presented a problem, for fresh fish was scarce inland. Castles, manor houses and monasteries had their own fish-ponds, full of freshwater bream, trout or pike, and often controlled the local fish traps and weirs as well. The kings of England even had a network of hunting lodges with fish-ponds attached. But the poor had to look elsewhere for their supplies. As in Greek and Roman times, dried and salted fish were more likely to be their everyday fare – usually cod or herring, found in great numbers around the coasts of Europe.

These fish-preserving techniques had been used for generations. During the declining days of the Roman Empire, Viking traders were to be seen in the Mediterranean, bringing fur and amber to the wealthy ports of Venice and Genoa. And sustaining them on their long journey southward was a strange dry food said to come from a fish that wasn't even caught in the Mediterranean, *Gadus morhua*, the cod.

The bitter climate of Scandinavia was ideally suited to drying fish. A cold, desiccating wind blows throughout much of the year and, just as winter is at its harshest, cod conveniently come to spawn in huge numbers off the Norwegian coast. Norway lacked grain but had fish in plenty, so trade between the north and the south, initially controlled by the powerful North

German Hanseatic League, supplied the north with wheat and the south with fish.

The Hansa also mined salt, and began to supply the Norwegians with enough to salt their cod, which was more to the taste of their southern customers than their somewhat indigestible dried fish. This was the beginning of an extraordinary link between the cold, fish-rich north and the southern Mediterranean for, as the Hanseatic League declined during the sixteenth century, salt from the natural pans of Iberia found a ready market with the salt cod producers far up north.

Up until the end of the fifteenth century, cod was almost exclusively supplied by Scandinavia. The big break on the cod front, though, came with John Cabot's discovery in 1497 of the cold green island of Newfoundland, where the sea was said to be so rich that fish could be caught by merely lowering a bucket over the side. The news soon filtered back to Europe. Portuguese, Basques, Normans and a few Bristolians set off to fish the cod, and the Grand Banks Fishery came into being. The conditions were perfect: cold, nutrient-rich water and a wide continental shelf. The only problem was the distance between this new-found land and Europe. The solution, once again, lay with salt.

There were two options: firstly, to salt the fish on board and, secondly, to dry or salt it on the shore. The Portuguese, Spanish and French had access to cheap domestic salt from their coastal salt-pans, so they tended to salt the fish on board and finish it off on land back home. The hot sun produced a much drier fish, preferred by Spaniards and Portuguese to this day, than the cod that was finished in Newfoundland and transported back ready salted.

Cod from America, both salted and dried, came flooding into Europe, upsetting the home-based fisheries. In 1506 the Portuguese king slapped a 10 per cent duty on all cod from America, and in 1542 Henry

VIII forbade the purchase of cod from foreigners, to encourage the English fleet to take advantage of what was an extremely lucrative fishery. By the end of the century the English presence in Newfoundland was as strong, if not stronger, than that of the Portuguese, who were the first to develop the fishery in a big way.

The English connection with Newfoundland has had a more lasting impact for, unlike the Spanish and Portuguese, they needed the land to process the cod. Every year, more settlers sailed out with the fleet. Shipwrights, merchants and opportunists settled in the harbours and spent the winters on the island. French and Portuguese fishermen were threatened and harassed so effectively by the English that quite quickly the names of the towns and harbours were anglicised, and have remained so to this day.

The fishing fleet became extremely important to the Crown. Not only did it provide the monarch with sailors and navigators of great skill but it also employed thousands of people. Queen Elizabeth I tried to make both Wednesday and Saturday fast days, in order to 'mayneteine fisshermen'. But such intervention wasn't popular, and laid her open to criticism for 'pro-Catholic' leanings. By Cromwell's time, fasting days were summarily dismissed as being 'rags of Rome'.

During the Reformation, fish consumption in Britain dropped. With the Church's reduced influence, people preferred eating meat, which was more readily available. Charles II tried in vain to prevent the fish trade from collapse. In 1677 amid much fanfare he set up the Royal Fishery Company, but this noble attempt came to nothing. Dukes and earls were on the board and promises were made to the industry, but almost all of the £12,000 capital – a vast sum in those days – was spent on equipment, which was captured by the French. In 1680 the company collapsed.

Pickled salmon and oysters as well as salt fish had fed the working classes for generations but fresh fish had always remained a luxury that they simply couldn't afford. During the Industrial Revolution, second-rate fresh fish became available, and were used by the growing fish and chip trade. Fish and chip shops, or chippies, appeared in all the major towns and cities of Britain, while costermongers continued to buy huge amounts of dubious-quality fish at the Friday market

at Billingsgate, then sold it fried in the streets of London.

It wasn't until the advent of the railway that fresh fish became more widely available. Much of it was caught using drift nets, nets that were simply laid in the sea, and into which the fish swam. In the middle of the nineteenth century, however, a seine net, an extremely efficient fishing method that involved *surrounding* a shoal of fish with a net, began to be used to catch Scottish herrings in the Firth of Forth. Violent disputes broke out between the seiners and the drift netters but seining was highly profitable and here to stay. Drift netters continued to protest that much of the juvenile stock was being destroyed, and in 1863 a Royal Commission was set up to look at the situation in detail.

It produced a momentous report, long in the making and typically Victorian in spirit. One of the Royal Commissioners, the Victorian scientist T. H. Huxley, became a vociferous spokesman for liberating all fisheries from any control whatsoever. 'Every legislative restriction,' he told the audience at the opening of the International Fisheries Exhibition in 1883, 'means that a simple man of the people, earning a scanty livelihood by hard toil, shall be liable to fine and imprisonment for doing that which he and his fathers before him have been free to do.'

The fishing fleet entered into this free-for-all with gusto. Steam trawlers replaced sailboats and Hull and Grimsby became the premier fishing ports of Britain. By 1909 there were 514 steam trawlers and 82 well smacks – boats specifically designed to keep fish alive – working from Grimsby alone. The boats became bigger and the fish and chip trade continued to grow but, almost as soon as Huxley's words were uttered, reports started coming back that perhaps this idea of unlimited largesse was mistaken. Many had assumed that fish were God's gift to man, and were available in infinite supply. Fishermen knew better and, as stocks diminished, they had to sail further afield to catch their cod. And so the distant-water fleet came into being. Based again in Hull and Grimsby, huge trawlers regularly steamed towards the far northern fisheries off the Faroes and Iceland.

By the 1970s catches were declining rapidly, and

when Iceland got tough, refusing to allow the fleet access to the fishing grounds, the resultant Cod War sounded the death knell for the distant-water fleet.

So far as most of the fishing industry was concerned, joining the Common Market was not a good idea at all. 'Our' fish became 'their' fish, and fisheries were perceived by many to be a sacrificial lamb offered to the gods in Brussels. The Common Fisheries Policy (CFP) was, from a British point of view, a stitch-up but, however you look at it, there is a fundamental problem in that there are simply too many boats fishing too few fish. The longer this over-capacity continues, the worse the situation will become.

But quite how one reduces the fishing effort, as it is called, is unclear. Laws may be fine in theory, mesh sizes and fishing times can be restricted, but what's missing is a vital sense of co-operation. Fishermen react with indignation when they are obliged under European law to throw away overquota fish. It is a complex and highly politicised debate, but there are some fundamental principles to bear in mind.

However fish are caught it is important that a viable population is left in order to reproduce and maintain the ecosystem (see page 19). At present, too much of the fish 'capital' is being eaten into; the interest went a long time ago. But what can be done?

It is, for example, technically possible to make fishing more selective. Nets can be fitted with special panels to allow juvenile fish to escape. Long lines can be made less destructive to sea birds. Turtle Excluding Devices (TEDs), whale and dolphin warning devices all exist, but must be combined with an overall policy that is effective, relevant and applicable.

Recently a new idea has come to the attention of the fishing industry which may provide a way forward. The WWF (World Wildlife Fund for Nature) and Unilever have come together to form the Marine Stewardship Council (MSC). The idea is that the MSC will allow fish and fish products from a sustainable, well-managed fishery to bear a logo that the consumer will recognise. Suppliers and producers would then have to prove that their products are up to scratch, before the potentially awesome force of the consumer moves into action. It is an attractive idea; so far no one else has managed to make this work. Perhaps you, the consumer, will.

The Bad News

- The FAO reports that 70 per cent of the world's commercially important marine stocks are fully fished, overexploited, depleted or slowly recovering.

- Worldwide, governments pay an estimated $54 billion per year in fisheries' subsidies to an industry that catches only $70 billion worth of fish.

- Contemporary fishing practices kill and waste 18–40 million tonnes of unwanted fish, seabirds, sea turtles, marine mammals and other ocean life annually – one-third of the total world catch.

The Good News

- People who eat a high level of fish tend to live longer; the Japanese, for example, have the lowest level of heart disease in the industrialised world, and their fish consumption is one of the highest.

- All fish, but particularly fatty fish such as mackerel and tuna, are a good source of Omega-3 fatty acids. These polyunsaturated fats make the blood less likely to clot, so people who eat fatty fish regularly have a lower risk of heart attacks. If you have had the misfortune to have one anyway, you should start eating fish, even cans of sardines, as soon as possible. A diet high in Omega 3 will significantly decrease your chances of another heart attack, so an oily fish diet is definitely to be recommended.

- In the book, fish that are rich in Omega 3 have been marked with a ♥.

What Is A Fish?

All manner of creatures can be found swimming in the seas and rivers of the world: flat fish, fat fish, carnivores, lethal fish, transparent fish, creatures with eight arms and some with ten legs. Tread on the stonefish, *Leucanthus horridus*, and it can kill you, while the charming *candirü*, a small Amazonian catfish, can swim up a stream of urine and lodge itself in your urethra. But most of the fish that concern us here are homely, everyday folk: the haddocks, pollacks and lings of this world.

Fish do everyday things such as sleep (a parrotfish constructs a nest of mucus as it goes to bed each night) and I have read that sharks fart to alter their natural buoyancy. The sea is not quite the peaceful haven you might have imagined. Apart from these shameless sharks, you may come across singing whales and grunting fish. The gurnard, for instance, is a notorious grunter, as is the cod, and there is a whole group of fish called croakers because, yes, you've guessed it, they croak.

Structurally, fish are fairly uniform. Being both surrounded and supported by water, they have no great gravitational force to deal with, so their muscles are mostly concerned with movement. They have an internal skeleton surrounded by muscle tissue, which is rich in protein; a vascular system; a swim bladder that controls buoyancy; and a two-chambered heart with blood like ours, which transports oxygen to muscle tissue. A fish's blood flows more slowly than our own and, since it would be very expensive to heat in fish terms, tends to be nearer the temperature of the surrounding water. This is why fish are basically cold blooded. However, it is not quite as simple as that. Some species of tuna, for example, have a body temperature higher than the water, which, as we will see, presents the buyer with particular difficulties.

Fish are mostly flat or round, with either a bony or a cartilaginous skeleton. Flat fish, with their eyes stuck firmly on top of their head, often sit indolently on the sea bed, eating the odd creature that passes by. Such fish have delicate, pristine white flesh, rich in what are called 'fast twitch fibres' which enable them to move rapidly in pursuit of prey. But these short bursts of energy, however intense, are just about all they can manage. Long-distance swimmers – bullet-shaped, super-fast fish such as mackerel and tuna – have redder, fattier flesh which contrasts starkly with the flat fish's virginal whiteness, and they can swim for much longer at a sustained high speed.

This redness of the flesh comes not from blood, as one might imagine, but from a substance called myoglobin, found in the muscle tissue. This stores vital oxygen, enabling the fish to convert its reserves of fat into energy. The structure of these muscles is important. When you cook a fish you can usually see that the meat falls into quite clear sections, or flakes. These flakes are simply blocks of muscle tissue, which in a live fish contract in a sort of syncopated rhythm right along the length of the fish like a piscine Mexican wave, causing it to swim. The muscle blocks, or myotomes, are only thinly connected to each other, giving the fish its characteristically fragile flesh.

A fish has a brain, a sense of smell, and a network of direction-finding, pressure-sensitive channels running along the side of its body. This is called the lateral line and, with a few exceptions, it is covered by scales. These scales serve a dual purpose. Firstly, they protect the body and, secondly, they help counteract the osmotic pressure from the sea, which continually draws out water from the fish. In the sea, a fish has a lower salt level than the surrounding water, so it has to increase its salt level to prevent dehydration caused by water being drawn out. This is why bony sea fish continually drink sea water, retaining much of the salt. Cartilaginous fish, such as rays and sharks, have come up with a different solution and actively retain salts from within (see page 92).

When you buy a fish, you may be amazed by the variety of colour on the skin. Brighter, brilliantly coloured fish tend to come from warmer waters, areas

rich in colourful seaweeds or coral. Some of these fish are herbivorous, and taste less pronounced than their meat-eating cousins. Others, such as the superb, multi-coloured groupers, are definitely carnivorous, and the mesmerising mahi mahi is no vegan. Colour, of course, is also used to attract a mate; the male coho salmon changes skin colour dramatically as it swims upstream during the spawning season, becoming quite a lurid shade of red. A surprising number of deep-water fish are also red, due to the properties of light at these murky depths, which actually makes red seem blue and so acts as a sort of camouflage.

Carnivorous hunting fish are positive dullards by comparison. Blending in with the background silver blue of the sea is critical for them, so a silvery underbelly and dark blue top are almost *de rigueur*. Such dullness is relative. A live tuna has an exquisite blue sheen on its upper side and a gloriously mottled silver underbelly – colours that meld perfectly when looked at from above or below. It is a transient beauty, fading fast when the fish dies, but you can get some idea of it by visiting an aquarium or, better still, by diving to see the fish in their purest, natural state.

Fish, of course, are not the sole inhabitants of the sea. There are the amazing molluscs, which include the single-shell gastropods, bivalves such as oysters and clams and, the most extraordinary of all, creatures called cephalopods which, as the Greek derivation suggests, seem to have their feet and head directly joined. These are the ten-legged squid and cuttlefish and the eight-legged octopus, the geniuses of the sea, whose prehistoric appearance belies a remarkable level of sophistication and intelligence.

Lastly there are the delicate-fleshed marine invertebrates called crustaceans, creatures with decidedly indelicate habits. They include lobsters and crabs, are mainly scavengers, and are found all over the world, primarily in shallow water.

Marine Ecosystems

Below sea fish, in an evolutionary sense, ranges a whole load of increasingly minuscule creatures that constitute the complex network known as the marine ecosystem. Some of the simplest are called phytoplankton, which live on the surface, need nutrients and sunlight to survive, and are carried by wind and currents. Phytoplankton are the breakfast, lunch and dinner of the more mobile zooplankton, which move between the surface and the lower levels of the sea. These zooplankton tend to avoid sunlight, and come to the surface at night, as do the creatures who live off them, which is one reason why so much fishing is done at night.

The nutrients upon which phytoplankton and zooplankton feed – mainly phosphates, nitrates and some silicates – are found in the shallower coastal areas where light is in good supply. There are also a few places around the world where currents well up from the deep, providing the phytoplankton with another rich source of food. So coastal zones and these upwelling areas are the richest places of all for fishing.

Around the Arctic, as the days lengthen and the temperature rises, a spring plankton bloom kickstarts the system into frenetic activity. Cod and other fish spawn in these warmer, nutrient-rich waters, feeding off the fish that feed off the zooplankton, which in turn feed off the phytoplankton. And that is the essence of what is called a food web.

The beach-bum's idyll of crystal-clear warm water is not as rich an area for fish as these rather more inhospitable cold-water seas. Heat causes a thermocline barrier in the water, above which phytoplankton are quickly used up and where there is little interchange between the lower and upper levels of water. The thermocline can work nearer home, too. On summer days when the sun shines and the wind blows feebly, fishing boats don't always come back with nets bursting (and this has nothing to do with the Spanish). As the water becomes cold again, and vital nutrients are stirred up by gales and currents, the system fares much better.

Some fish travel enormous distances to follow seasonal variations in food supply. The adult European eel leaves fresh water in the autumn to travel the 3,000-odd miles to the Sargasso Sea (in the Atlantic) to spawn. It seems at first to be a most peculiar thing for a fish to do, but the Sargasso is particularly rich in seaweed and provides an excellent basis for this eel love-park. Newborn elvers set out to swim back to the rivers their parents inhabited, a journey that takes them three years to complete. Somehow they make it, swimming and riding the ocean currents, a remarkable feat for such apparently insignificant, minuscule fish.

Pelagic fish, which live on or near the surface, also follow the ocean's currents. Herring and mackerel are pelagic, fatty and fast-moving fish that often congregate in huge shoals in the upper levels of the sea. The smaller the fish, the bigger the shoals tend to be; larger fish such as tuna become increasingly solitary the older they get.

The dynamics of a shoal of fish are fascinating. Recent research has shown that the mesmerising syncopated movement of a shoal of anchovies relies on each fish looking at the angle of the scales on the lateral line of the others and reacting accordingly. This weaving, ducking and diving of thousands of fish almost simultaneously is one of the most captivating sights under the water.

Demersal fish live on or near the bottom of the sea. They include cod and haddock as well as all the flat fish. One way of telling how fish feed is to see whether they have barbels under their chins, as, for example, cod do. These barbels are used to feel around the murky depths for things to eat. As the sea bottom can also be quite near the surface, reef-dwelling fish such as snappers and groupers are also called demersal.

Further down in the deepest depths of the ocean there is a mysterious world that remains largely unexplored. Bizarre worms have been found living off hot sulphurous underwater springs thousands of feet below the surface. Although there are few fish living this far down, some species, such as orange roughy and grenadier, can live at depths below 1,000m (3,280 ft) and are fished by enormously powerful boats. We don't really have enough information about what goes on at this level. We know that fish grow slowly, but their life cycles are still somewhat mysterious. We need to tread carefully when exploiting these deep waters which are particularly sensitive to overfishing.

PART TWO

BUYING, PREPARING AND COOKING FISH

On Buying Fish

You don't need any great skill when buying fish. It all boils down to common sense. Ideally, fish should be eaten within two or three days of being caught, but there are clear, easily remembered indicators that will guide your choice. Be an utterly ruthless buyer. Shop in a different way: go and see what's good and then choose. It's well worth cultivating your suppliers. They appreciate interest and the more interested you are the better service you should get. Ask your local shop, or fish counter at the supermarket, to tell you when the fish gets delivered, and then make sure you buy that day. Try not to store it for more than 24 hours in a domestic fridge; it's always better to eat fish on the day you buy it.

Buying: A Quick Guide

Fresh whole fish Bright, full eyes, clear skin, hard to the touch, clean smell, clear slime, no missing scales, bright red gills, clean gut cavity.

Fresh fillets, steaks etc. Clean, unfishy smell, firm to the touch, clear colours on skin.

Fresh squid etc. Clear white colour to body. Clear, bright eyes, fresh smell. No red tinge to skin.

Fresh shellfish Tightly shut shells, clean smell, shells shut if touched. Should feel heavy and full.

Live crustaceans Lively, tail springs back under body when picked up, well-worn feet in lobsters and crabs. Avoid any with frothing mouths.

Preserved fish

Salt cod Thick, white fillet, cleanly cut and split at head end. No gashes or blood spots on the flesh.

Smoked fish Good smoky smell, firm texture, consistent colour.

Caviar Clean smell, unbroken eggs.

Frozen fish No freezer burn. Prawns not too heavily glazed.

The Basic Rules: Look/Touch/Smell

It helps to understand what happens to a fish when it dies so let's look at the fish and its post-death experience.

As soon as any animal dies, the process of decomposition begins. A natural product of converting energy in muscles is lactic acid, which is normally carried away in the bloodstream. As the fish dies and the blood stops flowing, lactic acid builds up in the muscle tissue, causing the muscle fibres to combine temporarily. This leads to a general stiffening of the flesh known as *rigor mortis*.

The longer the fish stays in *rigor*, then the longer the whole process of decomposition is delayed. Much depends on the way it died. Fish that have been trawled or that have flapped around a lot use up glycogen and don't stay in *rigor* for long. But beware. If you cook the fish in *rigor*, not only will it be tricky to fillet but it also tends to fall apart when cooked.

The muscle fibres of fish have very little interconnecting tissue and what there is is very delicate. During *rigor* these fibres appear to be particularly weak and the larger flakes of fish – the broad band of muscles known as myotomes – easily separate. In order to get things just right when cooking, this delicacy has to be respected. Wait until the *rigor* disappears, which it will in a matter of hours. This is when you should cook your fish: immediately post *rigor mortis*.

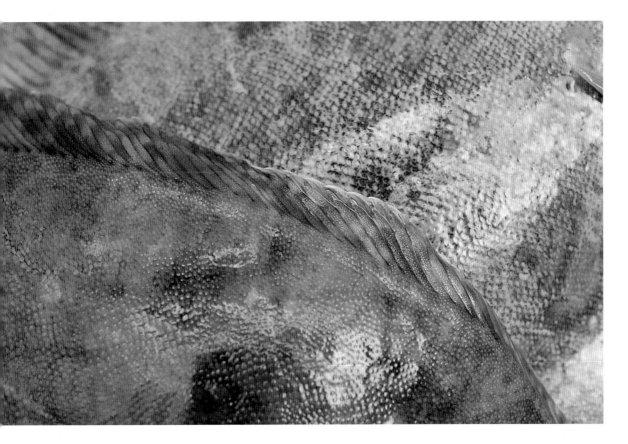

Fresh Fish

Look

Look a fish straight in the eye and if its eyes are bright, clear and lively, this could be the fish to go for. In time you will really need to do little else, since experience will give you a sixth sense. But to support your choice, check out the gills (they should be bright red, not a dull brown) and the colours on the skin, which should be bright and look natural. The slime that covers fish in water becomes opaque when old and stale, so only buy if the slime is clear. If you're buying a gutted fish, make sure that the gut cavity, which can harbour a lot of bacteria, is clean and dry.

Touch

A fresh fish should feel hard to the touch and your finger shouldn't leave a mark when you press it into the flesh. The flesh of fresh fish quickly springs back to its original shape.

Smell

Fresh fish don't necessarily smell of ocean breezes and seaweed. They often have a quite characteristic smell but what amazes many people is just how un-'fishy' it can be. This classic fishy smell comes from decomposition, and the art of buying is to outmanoeuvre the action of bacteria and enzymes.

As described elsewhere, cartilaginous fish – skate and shark etc. – retain salts such as urea within their bodies in order to counteract the osmotic pull from the sea. This urea can quickly turn to ammonia, and if you ever catch a whiff of it from a skate wing or shark steak, stay away, whatever anyone says.

Shellfish

Shellfish should be alive when bought. The exception is scallops, which are often sold out of the shell, or 'shucked', and are fine unless they have been soaked in water to plump them up.

Oysters, clams and mussels should be tightly closed and feel heavy and full rather than empty and hollow. Tap the shell and if they sound hollow don't use them. The shellfish should be full of liquor, i.e. sea water. If you touch them they should shut tightly and not twitch vaguely.

Crustaceans

Lobsters and crabs are sold alive or freshly cooked. Only buy a cooked crustacean from a regular, trustworthy supplier. A lobster or crayfish that has been cooked alive will have its tail tightly curled in towards its body. One with a floppy tail may have been cooked when dead, and should be avoided.

Live crustaceans should be lively and react vigorously to being picked up. A lobster or crayfish will thwack its tail and hold it tightly into its body; a crab should try and pinch you. Just before they expire, they tend to froth at the mouth so these will need to be cooked immediately. Langoustines are rarely sold alive, and can be used fresh.

Where to Buy Fish

An island surrounded by some of the richest fisheries in the world, blessed with sophisticated roads and railways, should be the ideal place to buy fish. Wrong. Great Britain Inc. is hopelessly served by fish shops and I am not altogether sure why. It's to supermarkets that many of us have to turn, not always happily, for our regular supplies of fish.

Supermarkets have to buy everything in massive quantity and purchases are centralised, computerised and somewhat remote. They appear to be trying hard to create a fishmonger's counter that appeals to us all and the quality can, let it be said, be excellent. The problem I have had with them is that the staff do not always appear to be specifically trained to deal with fish, and therefore cannot match the service provided by a high-street fishmonger.

For those of you with a good local fishmonger the situation may be easier, for it's likely that he/she will have a wealth of knowledge and experience to guide you, and a fishmonger can be more flexible about

supplies. But times are hard. The prices offered by supermarkets constantly undercut them, so the only way fishmongers can survive is to sell a top-quality product and service.

Markets

I have a great love and passion for fish markets. I hope I won't put you off in the pages to come by too many mentions of France and Spain but you have to admit their street markets are on a level far above our own.

Sophie's house in France is far from the sea, in the Loir valley, and the local town, Montoire, is neither too touristy nor too twee. It is a standard country town, where everyone knows M. le Maire, and the market comes twice a week to the Grande Place. Old ladies drive Deux Chevaux too fast through the narrow streets and clutch squawking chickens to their ample bosoms. The fishmonger, a ruddy-faced Breton called M. Delépine, bends over backwards to buy the best and, possibly because he knows I'm a fussy customer, will sometimes keep a perfect *turbotin* aside for me in his enormous truck, iced up and ready to go. This may be the stuff of summer holidays but why can't we have it here, *now*!

I would love to see street markets take off in this country. I would love to walk between stalls of glistening fish and sweet-smelling oysters. I would love to struggle past hysterical fathers squabbling over the last line-caught bass but, sadly, we are a little far away from this fishy paradise.

Fish markets exist on several levels. Wholesale markets supply the fish shops and market stalls, and are mostly found away from the city centres. Many are being forced to spend huge amounts of money on plastic walls and refrigerated stalls to conform to what *grand frère* in Brussels deems necessary.

They, in turn, are supplied by coastal fish markets, which can send fish to just about anywhere using the network of enormous trucks that ply the Continent. Some of these markets might let you wander in, but do try to let everyone get on with the business in hand. Fish auctions can be feverish, and much rushing around isn't conducive to a leisurely inspection. If you do want to visit one, a) check that it's allowed and b) try and look at the fish just before the auction starts.

Some of the best markets are found in small towns or cities, where the public are welcome and are the market's *raison d'être*. Take La Boquería in Barcelona. It's one of those buildings that buzzes. Turn the corner and walk into the market, where lights blaze and fish glint; there are piles of wild mushrooms, huge hams, cheeses and vegetables aplenty. This for a city seems an eminently practical and much more human way of buying food.

Thousands of miles away in Sweden, there's another market, in a fine building of brick, iron and glass, which has an entirely different range but the same vibrancy and bustle. Stockholm's Östermalms Saluhall not only has stalls that sell food but also has many where you can actually eat it. This is the land of herring, crispbread, lingonberries and reindeer, but in the fish department it is the herring that reigns supreme. You can snack on S.O.S. – a plate of *sill* (herring), *ost* (cheese) and *smör* (butter) – or dip into some delightfully named *sikrom*, or whitefish roe.

Markets should thrive on local variety and tastes. We have some over here that work well. Shrewsbury market sells local bacon, hams and cheese, and is more than just a source of cheap food. There are people there both knowledgeable about and interested in produce, which always helps in a food market. Let's hope that producers get their marketing act together and transform Britain's dull streets into markets of astonishing variety. End of market diatribe.

- This book will, I hope, be taken on holiday and used whenever you have time for a bit of market wandering. Where possible, I have given local names to guide you but if there's anything you've never seen before, be adventurous and give it a go.

Keeping Fresh Fish Fresh

Fish are cold blooded and their metabolism functions at a lower temperature than that of warm-blooded animals. Their enzymes also function at a lower temperature, so particular care must be paid to keeping fish cool at all times; if you don't you will unleash awesome forces. Enzymes are released by the action of lactic acid on cell walls. When liberated, they start acting on all the muscles, causing them to break down and decompose into amino acids, which can taint the fish.

As the fish ages, an amino acid called trimethy-lalamine, widely found in fish from the sea, degrades under the influence of lactic acid into trimethylamide, which gives that nasty smell so many (wrongly) attribute to fresh fish. As well as this we have to watch out for the action of bacteria, which can also lead to the degradation of amino acids. Cleanliness is not only next to godliness it is also good practice when dealing with any food.

Cross-contamination, dirty knives, hands and work surfaces are all good news for bacteria, which will happily jump from meat to fish with at times dire, even

fatal, consequences. Bacteria exist in the gut cavities of fish, in ice, in fridges and on other foods, so great care and attention must be paid at all times to simple hygiene. Bacteria multiply rapidly in the warm, so be doubly sure to keep the fish well iced and cool at all times. You could easily spend a lot of money on some fish, leave it in a hot sunny car for a few hours and it will begin to spoil alarmingly fast.

Storing Whole Fish and Cephalopods

Fridge temperature: between 0 and 2°C
If possible, keep whole fish on the bone, but try and make sure that they are gutted and gilled; they keep better that way. If you can't arrange the gilling, then go for the gutting. Check that the inside of the gut cavity is clean and dry. Wash it out under gently running cold water, and pat dry with a kitchen towel before you put the fish in the fridge.

Fish should be kept under cling film, or under a clean damp cloth which should be changed every twenty-four hours. Do not keep fish for more than forty-eight hours, absolute maximum, in a domestic fridge. If at all possible, eat it on the day of purchase.

Make sure that if the fish is sitting on a dish or plate it isn't lying in a pool of smelly melt water, which will also be rich in bacteria.

Storing Fish Fillets

Fridge temperature: between 0 and 2°C
Keep the fillets on a clean plate or tray in the fridge, under cling film or a clean damp cloth, for no more than forty-eight hours. The optimum fridge temperature is just above 0°C.

Storing Shellfish

Fridge temperature: 2°C
Live shellfish should be stored in the salad compartment of a fridge under a wet tea towel (or seaweed if available). Oysters will keep for several days and, as with all large bivalves, should be stored cup-side down.

This is because they can lose their liquor if stored at an angle, when they naturally relax their muscles every now and again. Scallops will stay alive on the shell for about twenty-four hours and should then be taken out of their shell and used. Never store shellfish, particularly fresh mussels, in fresh water, which kills them.

Storing Live Crustaceans

Fridge temperature: cold water: 2–4°C
warm water: minimum 6°C
Cold-water crustaceans such as the lobster and crab can be kept alive in a cool part of the fridge but must be kept moist. Use a damp cloth or seaweed. Warm-water crayfish will be killed at temperatures below 6°C. If they appear to be floppy when you pick them up, they should be cooked immediately.

Storing Preserved Fish

Salt or dried fish Store dried or salt cod in a cool dry place, out of direct sun.
Store wet salt cod in either a cool dry place or the fridge, depending on the amount of salt surrounding it.

Smoked fish Store in the fridge, wrapped to prevent it drying out.

Caviar Store sealed tins in the fridge, but if you open a tin it should be eaten within 2 or 3 days. Freeze if it is to be kept long term.

Storing Frozen Fish

Chest freezers are more suitable than fridge-freezers and bought-in frozen fish can be stored in them for several months, but respect the sell-by and packing dates. Fish that you have frozen yourself should be well wrapped and stored for no longer than two months. All fish deteriorate in the freezer but it is a useful way to extend the shelf life if you have bought some very fresh fish in bulk.

Never re-freeze previously frozen fish. Fatty fish do not freeze well.

On Preparing Fish

I'm a firm believer in leaving this side of things to the professionals. But for those of you of the muck-in school of thought, here is a brief guide to preparing your fish.

You will need the following to see you through:

- A sharp filleting knife, with a slightly bendy blade.
- A stout, sharp, solid, large knife for cutting through bone and for chopping crabs and lobsters in half.
- A fish scaler.
- Strong kitchen scissors.
- A large pair of tweezers or a small pair of narrow-ended pliers (free of oil and rust). The pliers are also useful if you have to skin skate wings.
- A pair of fine, long-bladed, sharp scissors if you are going to deal with sea urchins.
- A stubby-bladed or long-bladed oyster knife, with or without guard.
- A chopping board, solid, thick and wooden for preference.

Round Fish

Some of the round fish that you're most likely to buy whole are salmon, mullet, sea bass and snapper. Treat John Dory as a round fish that – like farmed trout, char and mackerel – doesn't need to be scaled. Some fish are more elliptical than round but the principles remain the same, and they are generally referred to as 'round' anyway.

Step 1: Trim and Scale

Cut off all the fins with a sturdy pair of scissors. Be careful; the dorsal fins on top can have sharp spines. Scale the fish (unless you're going to bake it in salt or eat the fillets skinned) by running the *back* (not the blade) of a strong knife or a scaler along the fish from the tail to the head, making sure you remove every last scale. You might like to cover the fish with a damp cloth to catch some of the scales, which have a habit of flying into the most obscure nooks and crannies of your kitchen. Running a tap over the fish to wet it thoroughly before scaling keeps the scales under control. There are special fish scalers available, which are definitely worth the cost if you're going to make a habit of scaling your own.

Whether you hold the fish by the head or tail depends upon you and the fish. If it's large or long, hold the tail and see how you get on. Scaling the fish before you gut it is easier, but if it's gutted anyway it must be scaled before filleting if you want to eat the fillets with the skin on.

Step 2: Gutting

Either: Take a sharp, short-bladed knife and slit the gut cavity from the anus to the head, gently pulling away the guts from the body. Cut them at the throat as near to the gills as you can, pull them out and cut at the anus. Try not to rupture anything, especially the green gall bladder which can spread some foul-tasting gall on to the flesh. Wash the cavity and pat dry. If you're going to store the fish you may like to remove the gills as well as the guts, both rich sources of flesh-rotting bacteria. Cut through the bone under the lower jaw and, with a pair of strong scissors, cut the gills where they join the head and mouth on both sides. Wash and clean.

Or: To gut a fish from the gills, cut the end of the gut away from the anus, then cut through the bone under the lower jaw. Cut the gills away from the head and mouth and draw the guts through the mouth. There is another way of doing this, called the *tsubo-nuki* technique by the Japanese, which involves twisting the guts around a pair of chopsticks and then drawing them through the mouth.

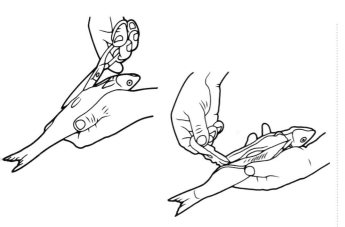

You will see a line of what appears to be coagulated blood running along the underside of the spine, on what was the top of the gut cavity. It is in fact the fish's kidney, and should be removed by running your thumbnail along its length, scraping it away from the bone. Wash and clean, then pat dry.

Step 3: Filleting

If you want to eat the fillets with the skin on, make sure that you have scaled the fish first (see Step 1). Take a very sharp knife with a fairly flexible, narrow blade and, with the back of the fish facing you, cut cleanly a little way down to the backbone, just behind the head, as if you were separating the head from the body. With smaller fish, such as red mullet, you can slide the knife just above the backbone, from the head to the tail in one sweep, and the fillet *should* come neatly off the bone. With larger fish such as salmon or bass, run the knife from the head towards the tail, but only as far down as the backbone, then lift the fillet up and cut more carefully, as if you were a surgeon rather than a butcher, to take the fillet away from the lower side. Turn the fish over and do the same on the other side.

To fillet smaller fish such as anchovies, sardines and herrings, see relevant entries.

Step 4: Skinning a Fillet

Place the fillet on a board with the tail end facing you and make a small cut between the skin and the flesh on the tail end. Taking a very sharp knife, slide it all the way along, separating the skin from the flesh. Hold the skin on to the board with your fingers while sliding the knife away from you.

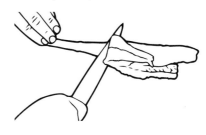

Step 5: Pinboning

There are some small bones on the fillets that need to be removed by hand. Get a stout pair of tweezers and lift out as many as you can. Run your finger along the fillet to check if you've left any bones in.

Flat Fish see page 104.

Shellfish see pages 192–4.

Crustaceans see pages 217–18.

Squid, Octopus and Cuttlefish see pages 247–8.

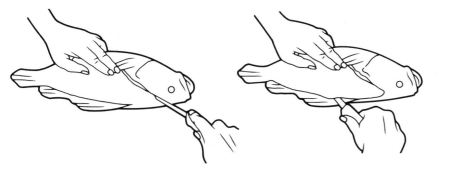
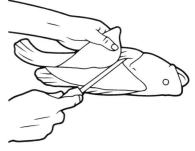

On Cooking Fish

The one simple rule to remember is don't overcook your fish. If you're stewing shad or tuna, where long cooking is called for, then that's fine, but otherwise be snappy and precise. If you have bought fish as fresh as it should be, having been harangued and cajoled by me throughout this book, then it should be good enough to eat raw, so it won't matter too much if it is a little on the underdone side while you're mastering your timing.

Before you enter the wonderful world of Sophie's recipes, you might like to familiarise yourself with the taste and texture of fish in its purest state. Try cooking different varieties with nothing more than a minuscule dribble of oil, some salt, pepper and maybe a squeeze of lemon. Buy yourself a non-stick oval fish pan; they're invaluable. If you get a taste for fish cooked this way, then you can add a little Thai fish sauce or chilli according to your mood, and something highly edible and incredibly easy will be ready in less than a minute.

And now William hands over to me. First of all, some general cooking notes. These are not specific to cooking fish but are useful in general when trying out the recipes in this book. First of all stick with one set of measurements, either metric or Imperial. All spoon measurements are rounded and all eggs are large unless otherwise stated.

All herbs are fresh and all spices are whole unless otherwise stated. Pepper should always be freshly ground, as should nutmeg. I always use extra virgin olive oil for cooking, since I find the flavour of plain olive oil (which has been chemically stripped of flavour, then had a little returned to it) disappointing. If you prefer a less powerful olive oil, then use it by all means, except where I have specifically called for extra virgin in a recipe.

Cooking times are meant as guidelines, not absolutes: all stoves vary, one cook's interpretation of medium or high heat will not match another's, a wider saucepan may change the cooking time of a sauce. If you use one of the suggested alternative fish you may well find that cooking times will vary more widely according to thickness and density of flesh. Use your eye, your sense of smell and your sense of taste to judge when food is done.

Before I'm let loose on cooking methods proper, let me hand on one invaluable tip which will improve nearly all fish, however you cook it. A good half an hour before it is to go into the pan, drain off any water it is sitting in, lay it on a plate and season it with salt. This pre-salting magically improves texture and boosts flavour, making really fresh, first-rate fish even more delicious and the not-quite-so-perfect specimens that we may have to resort to occasionally that much more enjoyable. I imagine that it works by drawing out some of the water lodged in the flesh but, believe me, whatever the reason, it's very effective.

And another small note, too. Try to remember to take your fish, particularly whole fish, out of the fridge about half an hour or so before cooking – unless the day is spectacularly hot in which case 15 minutes will suffice – so that it has time to come back to room temperature before it heads into the pan. Fish that is too cold will not cook evenly.

COOKING FISH ON TOP OF THE STOVE

Searing and Griddling

These are two of the best ways of cooking fish, producing crisp, browned skin. Since very little oil is used, it is also healthily and comfortingly low in calories. These methods are most suitable for thicker fillets, with skin on, though smaller whole fish (such as red mullet or sardines) can also be seared and griddled. The main difference between the methods is the pan.

To sear fish you will need a good frying pan with a solid, heavy base. An oval one is ideal as you will be able to fit more fish more comfortably in it. Wipe the pan out with a little oil (generally I use olive oil but sunflower or a similar neutral oil may be more appropriate for some recipes), but don't leave puddles of it. Place over a high heat and leave until horribly hot. Brush the fish with oil and lay it on the pan (if it is a fillet, then skin-side down first). Leave for 2–3 minutes *without moving*, then turn over and complete cooking on the other side. Alternatively, you can finish the cooking in a very hot oven in a matter of a few minutes, which may make more sense for very thick fillets or whole fish.

The cooked fish will have the most superb, slightly smoky flavour. Excellent served with little more than a wedge of lemon, though also eminently suitable for salsas and mayonnaise-based sauces.

To griddle, use the same method with a ridged, cast-iron griddle pan. The effect will be slightly different, with its stripes of brown-black from the ridges, but the taste and theory are much the same.

Frying

Shallow-frying

Always use a good-quality fat – there's no point ruining good fish with second-rate oil or, worse still, margarine. Extra virgin olive oil, or sunflower or groundnut oil are all good for shallow-frying. Butter is lovely but has a mean tendency to burn. Unsalted butter is a little safer but better still is clarified butter (see page 307). If you don't happen to have any handy (I rarely remember to clarify any in advance), then compromise without too much loss by using equal quantities of butter and oil, which will raise the burning point a little higher, usually enough to cook most fish. With thin, quick-cooking fillets you may be able to get away with butter alone.

If you are cooking with butter, heat until foaming, then add the fish. With oil, just make sure that it is good and hot so that the fish browns before it overcooks. Never overcrowd the pan or you will lower the temperature of the fat. When frying whole fish, lower the heat a little once the fish is beginning to brown so the heat can penetrate right through without

burning. As with searing and grilling, one of the keys to successful frying (and this holds true for meat and vegetables, too), is to staunch the temptation to move the fish around as soon as you've laid it in the pan. Leave it alone. Don't wiggle it around. After a couple of minutes, the underneath will have browned appetisingly (assuming your fat is hot enough, that is), forming a kind of non-stick crust, which allows you to turn the fish over in more or less one piece. However, if you give in to the innate urge to fiddle from the first fizz of fat meeting food, your fish will stick to the pan, and end up a right mess.

Flouring the fish is not necessary but does give a lovely finish and more of a light crust. Season the flour with salt and pepper (be generous with it), and coat the fish literally seconds before it goes into the pan, shaking off excess first.

Deep-frying

I usually use a wok for deep-frying. With its sloping sides, it's economical on oil, and it conducts heat well and evenly. For most fish dishes, the oil will need to be extremely hot, around 180–190°C/350–375°F. The easy way to test it is to drop a piece of bread into the oil. It should fizz vigorously straightaway and brown within about 30 seconds. Oil that is not hot enough will give greasy results.

There must be some sort of barrier between the fish and oil in order to protect the fish and stop the moisture escaping. This may be as light as a coating of flour or something more substantial, such as a batter. Either way, make sure that it coats the fish completely. Again, leave the coating until the last minute – with the exception of egg and crumb jackets, which are best prepared in advance so that the crumb has time to 'set'.

Slide the fish carefully into the hot oil so that it doesn't splash. Don't overcrowd the pan or the temperature of the oil will drop too far. When cooked, drain the fish briefly on kitchen paper, sprinkle with salt and serve immediately with lemon wedges or a suitable sauce or dipping sauce.

Stir-frying

Essentials for stir-frying are a wok (whatever you've read, a roomy frying pan does not work anywhere near as well) and violent heat. The sad truth is that few electric hobs are adequate for stir-frying, and smug, snug, Aga-owners (I'm one, so I can say that without being too rude) don't stand a chance. Gas is the thing, even though domestic gas can never give the intense heat generated in Chinese restaurant kitchens. Woks can be purchased very cheaply from Chinese super-markets and you really don't need to shell out on expensive, heavy, non-stick versions.

When stir-frying fish, what usually works best is to cut it into strips and toss these in cornflour, which gives them a better chance of holding together. Even so, it is wise to stir-fry them with a little less vigour than you might accord meat or vegetables, so that they don't collapse into a flurry of flakes. Stir-frying is brilliant for squid, which needs only the speediest of cooking.

Poaching

To show off the pure flavour, unadorned and untampered with, of truly fresh fish, poach it. Poached fish, done properly, can be sensational; done badly, it is disastrous. It is also a good method to use in more complicated composed dishes, such as fish pie. Ideally, you should make a *court-bouillon* (see page 309) in advance, which will enhance the taste of the fish without masking it. If you are pushed for time, then use water with the addition of a spoonful or so of wine vinegar, a few slices of onion, bay leaf, and/or dill or fennel, maybe some peppercorns and other gentle aromatics that take your fancy. Water on its own is not a good medium for poaching. In some recipes, particularly for preserved fish, milk and aromatics are used.

To poach the fish, place it in a single layer in a shallow flame-proof dish that is not too much bigger than the fish itself. Add cold liquid to cover, together with any aromatics. Heat gently until almost but not quite simmering. The surface of the liquid should be trembling and shuddering. Never let it reach a rolling boil. Thin fillets of fish may well be done by the time full temperature is reached but thicker pieces will not take a great deal longer. To help keep the fish under water, and to reduce evaporation, lay a circle of greaseproof paper over the surface of the water once

the temperature is correct. This is a particularly helpful trick for thicker fillets, which may require as much as 7–10 minutes' poaching.

Steaming

A gentle, fish-friendly method of cooking. For some time, it was considered suitable only for invalids, with the implication that the fish would turn out miserably bland but very digestible. Digestible maybe, but it doesn't have to be bland. If the fish is very fresh, steaming will show it to great advantage, keeping it moist without draining off any flavour.

Ideally, you should use a purpose-made steamer, or a wok with bamboo-steaming baskets and lid. If desperate, you can rig up a makeshift steamer out of a saucepan, a sieve and some foil.

Pour about 5cm (2 inches) of water into the lower part of the steamer (adding herbs or flavourings to the water will make the room smell nice but won't improve the fish at all) and bring up to a simmer. Either line the steamer basket with foil, leaving a gap around the edge so that steam can circulate freely, or find a plate that fits in comfortably, again allowing the steam to circulate. Make a bed of aromatics, if you wish (if you are cooking a piece of salmon, a bed of samphire is even better – fish and samphire will be perfectly cooked together, needing only a slug of *beurre blanc* or hollandaise to create a magic dish), and lay the fish on top. Lower the fish into the steamer, checking that the water does not bubble up and over on to the fish. Lay a folded tea towel over the top of the basket (not in contact with the fish). This is not mandatory but it does absorb some of the condensation that might otherwise drip down on to the fish, leaving it in a pool of warm water. Clamp on the lid and steam for a few minutes until the fish is just cooked through.

This is also an excellent method for cooking shellfish, such as mussels.

Braising

With meat, braising means long slow cooking, but braising fish is rather different. Piscine braising means a short spell in a heavy pan, the fish laid on a bed of

vegetables and flavourings, with a little liquid (not a deluge – it is there to moisten, not flood), lid on. You can braise fish in this way over a gentle heat on the top of the stove or at a moderate heat in the oven, whichever is most convenient. Do not let it overcook.

Stewing

When making fish stews or soups that include chunks of fish and shellfish, you will usually find that you can prepare the sauce/soup base well in advance, and that the seafood only needs to be added right at the very end of the process and stewed for the bare minimum required. This is best done shortly before you sit down to eat, so that the fish is not overcooked by the time it reaches the table. Most fish will need little more than 5 minutes in the hot sauce or soup, and possibly not even that. To minimise the chance of overcooking, cut the flesh into larger rather than smaller pieces – I'm talking roughly around 4cm (1½ inches) but this depends on the recipe in question.

Grilling and Barbecuing

A truly excellent way of cooking fish, most suitable for chunky steaks sliced from larger fish (tuna and monkfish, for instance, grill very well) and smaller whole fish, such as red mullet, sardines and the like. An hour or more's bath in a marinade before the fish meets the heat is always a boon, even if it consists of nothing more complicated than the juice of a lemon, 3 or 4 tablespoonfuls of olive oil, a couple of chopped cloves of garlic and a spoonful or two of chopped herbs of some sort.

Make sure that the grill is thoroughly preheated – give it at least 5 minutes to heat through. With a barbecue, allow plenty of time for the flames to die down, so that the coals are at the peak of their searing power. Brush both the grill rack and the fish with oil to prevent sticking. Lining the grill pan with foil will reduce the labour of washing up. Grill the fish close to the heat so that it browns on the exterior without overcooking on the interior. Turn it once and once only.

Too much handling and turning is likely to end in disaster, particularly with small whole fish.

The long-handled double-sided hinged grill racks that you can buy from kitchen shops make grilling fish infinitely easier. The pretty flower-like ones for holding smaller fish are lovely to look out, but for general use a plainer square or rectangular one is a better investment.

COOKING FISH IN THE OVEN
Roasting

Roasting implies that the fish is uncovered, cooked directly in the heat of the oven. This is a good way to cook larger chunks of fish (perhaps a joint of swordfish) or bigger whole fish (e.g. a whole monkfish tail). The fish will need some sort of lubrication (usually oil, preferably olive) to offer a little protection and may well benefit from being cooked on a bed of vegetables, moistened with, say, a splash of white wine, which can form the basis of a sauce when the fish is done. Fish should always be roasted at a relatively high temperature, so that it has a chance to take some colour on the outside before it is done.

Baking

What generally distinguishes baking from roasting, at least in the case of fish, is that the dish, or the fish itself, is covered in some way. This makes it a good method, and very convenient too, for cooking thinner fish, smaller fish or fillets. The fish may either be wrapped entirely in its own little shroud of greaseproof paper or foil (in other words, *en papillote*) or sit in a dish, possibly with other ingredients, that is itself covered in foil, trapping in steam and protecting the fish from the heat. I usually bake fish at around 180–200°C/350–400°F/Gas Mark 4–6. It won't take too long to cook, depending of course on thickness, though it tends to take a little longer than frying or searing.

Microwave

If it is used carefully the microwave is an excellent tool for cooking fish, though not quite as easy as manufacturers would have us believe. Either the fish needs to be cut into pieces all of the same thickness, so that they cook evenly, or else thinner parts need to be protected from the heat halfway through cooking with a shield of foil. For specific instructions, refer to the manufacturer's instructions or specialist microwave cookery books.

How to Tell if Fish is Cooked

- White fish: White fish becomes opaque when cooked. Ideally, the middle should be *just* cooked, white and moist, so to check, poke a knife into the centre to see if it has just turned.
- Fatty fish: Red coloured fish such as tuna can be eaten with the middle still rare, just like a steak. If you cook them through do not overdo it or the flesh will toughen and become dry and inedible.
- Shark and Skate: Cook through.

Quantities: How Much Fish to Buy per Person

- Allow 150–175g (5–6 oz) fillet for a main course.
- Allow 85–110g (3–4 oz) fillet for a starter.
- Allow 500g (1 lb 2 oz) gross for shellfish.
- Allow 500g (1 lb 2 oz) gross for large crustaceans.
- Allow 300g (11 oz) for small crustaceans such as prawns or shrimps.
- Allow 30–60g (1–2 oz) caviar.
- Allow 110g (4 oz) unsoaked salt cod.

Guide to Symbols

We have used a highly subjective system of stars ★ to indicate what we consider to be the best buys. The system may remind you of the three rosettes that Michelin use in their guides: it's supposed to. So, a great fish such as turbot will have three stars, very good fish will have two and a good fish will have one.

Obviously, freshness is more crucial than the type of fish, but given the same standards of freshness, the starred fish merit your attention over the unstarred.

On top of that, fish marked with an ® are especially recommended as being affordable, underrated and particularly good fish.

Fish marked with a ♥ are high in Omega-3 fatty acids.

We have included guides to price and yield. A fish with one £ is cheap, whereas ££ means moderately priced, and £££ means expensive. Yield is described as an approximate percentage of usable fillet from a whole gutted fish.

PART THREE

FISH TYPES AND RECIPES

Flaky Fish

The fish in this section are the regular guys, the lumpen proletariat of the fish world. Found in huge shoals, they became the backbone of the European fishing industry long ago, and their well-being is vital for chippies, merchants and fishermen all over the country. They are powerful swimmers, often living in quite deep water, but lack the dark, dense flesh of fatty hunting fish such as tuna. Their shape is classically round and fishy, and their flesh when cooked tends towards flakiness.

Flaky fish tend to come from the cold northern seas, and many of the recipes in this section are quite interchangeable. The exception is hake, which is still fished in the Mediterranean and seems to need a southern, Mediterranean touch for it to taste its best. As a general rule, flaky fish are improved by salting for an hour or so (see page 30).

Cod*

French: Cabillaud, Morue fraîche
Italian: Merluzzo bianco
Spanish: Bacalao
Portuguese: Bacalhau-do-Atlântico
German: Kabeljau, Dorsch

Atlantic Cod
Gadus morhua

Pacific Cod
Gadus macrocephalus

There is something quite beguiling about cod. Gracious, sleek creatures, with voracious mouths and large eyes, these are bottom-feeding fish that inhabit the murkier depths of the sea. Cod is the classic fish to accompany a chip, and is everyone's favourite flaky fish.

The Norwegians aren't too complimentary about them either and, oddly, think that eating cod makes you sleepy. There's a bit of wordplay here, for the Norwegian for cod, *torsk*, rhymes with *dorsk*, or sleep. Sophie and I have had the pleasure of sitting through a whole evening of Lofoten dialect jokes all about sleep, cod and drink, and even some just on cod. Unforgettable, especially if you don't speak Norwegian.

Enormous cod, weighing 50kg (111 lb) or more, once swam the oceans but, sadly, they swim no more, or if they do no one knows where. Today it's more likely to be a 5kg (11 lb) specimen that graces your table in some form or other.

There was once a thriving fishing port on the Thames estuary, the then rural backwater of Barking, Essex. Live fish were landed in boats called well smacks, which were specifically designed to keep fish alive. The cod were off-loaded and stored in wooden tanks in the estuary to be sent down to the fish markets as demand required. In the distant days when North Sea cod was still plentiful, Barking was the biggest fishing port in the UK. And what happened to its brilliant fishy career? Ice, and the railway, happened. Cod became even bigger business and supplies were eventually sent by train, iced rather than alive, from the newly developed ports of Hull and Grimsby, which were closer to the main fishing grounds.

There is an Icelandic saying that cod is at its best when there's snow in its mouth, and it does seem to need very cold water to firm it up. On the other side of the Atlantic, one of the finest cod fisheries of all, the Grand Banks, has collapsed and fishing has been forbidden temporarily. A stark warning to us all. On the plus side, cod are fertile fish, spawning in the spring, and reach maturity quite quickly so, in theory at least, overfished stocks that are left alone should recover.

With cod, the fishing method used is very important. Line-caught fish are not generally damaged during fishing, whereas netted or trawled fish can be bruised both inside and out, losing that superb taste of absolute freshness.

COD

Whether you buy cod in fillets or as steaks, look at the skin to check that it is fresh. The colours should be bright and clear. The average cod is between 50 and 90cm (20–36 inches) long, so even now it's found mostly in fillet form. For most recipes a thick fillet is essential, and the shoulder end is the best. Allow about 175–200g (6–7 oz) per person. Only very fresh cod should be poached, otherwise it tastes too bland.

See also Preserved Fish (pages 276–83).

Season: All year round.
Price: ££
Yield: 50%
Fishing method: Various. Line-caught for preference.

HADDOCK

Coley, Saithe, Coalfish, Pollock

Pollachius virens
French: Lieu noir, Colin noir (north)
Italian: Merluzzo nero
Spanish: Carbonero
Portuguese: Escamudo
German: Seelachs, Köhler

The coley is not a particularly fine fish. After death, its texture and taste deteriorate rapidly, taking on the subtlety and looks of grey cotton wool. Its dark-coloured fillets have made it a natural for fish and chips, for fillets covered in batter all look the same.

Coley usually weigh between 5 and 10kg (11 and 22 lb), and resemble elegant cod and pollack. They move shorewards in the spring, returning to deep water in the winter. They are quite manic if you ever catch one, flapping about like a high-speed fan. If you're holidaying in Bergen, hurry down to the fish market where you may be able to buy them alive.

Smaller than cod, coley are once again found mainly in fillet form. Any cod or haddock recipe will do for coley so long as it is extremely fresh.

Season: All year round.
Price: £
Yield: 60%
Fishing method: Trawl, seine and gill net.

Haddock®

Melanogrammus aeglefinus
French: Eglefin, Anon, St Pierre (north), Haddock (smoked fish)
Italian: Asinello
Spanish: Eglefino
Portuguese: Arinca
German: Schellfisch

Grey to brown, and rather dull looking, the haddock is unloved, or perhaps unknown, by most southern Europeans. However, the English and Scots adore them, as do the Scandinavians, so you won't be surprised to learn that this is a northern, deep-water, shoaling fish. Haddock resemble cod but are considerably smaller, weighing on average about 2 kg (4½ lb). The haddock has a tell-tale black mark on its side. It may seem quite ludicrous but I have read, admittedly in a book published in 1836, that this mark, as with the thumbprint on the John Dory, was associated with the hand of St Peter. The idea of haddock in the Sea of Galilee stretches even the staunchest Christian imagination.

Although it is often eaten smoked in France – there any dish labelled *haddock* always uses smoked rather than fresh fish – haddock is another fish 'n' chips classic over here. Supplies are primarily from the north, and Scottish fish have the best reputation. But with much of the demand being for haddock fillets of a very particular size, the fishing industry is deeply troubled by the huge numbers of undersized fish that are landed, and sold for far too little. In the south-west you occasionally see 'chats', or small haddock, for sale, which are caught with whiting.

If you happen to be wandering around the Faroe Islands, you may notice small haddock hanging on the rails, left outside to 'mature'. The Faroese like fish in a semi-rotten state, or *rost*, which surprisingly can taste quite good. This is similar to Norwegian *boknafisk*. For some peculiar reason, the idea that fresh fish isn't good for you took root in Scandinavia centuries ago, and many still believe it to be true.

Haddock is another species under great pressure from overfishing but, unlike the cod, haddock reproduce slowly.

Haddock fillets are widely available in the UK, and can be used in any cod or coley recipe. When poaching haddock, leave the skin on, since it holds the flesh together.

See also Preserved Fish (pages 276–83).

Season: All year round.
Price: £
Yield: 50%
Fishing method: Mainly trawled.

Hake*

Merluccius merluccius
French: Merlu, Merlu commun, Merluchon or Chon (small), Merlan (large, Mediterranean)
Italian: Nasello
Spanish: Merluza
Portuguese: Pescada
German: Seehecht

It is a shame that more hake isn't used in Britain, for it is a truly fine fish. The Spanish can't get enough of it, and swallow tonne upon tonne of our finest hake, paying far more than the domestic market ever will. Its soft flesh can be quite difficult to use and its very softness causes a bit of misunderstanding, for even the freshest hake tend to give slightly to the touch. A look at the eyes and a quick sniff should reassure the buyer but, wherever possible, line-caught fish should be used, although they are not easy to find over here. Trawled fish can be flabby and dull.

Hake are long, thin carnivorous fish, quite widely distributed throughout temperate waters. The European hake fishery in the Bay of Biscay is in trouble, and it hasn't been helped by the French, and their liking for little *merluchon*. Male hake don't reach sexual maturity until they're about 40cm (16 inches) long, and females until they are a hefty 50cm (20 inches), or about seven years old. Since fish bigger than that constitute such a small part of the catch, things are looking very bleak indeed.

WHITING

Young fish congregate in narrow areas of the sea and are an easy target for the fishing fleet. Some studies indicate that only about 4 per cent of them ever reach sexual maturity, a situation that, if correct, clearly cannot continue for long.

The answer to the problem of supply has been to exploit the stocks of closely related species in the southern hemisphere, notably *Merluccius hubbsi* off the South African and Namibian coasts, and *Merluccius gayi* off the Peruvian and Chilean coasts. Both are good fish, and will hopefully be better managed than the European hake fishery.

Hake fillets are difficult to handle, so it's better to cook the fish on the bone. A larger fish can be cut into steaks but smaller fish are best cooked whole. To feed four, you will need a fish about 1.2–1.5kg (2¾–3¼ lb).

Season: Best in summer.
Price: ££
Yield: 60%.
Fishing method: Line-caught fish superior. Mainly trawled.

Ling®

Molva molva
French: Lingue, Julienne
Italian: Molva
Spanish: Maruca
Portuguese: Maruca
German: Leng, Lengfisch

I have a liking for ling. It is perfect for a fish pie, having relatively few bones and no scales. Ling are long, brown skinned, and definitely underrated, with remarkably firm flesh when cooked. The problem is you rarely see ling in fish shops in this country. Nag your fishmonger to get some. Ling tend to live over rocky ground, so are seldom trawled, which means that they are mostly caught by line and, as we all know, line-caught fish are worth a detour.

Small ling are available, and fish of all sizes give an excellent firm fillet that can withstand a bit of manhandling.

See also Preserved Fish (pages 276–83).

Season: All year round.
Price: £
Yield: 55%
Fishing method: Line, inshore fish.

Pollack®

Pollachius pollachius
French: Lieu jaune, Colin jaune
Italian: Merluzzo giallo
Spanish: Abadejo
Portuguese: Juliana
German: Pollack

Not 'pollock' please (which refers to either coley or a deepwater American species, the Alaska Pollock), but pollack. It is an excellent alternative to cod, generally smaller, but less widely distributed and caught closer to the shore. In Brittany, there has been a concerted effort to boost the sales of pollack, which has meant that much of the UK catch gets sent out to France. The main pollack fisheries are around the Channel Islands and to the south-west of England, where some of the finest fish are hand-lined off wrecks. In some parts of the country, 'pollack' refers to coley.

A smaller fish than the cod, the usual length is between 25 and 75cm (10–30 inches), so the fillets tend to be thinner than cod, but of more even thickness. Cod recipes work well for pollack, as do haddock, ling and hake.

Season: Spring/autumn.
Price: £
Yield: 55%
Fishing method: Various.

Pouting, Pout

Trisopterus luscus
French: Tacaud
Italian: Merluzzo francese
Spanish: Faneca
Portuguese: Faneca
German: Franzosendorsch

You can't deny that fish can have wonderful names. This may sound like a tarty teenager to you but it's not really tarty at all, either to look at or to eat. What it lacks in charisma it certainly makes up in affordability. It is a rather dull, light-brown fish, about 25cm (10 inches) long, with a very fragile fillet. Pouts are considered to resemble whiting in both looks and taste, and tend to be caught with whiting as a by-catch. They have a curious membrane covering the eyes, which explains why they used to be called 'bibs', or 'blens', derived from an old word for blister. Best eaten as a fillet, the pout can be a surprisingly good fish in the right hands but must be eaten when *extremely* fresh, as the fillets keep very badly. It's best to buy a whole fish and have it filleted for you. Soft and difficult to handle, the flesh resembles a whiting and the two are largely interchangeable.

Season: All year round.
Price: £
Yield: 50%
Fishing method: By-catch.

Whiting

Merlangius merlangus
French: Merlan
Italian: Merlano
Spanish: Merlán
Portuguese: Badejo
German: Wittling, Merlan

Whiting (illustration page 39) are old, bespectacled fish that sit under woolly shawls. They have suffered too long from being the archetypal invalid food, together with warm tea and Rich Tea biscuits, and don't seem to be taken very seriously in the UK at all.

They are widely distributed, fairly small, soft-fleshed fish that need to be bought with extreme discretion. Serious enthusiasts swear by a really fresh whiting, and I particularly like the French term *merlan brillant*, for brilliantly fresh whiting, which adds a bit of glamour to this rather bland fish. If you really loathe it you can always chuck it about and say that the whiting's on the wall.

Given the whiting's notorious fragility, you may think you'd be better off with a whole fish and fillet it yourself. However, you can buy them as fillets if you're sure they're fresh. Smaller fish are often 'butterflied' giving one fillet from a single fish, which is a little tricky to do on a whiting. Keep the skin on. There are very few scales. Poached whiting should be cooked at a very gentle simmer, and can be served with a variety of buttery sauces.

Season: All year round.
Price: £
Yield: 50%
Fishing method: Mainly trawled.

Henningsvaer Fiskesuppe

Henningsvaer Fish Soup

Alternatives: coley, haddock, pollack, wrasse

When we were filming, some years ago, in the north of Norway, the snow thick on the ground, this superb, creamy, fish soup became something of a saving grace; there's only so much prime boiled cod, however fresh, that one can stand in ten days. We ate it in a fish restaurant in the picturesque fishing port of Henningsvaer, looking out over icy bobbing boats from the snug, wood-lined room. I'd been warned that the chef guarded his recipes fiercely but I found quite the contrary. He took me to the kitchen, ran through the method and told me that it was based on fish soups from the south of the country. It has remained a favourite, especially on cold, snowy days.

SERVES 6–8

1.3 litres (2¼ pints) Fish Stock (see page 308)
350g (12 oz) cod fillet
60g (2 oz) butter
1 onion, finely chopped
1 large carrot, finely chopped
1 large leek (both white and green parts),
    finely chopped
2 teaspoons caster sugar
2 tablespoons white wine vinegar
300ml (½ pint) *crème fraîche* or soured cream
    and double cream mixed
salt and pepper
chopped fresh parsley, to garnish

Bring the stock to the boil. Add the cod, bring gently back to the boil and then draw off the heat. When tepid, lift out the cod and flake, discarding the skin and any stray bones. Reserve the flesh and the stock.

Melt the butter in a large pan and add the vegetables. Stir to coat nicely in fat, cover the pan, reduce the heat to a mere thread and leave to sweat for 20 minutes, stirring once or twice. Add the stock, sugar, vinegar, salt and pepper and bring up to the boil. Simmer for 10 minutes. Stir in the cream and the flaked fish. Taste and adjust the seasoning and then re-heat gently, without boiling. Serve immediately, sprinkled with a little chopped parsley.

Seared Cod with Caramelised Shallot and Red Wine Sauce

Alternatives: bass, haddock, coley, pollack

Putting red wine with white fish still comes as a bit of a shock to the system but it can work and, in this case, it does work extremely well. Get the sauce going in advance; the final dish takes only about 7 minutes to cook. Quick but very stylish. Serve with plenty of creamy potato purée and maybe some lightly cooked spinach.

Kecap manis is an Indonesian sweet soy sauce, now available from many of the bigger supermarkets and from most oriental food shops. It has become an indispensable ingredient in our kitchen: great in salad dressings and superb as a last-minute condiment with both fish and meat.

SERVES 4

olive oil
4 thick portions of cod fillet, with skin on,
    weighing about 150–175g (5–6 oz)
coarse salt
pepper

For the Sauce:
60g (2 oz) shallot, thinly sliced
60g (2 oz) unsalted butter
1 tablespoon olive oil
½ tablespoon caster sugar
150ml (¼ pint) well flavoured Fish Stock
    (see page 308)
150ml (¼ pint) good, fruity red wine
1 tablespoon *kecap manis*, or soy sauce with a
    pinch of sugar
½ teaspoon Worcestershire sauce

Prepare the sauce before you start cooking the fish. In a shallow frying pan, fry the shallot gently in half the butter and all the olive oil, until tender, without browning. Put the remaining butter back in the fridge to chill. Sprinkle the sugar over the shallot, stir, and then cook for a further 1–2 minutes. Add the fish stock and wine and boil hard until reduced by two-thirds. Stir in the *kecap manis* or soy sauce and sugar and the Worcestershire sauce. Draw off the heat until needed.

Preheat the oven to 220°C/425°F/Gas Mark 7. Wipe a heavy, ovenproof frying pan with a touch of olive oil. Set over a high heat and leave to heat for 3–4 minutes. Dry the fish thoroughly with kitchen paper. Rub coarse salt into the skin. Place the fish skin-side down in the frying pan. Leave for 3 minutes without turning. Brush the upper side lightly with olive oil, then turn the fish over (the skin should be well browned) and transfer to the oven for a further 3–4 minutes, by which time it should be just cooked.

Meanwhile, re-heat the sauce. Cube the remaining chilled butter and add to the pan a few cubes at a time, whisking it in to thicken the sauce. Taste and adjust the seasoning and spoon the sauce around the slabs of seared cod. Serve immediately.

Roast Cod with a Lemon, Garlic and Parsley Crust

Alternatives: haddock, coley, pollack, hake, bass, toothfish, red mullet

Roasting cod in a hot oven, topped with a crisp crust, is a simple, quick trick and open to endless variations. In my last book, *Taste of the Times*, I flavoured the crust with coriander. Here I've come closer to home, with lots of parsley, a little garlic and the scent of lemon. You will need good, thick chunks of cod fillet for this – there's no point in doing it with measly, thin little pieces, which will be overcooked by the time the crust is crisp.

This makes perfect mid-week dinner-party food, or you might just want to save it for yourselves (it's easy to halve quantities if there are only two of you).

SERVES 4

700g (1½ lb) skinned, thick cod fillet
   (at least 3cm (1¼ inches) thick)
85g (3 oz) soft or slightly stale white breadcrumbs
3 generous tablespoons finely chopped fresh
   parsley
2 garlic cloves, crushed
finely grated zest of ½ lemon
60g (2 oz) butter, melted
lemon juice
salt and pepper
lemon wedges, to serve

Preheat the oven to 220°C/425°F/Gas Mark 7. Season the cod with salt and pepper. Mix the breadcrumbs with the parsley, garlic, lemon zest, salt and pepper, then add the butter and a squeeze of lemon juice. Mix thoroughly with your fingers. Place the cod in a greased, shallow ovenproof dish and press the buttered crumbs firmly on to the upper side to form an even crust. Bake for 20 minutes, until the crust is browned and the fish just cooked through. If the crust is still pale, pop under a hot grill to finish browning. Serve immediately, with lemon wedges.

Mrs Johannesen's Frikadellur

Alternatives: haddock, cod, pollack and most white fish

This recipe for fish *frikadellur* – essentially, fish rissoles – comes from the mother of a colleague of William's in the Faroe Islands. All William managed to extract for me was the bare bones of the recipe (if you'll excuse the weak pun) – a list of ingredients including *talg*, which is salted fat, and the following minimal method: 'Spoon mix, fry butter'. I hope Mrs Johannesen will forgive me for any errors I may have made but I didn't have a great deal to go on. The end result, though simple, is rather good. Children, by the way, love these *frikadellur*.

As with all dishes using cooked potato as a binder, you will achieve a better, firmer mixture if you bake the potatoes or cook them in the microwave. If you must boil them, boil them whole in their skins so that the flesh is less waterlogged.

SERVES 6

400g (14 oz) skinned coley fillet
125g (4½ oz) *lardons* (short, thick bacon batons)
30g (1 oz) bacon fat or dripping
½ large onion, chopped
400g (14 oz) cooked potato
1 egg, lightly beaten
85–110ml (3–4 fl oz) milk
butter, bacon fat or dripping, for frying
salt and pepper

Cut the coley up roughly and season with salt and pepper. Fry the *lardons* in the bacon fat or dripping over a brisk heat until browned. Scoop out and reserve. Add the onion to the pan and fry over a moderate heat until soft and translucent. Put the onion and its fat into the bowl of a food processor with the fish and the potato. Add the egg, salt and pepper. Process in short bursts, scraping down the sides between bursts, to give a fairly smooth mixture, gradually adding enough milk to give a soft, but not sloppy, texture. Stir in the *lardons*.

Dip two dessertspoons into cold water and use one to scoop out a nice ball of the mixture. Form it into a neat rugby-ball shape using the second spoon. Continue until all the mixture is used up. When all the *frikadellur* are made, heat a little butter, bacon fat or dripping and, when foaming, add the *frikadellur*. Fry gently until golden brown all over. Serve at once, with a little extra melted butter as a sauce, or the Norwegian Shrimp Sauce on page 246.

Fish Bobotie

Alternatives: pollack, cod, haddock, and most white fish

The Cape Malay dish *bobotie* is a curious enough (but decidedly good) combination of meat, curry, raisins and savoury custard, but I was even more surprised to read of a version made with fish in *South African Cape Malay Cooking*, by Sonia Allison and Myrna Robins (Absolute Press). In South Africa it would probably be made with *snoek*, their commonest flaky fish, but since that is almost impossible to find here, I tried it with coley, making minor personal alterations as I went along. Indeed, it turns out to be a fine way of using some of the lesser flaky fish, though perhaps it would be a shame to mask the flavours of classier white fish with so many unorthodox ingredients.

The *bobotie* is served with Apricot and Chilli Blatjang (see page 312), a humdinger of a sauce made, bizarrely enough, from apricot jam. It is essential, we think, with the *bobotie* itself but also goes extremely well with fried fish, being hot and sweet and sharp all at the same time. Thank you, Sonia Allison and Myrna Robins.

SERVES 6–8

2 onions, finely chopped
2 garlic cloves, chopped
1 tablespoon sunflower oil
1 tablespoon mild curry powder
½ teaspoon ground turmeric
3 thick slices of white bread weighing about
    175g (6 oz), crusts removed
300ml (½ pint) milk
1kg (2¼ lb) skinned coley fillet, very finely
    chopped or minced
1 teaspoon *garam masala*
3 tablespoons lemon juice
85g (3 oz) raisins
4 tablespoons apricot jam
2 large eggs, beaten
salt and pepper
lime wedges, to serve

For the Topping:
2 large eggs
15g (½ oz) flaked almonds
4 lime leaves or fresh bay leaves (optional)

Preheat the oven to 180°C/350°F/Gas Mark 4. Fry the onions and garlic gently in the oil, without browning, until tender. Towards the end of the cooking time, stir in the curry powder and turmeric and cook for a further 1–2 minutes. Tear the slices of bread up roughly and soak for 5 minutes in the milk. Squeeze the milk out of the bread and reserve the milk and bread separately.

Mix the onions and garlic thoroughly with the minced fish, bread, *garam masala*, lemon juice, raisins, apricot jam and eggs. Season with salt and pepper. Spoon the mixture into an ovenproof dish, about 7.5cm (3 inches) deep and 23cm (9 inches) diameter (I use a soufflé dish, which is perfect) and smooth down. Use a fork to make ridges and grooves in the surface, so that the topping has something to grip hold of.

Beat the reserved milk with the eggs for the topping and pour over the mixture. Sprinkle with almonds and dot the lime or bay leaves on top. Bake for 40–45 minutes, until the topping is golden brown and lightly puffed. Serve with apricot and chilli *blatjang* and the lime wedges.

Norwegian Fishcakes

Alternatives: cod, coley, pollack, and most white fish

The basic mixture for these fishcakes is a multi-purpose one that we came across on travels in Norway. The same purée is poached to make fish balls (no jokes, please) or steamed to make fish pudding but, best of all, it's fried to a golden brown to transform it into fishcakes. In Norway we ate them smothered in a creamy shrimp sauce, the recipe for which you will find on page 246. I recommend it.

SERVES 6–8

900g (2 lb) skinned haddock fillet
225ml (8 fl oz) milk
2 tablespoons cornflour
freshly grated nutmeg
3 tablespoons chopped fresh parsley
about 225ml (8 fl oz) *crème fraîche* or soured
 cream mixed with double cream
salt
butter or butter and oil, for frying

Cut the fish up into rough chunks and process in three batches, with just enough of the milk to smooth it out. Keep processing in several long bursts, scraping down the sides of the bowl every now and then, until the purée is very smooth. Scoop into a bowl to finish the mixing by hand – this, we were told, is where the skill comes into it and cannot be replicated in a processor. Sprinkle over the cornflour, plenty of nutmeg and the parsley, season with salt and mix evenly.

Mix the remaining milk with the cream and slowly beat it into the fish mixture, a little at a time, until it is light and fluffy (you may not need it all). Chill the mixture for 30 minutes in the refrigerator.

Shape generous tablespoons of the mixture into small, flat, round cakes about 1cm (½ inch) thick. Fry in butter, or butter and oil, until browned. Serve immediately, with the Norwegian Shrimp Sauce, on page 246.

Sweet Potato and Fish Pie

Alternatives: ling, cod, coley, pollack, smoked haddock

White-fleshed sweet potatoes have an unexpected and most delightful affinity with fish and, once you discover it, you'll find yourself swapping sweet potatoes for ordinary potatoes whenever opportunity allows. This is nothing more nor less than a recipe for a classic fish pie, always a great favourite when well made, with sweet potatoes giving it an updated image, and a hint of dill instead of plain parsley.

Finding white-fleshed sweet potatoes, with their fluffy, pale flesh and chestnutty flavour – not as intense and cloying as that of orange-fleshed tubers – is not always easy. Ask your greengrocer to get some in. The only way to tell the difference between the two if they are not labelled is to scrape a small fleck of the purple skin away to reveal the interior colour. If you can't get white-fleshed sweet potatoes, settle for ordinary, floury main-crop potatoes and enjoy a classic British fish pie instead.

SERVES 4

700g (1½ lb) sweet potato
4 eggs
60g (2 oz) butter
300ml (½ pint) milk, plus a little extra for
    the potato
3 branches of fresh dill
1 small onion, sliced
5 peppercorns
1 bay leaf
700g (1½ lb) haddock or other white fish fillet
110g (4 oz) shelled, cooked fresh peas or thawed
    frozen peas
15g (½ oz) plain flour
salt and pepper

Preheat the oven to 180°C/350°F/Gas Mark 4. Cut the sweet potato into chunks and cook in salted water until soft. Peel and mash 500g (1 lb 2 oz) of the potato with 1 egg, 30g (1 oz) of the butter and enough milk to give a soft consistency. Chop the fine, feathery parts of the dill, reserving the stalks separately.

Hard-boil the remaining 3 eggs and then run them under the cold tap. When they are cool enough to handle, remove their shells and cut them into quarters. Put the 300ml (½ pint) milk into a pan with the sliced onion, peppercorns, bay leaf and dill stalks. Bring gently to the boil. Put the fish fillets in an ovenproof dish and pour the hot milk and seasonings over them. Bake for 15–20 minutes, until the fish is cooked. Turn up the oven to 220°C/425°F/Gas Mark 7.

Strain off the milk and discard the onion and seasonings. Flake the fish, discarding the skin and any bones, and put it on the base of a pie dish. Scatter over the peas, then dot with the quartered eggs. Sprinkle the chopped dill over the top.

Make a white sauce (see page 306) with 15g (½ oz) of the remaining butter, the flour and the milk from cooking the fish. Simmer for 5 minutes and season well. Pour the sauce over the fish, shaking the dish gently to distribute it. Spread the mashed potato thickly over the top and make a wavy pattern on the top with a fork. Dot with the last of the butter. Bake for 15–20 minutes, until lightly browned.

Deep-fried Battered Haddock

Alternatives: cod, coley, pollack, halibut, huss

Here's one half of the most famous, most widely eaten British fish speciality, good old fish and chips. It's not much hassle to turn your kitchen into the local chippy for an evening: I reckon that you can probably manage your own chips, so here is a recipe for their partner, deep-fried fish in a crisp batter. Made with really fresh fish and eaten hot from the pan, it is a dish to be proud of. I love deep-fried haddock but all manner of fish take well to the chip-shop approach. Whatever you use, make sure it is really fresh and you instantly lift your battered fish above the average offering. Serve it with Tartare Sauce (page 315), or wedges of lemon, or tomato ketchup or vinegar – whatever takes your fancy (and chips, of course).

SERVES 4

oil or dripping, for deep-frying
4 skinned haddock fillets, weighing about 175g
  (6 oz) each
lemon wedges, Tartare Sauce, malt vinegar and/or
  tomato ketchup, to serve

For the Batter:
225g (8 oz) plain flour, sifted
300ml (½ pint) lager or brown ale
1 egg, separated
1 tablespoon sunflower oil
110ml (4 fl oz) water
salt and pepper

To make the batter, season the flour with salt and pepper. Make a well in the centre and add the lager, egg yolk and oil. Gradually whisk into the flour to make a smooth batter. Stir in the water. Leave to rest for at least half an hour. Shortly before using, whisk the egg white until it forms stiff peaks and fold into the batter.

Heat the oil to 180°C/350°F, or until a cube of bread dropped into it sizzles fairly vigorously straight away. One by one, dry the haddock pieces. Then dip into the batter, making sure that they are completely coated. Slide into the oil and fry for about 5–6 minutes, depending on the thickness of the fish, until golden brown. Drain briefly on kitchen paper and sprinkle with salt. Eat immediately.

Roast Hake with Red Pepper Mayonnaise

Alternatives: cod, pollack, bass, grey mullet, halibut

With its soft, tender flesh, hake is every bit as good cold as it is hot. It makes a glorious summer lunch dish served with a pretty red pepper mayonnaise.

SERVES 4–6

1 hake, weighing around 1kg (2¼ lb), cleaned
    and trimmed
1 onion, sliced
1 carrot, thinly sliced
1 bay leaf
2 fresh parsley sprigs
glass of dry white wine (about 110ml/4 fl oz)
salt and pepper

For the Mayonnaise:
1 red pepper
1 egg yolk
½ tablespoon white wine vinegar
½ teaspoon Dijon mustard
60ml (2 fl oz) extra virgin olive oil
110ml (4 fl oz) sunflower or groundnut oil
salt and pepper

Preheat the oven to 180°C/350°F/Gas Mark 4. Trim the fins off the fish but leave the head and tail in place. Make a bed of the onion, carrot, bay leaf and parsley in an ovenproof dish. Lay the hake on it, curving it round to fit snugly. Pour over the wine and season with salt and pepper. Cover with foil and bake for 30–40 minutes, until the hake is barely cooked (it will continue to cook a little as it cools), basting every now and then. Uncover and leave to cool, basting with the pan juices when you remember. Skin the fish if you wish, though, being a soft-fleshed fish, hake can look a little ragged by the end of the process. Carefully transfer to a serving dish and cover.

Begin the sauce by grilling the pepper: cut into quarters, discard the seeds and then grill, skin side to heat, close to a thoroughly preheated grill until blackened and blistered. Drop into a plastic bag, seal and leave until cool enough to handle. Pull off the skin and discard. Chop the flesh of the pepper roughly.

Beat the egg yolk lightly with the vinegar and mustard, then gradually whisk in the two oils, in a slow, continuous trickle at first, gradually increasing the flow as you get about halfway through. Put the grilled pepper into a food processor with a few spoonfuls of mayonnaise and process until smooth. Stir back into the remaining mayonnaise. Taste and adjust the seasoning. Serve alongside the hake.

Nasello all' Palermitana

Roast Hake with Anchovy and Rosemary

Alternatives: bass, grouper, grey mullet

This Sicilian recipe for hake roasted with rosemary, anchovies and garlic is one of the best of all ways to cook hake. It may not look as snazzy as hake dishes brightened with greenery and the red of peppers or tomatoes but don't let that put you off. The crunch of the breadcrumbs, sozzled in olive oil, and the blissful marriage of a judicious helping of anchovies and rosemary, set off the soft, sweet hake flesh to perfection – and for once this over-used and often misused phrase is absolutely right.

SERVES 4

1 hake, weighing about 1kg (2¼ lb), cleaned
extra virgin olive oil
1 fresh rosemary sprig
2 garlic cloves, finely chopped
8 tinned anchovy fillets, chopped
2 teaspoons finely chopped fresh rosemary leaves
30g (1 oz) slightly stale breadcrumbs
salt and pepper
lemon wedges, to serve

Preheat the oven to 170°C/325°F/Gas Mark 3. Brush the insides of the fish with a little olive oil, season with a little salt and plenty of pepper and tuck the sprig of rosemary inside. Lay in an oiled ovenproof dish, curving it round if necessary to fit neatly.

Heat 5 tablespoons of olive oil in a pan over a low heat and add the garlic and anchovies. Cook until the garlic is lightly coloured, mashing down the anchovies as they dissolve into the oil. Draw off the heat and drizzle over the fish, trickling a little into the stomach cavity as well. Season with pepper and sprinkle with the chopped rosemary. Now scatter over the breadcrumbs and bake for about half an hour, until the fish is just cooked through and the breadcrumbs have formed a nice crust. Check the fish once or twice as it cooks and, if it is looking dry, baste with its own juices or drizzle with a little extra oil. If necessary, pop the fish under a hot grill for a few minutes to brown the breadcrumbs. Serve piping hot, with lemon wedges.

Goujons of Pollack with Tamarind or Vietnamese Dipping Sauce

Alternatives: Dover sole, lemon sole, bass, grey mullet, cod, grouper, zander, barracuda

Goujons are long, thin strips of fish, deep-fried until crisp on the outside, tender inside. They must be eaten virtually straight from the pan, allowing only a few minutes for them to cool down enough not to burn the mouth. Though more expensive fish, like sole, are often used for goujons, pollack works just fine.

Whatever the fish, some kind of fairly punchy dipping sauce is definitely required. A lively tartare sauce is the stuff of tradition but I also love the Spicy Tomato Ketchup on page 58 or even the Apricot and Chilli Blatjang on page 312. Best of all, though, I like the strong flavours of South-east Asia with goujons. The four members of our household, who all dipped keenly, were evenly divided on which of these two dipping sauces went best with the goujons. Two of us liked the lighter but bright tones of the thin Vietnamese sauce; the other two preferred the thick, fruity tartness of the tamarind and ginger sauce. The one thing we all agreed upon was that we would have been perfectly happy with either.

SERVES 6 AS A FIRST COURSE,

4 AS A MAIN COURSE

500g (1 lb 2 oz) skinned pollack fillet, cut into
    strips about 1cm (½ inch) wide and 7.5cm
    (3 inches) long
juice of 1 lime
5 tablespoons plain flour
1 teaspoon ground coriander
salt and pepper
sunflower oil, for deep-frying

Season the pollack with salt and pepper, pour on the lime juice, stir quickly and set aside for half an hour.

Mix the flour with the coriander, salt and pepper. Heat the oil to 185°C/370°F (to test, drop in a cube of bread – if the oil fizzes with gusto and the bread begins to brown speedily, it is about right). Roll the pieces of pollack in the flour and then slide a small handful at a time into the hot oil. Use chopsticks to separate the pieces, if necessary, and fry until golden brown – a matter of a couple of minutes. Drain briefly on kitchen paper and serve piping hot, with one of the dipping sauces opposite, spicy tomato ketchup or apricot *blatjang*.

Vietnamese Dipping Sauce

SERVES 4–6

2 garlic cloves, roughly chopped
1 small fresh, red Thai chilli, de-seeded and
    finely chopped
2 tablespoons caster sugar
1–2 limes
4 tablespoons fish sauce (Vietnamese if you
    can get it, but Thai will do fine)
60ml (2 fl oz) water

Pound the garlic to a paste with the chilli and caster sugar in a mortar or strong, small bowl, using the pestle or the end of a rolling pin. Squeeze the limes and add not only the juice but also the pulp that has gathered in the citrus squeezer (minus pips). Stir in the fish sauce and water.

Tamarind Dipping Sauce

These days you can buy blocks of compressed tamarind from some large supermarkets, but otherwise you'll have to aim for an oriental food store. It keeps for ages in the fridge, even when opened, so please do buy some and try it if you can. It has the most heavenly fruity flavour and adds a velvety thickness to oriental sauces.

SERVES 4–6

60g (2 oz) lump of tamarind
110ml (4 fl oz) boiling water
1 garlic clove, chopped
1 small fresh, red Thai chilli, de-seeded and
    chopped
1 tablespoon granulated sugar
1cm (½ inch) piece of fresh root ginger, grated
2 tablespoons fish sauce (again, Vietnamese for
    preference but Thai is fine)

Soak the tamarind in the boiling water for about 30 minutes, until softened. Mash down, then rub the tamarind and water through a sieve. Pound the garlic, chilli, sugar and ginger to a paste in a mortar or bowl and then gradually work in the tamarind liquid. Stir in the fish sauce and it's done.

Pollack, Caramelised Onion, Aubergine and Tomato Pie

Alternatives: cod, hake, grouper, grey mullet, halibut, ling

I am inordinately proud of this pie. I don't quite know why I thought the various ingredients might work together. Indeed, I'll admit that I had doubts even as I was trying the recipe out for the first time. The result, however, is tremendously good, and I've already had to part with several advance copies of the recipe to friends who have tried it. The sweetness of the onions, the hint of basil from the pesto, the tender aubergine and the flaky fish all come together in complete harmony, and it even tastes good cold.

SERVES 4–6

500g (1 lb 2 oz) skinned pollack fillet
1 large aubergine, diced
5 tablespoons extra virgin olive oil
1 onion, chopped
4 garlic cloves, chopped
2 tablespoons caster sugar
400g (14 oz) tin of chopped tomatoes
1 large fresh thyme sprig
1 tablespoon tomato purée
2 tablespoons pesto
500g (1lb 2 oz) shortcrust pastry
12 cherry tomatoes (optional)
1 egg yolk, beaten with 1 tablespoon water
salt and pepper

Cut the pollack into 2–2.5cm (¾–1 inch) cubes and season with salt and pepper. Set aside. Place the aubergine in a colander and sprinkle lightly with salt. Set aside to drain for at least half an hour. Rinse and pat dry.

Meanwhile, heat 2 tablespoons of the oil in a frying pan and add the onion and garlic. Cover and cook slowly for about 30 minutes, stirring occasionally, until very tender. Stir in the sugar and continue cooking, uncovered, until all the liquid has evaporated and the onions have caramelised slightly to a nice brown. Scoop out the onions and reserve. Tip the tinned tomatoes into the pan you cooked the

onions in (so that they pick up the delicious oniony sweetness), add the thyme, stir in the tomato purée and boil down hard, stirring occasionally to prevent it from catching, to give a thick sauce without a hint of wateriness.

Meanwhile, fry the aubergine in the remaining oil in a clean frying pan until very tender and browned. Season the tomato sauce with salt and pepper and stir in the pesto. Discard the thyme stalk if you come across it. Mix the tomato sauce, aubergine and onion together and then add the pollack. Taste and adjust the seasoning and leave to cool.

Roll out just over half the pastry and use to line a 20–23cm (8–9 inch) pie plate. Roll the remaining pastry out to form a lid. Fill the pie with the filling mixture and dot the cherry tomatoes around in it, if using. Brush the edges of the pastry with the egg wash. Lay the lid over the top and trim off the excess pastry. Press the edges together firmly to seal, then make a pretty edging by crimping. Make a hole in the centre. Rest the pie in the fridge for half an hour before cooking. Place a baking tray in the oven and preheat to 190°C/375°F/Gas Mark 5.

Brush the pastry with the remaining egg wash and then bake for about 30–35 minutes, until browned on top. Serve hot or warm, with boiled new potatoes and a big green salad.

Curried Potato and Ling Turnovers

Alternatives: conger eel, catfish, pollack, cod, coley

This is a sturdy way of using ling, beefing it up with finely diced potatoes and a lick of not-too-hot curry paste and then wrapping the whole up in crisp puff pastry. A spoonful of mascarpone keeps the filling moist, adding a hint of sweetness. These pasty-shaped turnovers look pretty and, in my kitchen at any rate, are greeted with considerable enthusiasm. All to the good for, although they can be reheated, they really taste best straight from the oven.

MAKES 4

350g (12 oz) puff pastry
1 egg yolk, beaten with 1 tablespoon water

For the Filling:
250g (9 oz) skinned ling fillet, diced
110g (4 oz) peeled prawns, raw if possible,
    roughly chopped
700g (1½ lb) firm potatoes, e.g. Cara, diced
1 onion, chopped
30g (1 oz) butter
1 tablespoon mild curry paste
4 tablespoons mascarpone cheese
salt and pepper

Make the filling first. Season the ling and prawns with salt and pepper. Blanch the potato dice in boiling salted water for 3 minutes, then drain thoroughly. Fry the onion in the butter, without browning, until tender. Add the potato and curry paste and fry for a further 2–3 minutes, without breaking up the potato. Draw off the heat and cool slightly, then stir in the ling and prawns.

Roll the pastry out on a lightly floured, cool surface. Cut out four 20cm (8-inch) circles. Place 3 heaped tablespoons of the filling on each one, dolloping it on slightly off centre. Put a spoonful of mascarpone on top of each mound of filling. Brush the edges of the pastry with the egg and water mixture, then lift the pastry over the filling to make a half-moon-shaped pasty. Press the edges together firmly and decorate with the tines of a fork. Place on baking sheets and brush with more of the egg wash. Leave to rest in the fridge for half an hour. Preheat the oven to 200°C/400°F/Gas Mark 6.

Brush the turnovers again with egg wash and then bake for 20 minutes. Serve hot.

Ling with Bacon and Saratoga Chips

Alternatives: conger eel, catfish

I once read, and I can't quite recall where, that ling used to be dished up with bacon and parsnips. The idea stuck; it seemed a pleasingly old-fashioned, warming combination. I still think that all three together might make a very good soup but, for the time being, I've brought them together in a way that retains more individuality. Rolls of ling fillet are held in place with a belt of bacon, served on a mildly acidulated bed of sweet onion and set off with a big helping of Saratoga chips or, in other words, parsnip chips. If you ever thought that ling was dull and barely worthy of attention, try this. It's a cheap dish to put together but it sure tastes good.

If you are not keen on getting out the chip pan (or indeed the chip oven), you could replace the chips with parsnip and potato mash (equal quantities of both, mashed with butter and milk and then seasoned with salt, pepper, nutmeg and perhaps a little grated Parmesan).

SERVES 4

500–600g (1 lb 2 oz–1¼ lb) skinned ling fillet
4 rashers of smoked streaky bacon, rinded
1 large onion, chopped
1 tablespoon dripping or butter
1 tablespoon white wine vinegar
2 tablespoons chopped fresh parsley
1 tablespoon melted butter
salt and pepper

For the Chips:
1kg (2¼ lb) large parsnips
sunflower oil or other bland oil, for deep-frying
salt

Preheat the oven to 180°C/350°F/Gas Mark 4. To prepare the chips, peel the parsnips and cut them into fairly chunky chips, removing the woody cores if the parsnips are particularly large.

Cut the ling into 4 portions and season with salt and pepper. Using the back of a knife, stretch the bacon to make a lighter jacket for the ling. Roll each portion of ling up neatly and then wrap a slice of bacon securely around it.

Fry the onion lightly in the dripping or butter over a moderate heat without letting it brown. Stir in the vinegar and half the parsley. Make a bed of this mixture in a shallow ovenproof dish.

Lay the ling on top of the onion with the ends of the bacon tucked neatly underneath the fish. Drizzle over the melted butter. Cover with foil and bake for 10 minutes. Remove the foil and cook for a further 10–15 minutes, until the bacon is looking less anaemic, and rather more attractive, and the ling is just cooked through.

Meanwhile, cook the Saratoga chips. To fry, heat a generous amount of oil to about 170°C/330°F. If you don't have a suitable thermometer or electric deep-fryer (I actually prefer to use my wok for deep-frying), test by dropping a cube of bread in. If it fizzes gently, the oil is about right. Deep-fry the parsnip chips in small batches until crisp and browned – 8–10 minutes. Drain briefly on kitchen paper, season lightly with salt and keep warm in the oven, if necessary.

To bake in the oven, toss the chips in 4 tablespoons of oil in a shallow metal roasting tin. Spread out and roast at 220°C/425°F/Gas Mark 7 for about 20–30 minutes, turning occasionally, until tender in the centre and browned and crisp on the outside.

Serve the parsnip chips alongside the ling and sweet onion, sprinkling the remaining parsley over the fish and onion.

Nagopa

Indian-Style Fried Fish with Spicy Tomato Ketchup

Alternatives: cod, hake, kingfish, grouper, bass, Dover sole, brill

This is the most brilliant way to turn rather plain, cheap fish into something that sets the tastebuds racing and dancing. The recipe is based on one given in Pat Chapman's *Balti Curry Cookbook* (Piatkus). I once tried to pin Pat (and Madhur Jaffrey, who was also filming with us) down to a precise definition of the term 'Balti'. He tried, she tried, and neither of them came up with anything more exact than a Birmingham-refined style of Pakistani cooking, usually applied to one-pot curries. This fried fish seems to be the exception to the rule – it's not a curry at all – but who cares? It is easy, lively and a delight to eat. Serve it with dhal and rice, as Pat suggests or, as I do, with a spicy tomato ketchup dipping sauce, mixed green salad or tomato salad, and new potatoes. A feast either way, and a cheap one at that.

SERVES 4

600g (1¼ lb) skinned pout fillet, cut into 8 pieces
salt
6 tablespoons ghee or sunflower or vegetable oil
lemon wedges and Spicy Tomato Ketchup (see
    page 58), to serve

For the Batter:
150g (5 oz) gram flour (chick-pea flour, from
    Indian shops, Italian delis and wholefood shops)
2 teaspoons salt
2 teaspoons sugar
1 heaped teaspoon cumin seeds
2 garlic cloves, very finely chopped
1 tablespoon white wine vinegar or malt vinegar
3 tablespoons Greek-style yoghurt
2 tablespoons medium curry paste
1 fresh green chilli, de-seeded and very finely
    chopped

Season the pout fillets lightly with salt. To make the batter, mix the gram flour with the salt, sugar and cumin seeds. Make a well in the centre. Mix together the garlic, vinegar, yoghurt, curry paste and chilli. Place in the well and add a slurp of cold water. Start mixing, gradually adding more water, until you have a very thick but pourable batter – about 110–150ml (4–5 fl oz) water in all will see you right. Add the fish fillets to the batter, stir in and then cover and leave in the fridge for 1–2 hours.

Heat the ghee or oil in two large frying pans over a moderate heat. Pick the fish bit by bit out of the batter, making sure each piece is thoroughly coated, and lay it in the hot ghee or oil without overcrowding the pan. Fry, not too fast, for about 4–6 minutes, until the batter is crisp. Then turn over and fry the other side for the same time. Drain briefly on kitchen paper and keep warm while you fry the other pieces. Serve with the lemon wedges and Spicy Tomato Ketchup.

Spicy Tomato Ketchup

In India they have no qualms about offering a bowl of tomato ketchup as a dipping sauce with fried snacks and foods. This is one easy way of spicing up straight ketchup to turn it into a sauce worthy of the finest food. It is best made 24 hours in advance so that the spices have time to merge and settle in. Serve it with Nagopa (see page 57) or with the Goujons of Pollack (see page 54) or, indeed, with any other fried fish (nice, too, with vegetable fritters).

SERVES 4

8 tablespoons tomato ketchup
1 teaspoon cumin seeds
1 teaspoon black mustard seeds
½ teaspoon coriander seeds
½ teaspoon fennel seeds
¼ teaspoon turmeric
¼ teaspoon cayenne pepper

Put the ketchup into a small bowl. Dry-fry all the whole spices until the mustard seeds start to leap out and escape. Tip into a bowl and leave to cool. Grind to a powder with the turmeric and cayenne, then stir half or more of the spices into the tomato ketchup, depending on your taste (I'd use the whole lot myself). If you can leave it for a few hours before serving, so much the better.

Whiting and Tomato Gratin

Alternatives: hake, cod, pollack, bass

In this gratin, the whiting is swiftly cooked in a blanket of raw sweet tomato and mild shallot, each element retaining the freshness of youth. It's a quick dish to put together and a pleasure to eat.

SERVES 4

450g (1 lb) skinned whiting fillets
2 tablespoons finely chopped shallot or red onion
450g (1 lb) tomatoes, skinned, de-seeded and
   chopped
4 fresh thyme sprigs
300ml (½ pint) double cream
85g (3 oz) farmhouse Cheddar cheese, grated
salt and pepper

Preheat the oven to 220°C/425°F/Gas Mark 7. Place a baking tray in the oven to heat through. Lightly grease an ovenproof dish and lay the whiting in it in a single layer. Season with salt and pepper. Scatter the shallot or onion over the fish.

Spread the tomatoes in a thick layer over the whiting. Season and sprinkle with the thyme leaves. Pour the cream over the top and finally top with the grated Cheddar. Place on the hot baking tray in the oven and bake for 25 minutes, until nicely browned.

Poached Whiting Fillets with Orange Butter Sauce

Alternatives: pollack, hake, lemon sole, grey mullet, brill, Dover sole

Whiting has earned a reputation as nursery food and, indeed, it is not one of the most electrifying of fish, but it is pleasant, and delicate, especially when very fresh. Serving the fillets lightly poached in a *court-bouillon* helps their flavour to emerge, while a rich, orange-scented butter sauce whisks them straight into the realms of fine dining (far too good to consign to children alone).

Beurre blanc, butter sauce, is often thought of as a rather daunting chef's sauce but don't be fooled. It is surprisingly easy to make and convenient, too. The lengthy bit – the softening of the shallot and the reduction of the liquids – can all be undertaken in advance. Finishing the sauce is then a matter of a few minutes away from the dinner table. Your guests won't think you rude at all.

During their short season in January and February, replace the orange and lemon juice with the juice of Seville oranges for an even more sublime sauce.

SERVES 4

1 quantity of *court-bouillon* (see page 307)
4 whiting, filleted
salt and pepper

For the Orange Butter Sauce:
1 shallot, finely chopped
125g (4½ oz) unsalted butter, diced
100ml (3½ fl oz) dry white wine
juice of 2 oranges
juice of ½ lemon
finely grated zest of 1 orange
pinch or two of sugar
5–6 tablespoons double cream
salt

For the orange butter sauce, soften the shallot in 15g (½ oz) of the butter over a gentle heat without browning. Put the remaining butter back in the fridge to chill. Add the wine, orange juice and lemon juice to the pan. Boil gently until reduced to about 3 tablespoons, with a marvellously syrupy consistency. Set aside if not serving the sauce imminently.

When you are ready to complete the sauce, re-heat the reduction. Reduce the heat to a thread (or, if it won't turn down sufficiently low, pull the pan back from the heat every now and then so that the sauce doesn't overheat). A few cubes at a time, whisk the butter into the sauce until all is incorporated. Add the orange zest, sugar and cream: 5 tablespoons at first, adding the last one only if the sauce seems a little on the tart side (a little more sugar can go some way towards rectifying this, too, as long as the sauce doesn't start to resemble sweet custard). Season with salt to taste and keep warm over a very low heat while the fillets finish cooking.

If, by any ghastly chance, your sauce seems on the edge of curdling, you are probably overheating it. Plunge the pan into a bowl of very cold water and keep whisking. With any luck, and fast action, it will be saved.

When your guests are all seated at table, and while you are whisking the sauce, bring the *court-bouillon* to just below simmering. Season the fillets, then lower into the *court-bouillon* as many of them as will fit comfortably into the pan. Poach for 2–3 minutes, until the fillets are just cooked through. Lift out with a slotted spoon and allow to drain thoroughly while you cook the remaining fillets. Serve with the orange sauce drizzled temptingly over the pallid flesh of the poached whiting.

Whiting, Leek and Prawn Turnovers

Alternatives: pout, cod, pollack, hake, conger eel, lemon sole, ling

When I was playing around with ideas for fish turnovers wrapped in flaky puff pastry, I came up with two completely different versions, both of which seemed extremely good. After some debate, we decided that the robustness of curried potato turnovers suited a fish like ling marginally better (see page 53), while these creamy leek turnovers with a hint of orange would set off whiting a little more elegantly.

MAKES 4

350g (12 oz) puff pastry
1 egg yolk, beaten with 1 tablespoon water

For the Filling:
250g (9 oz) skinned whiting fillet, diced
85g (3 oz) peeled prawns, raw if possible, roughly chopped
2 leeks, sliced
20g (2/3 oz) butter
juice of ½ orange
110g (4 oz) cream cheese
1 egg, lightly beaten
salt and pepper

To make the filling, season the whiting and prawns with salt and pepper and set aside. Sweat the leeks in a covered pan with the butter and orange juice for 5 minutes, stirring once or twice. When they are almost tender, remove the lid and continue cooking, stirring frequently, until all the liquid has evaporated, leaving a moist mixture. Draw off the heat and cool slightly. Stir in the cream cheese and all the remaining filling ingredients, including the whiting and prawns, but adding only about half the egg.

Roll the pastry out on a lightly floured, cool surface. Cut out four 20cm (8-inch) circles. Divide the filling between them, dolloping it on slightly off centre. Brush the edges of the pastry with the egg and water mixture and then lift the pastry over the filling to make a half-moon-shaped pasty. Press the edges together firmly and decorate with the tines of a fork. Place on baking sheets and brush with more egg wash. Leave to rest in the fridge for half an hour. Preheat the oven to 200°C/400°F/Gas Mark 6.

Brush the turnovers with egg wash again and then bake for 20 minutes. Serve hot.

Inshore and Prime Fish

The closer fish are to the shore, the quicker they can be landed, which is what inshore fish should be all about. With the pressure on fish stocks being so great, boats now have to go further and further afield to catch any fish at all, but there are still some ports where bigger boats simply cannot land. Looe in Cornwall, in the south-west of England, is one of the few active fishing harbours that dries out at low tide, so no beam trawlers – in fact nothing of any great size at all – can operate from there and the fleet has to be in and out as quickly as the tides allow. These days boats can land fish of exceptional quality.

We are still a little behind over here when it comes to appreciating how our fish are caught but the French will quite happily pay higher prices for fish caught by these *petits bâteaux*, and are even quite happy to pay high prices for Looe fish. Much of it goes for export to either France or Spain. But we're talking more than just freshness here. Fish can suffer from the stress of being caught, and small boats, especially those using hand lines, can dispatch their catch relatively quickly. The endless tumbling and crushing of a large trawl not only bruises and damages the fish but also affects its keeping quality. Stress in animals lowers the glycogen level, which in turn lowers the pH (the level of acidity or alkalinity). This reduces its shelf life and, some believe, alters the taste.

The Japanese have got around this by perfecting a fishing method called *iki jimi*, where a spike is quickly pushed through the fish's brain. It might sound a bit, well, Japanese, but it gives a remarkably good piece of fish. There is even a fishery off Poole where spectacularly fresh (and large) plaice are spiked. Sadly, they rarely find their way on to the retail market – there are too many chefs greedily waiting for them.

Some of our finest sea fish are included in this section: John Dories, sea bream and red mullet. They are found more frequently in late summer when they swim with the Gulf Stream but, as winter begins, they chill out and hurry to deeper, warmer waters further south.

Conger Eel

Conger conger
French: Congre
Italian: Grongo
Spanish: Congrio
Portuguese: Congro
German: Congeraal, Meeraal, Conger

Conger eel are rather large, slightly off-putting, serpentine fish with a fearsome reputation. Years ago when I was working on an Irish oyster farm, we used to clean up the nets every now and again. These should have been full of fat young oysters but young conger, equally fat, hid in the nets too, growing too thick to slither out. Sorting out the oysters became an even less attractive job.

Congers, like their flash cousin the moray eel, are ferocious beasts, much loved by sea anglers. They have thick, long bodies, firm flesh, and are not bad to eat. They also have the advantage of being cheap.

Conger was once one of the staples of Cornish cooking, for it was easy to catch along the rocky coastlines. It made an excellent pie and was sometimes dried and grated to make or flavour soup.

Although conger are usually relegated to the soup pot, they can also be roasted, or baked with a strong-flavoured sauce. They are bony, so buy middle cuts off a large fish. Allow 175g (6 oz) per person on the bone. The heads and bones make excellent stock.

Season: All year round.
Yield: 60%
Price: £
Fishing method: Line. They are solitary fish.

John Dory★★

Zeus faber
French: St Pierre
Italian: Pesce San Pietro
Spanish: Pez de San Pedro
Portuguese: Peixe-galo
German: Petersfisch

The solitary Dory is a slimline hunter with

JOHN DORY

a telescopic mouth and a profile so petite that it hides itself from its prey simply by being thin. Quite a feat for one so ugly, but what a pleasure to eat! The name John Dory (it's called Dory for short, by the way) is thought to come from the French *jaune doré*, golden yellow, which well describes the colour of a very fresh specimen. This golden sheen quickly fades, so if your Dory has a glint of gold, then count yourself lucky.

It is a first-class fish but you may feel a little cheated if and when you come to fillet your Dory because there is a phenomenal amount of waste – and precious little fillet. But, *tant pis*, keep the bones, they make a wonderful stock. You may also feel a little sore fingered, since the Dory has a series of nasty projections running along the top that need to be treated with care.

The curiously shaped *Zeus faber* is known by virtually everyone (apart from the Brits, the Portuguese and the Greeks) as St Peter or St Pierre, or a local variation thereof, due to the alleged thumb print of St Peter on its side. The kindly John Dory was thus marked for offering the good saint some money to pay a tax bill, which makes one wish that it could do the same for us lesser mortals. As with the haddock, this story is totally implausible since neither is found in the Sea of Galilee – although, in the Dory's case, they at least live in the sea nearby.

John Dory is fished from England all the way down to the Moroccan Atlantic coast (indeed, Moroccan fish are often extremely good). In the southern hemisphere it is found in virtually indistinguishable form in the waters off New Zealand. It is an excellent, highly adaptable fish that goes well with almost anything. To avoid the fillet curling up in the pan, lightly slash the skin with a sharp knife before cooking. Expect to get little more than 300–350g (10–12 oz) of fillet off a 1kg (2¼ lb) fish, which will feed two; larger fish are becoming hard to find.

Season: In the UK the fish are at their best in autumn. From Morocco, fish available all year round.
Price: £ small, ££ medium, £££ large
Yield: Exceptionally low, 35%
Fishing method: Net.

Grey Mullet®♥

Mugilidae spp.
French: Mulet, Muge (Mediterranean)
Italian: Cefalo, Muggine
Spanish: Lisa, Mujol
Portuguese: Tainha, Mugem
German: Meeräsche

Common grey mullet
Mugil cephalus
French: Mulet cabot

Thin-lipped mullet
Liza ramada
French: Mulet porc

Golden grey mullet
Liza aurata
French: Mulet doré

Thick-lipped grey mullet
Liza labrosus

There are several species of grey mullet that swim in our waters, although I have never once seen any distinction made between them in the UK. The French pay more for the finest species, the golden grey mullet, *Liza aurata* – a fine, delicate-looking fish compared to the largest fish, the big-headed common grey mullet that we most commonly see in the UK. The thin-lipped mullet is distinguished by a light yellow mark on the operculum and a black mark on the pectoral fin. The golden grey mullet has a golden mark on the operculum.

Grey mullet have a grey reputation but there is more to them than meets the eye. The key is their origin. When grey mullet are fished in the open sea they can taste very good, but the fish that moon around harbour mouths eating nasty things, can taste, let's say, a little muddy. Grey mullet have a remarkable ability to thrive in brackish and polluted water and, like ants, would probably survive a nuclear holocaust.

Along the Mediterranean coast, lagoons have been a useful source of fish for generations, and the grey mullet, along with bass and various sea breams, still spawn and are fished there. The mullet's popularity is helped by its excellent roe. Fresh, it can be used to make *taramasaláta* (see page 73) (which, by the way, doesn't have to be livid, pink and glutinous), and you may come across it in dried form as *poutargue* (or *bottargo*), a Mediterranean oddity that retains the very particular pungency of the roe (see page 280).

Perhaps the most remarkable of all the world's mullet fisheries was practised by the Imraguen on the Mauritanian coast in West Africa. When the mullet arrived, the village would move *en masse* down to the sea and start a rhythmic slapping of the water. The local dolphin population knew that this meant mullet, and herded the fish shoreward into the nets. In the general mêlée, the villagers got their fish, and the dolphins either a wild time or some fish for themselves, possibly both. Who knows, but one day I must go to Nouadhi'boue . . .

The large scales of grey mullet are easy to remove, so scale and then fillet the fish, keeping the silver skin to add some colour. A 1.5kg (3¼ lb) fish will feed four with ease. Strong flavours suit this fish and you can use any bass recipe for it. The fillet holds together well when cooked but it's not at its best steamed.

Season: Spring/summer.
Price: £
Yield: 55%
Fishing method: Various.

Gurnard®

French: Grondin, Rouget grondin, Rouget (north), Tombe (large specimens)
Italian: Capone
Spanish: Rubios
Portuguese: Cabra
German: Knurrhahn

Red gurnard
Aspitrigla cuculus
French: Rouget grondin, Galinette
Italian: Capone coccio
Spanish: Rubios, Garneos
Portuguese: Ruiro, Bobo
German: Knurrhahn

Grey gurnard
Eutrigla gurnardus
French: Grondin gris
Italian: Capone gurno
Spanish: Borracho
Portuguese: Cabra morena
German: Grauer Knurrhahn

Tub gurnard
Trigla lucerna
French: Grondin perlon
Italian: Capone gallinella
Spanish: Bejel, Alfondega
Portuguese: Cabra-cabaço
German: Knurrhahn

Flying gurnard
Dactylopterus volitans

There are quite a few species of this fish but, discounting minor variations such as the angle of the slope of their nose and the colour of their skin, they all look like Donald Duck. They have a tough armoured head and three pectoral spines that look like legs protruding from the underside; these are used to feel and, it is thought, 'taste' their way along the sea floor. Of them all, the flying gurnard is the most spectacular, with its brilliant red, wing-like pectoral fins, touched with blue, green and black.

Although gurnard are notorious underwater grunters, no one has, as yet, translated what they're saying . . .   Gurnard are essentially a stock and soup fish: cheap, well flavoured but still good enough to eat in fillet form despite being quite bony. Although most are quite small, you can sometimes see some big fish weighing in at a hefty 2kg (4½ lb) or so, which can be wonderful to eat. The red-coloured skin has few scales. The fish can be cooked with its skin on, but prepare as usual by running a knife from the tail to the head to clean and level the lateral line, which can be a little rough.

Can be cooked as red mullet or grey mullet, or served *meunière* (see page 116).

> **Season:** Spring/summer.
> **Price:** £
> **Yield:** Poor, 40%
> **Fishing method:** Various.

Monkfish, Monk, Anglerfish*

Lophius piscatorius, Lophius budegassa
French: Lotte, Baudroie
Italian: Rana pescatrice, Rospo
Spanish: Rape
Portuguese: Tamboril
German: Seeteufel, Angler

Although these fish do 'angle', I wonder quite why they are called monks? They are ugly, and have a high water content, surely no connection there. They are aggressive and carnivorous but they taste uncommonly good. Still can't get it.

Lophius piscatorius behaves in a most un-Christian fashion. Its vast head has a cavernous mouth edged with needle-sharp teeth and topped by a strange, dangly fishing rod. Hence 'angler', for it sits camouflaged on the sea floor, dangling its rod, waiting for something to swallow the bait. (They are so indolent that their breathing rate can be as low as two breaths per minute.) Any fish unwise enough to fall for this ancient deception will be crunched up, processed and recycled by those menacing jaws. Monkfish heads are thought to be sufficiently ugly to put the fear of God into anyone passing by, which is a shame. Every time I've seen a whole fish, or had the good fortune to buy one, people flock to this monster from the deep, fascinated.

I suspect the reason we seldom see whole monkfish for sale is more prosaic. The head weighs in at well over 50 per cent of the body weight and has little food value, apart from the cheeks. (It does, however, make wonderful stock.) It's sad too that we practically never see monk livers for sale; they are perfectly wholesome, in fact quite excellent. What is the sense in chucking them away? The Spaniards highly rate their *rape*, and rightly so. But they don't seem to be bothered by its looks and are far less wasteful when dealing with it. They sell monk head on and livers in. The head goes into a soup, the liver provides a meal in itself, and the tails are one of the finest pieces of fish you can buy.

Monkfish can live in very deep water – up to about 1,000m (3,280 ft) deep – as well as in the shallower areas worked by the inshore fleet and, as demand is continually increasing, fishing boats are looking further and deeper for this valuable species. Recently, enormous quantities of fish have been found off the south-west of Ireland, provoking a positive monkfish klondyke.

Monkfish are said by the Spanish to have seven layers of skin. They prefer the fish with a dark belly lining, which some people believe are females but which are in fact a separate but related species, *Lophius budegassa*. This lives in shallower water and, as well as having a black lining to its gut cavity, has between eight and ten spines to its dorsal fin, compared to between eleven and thirteen in *Lophius piscatorius*.

By the way, American monk tails are not as good as the European monk; ask any Breton fisherman. Their fish,

MONKFISH

L.americanus, closely resembles *L.piscatorius* but lacks finesse. New Zealand monk (*Kathetostoma giganteum*) is more closely related to a stargazer, and should go straight into the soup pot.

Like all fish, monks get thin and watery after spawning, and if you ever see a particularly scraggy-looking tail it's likely to be what is called a slink, or slinky (a spent or spawned fish). Avoid them.

Although monk are fished from the south of England right up to the north of Scotland, and far off the west coast of Ireland, there is a big difference in how the tails are cut. Fish from the north have more belly and shoulder left on them, which is often trimmed off at a later stage.

Because of their high water content, monk tails should be cooked with very little liquid. They are particularly well suited to being roasted, or served as part of a soup such as the Portuguese *Caldeirada*. A small tail of 200g (7 oz) will feed one, while a 900g–1.35kg (2–3 lb) tail should feed four to six. Remember to remove the skin before cooking, by peeling it back from the head end towards the tail. It comes off easily.

Season: Spring/summer.
Price: ££
Yield: 65%. From tail.
Fishing method: Various.

Rascasse, Scorpion Fish*

Scorpaena scrofa, Scorpaena porcus
French: Rascasse, Chapon
Italian: Scorfano
Spanish: Cabracho, Rascacio
Portuguese: Rascasso, Cantarilho
Catalan: Escorpa roja
Majorquin: Cap roig
German: Drachenköpfe

This red, devilish fish is absolutely essential if you're having the folks round for a quick *bouillabaisse*. The problem is handling it. The *rascasse* might have sweet, succulent flesh, and it might make the most beautiful soup in the world, but it has poisonous spines which, even when the fish is dead, can cause a nasty swelling.

Rascasse are mainly fished in the Mediterranean and off the North African coast but can occasionally be found as far north as Brittany. Possibly because of global warming, they have been seen swimming off the Cornish coast. The first time I ate a *rascasse* was in St Tropez, just before Bardot had begun rescuing abandoned poodles there. The fish, called a *chapon* down in that part of the world, was baked in fennel and served whole, dramatically, with head, spikes and fins intact. It tasted wonderful.

Beware of buying *rascasse* in fillet form. It usually comes from northern France and their *rascasse* is nothing more than the redfish (see page 184), a rather bland and far less exciting creature.

The yield from a true *rascasse* is alarmingly low, which is one reason why it is used so often in fish soups, although, of course, it does have an excellent taste. Unlike the northern Gallic imposter it is not a deep-water fish, and is still caught in nets by smaller Mediterranean fishing boats that work the inner shores.

If you want to eat a *rascasse* whole rather than in a soup, then you'll need a fairly large fish, say a 1.5kg (3¼ lb) one to feed four. To bake whole, add some seasoning, garlic and olive oil to the dish and fish, and stuff the cavity with as much wild or cultivated fennel as possible. Bake in a hot oven for 15–20 minutes until done.

Season: Spring/summer.
Price: £££
Yield: 35%
Fishing method: Various.

Red Mullet***♥

Mullus surmuletus, Mullus barbatus
French: Rouget barbet, Rouget de roche (*Mullus surmuletus*), Rouget de vase (*Mullus barbatus*)
Italian: Triglia
Spanish: Salmonete
Portuguese: Salmonete
German: Meerbarbe

Of the two species of red mullet (illustration on page 66) found in European waters, the one we are most likely to see in the UK is *Mullus surmuletus*, technically known as the surmullet. This fish is distinguished by a narrow yellow band that runs along the length of its body and a stripe on its first dorsal fin. When you see this as a clear, unbroken line, the fish is almost always fresh, and it may tell you something about how it was caught. The French say that the best red mullet *manquent pas une écaille* – don't have a scale out of place. Exactly right. Fish that have tumbled through trawls for hours are a sorry sight; guts split, red eyed and dull. So your bright-eyed, still stripy red mullet would almost certainly have been fished by a small boat close to port.

The other variety of mullet, found mainly in the Mediterranean, is *Mullus barbatus*, what the French call *rouget de vase*. It has a lovely mottled skin which changes its pattern at night – the blotchier the mottle on your fish, the darker it was when caught – and, as the Romans noticed, the colours also change as the temperature increases. Classical texts tell us that this unfortunate fish was once slowly boiled in a glass bowl by a wealthy Roman so that he could marvel at the miraculous changes in its colour as it died. The Romans were mad about mullet – one fish fetched the price of nine bulls in a Roman market – but they showed a distinct preference for large fish, the size of which you would never see in the Mediterranean these days: 'Do not dishonour your gold serving-dish by a small mullet: none less than two pounds is worthy of it.' Such fish were quite clearly not destined for the tables of the poor.

Today, Mediterranean red mullet are few and far between. There are some *rougets vendangeurs* caught on the Catalan coast (as the name would suggest, during the grape harvest) but you really need to be on the rocky coast at Banyuls, sipping wine and talking grapes to get into such an esoteric speciality.

The red mullet has a loyal following in Europe. To the uninitiated, it may look like little more than a stretched goldfish, but it is in the eating that it excels. Once they were known as *bécasse de mer*, woodcock of the sea, because they were often cooked, as is the woodcock, with the liver left in. The Romans made a type of fish sauce, or *garum*, from the red mullet livers alone, and it was said to be the finest of them all.

You really need to grill a red mullet to appreciate it at its best, so ask for it to be scaled and gutted. Before you grill it, slash the body on both sides diagonally down to the bone to help it to cook more quickly and evenly. Rosemary goes particularly well with red mullet, so add a sprig or two if possible. A 200g (7 oz) fish will feed each person well. If you want to fillet a red mullet, ask your supplier to look out for a larger fish, but you'll rarely find red mullet bigger than 500g (1 lb 2oz), and smaller fish are tastier anyway. (To tell the difference between the species, *Mullus barbatus* has a steeper profile, and three scales under its eye; its cousin has two.)

There are two warm-water species of red mullet that appear for sale over here and which should more properly be called goatfish. Neither the West African Red Mullet (*Pseudopeneus prayensis*) nor the Yellowfin Goatfish (*Mulloidichthys varicolensis*) from the Arabian Sea rivals the native European species for taste or looks.

Season: Throughout much of the year. Spring, summer for French (La Turballe, Boulogne); autumn for Catalan and UK fish, although the latter are available in smaller quantities during summer.
Price: £££
Yield: 50%. Serve whole.
Fishing method: Beam-trawled fish to be avoided. Use day-boat fish if possible.

Sea Bass★★★ Bass

Dicentrarchus labrax
French: Bar (north and west), Loup de mer (Mediterranean)
Italian: Branzino, Spigola
Spanish: Lubina
Portuguese: Robalo
German: Zackenbarsch

Sea bass (illustration on page 67) are sleek, intelligent fish. Fishermen like

them, anglers love them, and gourmets, restaurateurs, chefs, the Japanese, Chinese and Italians all rate them as amongst the finest fish in the sea.

Bass appear to be quite aware that our intentions towards them are not always honourable. When the sun is shining and the days and nights are clear, landings are usually down, for the fish can clearly see the boats and tend to scarper. But as soon as it gets rough and visibility goes down, the landings conversely go up.

In Britain, most bass are caught in the southern half of the country, increasingly by hand lines. Fresh line-caught bass are ravishingly beautiful – bright silver, bright eyed, superbly hard to the touch. There is an excellent fishery off Dorset, and you can also find them off Jersey, south Wales and even the Essex coast.

In the summer, bloated bass are a problem, and this is due not just to overeating but a tendency of females in roe to absorb a large amount of water. Some bass shoal and gorge themselves on pilchards and herring and are targeted by trawlers, who bring back huge amounts of dubious-quality fish that have a tendency to decompose alarmingly quickly.

Inevitably, demand pushed up its price so much that sea bass became just too expensive for most of us. Notice, however, the use of the past tense here, for help has come from an unlikely quarter: aquaculture. The Italians and the French have been saved from bass starvation by the recent explosion in bass farming in the Mediterranean. Despite this, farmed fish have managed to hold their price quite well but, much to the fishing community's annoyance, the price of wild fish has actually fallen. The French bass fishery, troubled by the consumer's inability to distinguish between wild and farmed fish, has taken to labelling each line-caught bass. It has to be said, differentiating farmed from wild fish isn't easy. If you happen to see a shop with a whole load of bass of almost identical size, and some with snubby noses, then they are almost certainly farmed.

Sea bass is one of the most

adaptable of fish but avoid using overpowering flavours with it. The skin is always good to eat, so keep it on, remembering to scale the fish before you clean it. This is a good fish to steam, or to eat raw if superbly fresh.

Season: Spring/summer.
Price: £££
Yield: 50%
Fishing method: Line, trawl.

Sea Bream

Atlantic and Mediterranean species

Gilt-head sea bream, Royal bream★★★
Sparus aurata
French: Dorade royale
Italian: Orata
Spanish: Dorada
Portuguese: Dourada
German: Meerbrassen, Goldbrassen

Red sea bream★★
Pagellus bogaraveo, Pagellus centrodontus
French: Pageot rose, Dorade (or Daurade) rose, Gros yeux
Italian: Pagro, Pagello
Spanish: Besugo
Portuguese: Besugo
German: Nordischer Meerbrassen

Black sea bream, Black bream
Spondyliosoma cantharus
French: Dorade grise, Griset
Italian: Tanuta
Spanish: Chopa
Portuguese: Choupa
German: Streifenbrassen

Ray's bream, Atlantic pomfret®
Brama brama
French: Castagnole, Brème de mer, Hirondelle
Italian: Pesce castagna
Spanish: Japuta, Palometa
Portuguese: Xaputa, Chaputa
German: Braschsenmakrele

Mediterranean and North-west African fish

French names are often used
Bogue
Boops boops

Dentex
Dentex dentex
French: Denté

Marbré
Lithognathus mormyrus

Oblade
Oblada melanura

Pagre®
Pagrus pagrus

Pageot, Pandora, Common pandora®
Pagellus erythrinus
French: Pageot, Dorade rose, Pageot commun, Breka
Italian: Pagello, Fragolino
Spanish: Besugo, Breca
Portuguese: Bica
German: Kleiner Rotbrassen

Saupe, Salema
Sarpa salpa
French: Saupe
Italian: Salpa
Spanish: Salema
Portuguese: Salema
German: Goldstrieme

White bream®
Diplodus sargus
French: Sar
Italian: Sarago
Spanish: Sargo
Portuguese: Sargo
German: Bindenbrassen

Sea bream, sea bream, wherefore art thou, sea bream? Everywhere and nowhere. Sea bream is as broad a category of fish as snapper, which admirably suits restaurant and dinner-menu planners, but *naming* sea bream deserves a book to itself. Above I offer a selection of the most commonly found species but I have no need to remind you that scientific accuracy sometimes has to take second place to common usage.

To me the red sea bream, *Pagellus bogaraveo*, is the true one. It's rare these days, but once flocked like a tourist to the Cornish coast, swimming up with the Gulf Stream. This is a marvellous fish, which you can tell apart from other bream by the light black mark just behind its head on the lateral line. It has a rounder profile than a snapper or any other fish masquerading as a sea bream. Attractively coloured, it's not a vulgar, but rather an elegant, red. Remarkably, as far as I can discover, this is one of the few European fish with a black mark that hasn't had the finger of St Peter story thrust upon it.

Red sea bream are strong, fighting to the last when caught – a gallant and tasty fish. They swim southwards with the onset of winter and have become a Christmas favourite with the Gallegans and Basques of northern Spain and southern France. There is a complex and highly ritualised fishery there which has given the fish, *besugo*, enormous local prestige.

There is a second related species, *Pagellus centrodontus*, which is a slightly paler version but lacks such a strong black mark and has smaller eyes. Both have powerful jaws and can crunch up molluscs and crustacea alike. On such a diet they are good to eat.

The fish that most would consider a lesser prize, the black sea bream (*Spondyliosoma cantharus*), has a particular fondness for the Sussex coast. If you happen to be strolling along the seafront of Littlehampton one fine May day, cast your eyes seaward and think of the thousands of little black bream having a wonderful time spawning not far from the shore. Stick to a fish of at least 500g (1 lb 2 oz), which will serve two well.

Rarer visitors to the UK are Ray's bream, *Brama brama*, which have a strong following in Portugal. They have excellent, tasty, firm flesh but can be riddled with parasites. They are trying to get us to call this fish the Atlantic pomfret, which more accurately suggests its looks and texture. The 'Ray', by the way, was John Ray, who lived in

GILT-HEAD SEA BREAM

the seventeenth century. He was the first to describe *Brama brama*, and also to record the peculiar mass strandings that once occurred along the British coast in late summer.

The finest of all sea breams is *Sparus aurata*, referred to by most in English as the gilt-head bream but by me, stubbornly, as the royal bream, from its French equivalent, *dorade royale*. It is an exquisite fish, both to look at and to eat. Don't be fooled into thinking that they have suddenly become common; like the sea bass, royal bream are being successfully farmed in the Mediterranean.

What's really 90s about these fish, or perhaps 80s come to think of it, is their bisexuality. Like many of the *Sparidae* family, they start off being male and transform themselves into females at a

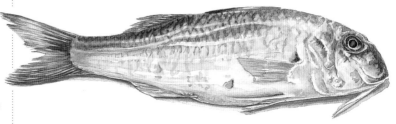

RED MULLET

SEA BASS

certain age, with testes developing first and ovaries next. What a life! And a crown and good looks to boot.

Both the *dorade royale* and red sea bream are found in the Mediterranean but there are quite a few sea bream that *we* don't have and *they* do. Although strictly speaking the term *pageot* refers to the pandora, it has become more usual to refer to *Pagrus pagrus*, a fish that one would expect to be called *pagre*. (In French, *pagre* more often refers to a larger specimen, sometimes of either species.) The majority of fish you see are caught in the Atlantic off the coast of Mauritania and Senegal, where they are neatly graded, packed and flown across to Europe. A delicate pink fish, in its freshest form it can be very good indeed, but it does tend to lack zing.

The Italians have a particular liking for the *sar*, or white bream. This is a good fish, certainly not white to look at, which actually resembles a slightly striped version of the black bream.

Most sea bream are on the small side and are best cooked on the bone. Any snapper, sea bass or red mullet recipe will do for this large family of fish, which are all good to grill or bake. Larger fish can be filleted but try to keep the skin on, slashed lightly across with a knife to stop the fillets curling up when cooking. Most species can be eaten raw, although the quality of imported *pageot* is seldom good enough for *sashimi*.

The cheaper fish such as *bogue*, *oblade* and *saupe* are best fried, but *pageot* and Ray's bream can be used for any pomfret or pompano recipe. Allow a 300–400g (11–14 oz) fish per person, or a 500–800g (1 lb 2 oz–1¾ lb) fish for two.

Season: Summer for black bream, autumn for gilt-head and red sea bream.
Price: ££/£££
Yield: 50%
Fishing method: Line. Trawled fish poor quality.

Weever*

Trachinus draco
French: Vive
Italian: Dragone
Spanish: Escorpión
Portuguese: Peixhe-aranha
German: Petermann, Petermännchen

These are fish to handle with care. The weevers may sound like an American sitcom family but they are good, indeed excellent, for soup, despite having poisonous spines. We recently ate one grilled on a barbecue, stuffed with savory, and it was quite delicious. If you can get hold of some, a 200g (7 oz) fish will feed one, but you rarely see fish bigger than 300g (11 oz).

Remember that live fish can inflict a serious wound from the venomous first set of dorsal fins (which are generally cut out before the fish are sold).
Season: Spring/summer.
Price: £
Yield: 40%. Eat whole or use in soups.
Fishing method: Various.

Wrasse

Labrus spp.
French: Labre, Vieille, Coquette
Italian: Labridi
Spanish: Merlo, Tordo, Gallano
Portuguese: Bodião
German: Lippfisch

Perhaps weighed down by the damning Latin name of one of their family, *Labrus turdus*, many of this large group of lippy, highly coloured fish are dismissed as 'having little culinary value' or words to that effect.

But there are, as always, exceptions. The Romans developed a positive mania for *Euscarus cretensis*, the parrotfish wrasse. Although more of a parrotfish than a wrasse, we can include it here – the orders are quite similar.

There are still corners of the world where wrasse are esteemed. The Majorcans love their *raor* (*Xyrichthys novacula*), an interesting wrasse which appears fitfully in the autumn, the Madeirans their *bodião* and the Catalans their *tort*. The French, however, wisely consign theirs to the soup pot. The tautog, from the eastern seaboard of the USA, is quite good, and I have been told that the Chinese love their *tsing ye*, another wrasse-type fish.

Of the wrasse that one sees for sale, most would indeed be best used in a soup. The rarer kinds can be baked or steamed, but be sure of your species.
Season: Spring/summer.
Price: £
Yield: 40%
Fishing method: Various.

Moroccan Conger Eel with Raisins and Onions

Alternatives: ling, monk (use skinned fillet and omit initial simmering)

A speciality of Safi, which was where we got stranded late one night as William sat talking in a freezing warehouse with like-minded Moroccan fish-dealers. The water was alive with phosphorescence, a beautiful evening, but quite foodless. If only they could have conducted business over a plate of conger eel.

It seems a most weird and ridiculous combination of ingredients to us but it's worth trying, out of curiosity if nothing else. You will be surprised. Serve it with warm Arab flat bread or pitta bread or, if you want a more substantial starchy accompaniment, boiled rice or even couscous. Moroccans like their conger cooked far beyond what we would consider done, to the point where it begins to collapse down into the sauce.

SERVES 4–6

1–1.5kg (2¼–3¼lb) conger eel, cut into 6 pieces
500g (1 lb 2 oz) carrots, thinly sliced
500g (1 lb 2 oz) red onions, halved and sliced
  into thin semi-circles
250g (9 oz) seedless raisins
1 teaspoon freshly ground black pepper
2 teaspoons ground cumin
1 teaspoon ground cinnamon
generous pinch of saffron strands
10 garlic cloves, chopped
4 tablespoons chopped fresh coriander
900ml (1½ pints) water
110ml (4 fl oz) sunflower oil
salt

Preheat the oven to 200°C/400°F/Gas Mark 6. Drop the fish into boiling water and let it simmer for 4 minutes. Lift out and scrape off the skin with a thin-bladed knife. Remove the large central bones and as many smaller bones as you can. Make a bed of carrots in a lightly oiled flameproof baking dish. Place the conger on top and then strew over the onion and raisins. Mix the pepper, cumin, cinnamon, saffron and some salt and sprinkle over, then scatter on the garlic and half the coriander. Add the water and oil, cover and bake for an hour, stirring occasionally.

Transfer to the hob and boil the sauce for about 15 minutes to give a fairly thick, stewy consistency. Taste and adjust the seasoning, scatter with the remaining coriander and serve.

Jersey Conger Eel Soup

Alternatives: ling, monk (reduce initial cooking time by 20 minutes)

This soup from the island of Jersey brings together the fine vegetables that grow on the island with rich milk from its pastures and fish from the seas. Not the smarter fish that can be so good there, but conger eel. It's sturdy peasant fare, a main-course chowder to fill hungry stomachs. There's one charming touch that marks it out and that's a scattering of marigold petals (perfectly edible, though not absolutely essential) to bring flashes of colour and a delicate taste.

SERVES 6–8

1kg (2¼ lb) piece of conger eel
1.7 litres (3 pints) water
½ green cabbage, shredded
1 large onion, chopped
2 carrots, diced
110g (4 oz) shelled fresh peas, or thawed
    frozen peas
300g (11 oz) small new potatoes, halved
2 tablespoons chopped fresh parsley
2 fresh thyme sprigs
2 marigold leaves, and the petals of 1 or 2
    flowers to garnish (optional)
1.15 litres (2 pints) full-cream milk
30g (1 oz) butter
30g (1 oz) plain flour
150ml (¼ pint) double cream
salt and pepper

Chop the conger eel up into large chunks and rinse. Put into a saucepan with the water and bring up to the boil. Simmer for 40 minutes, skimming off any scum that rises to the top. Strain off the liquid and reserve. Remove the skin of the conger and pick off the edible flesh left on the bones. Reserve the flesh and discard the skin and bones.

Return the liquid to the cleaned saucepan and add all the vegetables plus the herbs, including the marigold leaves, and salt and pepper. Simmer until the vegetables are tender. Add the milk to the pan and bring back to the boil. Mash the butter with the flour to form a paste. Dot little bits into the soup and stir until dissolved. Return the fish to the pan and simmer the soup gently for 5 minutes, until lightly thickened. Stir in the cream and then taste and adjust the seasoning – it needs a fair amount of salt to save it from blandness. Scatter with marigold petals, if using, and serve.

Saint-Pierre à la Menagère

John Dory Baked in Potato Gratin

Alternatives: bass, grouper, snapper, emperor, turbot, halibut, monk

This is one of the classic French ways of cooking John Dory and no wonder. It is so very good, with its layers of potato protecting the fish, the whole kept moist and beautifully flavoured with liberal dousings of melted butter and white wine. From the thin slices of potato it derives an alternative name, *Saint-Pierre à Parmentier*, the title given to many fine potato-laden dishes in honour of the brilliant man who popularised the potato in France, against the odds.

With smaller fish, you will need to blanch the potato slices so that the fish doesn't overcook before the potato is tender. If you can lay your hands on one large John Dory, big enough to feed four (we're talking around 2.5–3kg (5–7 lb), which is pretty rare), then you can just get away without the blanching, since the fish will require that much longer to cook through.

SERVES 4

2 John Dory, weighing about 700g (1½ lb) each, cleaned
700g (1½ lb) waxy potatoes, peeled and very thinly sliced
60g (2 oz) butter, melted
150ml (¼ pint) dry white wine
salt and pepper
chopped fresh parsley, to garnish

Preheat the oven to 190°C/375°F/Gas Mark 5. Leave the heads on the John Dory. Blanch the potato slices in boiling water for 2 minutes, then drain thoroughly. Brush a baking dish with a little of the butter and then lay just under half the potato slices in it in a thin layer (better to leave some out than overload the dish with too thick a layer). Season with salt and pepper and then drizzle over about one-third of the melted butter. Lay the fish on top, season with salt and pepper, drizzle with a little more butter and then cover with the remaining potato slices, laying them on neatly. Season and spoon over the last of the butter; pour over the wine.

Bake for 30 minutes, until the fish and potatoes are just cooked through, basting frequently with the juices of the dish. If you wish to brown the potato slices to a rather more becoming state, whip the dish under a thoroughly preheated grill for a few minutes. Grilled or no, sprinkle with parsley and serve.

Salad of John Dory, Orange and Beetroot

Alternatives: bass, grouper, snapper, emperor, turbot, halibut, monk, zander, barracuda

Unlike other fish, the filleted side of a John Dory divides neatly into three strips, rather than the more usual two. You'll see exactly what I mean when you take a look at it. In this recipe, the strips are quickly pan-fried to top a salad of peppery watercress and rocket, sweet beetroot and tart oranges: a surprisingly good combination.

SERVES 4

2 John Dory, weighing about 700g (1½ lb) each, skinned and filleted
2 tablespoons olive oil
plain flour
salt and pepper
snipped fresh chives, to garnish

For the Salad:
large handful of watercress
large handful of rocket
1 large or 2 small beetroot, preferably home-cooked, skinned and diced
2 oranges, peeled and segmented

For the Dressing:
1½ tablespoons lemon juice
3 tablespoons lemon olive oil and 2 tablespoons olive oil, or 5 tablespoons olive oil
salt and pepper

Divide each fillet neatly into three along the natural lines. Cut the larger pieces in half. Season with salt and pepper and set aside while you prepare the rest of the salad.

To make the dressing, season the lemon juice with salt and pepper and then whisk in the oil(s) a tablespoon at a time. Taste and adjust the seasoning.

Shortly before serving, toss the greenery with this dressing. Arrange on a plate and scatter with the beetroot and orange.

Heat the remaining oil over a high heat. Dust the fillet pieces lightly with flour and fry very quickly, until just firm. If you got the oil hot enough in the first place they will also be patched with brown. Lay the fried fish over the salad, sprinkle with chives and serve at once.

Grilled John Dory with Salsa Verde

Alternatives: bass, grouper, snapper, emperor, halibut, monkfish

The Italian *salsa verde*, literally 'green sauce' – with its armfuls of fresh herbs, enlivened by the piquancy of olives, capers and anchovies and bound by breadcrumbs – goes well with many fish but it is especially good with the firm flesh of John Dory. It looks beautiful, too, drizzled across the robust lozenge of its body, burnished in the heat of the grill.

The *salsa verde* is at its best when freshly made but it keeps happily in the fridge for a day or two (and up to a week if you put it into a clean jar and cover the surface with a layer of oil to seal out impurities). The quantities sound vague – how big is a bunch of parsley? – but that is in the nature of the sauce. Variations abound, and the key is to taste and play with the balance of flavours until it pleases you. This recipe is meant only as a basis for your own creation.

SERVES 4

4 John Dory, weighing about 350g (12 oz) each,
    cleaned
extra virgin olive oil
salt and pepper

For the Salsa Verde:
bunch of fresh parsley
handful of fresh basil leaves
4 tinned anchovy fillets
2 tablespoons capers, rinsed, or thoroughly
    soaked if salted
2 garlic cloves, chopped
45g (1½ oz) pitted green olives, roughly chopped
    (optional – can be replaced with an extra
    2 anchovy fillets and another tablespoon
    of vinegar)
1 tablespoon white wine vinegar
slice of good-quality white bread, crusts
    removed, torn into pieces
150–250ml (5–9 fl oz) extra virgin olive oil
salt and pepper

Make a couple of diagonal slashes across each side of the body of each John Dory. Season the fish with salt and pepper.

To make the *salsa verde*, slash the leaves from the bunch of parsley. Put them into a food processor with all the other ingredients except the olive oil and seasoning. Process in short bursts, scraping down the sides, until finely chopped. Keep the blades whirring as you trickle in enough olive oil to give a thickish sauce. Taste and adjust the seasoning.

Preheat the grill. Brush the fish with olive oil, then grill about 10cm (4 inches) away from the heat, until browned and just cooked through, turning once. Serve straight away, with the *salsa verde*.

Taramasaláta

Alternatives: tuna roe

If you are lucky enough to gather roes from the insides of grey mullet it is easy to make your own *taramasaláta*. It is so much nicer – and quite different from – the bought stuff with its unnatural, bright pink hue. I usually begin by covering the roes in equal quantities of sugar and salt, which as well as seasoning them partially cures them, giving a longer fridge life. A form of *taramasaláta* can be made using fresh cod's roe if grey mullet roe is out of the question.

Since this recipe is largely a matter of balance and tasting, the exact quantity of roe that you start with doesn't matter too much. If it is a little less or a little more, just adapt the recipe as you go along, adding more lemon, oil or water to get a good consistency and a pleasing taste. If you wish, try adding a little chopped onion to the processor with the roes and breadcrumbs, or replace the crumbs with a few spoonfuls of cooked potato.

Traditionally, *taramasaláta* is a winter dish in Greece, made with dried salted roes, or *taramá*. Some Middle Eastern and Greek shops sell it. Break it up into lumps and soak in cold water for a good half an hour before using. You will need to increase the ratio of breadcrumbs to roe to make up for its more intense flavour, and you may need extra oil as well.

SERVES 4–6

225g (8 oz) fresh grey mullet roes
coarse salt
granulated or caster sugar
60g (2 oz) fresh white breadcrumbs
juice of ½ lemon
150ml (¼ pint) olive oil
60ml (2 fl oz) cold water
chopped fresh parsley and cayenne pepper,
   to serve

Place the roes in a shallow bowl. Mix equal quantities of salt and sugar and dredge over the roes, covering them entirely. Cover with cling film and leave in the fridge for at least 24 hours. They'll keep well in their brine for 3 or 4 days at least.

When you are ready to use them, drain and rinse thoroughly. Place in a bowl and break up into pieces, pulling away as much of the skin as comes off easily.

Then cover with cold water and leave for 10 minutes. Tip into a sieve lined with muslin and leave to drain. Squeeze out the last of the water.

Put the roes into a food processor with the breadcrumbs. Start the blades whirring and add the lemon juice, then trickle in the oil slowly until about two-thirds of it is incorporated. Keep the motor running and add the water, then carry on with the oil until it is all used up. If the taramasaláta is too thick, add a little more water. The final consistency should be that of very thick double cream. Taste and add a little more lemon juice if you want it sharper, or process in a little more oil if the flavour is too strong. Scrape into a bowl.

Just before eating, sprinkle with parsley and a light dusting of cayenne. Serve with warm pitta bread.

Samak Harrah

Lebanese Baked Grey Mullet with Coriander and Nut Stuffing

Alternatives: bass, snapper, grouper, emperor

I love this Lebanese stuffing of coriander, garlic and nuts, which goes so well with grey mullet. Roasting the garlic softens it, but otherwise I've borrowed the recipe lock, stock and barrel from the Lebanese food writer Anissa Helou. It appears in her book *Lebanese Cuisine* (Grub Street), an essential for anyone interested in the cooking of the Middle East.

One small word of warning – rinse the coriander thoroughly under the cold tap to make sure that all grit has been washed away. You would be surprised how much grit and grime lurks amongst those innocent-looking leaves and, if you don't wash it out, you will only discover it too late, as you take your first mouthful of stuffing. Be warned.

SERVES 4

1.5kg (3¼ lb) grey mullet, or 2 x 900g (2 lb) grey mullet, scaled and cleaned

For the Stuffing:
1 head of garlic
olive oil
60g (2 oz) pine nuts
60g (2 oz) shelled walnuts
1 heaped teaspoon coriander seeds
leaves of 2 bunches of fresh coriander, finely chopped
1 onion, finely chopped
2 plum tomatoes, de-seeded and finely diced
1 teaspoon ground cumin
juice of 1–2 lemons
½ teaspoon cayenne pepper
8 small firm tomatoes, to take leftover stuffing
salt and pepper

To make the stuffing, preheat the oven to 200°C/400°F/Gas Mark 6. Place the head of garlic in an oiled small, shallow dish and drizzle over a teaspoon of olive oil. Add 3 tablespoons of water. Roast for an hour, until tender. While it is cooking, dry-fry the pine nuts, walnuts and coriander seeds over a medium heat for a few minutes, to toast them. Leave to cool. Drop them into a food processor and grind in short bursts, so that they are still slightly knobbly. When the garlic is done, squeeze the roasted garlic out of the individual skins into a bowl with the nuts. Add the coriander leaves, onion, tomatoes, cumin, lemon juice to taste, cayenne, salt, pepper and about 8 tablespoons of olive oil. Mix thoroughly.

Cut lids off the top of the small tomatoes, scoop out the insides with a spoon, then season with salt and leave upside-down on a rack to drain for at least 20 minutes.

Reduce the oven to 180°C/350°F/Gas Mark 4. Fill the fish with the stuffing and either sew up with thick thread or secure with wooden cocktail sticks or metal skewers. Place the fish in an oiled baking dish. Scatter about 2 tablespoons of the remaining stuffing over the fish, then fill the tomatoes with the last of the stuffing.

Bake the fish for about 30–40 minutes, until just cooked through, adding the tomatoes after 20 minutes. Serve warm or at room temperature.

Baked Gurnard with Chicory and Orange Compote

Alternatives: red mullet, redfish, rascasse, John Dory, bass

The bitterness of chicory (choose spears that are edged with yellow, not those tinted green, which will have been over-exposed to the light, making them too bitter for enjoyment), softened by cooking and the citrus sweetness of orange juice, is a lovely foil for gurnard or red mullet. Here I've partnered it with baked gurnard but you might well prefer to grill the fish.

SERVES 2

2 gurnard or red mullet, weighing 175–225g
(6–8 oz) each, scaled and cleaned
olive oil
salt and pepper
chopped fresh parsley, to garnish

For the Compote:
1 large orange
15g (½ oz) butter
1 tablespoon finely chopped shallot or onion
2 spears of chicory, sliced 5mm (¼ inch) thick
1 tablespoon lemon juice
1 teaspoon sugar
salt and pepper

Preheat the oven to 200°C/400°F/Gas Mark 6. Make the compote first. Pare 4 strips of zest from the orange and cut them into thin shreds. Blanch in boiling water for 2 minutes, drain and set aside for the garnish. Cut the orange in half and squeeze the juice from one half. Cut the other into wedges and reserve. Melt the butter in a small pan over a fairly low heat. Add the shallot or onion and cook gently, without browning, until tender. Add the chicory and continue cooking, stirring, for a further 2 minutes or so. Add the orange juice, lemon juice and sugar. Stir to mix and simmer, stirring occasionally, until the mixture is moist rather than liquid – about 5 minutes. Season and keep warm.

Meanwhile, make two deep slashes on each side of each fish. Season and brush with oil, then wrap each one securely in a square of silver foil. Bake for about 20 minutes, until cooked through. Unwrap and serve with the chicory and orange compote, scattered with the reserved orange zest and parsley, with the orange wedges tucked alongside.

Lotte Dunkerquoise

Monkfish with Beer and Cream

Alternatives: cod, bass, brill, plaice

This recipe from the north of France brings monkfish head-on to a glass of beer. Not the most obvious collusion, but shelve any doubts: it turns out remarkably well. The beer forms the basis of the sauce, along with the copious juices thrown out by the fish itself, but both are aided and abetted by a touch of tomato purée and a good slurp of cream.

SERVES 4

900g (2 lb) monkfish tail, filleted and cut into
    4cm (1½-inch) chunks
2 fresh parsley sprigs
1 bay leaf
2 fresh thyme sprigs
30g (1 oz) butter
3 shallots, chopped
200ml (7 fl oz) lager
3 tablespoons tomato purée
4 tablespoons *crème fraîche* or double cream
salt and pepper

Season the monkfish with salt and pepper. Tie the herbs together with string to make a *bouquet garni*.

Melt the butter in a frying pan large enough to take the monkfish in a single layer. Fry the shallots gently until translucent. Lay the monkfish pieces on top and tuck the *bouquet garni* amongst them. Pour over the beer. Cover and cook over a very gentle heat for 10 minutes or so, until the monkfish is barely cooked. Transfer the fish to a warmed serving dish, using a slotted spoon, and keep warm while you finish the sauce.

Return the pan to the heat and stir the tomato purée and cream into the beer and juices. Boil until reduced to a moderately thick sauce. Stir in any liquid given off by the monkfish and reduce a little more if necessary. Taste and adjust the seasoning, pour over the fish and serve.

Gigot de Lotte

Roast Monkfish Tail

Alternatives: tuna, swordfish

A skinned and beheaded tail of monkfish bears a passing resemblance to a leg of lamb and is sometimes known, therefore, as a *gigot*. The piscine *gigot* can, as it happens, be cooked in a similar fashion to the meaty one: studded with slivers of garlic and needles of rosemary and roasted in a hot oven.

SERVES 4–6

900g–1.35kg (2–3 lb) monkfish tail
2 garlic cloves, cut into fine shards
leaves of a small fresh rosemary sprig
½ red onion, thinly sliced
glass of dry white wine (about 110ml/4 fl oz)
110ml (4 fl oz) extra virgin olive oil
salt and loads of freshly ground pepper

Make slits all over the monkfish tail and push in slivers of garlic and rosemary leaves, using the handle of a teaspoon or some other thin, blunt instrument. Place in a hole-free plastic bag with the onion, pour over the wine and oil and season with a little salt and lots of pepper. Knot the bag tightly and sit it in a dish, to catch any escapologist drips. Marinate for at least an hour and up to 12 (in the fridge), turning the bag occasionally. If necessary bring back to room temperature before cooking.

Preheat the oven to 190°C/375°F/Gas Mark 5. Place the onion slices in an ovenproof dish and sit the monkfish on top. Pour over the marinade. Roast for 25–30 minutes until just cooked through, basting occasionally with the pan juices.

Fried Monkfish with Salsa Verde

Alternatives: John Dory, cod, any flat fish

Cut into thin slices, monkfish takes well to flash-frying over a beltingly high heat. If the temperature is ferocious enough the flood of liquid that usually emerges will evaporate as it hits the pan, leaving beautifully moist, tender little sippets of fish. Cooked like this, they go particularly well with the herby sharp Italian sauce, *salsa verde*.

SERVES 4–6

900g–1.35kg (2–3 lb) monkfish tail, filleted
1 quantity *Salsa Verde* (see page 72)
olive oil, for frying
salt and pepper

Make the *salsa verde* as on page 72.

Slice the monkfish fillets across the grain into pieces about 5mm (¼ inch) thick. Just before you eat, season and fry the monkfish slices briskly in olive oil over a high heat. Drain briefly on kitchen paper and serve with the *salsa verde*.

Provençal Fish Soup

I adore this intensely flavoured, smooth, brick-red soup, which comes with little garlicky croûtons and *rouille*, a peppery, thick sauce, to stir into it. It is the most reviving ambrosia after a long day doing anything at all. It's made its way on to many restaurant menus and, even if they do take it out of a jar, it is still a great pleasure to eat.

It also happens to be a great pleasure to make and, though it requires a few leaps of faith if you are not familiar with the recipe, there is nothing difficult about it at all. Two things are crucial. The first is a good mix of fish, amongst them, for preference, a brace of rascasse for the most authentic of flavours, or at least a couple of fine red mullet for the next best thing. Some recipes sanction water as the liquid but I think it is essential to use a good fish stock, to give depth to what is a smooth, thin soup.

There are several different versions of *rouille*. Often, you will be served a garlicky, saffron and pepper mayonnaise but the original is based on bread and remains, to my mind, by far the best choice. If you have any left over, use it as a dip with prawns or spoon it over baked or boiled potatoes. Delicious.

SERVES 6-8

1.8kg (4 lb) mixed fish (rascasse, if you can get them, and/or a few red mullet, but also conger eel, wrasse, monkfish, gurnard, sea bream or any fish that is not oily)
250g (9 oz) shell-on raw prawns
110ml (4 fl oz) extra virgin olive oil
1 onion, chopped
1 carrot, sliced
1 leek, white part only, sliced
1 red pepper, de-seeded and chopped
1 celery stick, sliced
1 large head of fennel, diced
8 garlic cloves, chopped
½ tablespoon coriander seeds, coarsely crushed
1½ × 400g (14 oz) tins of tomatoes
2 tablespoons tomato purée
bouquet garni of 1 fresh rosemary sprig, 2 fresh thyme sprigs, 3 fresh parsley sprigs, and 2 bay leaves, tied together with string

juice of 1 orange
1 strip of dried orange zest
2.5 litres (4 pints) Fish Stock (see page 308)
generous pinch of saffron threads
3 tablespoons Pernod
½–1 teaspoon cayenne pepper
salt and plenty of pepper

To Garnish:
8–12 slices of French bread
olive oil
Rouille (see opposite)
freshly grated Gruyère or Parmesan cheese

Cut the fish into chunks that are roughly 5cm (2 inches) across. Set aside with the prawns.

Put the oil in a large pan and add the vegetables, garlic and coriander seeds. Stir to coat in oil and then cover and sweat over a low heat for 15–20 minutes. Now add the tomatoes, tomato purée, *bouquet garni*, orange juice, orange zest, fish, prawns, salt and pepper. Cook over a high heat for 5 minutes, stirring occasionally to prevent it from catching. Now add the stock, bring up to the boil and simmer for 45 minutes. Add the saffron, Pernod and cayenne and simmer for another 10 minutes. Cool slightly and fish out the bundle of herbs, then liquidise the whole contents of the pan (yes, including the prawns in their shells) to a smoothish sludge. Now pass the soup through the fine blade of a vegetable mill or rub through a fine-meshed sieve, pressing through all the juice. Taste and adjust the seasoning, adding a generous grinding of black pepper.

Meanwhile, for the garnish, preheat the oven to 200°C/400°F/Gas Mark 6. Brush the slices of French bread generously with olive oil, then bake until golden brown and crisp, turning once. Place in a plate or bowl and pass around as the soup is served, along with a bowl of *rouille* and another filled with grated cheese, so that everyone can help themselves.

Rouille

SERVES 6–8

2 x 2.5cm (1 inch) thick slices of French bread
pinch of saffron strands
1 tablespoon hot water
1 red pepper, grilled and skinned (see page 49)
½–1 medium fresh red chilli, de-seeded and
   roughly chopped
3 garlic cloves
¼ teaspoon salt
110ml (4 fl oz) olive oil

Tear the bread up roughly and place in a bowl. Add enough water barely to cover and leave for 5–10 minutes. Put the saffron in a small bowl and spoon over the hot water. Leave to steep. De-seed the pepper and chop roughly. Place either in a mortar or the bowl of a food processor with the chilli and garlic. Drain the bread and squeeze out the water with your hands. Add to the pepper and chilli, seasoning with the salt. Pound or process to a smooth paste and then gradually work in the olive oil as if making mayonnaise (though you can afford to be a little more heavy-handed). Stir in the saffron and its water, then taste and adjust the seasoning.

Fried or Grilled Red Mullet with Warm Tomato Vinaigrette

Alternatives: bass, sea bream, emperor, snapper, grey mullet, Dory

A vinaigrette, softened with the sweetness of raw summer tomatoes and gently warmed through, makes a delicious dressing for fried or grilled red mullet. Better still, try it with mullet that have been barbecued to a smoky turn.

SERVES 4

4 red mullet, weighing 175–200g (6–7 oz) each, cleaned and scaled
juice of ½ lemon
olive oil or olive and sunflower oil
salt and pepper

For the Vinaigrette:
3 tomatoes, peeled, de-seeded and chopped
1 teaspoon chopped fresh tarragon, basil or chives
1 shallot or ½ small onion, very finely chopped
85ml (3 fl oz) olive oil
1 tablespoon fresh lemon juice
salt and pepper

Snip the fins off the red mullet and make two diagonal slashes across the thickest part of the body of each fish on each side. Season inside and out with salt, pepper and the lemon juice. Leave for at least half an hour before cooking.

If you want to fry the fish, pour enough olive oil (or olive oil mixed with sunflower oil) into a large, heavy frying pan to fill it to a depth of about 2cm (¾ inch). Heat up over a high heat. Dry the fish and lay them in the hot oil. Fry for about 4–5 minutes, until browned and cooked through on the underside. Turn and repeat on the other side. Drain briefly on kitchen paper.

If you wish to grill the fish, preheat the grill thoroughly. Dry the fish on kitchen paper. Brush the grill rack and fish with olive oil, then lay the fish on the grill rack and season generously. Grill for about 4–6 minutes on each side. Check to make sure that they are cooked through to the bone.

Mix the vinaigrette ingredients in a small pan and heat gently. The dressing should be warm, not hot. Serve the hot fish with the warm dressing.

Tarte Fine of Red Mullet and Fennel

Alternatives: bass, sea bream, emperor, snapper, grey mullet, Dory

A *tarte fine* is a thin disc of puff pastry with a topping of some sort, baked at high heat until puffed and brown. It requires last-minute assembly and cooking but the results, in this case at least, more than justify the bother.

SERVES 4

4 medium red mullet, weighing 175-200g
  (6-7 oz) each, scaled and filleted
2 small or 1 large head of fennel
extra virgin olive oil
1 generous tablespoon finely chopped fresh basil
½ tablespoon finely chopped fresh parsley
1 teaspoon capers, rinsed (soaked if salted) and
  finely chopped
1 garlic clove, crushed
1 tablespoon tomato purée
pinch of sugar
250g (9 oz) puff pastry
salt and pepper

Preheat the oven to 230°C/450°F/Gas Mark 8. Season the red mullet fillets with salt and pepper and set aside. Trim the fennel, reserving the feathery fronds to use as a garnish. Halve the fennel lengthways and slice finely. Put into a pan with a tablespoon of oil, a tablespoon of water and a little salt. Cover and sweat gently for 5–10 minutes, until the fennel is tender. Drain and reserve. Mix the basil, parsley, capers, garlic, tomato purée and sugar with 1½ tablespoons of olive oil.

Roll the puff pastry out very thinly and cut out four 20cm (8-inch) circles. Lay them on oiled baking sheets and prick all over with a fork. Brush or smear the olive oil and herb mixture over the circles, leaving a 1cm (½-inch) border all around the edge. Now divide the fennel between the circles – it should cover them more or less but don't start heaping it up if you have a lot to spare. Cut the red mullet fillets into strips, wipe them dry and arrange, skin-side up, over the fennel, pressing down gently. Brush the red mullet, fennel and edges of pastry with olive oil.

Bake for 5 minutes. Whip the tarts out of the oven, brush the edges of the pastry with olive oil again and then return to the oven for a further 5 minutes, until the fish is just cooked through. Serve immediately, scattered with the reserved fennel greenery.

Grilled Red Mullet with Tapenade

Alternatives: gurnard, sardines, bass, sea bream, emperor, snapper, grey mullet, John Dory

Tapenade, the powerful caper and olive paste from the South of France, could have been tailor-made for red mullet, with a punchy saltiness that is a perfect match for the fish's gaminess. Together they work wonders – a pungent, exuberant marriage which reeks of Provence. Use the best-quality black olives and take the trouble to pit them yourself; the ready-stoned ones are often soapy and second rate and will produce a miserable apology for tapenade.

You'll end up with more tapenade than you need for this recipe but the remains will keep in the fridge for a week or more if you spoon it into a screwtop jar and cover it completely with olive oil before sealing and stashing. Spread it on grilled bread for a quick first course, perhaps with slices of sweet tomato on top, or dollop into baked potatoes with scoops of soured cream. Or you could make the famous *oeufs tapenade*, by mashing the yolks of halved hard-boiled eggs with tapenade and then piling the mixture back into the shells.

SERVES 4

4 medium red mullet, weighing 175–200g
  (6–7 oz) each, scaled and cleaned
3 tablespoons olive oil
juice of ½ lemon
¼ teaspoon cayenne pepper
2 handfuls of rocket leaves
French dressing
salt
lemon wedges, to serve

For the Tapenade:
250g (9 oz) black olives, pitted
4 tinned anchovy fillets
2½ tablespoons capers, rinsed
  (and soaked, if salted)
2 garlic cloves, chopped
½ tablespoon chopped fresh basil leaves
½ teaspoon fresh thyme leaves
½ teaspoon freshly ground black pepper
4 tablespoons olive oil

Make two diagonal slashes across the thickest part of each side of the fish. Whisk together the olive oil, lemon juice, cayenne and some salt. Brush over the red mullet and then drizzle what remains over them. Cover and leave for an hour or two.

To make the tapenade, put all the ingredients except the oil in a food processor and process in brief bursts to give a slightly knobbly purée. Add the olive oil and process briefly to mix in.

Preheat the grill thoroughly, then grill the red mullet fairly close to the heat for 4–6 minutes on each side, until just cooked through.

Toss the rocket leaves in the dressing and then divide between 4 plates. Lay the grilled mullet on the leaves and heap a little mound of tapenade beside each. Add lemon wedges and serve.

Chinese Steamed Sea Bass with Soy Sauce and Sesame Oil

Alternatives: sea bream, snappers, emperors, grouper, grey mullet

If you've ever eaten this dish in a Chinese restaurant, you'll know how very glamorous it is: a whole silvery sea bass, sizzling under its scattering of green spring onion and threads of red chilli. The moist, steamed flesh tastes superb, with its seasoning of soy sauce. The hot oils release the fragrance of the ginger and garlic, keeping it fresh and immediate.

As long as you have a steamer that will take a whole sea bass, this dish is remarkably easy to prepare at home; a spectacular way to begin a dinner party.

SERVES 2 AS A MAIN COURSE,

4 AS A STARTER

1 sea bass, weighing about 1–1.5kg (2¼–3¼ lb), cleaned and scaled, but head on
2cm (¾ inch) piece of fresh root ginger, peeled and cut into fine matchsticks
2 garlic cloves, finely chopped
1 fresh chilli (mild–medium hot), de-seeded and cut into fine threads
4 spring onions, cut into fine threads
2 tablespoons sesame oil
2 tablespoons sunflower or vegetable oil
2 tablespoons soy sauce
small handful of roughly chopped fresh coriander leaves
salt and pepper

Trim the dorsal and side fins off the fish. Season the stomach cavity lightly. Make three diagonal slashes across each side of the sea bass so that it cooks more easily. Find a heatproof plate that will just fit into your steamer, allowing a little room around the edges so that the steam can circulate. If the fish is too big to curl up on the plate, cut it in half so that it will fit neatly.

Place the steamer over a pan of boiling water and put the plated fish in the basket. Cover the basket with a cloth (making sure that the ends don't trail down on to the hob and burst into flames) and then put the lid of the steamer firmly on top of that. Steam for about 8–12 minutes, until the fish is just cooked through but no more than that. If you really have to transfer the fish to a more glamorous serving dish, do it quickly, now. Sprinkle the ginger, garlic, chilli and spring onions over the fish.

Put the two oils quickly into a saucepan and heat until smoke rises, then pour the oil over the fish and flavourings. Drizzle on the soy sauce, scatter with coriander and rush to the table forthwith.

Sea Bass Baked in Salt

Alternatives: bass, grey mullet, snapper, emperor

There is nothing to match this method of cooking a whole fish buried in a hummock of salt. It is the purest, most perfect recipe in the book, with only two essentials: very fresh fish and a big bag of coarse sea salt. Like a protective blanket, the salt envelops the fish without oversalting the flesh (the scales form a light barrier), trapping all its goodness inside. William and I often cook it in our house in France, where we can buy sacks of coarse salt for a few pence (the grey coarse sea salt is lovely stuff, and you can buy it in most French supermarkets – stock up while you are on your holidays). The cliff around the house is strewn with wild fennel plants, so I always tuck a handful of fronds inside the fish to give it a gentle aniseed scent. Not absolutely essential, by any means, but a good addition if you grow fennel in your garden.

SERVES 2

**1 sea bass (or sea bream), weighing around
   1–1.5kg (2¼–3¼ lb), cleaned but not scaled
handful of sprigs of fresh fennel or dill (optional)
plenty of coarse sea salt**

Preheat the oven to 200°C/400°F/Gas Mark 6. Take the sea bass and fill the stomach cavity with fennel or dill, if using. Find an ovenproof dish just large enough to take the fish and make a thin but thorough bed of salt on the bottom. Lay the fish on top and then bury it entirely under a thick layer of salt. Sprinkle a little water over the salt – just a few flicks of the hand after you've run it under the cold tap, or a quick spritz with a water sprayer. Bake for 25–30 minutes, depending on size. Sea bream takes a little longer – add on another 5 minutes.

Take the fish to the table in its mound of salt. Break open the salt crust to reveal the fish hidden underneath. Scrape away the salt and pull off the skin to reveal the perfectly cooked, moist flesh in all its glory. (It's a good idea to have a second dish on hand to take the spent salt and the skin and bones.) Serve the fish immediately.

Seared Sea Bass Fillet with Plum and Star Anise Compote

Alternatives: cod, halibut, salmon

The tart and slightly bitter flavour of cooked plums goes very well with sea bass, working as lemon might, but in a rather fruitier way, to emphasise its flavour. Here, the plums are cooked lightly in their own juice and then given a final lift with a splash of balsamic vinegar. A twelve-year-old, more mature – and, yes, more expensive – balsamic gives a marvellous richness, so use the full tablespoon if you have it. The cheaper, younger balsamics tend to be sharper, though the flavour is still good. Start off by adding just half a tablespoon, increasing the amount slightly if you think the compote can take it.

SERVES 4

4 portions of sea bass fillet, weighing about
   110g–175g (4–6 oz) each, with skin on, scaled
sunflower oil
salt and pepper
roughly chopped fresh chives, to garnish

For the Compote:
2.5cm (1 inch) piece of fresh root ginger, grated
1 small red onion, chopped
2 garlic cloves, chopped
30g (1 oz) butter
500g (1 lb 2 oz) red plums, halved and stoned
60g (2 oz) caster sugar
2 whole star anise
½–1 tablespoon balsamic vinegar
salt and pepper

Preheat the oven to 240°C/450°F/Gas Mark 8. If you have whole fillets, long and tapering, cut them in half (easier to handle in the pan). Season the fish on both sides with salt and pepper. Set aside.

To make the compote, cook the ginger, onion and garlic gently in the butter, without browning, until tender. Add all the remaining ingredients except the balsamic vinegar, salt and pepper. Cook gently over a low heat without covering for 5 minutes, stirring once or twice, until the plums are just tender but still holding their shape more or less. Stir in the vinegar, then taste and adjust the seasoning. Re-heat gently, until warm rather than hot, just before serving.

Put a heavy ovenproof pan or griddle over a high heat to heat through. Pat the fish dry on kitchen paper and then brush the skin side with oil. Place, skin-side down, on the pan or griddle and leave for 2 minutes. While it cooks, brush the upperside with oil. Turn over, immediately pop into the oven and roast for a further 3 minutes.

Warm up the compote. Serve the hot bass, crisp skin-side up, sprinkled with chives, with the compote on the side.

Grilled Coconut-marinated Pageot

Alternatives: pomfret, sea bream, snapper, parrotfish

This is a recipe I came up with when I lived in an area of London with strong West Indian, Greek and Irish communities. There's not much of the Irish in it, I'll grant you, but the exuberance of coconut milk and chillies, the heat of the grill, or better still the barbecue, take me back to the small shops full of exotic ingredients that lined the grey streets.

SERVES 4

4 pageot, weighing 300–400g (11–14 oz) each,
    or other whole fish (pomfret is good), cleaned
2 medium onions, finely chopped
4 garlic cloves, finely chopped
4 small red or green chillies, de-seeded and
    finely chopped
300ml (½ pint) coconut milk (see page 308)
1 lime or lemon, cut into wedges

Make three or four slashes across the thickest parts of the fish on each side. Mix the onions, garlic, chilli and coconut milk. Pour over the fish and leave to marinate for at least an hour and up to 4 hours in a cool place, turning occasionally.

Grill the fish, close to the heat at first, to brown on both sides, moving them about 2.5cm (1 inch) further away to finish cooking until opaque through to the bone. Warm the marinade gently and brush it over the fish occasionally as they cook. Serve with lime or lemon wedges.

Besugo al Horno

Alternatives: bass, grey mullet, snapper, emperor

Besugo al horno just means 'bream baked in the oven'. Not much of a giveaway. Even if I were to tell you that it was whole bream baked on a bed of potatoes you would still have little inkling of the excellence of this dish. In fact, it deservedly takes pride of place at Christmas in Spain. It is served on Christmas Eve, an essential part of what is, for the Spaniard, the major feast of the whole festivities. And what a star it is, too. The potatoes are garlicky and enriched with olive oil and the juices of the bream, while the fish itself sits proudly atop them in full glory. If you only ever cook bream once, this is the way to do it.

SERVES 6

1 royal sea bream, or red snapper or emperor,
    weighing about 1.8–2kg (4–4¼ lb)
juice of 1 lemon
1kg (2¼ lb) potatoes, peeled and thinly sliced
1 large onion, thinly sliced
4 garlic cloves, roughly chopped
pinch of saffron strands (optional)
5 tablespoons roughly chopped fresh parsley
6 tablespoons extra virgin olive oil
4 tablespoons water
salt and pepper

To Serve:
fresh parsley sprigs
fine curls of lemon zest

Preheat the oven to 190°C/375°F/Gas Mark 5. Make a couple of deep slashes on either side of the bream, across the thickest part, so that it cooks evenly. Season inside and out with salt and pepper and then squeeze over the lemon juice and rub it in well, again inside and out. Set aside.

Arrange the potatoes and onion in layers in a greased ovenproof dish, large enough to take the bream as well eventually (I use a shallow rectangular dish about 34 x 23cm, (13½ x 9 inches). Put the garlic, saffron, parsley and a teaspoon of salt into a mortar. Pound vigorously to a paste. Gradually work in 4 tablespoons of the olive oil and then the water. Give it a final stir and spoon over the potato and onion. Bake in the oven for 40 minutes, until the potato and onion are almost cooked.

Lay the bream on top and spoon over the remaining 2 tablespoons of olive oil. Return to the oven and bake for another 25 minutes or so, until the bream is just cooked through. Tuck in a few decorative sprigs of parsley, scatter with lemon zest and serve immediately.

Flambéed Sea Bream with Fennel and Coriander

Alternatives: bass, grey mullet, snapper, emperor

A dish full of drama, this, and very fitting, too, for one of the finest and most beautiful fishes around. The whole bream is baked in foil but the excitement comes right at the last minute when, surrounded by a small thicket of fresh herbs, it quite literally goes up in flames, spitting and sparking in the heat of an alcohol-induced haze. The haze is a heat haze and it is flaming brandy that ignites the excitement. By the time the flames have died down, the cooking juices are nicely flavoured with brandy (but without the alcohol, now that it has burnt off), while the fish takes on some of the scent of the charred herbs.

SERVES 4

1 sea bream or red snapper, weighing about
   1.5kg (3¼ lb), scaled and cleaned
olive oil
30g (1 oz) fresh fennel or dill sprigs
10 fresh coriander sprigs
juice of ½ lemon
85ml (3 fl oz) brandy
salt and pepper

Generously oil a sheet of foil large enough to wrap around the fish and lay the bream in the centre. Season the inner cavity and tuck 2 fennel or dill sprigs and a coriander sprig inside. Trickle the lemon juice over the fish, rub it in with your hands and then season with salt and pepper. Wrap the bream up in the foil, sealing tightly. Lay it on a baking sheet and keep cool in the fridge until ready to cook if not cooking straightaway. Bring back to room temperature before cooking.

Preheat the oven to 200°C/400°F/Gas Mark 6. Bake the fish for 25 minutes or until just cooked through to the bone. Transfer to a warmed serving dish, pouring its juices over it. Cover with the whole sprigs of fennel or dill and coriander.

Heat the brandy gently in a small pan until warm but not hot, and certainly not boiling. At arm's length, set a lighted match to it and then pour it over the fish and herbs in a flaming stream. Serve once the flames have died down.

Fish with No Bones – The Cartilaginous Fish

There is a weird and wonderful collection of fish that don't have a bone to their body. Skeleton yes, but true bone, no. Called Chondrichthyans, they have skeletons of cartilage instead of bone, and include sharks, rays and some bizarre, soft-headed fish called chimaera. They have evolved different solutions to those everyday problems that fish confront: how to survive in sea water, how to float and how to reproduce. While bony sea fish increase the salt content of their bodies by continually drinking sea water, Chondrichthyans retain salts from within. Among these salts is urea, a natural product of the breakdown of proteins, which is found in high enough levels to counterbalance the osmotic pressure from the sea.

Soon after the fish dies, the urea begins to break down and forms ammonia, which makes the whole shebang quite offensive and definitely inedible. Whatever anyone says in any book, or in any circumstance at all, this smell does *not* go away. If the fish is handled correctly, there shouldn't be a problem, and that means that it must be bled, since the urea is found in the blood. Another option, used widely where shark is dried in the sun, is to bleed the fish and then soak the flesh in brine.

Cartilaginous fish don't have a swim bladder, which controls buoyancy, so in order to avoid sinking like a stone they have developed large livers which are rich in oil. These have a double function: they act as a liver should and also as a sort of internal floatie, with the high level of oil tending to pull the fish to the surface.

Sadly for them, shark and many of their relations are simply not very cuddly. Even though shark stocks are under great pressure, no one seems to get very worked up about them. Demand for sharks' fins and even shark meat is on the up. To compound their problems shark take a long time to reach sexual maturity, laying small numbers of eggs and, in some cases, giving birth to live young. Even the oil from the liver and the rough skin have important specialist markets; there is also a belief that extracts from the cartilage may help fight cancer, a claim as yet unproven. Things will, I suspect, get worse for these troubled fish.

SHARKS AND DOGFISH

Cooking Hints

Mako and porbeagle are considered the best sharks to eat but they are far from being everyone's favourite fish. Porbeagle, or *taupe* in French, is eaten in France as *veau de mer*, which nicely hints at its meatiness and rosy colour. A long meeting with a marinade makes shark easier to eat. Strong spices and chilli are quite permissible. Thinly sliced shark is more palatable than great chunks.

Blue Shark

Prionace glauca
French: Peau bleu
Italian: Verdesca
Spanish: Tintorera
Portuguese: Tintureira
German: Grosser Blauhai

The blue shark is migratory, appearing off the Cornish coast in summer. A slow-swimming shark that drifts with the ocean currents, it isn't particularly wonderful to eat but if you're fond of shark you'll like the blue shark's teeth; it has a particularly fine set. The meat from a blue is very white.
Season: Summer.
Price: ££
Yield: Fair, 40%
Fishing method: Line.

Dogfish, Huss, Rock Salmon®♥

Lesser-spotted dogfish
Scyliorhinus caniculus
French: Petite roussette
Italian: Gattopardo
Spanish: Pintarroja
Portuguese: Pata-roxa
German: Katzenhai

Nursehound
Scyliorhinus stellaris
French: Grande roussette, Saumonette
Italian: Gattopardo
Spanish: Alitan
Portuguese: Pata-roxa-gata
Catalan: Gató
German: Katzenhai

Dogfish can be many things but, whether it's a cat, dog or huss, is a type of small shark, and can be a surprisingly good fish to eat. Since eating dog is taboo in this country, the dogfish was cannily renamed rock salmon by some bright spark. In France, this relatively common fish has been similarly upgraded to *saumonette*, or little salmon.

Wherever you find them, dogfish are sold skinned, devoid of any sharkiness, looking curiously unlike anything that lives in the sea. They are used in the most curious places too. In the UK dogfish go almost entirely to the fish and chip trade, but in Germany there is an insatiable demand for smoked dogfish stomach flaps. In Catalonia, the *gató* is often cooked with a heavy emphasis on black pepper.
Season: All year round.
Price: £
Yield: 75%, as skinned
Fishing method: Various.

Mako Shark

Isurus oxyrinchus
French: Mako, Taupe bleu
Italian: Squalo mako, Ossirina
Spanish: Marrajo
Portuguese: Tubarão-anequim
German: Mako, Makrelenhai

Sharp nosed and beautiful, mako are thought by some to be the best shark available. Widely distributed, they have good white flesh but they are not fish to go swimming with. They seem to sell quite well in supermarkets, although quite why is beyond me. I think they are rubbery and tasteless, and need a good dose of chilli to make them palatable. Sorry, thumbs down from me, but go for it if you're a rubber fetishist.
Season: All year round.
Price: ££
Yield: Sold as loin or fillet, 40%
Fishing method: Long line, net.

Porbeagle

Lamna nasus
French: Taupe
Italian: Smeriglio
Spanish: Cailón, Marrajo
Portuguese: Tubarão-sardo
German: Heringshai

A stocky, classic-looking shark, the porbeagle is fished in seas off countries as far apart as Lebanon and Iceland. To shark-fishers off the coast of Cornwall it has a reputation as a lazy fish, easy to land, but it is an impressive catch all the same. It tends to swim near the surface when the weather is calm, and wanders around the oceans following a pattern as yet to be understood by *homo sapiens*.
Season: All year round.
Price: ££
Yield: Sold as loin or fillet, 40%
Fishing method: Line, net and trawl.

Tope

Galeorhinus galeus
French: Requin-hâ
Italian: Cane
Spanish: Cazón
Portuguese: Perna-de-moça
German: Hundshai

Typically what we call tope is not what the French call *taupe*. They are both sharks, however, and our tope is as widely distributed as the French *taupe*, our porbeagle. It is a slimmer, browner shark, giving birth to as many as twenty live young at a time. Not a great shark to eat.
Season: All year round.
Price: £
Yield: Sold as loin or fillet, 40%
Fishing method: Line, net and trawl.

SKATES AND RAYS

Common skate
Raja batis
French: Pocheteau gris, Tyre (Boulogne)
Italian: Moro
Spanish: Noriega
Portuguese: Raia-oirega
German: Glattrochen

Thornback ray, Roker
Raja clavata
French: Raie bouclée
Italian: Razza spinosa
Spanish: Raya de clavos
Portuguese: Raia-lenga
German: Keulen-Stachel

Blonde ray
Raja brachyura
French: Raie lisse
Italian: Razza
Spanish: Raya boca de rosa
Portuguese: Raia-pontuada
German: Rochen

When is a skate not a skate? When it is a ray. There's a longstanding deception. Since skinned wings of indeterminate type are generally all that one sees of the fish, the intricacies of what is ray/skate are best left to the supplier. The true skate, *Raja batis*, has a longer snout and smoother skin than all the other species but blue skates, grey skates, spotted rays, starry skates etc. all look very similar when skinned and cut . The thornback ray (*Raja clavata*) is considered to be one of the finest rays. It is a confusing world, but since skates and rays all taste fairly similar, thorns and knobbles are largely irrelevant.

They are an unadventurous group of fish, and tend to sit camouflaged on the sea bed, waiting for prey to pass by. Migration or long-distance swimming is not one of their favourite pastimes, and stocks are so localised that there are even species unique to Malta and Madeira. They have evolved a clever way of breathing without opening their mouths which, since they are often buried in the sand along with the rest of the fish, seems eminently sensible. On their top side they have a vent, and it is through this that the water passes over the gills to provide oxygen for the body.

Reproduction with all the cartilaginous fish is a sexier affair than with most of the bony fish. The male – almost always smaller than the female, by the way – grips his mate tightly, often by the teeth as well as by his rather lewd-looking claspers. Coupling can go on for some time but the fertilised eggs won't be passed out for a month at least, and do so as neat little packages, an overnight bag with all that a baby ray requires – food, protection and a relatively stable home. At each corner there is a filament which grips on to seaweed, or something solid, and stops the eggs being swept away by the current. When the juvenile fish hatches it can be about 20cm (8 inches) long, and is quite capable of getting on with life, eating small crustaceans and minding its own business straight away.

The wing is the fish's pectoral fin, flattened by millions of years' evolution, and has sweet flesh that's easy for anyone to eat. One of the nicest skate dishes I have had uses raw skate, a dish we ate in a Korean restaurant in Camden, north London, years ago. Sophie has been nagged into experimentation and has come up with something that approximates it (see page 96). Ray is an immensely versatile fish but let me put a word in for skate knobs, which are very good and are cut from the tail end, and skate cheeks which give an excellent nugget of flesh.

A wing weighing 225–250g (8–9 oz) will feed one but larger wings have a higher meat to bone ratio. Allow about 225g (8 oz) per person. The classic dish of *Raie au beurre noir*, or skate with black butter (see page 95), works well, and many shark recipes can be quite easily adapted to skate. You could just as well serve shark *au beurre noir*! If you are ever unfortunate enough to have to deal with an unskinned wing I suggest that you remove the skin after cooking. Otherwise, you'll need a stout pair of pliers to grip the skin and peel it off.

Season: Most of the year.
Price: ££
Yield: Bought as wings, 50%
Fishing method: Trawl.

Skate with Black Butter

This remains one of the very best ways to cook skate. Prime skate, butter, lemon juice and capers are the essential, perfect companions. This is a dish for a homely weekday supper *à deux* (as long as you are not too cholesterol-conscious) but just as suitable for a smarter dinner party – just double or treble the quantities (though you can cut down a bit on the vinegar in the poaching water) and allow a little extra time for the butter to brown.

SERVES 2

450g (1 lb) skate or ray wings, skinned
3 tablespoons white wine vinegar
1 tablespoon lemon juice
45g (1½ oz) unsalted butter
1 tablespoon capers, rinsed (soaked if salted)
1 tablespoon chopped fresh parsley
salt and pepper

Place the skate wings in a large pan and pour over the vinegar. Season with salt and pepper. Add enough water to cover and bring slowly to a gentle simmer. Turn the heat down and poach for 10–15 minutes or until the skate wings are just cooked through. Drain well, arrange on a serving dish, sprinkle the lemon juice over the fish and keep warm.

Place the butter in a small pan to melt. Turn up the heat and cook until it begins to turn brown. As soon as the colour begins to deepen, remove from the heat and add the capers and parsley. Pour quickly over the hot skate and serve.

Spiced Skate

Alternatives: brill filet, sole fillet, cod fillet

Coated with a mixture of crushed black peppercorns, coriander and oregano, these skate wings are fried until crisp on the outside and tender inside. All they need after that is a squeeze of lemon juice and a few new potatoes on the side. Delicious.

SERVES 2

2 portions of middle skate or ray wing,
    weighing about 175g–225g (6–8 oz)
    each, or 2 small wings, skinned
1½ teaspoons black peppercorns
1½ teaspoons coriander seeds
1½ teaspoons dried oregano
plain flour
1 egg, beaten
2 tablespoons sunflower oil
salt
lemon wedges, to serve

Season the skate wings with salt. Crush the peppercorns and coriander seeds coarsely and mix with the oregano. Spread out on a plate. Coat the wings lightly with flour, shake off the excess, and then dip into the beaten egg. Press the spice and herb mixture gently on to the wings, coating them evenly on both sides. Heat the oil in a frying pan large enough to take both portions. Fry fairly gently, turning once, until they are just cooked through. Serve immediately, with the lemon wedges.

Korean Skate Salad

Alternatives: monk, John Dory, pomfret

This is based on a salad we used to eat in a small Korean restaurant in Camden, where it was hidden away in the Korean section of the menu, not translated into English. They used raw skate but my Korean cookbooks also suggest sea bream, Dover or lemon sole or even plaice. Whichever you choose, make sure that it is extremely fresh and use it on the day it is bought. Ask your fishmonger to fillet and skin it for you (take the cartilage home, too, to make stock), and then all you will need to do is slice it very thinly.

Kochu jang is the essential, very powerful, Korean chilli paste used widely to season Korean food. It is not easy to find, which is a pity, as it has a very particular, rich, velvety consistency. Chinese chilli paste with garlic is a fairly good substitute if you can't get the proper thing, or you could even try the fiery Moroccan harissa. Whatever you use, it should be thick rather than runny.

SERVES 6

500g (1 lb 2 oz) fresh skate or ray wings, skinned and filleted
½ large cucumber
1 large carrot
15cm (6 inch) length of white radish (daikon or mooli)
1 tablespoon pine nuts, lightly toasted

For the Sauce:
2 tablespoons *kochu jang* (Korean chilli and soy bean paste) or Chinese chilli paste with garlic
1½ tablespoons caster sugar
1 tablespoon sesame oil
1 tablespoon rice vinegar
1½ tablespoons soy sauce
1 heaped teaspoon sesame seeds, lightly toasted
2 garlic cloves, crushed
1cm (½ inch) piece of fresh root ginger, grated
4 spring onions, white part only, chopped

Cut the fish into very fine slivers, no more than about 5mm (¼ inch) wide and around 4–5cm (2 inches) long.

Cut the cucumber, carrot and white radish into fine matchsticks, about 4–5cm (2 inches) long. Mix all the sauce ingredients together. Shortly before serving, mix the sauce with the fish and vegetables. Pile on to a serving dish and scatter with the pine nuts. Serve straightaway.

Terrine of Skate with Grilled Vegetables

Skate is naturally gelatinous and sticky so, with its distinct, firm texture, it is perfect material for a cool summer terrine, to be served in slices as a first course. Here the terrine is fleshed out with grilled vegetables, giving it a smoky flavour that emphasises the sweetness of the fish.

You will need to allow plenty of time for preparing this terrine, though it can be done in stages, so tackle it the day before you intend serving it, and enjoy yourself.

SERVES 8

1.35kg (3 lb) skate wings, skinned
juice of 1 lemon
1 large aubergine, sliced thinly lengthways
olive oil
2 large tomatoes, peeled and quartered
2 red peppers, grilled and skinned (see page 49)
1 yellow pepper, grilled and skinned (see page 49)
salt and pepper

For the *court-bouillon*:
big glass of white wine (about 150ml/¼ pint)
4 black peppercorns
½ teaspoon coriander seeds, bruised
1 fresh parsley sprig
2 shallots, sliced
1 carrot, sliced
¼ fennel bulb, sliced
2 strips of lemon zest

To Serve:
best extra virgin olive oil, Pesto Dressing (page 184) or Lemon Mayonnaise (page 311)
lemon wedges
chopped fresh parsley or chervil or whole fresh basil leaves

To make the *court-bouillon*, put all the ingredients into a pan with 450ml (16 fl oz) of water and bring up to the boil. Simmer for 5 minutes, then leave to cool. Strain. Place the skate, cut up if necessary, into a shallow, close-fitting pan and pour over the *court-bouillon*. Bring gently up to the boil, reduce the heat and poach for 5–10 minutes (depending on the thickness of the wings), until the skate is just done and pulls easily away from the inner cartilage. Lift the skate out and strip off the bones. Add the bones to the poaching liquid, return to the heat and boil until reduced by half. Strain, taste and season, adding a little lemon juice to invigorate.

Meanwhile, salt the aubergine lightly and leave for at least half an hour. Rinse and dry. Brush the pieces with olive oil and grill until browned and tender. Remove the inner core of the tomatoes completely, along with the seeds, and cut the flesh into strips that can be comfortably flattened down. Season lightly with salt and leave to drain for at least 30 minutes.

Now the fun part. Find a loaf tin or terrine with about 1 litre (1¾ pint) capacity. Long and thin is better than short and wide – the one I use is about 25cm (10 inches) long. Line it with cling film and then brush with olive oil and start building up layers of aubergine, skate, peppers and tomato, seasoning well between layers with salt, pepper and a squeeze of lemon juice. Spoon a little of the reduced, cooled poaching liquid over each layer. Order doesn't matter much but think about the effect when you slice it. Cover with cling film and then foil, and weight down with tins or other weights. Leave overnight in the fridge to set.

To serve, unmould and slice with a very sharp knife. Serve with a drizzle of olive oil, puddles of pesto dressing or a dollop of home-made lemony mayonnaise. Add a wedge or two of lemon and a little parsley, chervil or basil to each plate.

Skate Fingers, Sauce Ravigote

Alternatives: turbot, brill, John Dory, monkfish, cod, pollack

These are kind of upmarket fishfingers, sure to delight adults and, more than likely, children as well. The skate is poached first to release it from the bone and then deep-fried briskly in a coating of breadcrumbs. Sauce ravigote, when it is a cold one like this, is really a mustardy vinaigrette seasoned vigorously with shallots, capers and lots of herbs. It's good with all kinds of fish dishes as well as with many cold meats.

SERVES 4

about 800g–1kg (1¾–2¼ lb) skate wings
2 tablespoons white wine vinegar
1 bay leaf
2 fresh parsley sprigs
½ teaspoon coriander seeds
6 peppercorns
2 eggs, lightly beaten
fine dry breadcrumbs, for coating
sunflower or vegetable oil, for deep-frying
salt
lemon wedges, to serve

For the Sauce Ravigote:
1½ tablespoons white wine vinegar
1 teaspoon Dijon mustard
good pinch of sugar
8 tablespoons grapeseed or safflower oil
1 heaped tablespoon very finely chopped shallot
1 tablespoon chopped capers, rinsed (soaked if salted)
1 tablespoon chopped fresh parsley
1 tablespoon chopped fresh chervil
½ tablespoon chopped fresh tarragon
salt and pepper

Put the skate wings into a shallow pan with just enough water to cover. Add the vinegar, bay leaf, parsley sprigs, coriander seeds, peppercorns and a pinch of salt. Bring gently up to the boil, reduce the heat and poach very gently for about 8–10 minutes, until the skate is barely cooked. Lift out of the poaching liquid and lift the flesh from the cartilage, trimming off the tiny bones around the edges. Cut into fingers about 2.5cm (1 inch) across and as long as you care to make them.

While the fish is cooking, put the eggs into a shallow bowl and spread out the breadcrumbs on a plate. Once prepared, and preferably while still warm, dip the skate into the egg and then coat in breadcrumbs, making sure that the 'fingers' are covered completely. Leave to cool and, if possible, chill in the fridge for an hour or two before finishing.

To make the sauce ravigote, whisk the vinegar with the mustard, sugar and some salt and pepper. Gradually whisk in the oil, then stir in all the remaining ingredients. Taste and adjust the seasoning.

To cook the 'fingers', heat the oil to 190°C/375°F and deep-fry a few at a time, until golden-brown. Drain briefly on kitchen paper and serve immediately with the sauce ravigote.

Shark Koftas with Yoghurt and Garlic Sauce

Alternatives: dogfish, monkfish and most white fish

Shark is an oddity amongst fish, as it has an unfortunate tendency to be tough. Marinating it in a mildly acidic mixture can counteract this to some extent, though you still have to take enormous care not to overcook the fish. Treating the steaks like veal escalopes – cutting them thin (1cm/½ inch or so), sandwiching them between greaseproof paper sheets and bashing them with a meat mallet or rolling pin until they flatten right down – is fairly effective but parts of them remain tough even so. By far the most effective method I've come up with is mincing the flesh up finely to make *koftas* or, in other words, Turkish-style fish balls, which can either be grilled or fried and served with a yoghurt and garlic sauce.

One small note – don't use commercial white sliced bread for this. It turns slimy when wet. You need some decent, sturdy bread – one of the *pains de campagne* that many supermarkets now sell will do nicely.

SERVES 4

2 slices of white bread, weighing about 60g
  (2 oz), crusts removed
milk
450g (1 lb) skinned shark fillet
finely grated zest of 1 lemon
2 garlic cloves, crushed
1 shallot, very, very finely chopped
2 tablespoons very finely chopped fresh parsley
1 level teaspoon ground cumin
extra virgin olive oil for cooking
salt and pepper

For the Yoghurt Sauce:
300ml (½ pint) Greek-style yoghurt
3 garlic cloves, crushed
1 tablespoon chopped fresh mint
2 tablespoons chopped fresh parsley
1 teaspoon sugar
salt and pepper

To make the yoghurt sauce, mix all the ingredients together and then taste and adjust the seasoning. Cover and chill until needed.

To make the *koftas*, tear the bread up roughly and then soak in milk for 10 minutes. Squeeze dry and discard the milk. Chop the shark up into large cubes, discarding any obvious tough threads (don't go overboard on this or you'll end up with precious little to eat). If you have a mincer, use that to mince the shark finely. Otherwise, pulse-process, scraping down the sides frequently, until very finely chopped. Add to the bread, with all the other ingredients apart from the oil. Mix thoroughly with your hands and then knead and squeeze the mixture until it becomes cohesive.

If grilling, divide the mixture into four portions and roll each one into a sausage shape about 10cm (4 inches) long. Place on the palm of your hand, flatten slightly and lay a skewer down the centre. Mould the mixture round the skewer to form a fat sausage. Chill until ready to cook but bring back to room temperature before cooking. Just before cooking, brush with oil and then grill fairly close to the heat, turning two or three times, until patched with brown. Allow about 5–6 minutes in all.

If you prefer to fry the *koftas*, divide the mixture into eight and roll each one into a ball. Cover and chill until needed. Bring back to room temperature before cooking. Heat a little olive oil over a brisk heat and then fry the balls, flattening them down a little in the pan to look like overstuffed cushions, until patched with brown on both sides, about 4–6 minutes in all. Don't be tempted to move the balls at all for the first 2 minutes on each side or you will find that they stick. Serve with the yoghurt sauce.

Blackened Shark Steaks

Alternatives: monkfish, dogfish, conger eel, cod, salmon, halibut

Blackened fish came to us from Louisiana, back in the Eighties. It was pioneered by that eminent New Orleans chef, Paul Prudhomme, and quickly embraced by his colleagues, then by many chefs over on this side of the Atlantic. The principle is simple – the fish is coated with a mixture of spices and dried herbs and then seared in an outrageously hot pan, so that the smoky scent of the flavourings penetrates right into the fish. It looks dramatic, too, with the blackened crust. Whether or not you eat the crust itself depends on the degree of blackening achieved and your personal taste for charred food, but the fish inside should stay moist and beautifully flavoured.

All kinds of fairly firm, 'steakable' fish benefit from this treatment but it does seem to be particularly kind to shark, which is as tough as old boots when overcooked. I like to marinate the shark with lemon and oil before cooking to soften some of the tough fibres (unless minced, it is rarely completely tender) before they meet the heat. With other fish, such as cod or even salmon, you can skip the marinating without enormous loss to the finished dish.

SERVES 4

juice of ½ lemon
2 garlic cloves, crushed
1 small onion, finely chopped
4 tablespoons oil, plus extra for cooking
4 porbeagle or blue shark steaks, about 2cm
   (¾ inch) thick

For the Blackening Spices:
1½ teaspoons whole black peppercorns
1½ teaspoons dried green peppercorns
2 teaspoons whole coriander seeds
2 teaspoons salt
1 teaspoon cayenne pepper
1 teaspoon dried marjoram
1 teaspoon dried thyme
1 tablespoon paprika

Mix the lemon juice, garlic, onion and 4 tablespoons oil. Coat the fish steaks evenly with this mixture, cover and leave in the fridge, turning occasionally, for 1–6 hours.

Mix the peppercorns and coriander seeds, crush them coarsely and mix with the remaining spices and herbs. Spread on a plate. Take the fish out of its marinade, brush off the pieces of onion and coat the fish evenly on both sides with the spice mixture.

Place a lightly oiled heavy cast-iron frying pan over a high heat until very, very hot. Place the steaks in it, drizzle a teaspoon of oil over the upper side of each one and cook, ignoring the smoke bravely, until the underneath is brown-black, about 2–3 minutes depending on the heat. Turn and cook for a further 2–3 minutes, until the other side is also blackened.

Check that the steaks are just cooked through (no more than that, though, or they will begin to toughen up) and serve immediately.

Baked Huss with Coriander and Garlic

Alternatives: ling, conger eel, halibut

This was the first dish I ever made with huss, or dogfish, and I remember how delighted I was with it at the time. Memories of school biology labs dispersed at the first mouthful and, if you didn't tell anyone, they'd never guess that they weren't eating rather a fine fish. Marinating with lemon or lime juice for a short while before cooking really improves the flavour, while the salt helps to firm the naturally rather soft texture.

SERVES 4

700g (1½ lb) skinned huss fillet, cut into 8 pieces
juice of ½ large lemon or 1 lime
1 garlic clove, chopped
1 small onion, finely chopped
1 green chilli, de-seeded and finely chopped
3 tablespoons olive oil
3 tablespoons finely chopped fresh coriander
salt and pepper
lemon wedges, to serve

Season the huss with salt and pepper and then pour over the lemon or lime juice. Turn to coat and then set aside for 20 minutes. Cook the garlic, onion and chilli gently, without browning, in the olive oil. Preheat the oven to 180°C/350°F/Gas Mark 4.

Oil an ovenproof dish large enough to take the fish in a close-fitting layer. Arrange the fish in it, with the marinating juices. Sprinkle evenly with the coriander and spoon over the garlic, onions and chilli and their oil. Bake, uncovered, for 15–20 minutes, until the fish is just done. Serve immediately, with lemon wedges.

Yucatan-Style Fish Tortillas

Alternatives: shark, ling, conger eel

In the Yucatan province of Mexico a paste of yellow *achiote* seeds (another name for annatto, which is what gives red Leicester and other orange cheeses their classic colour), diluted with sour orange juice and sometimes grapefruit juice, is used as a marinade for grilled fish. You can get *achiote* here, if you've a persevering nature, but it is not that easy to find. It has a mildly resinous flavour but it's the colour that really startles, so I've adapted the basic principle and made a marinade that echoes the original.

Serve the fish straight from the barbecue or grill, with a mound of rice and lime wedges if you wish, but it's even nicer wrapped in a warm tortilla with a tomato salsa and a big spoonful of soured cream.

SERVES 4

700g (1½ lb) dogfish fillet

For the Marinade:
¼ teaspoon black peppercorns
½ teaspoon each of cumin seeds, coriander seeds, dried oregano, ground turmeric and paprika
¼ teaspoon cayenne pepper
3 garlic cloves, chopped
½ teaspoon salt
juice of 1 lime
juice of 1 Seville orange or ½ grapefruit

For the Tomato Salsa:
450g (1 lb) ripe tomatoes, de-seeded and finely diced
½ red onion, finely chopped
1 garlic clove, very finely chopped
2 green chillies, de-seeded and finely chopped
juice of ½ Seville orange or ½ grapefruit
1 teaspoon sugar
4 tablespoons chopped fresh coriander
salt and pepper

To Serve:
8 soft flour tortillas
150ml (¼ pint) soured cream
lime wedges

Cut the fish into eight portions. To make the marinade, dry-fry the peppercorns and the cumin and coriander seeds over a moderate heat until they turn a shade darker and give off a waft of incense. Tip into a bowl and cool slightly. Grind with the oregano, turmeric, paprika and cayenne. In a mortar, mash the garlic to a paste with the salt, then gradually work in the spices and the citrus juices. Smear this mixture over the fish and leave to marinate for at least an hour and up to 4.

To make the salsa, mix all the ingredients together, then taste and adjust the seasonings. Chill in the fridge until needed.

Preheat the grill or, better still, the barbecue. Wrap the tortillas in foil and warm through in the oven or on the edge of the barbecue. Grill the fish, turning carefully once, until just cooked through. If you're feeling loving and generous, lay each piece of fish on a warm tortilla, top with a good dollop of salsa and a spoonful of soured cream, fold the tortilla round the filling and then hand out to your guests. Alternatively (and your friends or family may well prefer the DIY approach) pass the fish, tortillas, salsa, cream and lime wedges around so that everyone can put together their own Yucatan fish tortilla.

Flat Fish

Flat fish have an easy bone structure and are ideal for people who need to be convinced that anyone who eats fish doesn't a) get a bone stuck in their throats or b) die of boredom. They range from the humble dab, which sadly is not called *Dabbus dabbus*, right up to the massive halibut, *Hippoglossus hippoglossus* – can that mean shiny horse, shiny horse?

Flat fish seem to be a peculiarly European forte. Although they exist in American waters they are mostly dull fare, and the Indian or African sole will disappoint. Everyone knows *Solea solea*, the Dover sole that you practically never see near Dover, an exquisite and rightly popular fish.

With all flat fish, it is as well to be aware that as they near the spawning season they can have a great deal of roe in them, which not only weighs a lot but can also affect the yield of fillet, and consequently the cost of the fish. On the plus side, a fish just prior to spawning is at its best, fat and tasty. But post-spawning fish are a different matter altogether, wasted in fact. Avoid them!

Preparing Flat Fish

Although flat fish are better for being cooked and eaten on the bone, filleting them is quite easy. They are almost always sold gutted, so you don't have to worry about cleaning them. You won't get four equal fillets because the structure is not entirely regular. Lay the fish eyes-up on a flat surface or a chopping board. Cut behind the head down to the bone on both sides of the spine. Cut along the middle of the fish from the head to the tail, following the line of the backbone to free the fillets on both sides. Finish off by cutting around the outer edge and lift the two fillets off. Repeat for the underside.

Skin flat fish fillets in the same way as round fish fillets (see page 30).

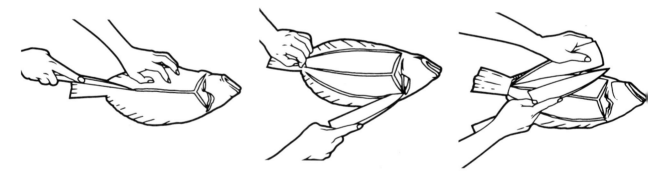

To prepare flat fish for cooking on the bone, you should make them 'pan-ready' by trimming the fins and cutting off the head. Dover sole to be grilled are traditionally skinned on the dark side only. Scale the white side. Make a small nick on the tail between the dark skin and the tail bone, then grip the skin tightly with a cloth and peel it off, pulling towards the head end. This can be difficult with a very fresh fish. You might need a little salt to stop the cloth slipping.

Brill★★

Scopthalmus rhombus
French: Barbue
Italian: Rombo liscio
Spanish: Rémol
Portuguese: Rodovalho
German: Glattbutt, Kleist

Brill do have a hint of rhombus about them but have to live, figuratively, in the shadow of their knobbly and rounder cousin, the turbot. It is an excellent flat fish and a firm restaurant favourite, easy to fillet and cook, but these days fish larger than 3-4kg (7-9 lb) are rarely caught.

Odd fishy facts about brill? Well, did you know that they are one of the very few flat fish to have a gap between their eyes wider than their diameter? Brill, like turbot, alter the colour of their skin according to where they are caught, so that lighter, almost lemon-sole-coloured fish are found on sandy sea floors and dark, rich chocolate-brown fish on a muddier substrate.

Brill is a wonderful fish to cook and eat. Its luscious white flesh can be poached, fried, steamed, seared, cooked in any way known to man. Smaller specimens (less than 1kg/2¼ lb) are best cooked on the bone but larger fish can easily be filleted. To feed four you will need a fish between 1.2 and 1.5kg (2¾–3¼ lb).

Season: All year, best April to September.
Price: ££
Yield: 50%
Fishing method: Trawl, net.

Dab

Limanda limanda
French: Limande
Italian: Limanda
Spanish: Limanda nordica
Portuguese: Solha-escura-do-mar-do-norte
German: Scharbe, Kliesche

This sweet little flat fish sounds so charming but tastes a little bland. It's very much a summer fish, practically coming on to the beach the hotter it gets. If you are lucky you may even find some live specimens flapping around on the odd fishmonger's slab.

To tell a dab from a flounder is challenging: a dab has a large curve in its lateral line around the head end, but no bony protuberances around its edge as does the flounder. They are both similar fish to eat, and are good if eaten very, very fresh, but are fast faders. For cooking methods, see Flounder.

Season: Best April to July.
Price: £
Yield: 50%
Fishing method: Inshore net.

Flounder, Fluke

Platichthys flesus
French: Flet
Italian: Passera pianuzza
Spanish: Platija
Portuguese: Solha-das-pedras
German: Flunder, Butt, Struffbutt

Another flat fish that swims very close to shore, the flounder used to be more widely recognised, since its tolerance of low salinity meant it was often fished far up the Thames estuary. I can't say I rate it highly but, given that a fresh flounder is better than a putrid turbot, don't ignore them if they are screamingly fresh.

Very simple cooking is recommended. Steam, grill or pan-fry smaller fish if very fresh. Dabs more than a day old can be bland. Fish are usually on the small side, weighing between 300 and 350g (11–12 oz).

Season: All year, best April to July.
Price: £
Yield: 50%
Fishing method: Small trawl.

Halibut★★★♥

Hippoglossus hippoglossus
French: Flétan
Italian: Halibut
Spanish: Halibut
Portuguese: Alabote-de-Atlantico
German: Heilbutt

Halibut can be enormous fish, at times weighing over 200kg (444 lb) and are fished in very deep cold water in the far north. During the winter they are difficult to find, but in the early summer months they cruise landwards and are particularly fond of eating seabird eggs that fall from cliff-top nests. There have been a few attempts to land halibut and store them alive in tanks. The fish were kept until the market prices were high, then flown in from Iceland and freshly killed according to demand. They were absolutely superb. However, there are no Icelandic halibut millionaires that I am aware of, so halibut broking was obviously not a profitable business. Supplies are now irregular.

The texture of halibut is very distinctive, almost meaty, which may explain why the fish is so popular in the UK. Sadly, it is becoming increasingly hard to find good-quality wild halibut but there are now regular supplies of farmed fish arriving from Norway. A wealthy shipping magnate fell in love with the idea of farming halibut and pumped millions of *kroner* into the business. Although early experiments resulted in fatty fish, the diet has now been adjusted to give a very fair and – most importantly – consistent quality.

Smaller fish, sometimes called chicken halibut, can be cooked whole but larger wild fish are almost always sold cut up in steaks. Cooking with the bones in gives the flesh added succulence, which counterbalances the dryness of larger fish; the larger the fish, the dryer the flesh tends to be. This is an excellent fish to bake, braise or poach. Allow 175g (6 oz) fillet per person or 200g (7 oz) steaks.

Beware of imitations! Greenland halibut (*Reinhardtius hippoglossoides*), known as turbot in Canada, is a fairly unexciting fish in any form, and is caught in waters so distant that it is either frozen or sits in a container for two weeks before it gets to market. The Pacific halibut, *Hippoglossus stenolepsis*, is a good alternative to the Atlantic fish, mostly long-lined, whose stock is under great pressure.

Season: Farmed: all year round but limit to size of fish. Wild: early summer best bet. Otherwise irregular.
Price: £££
Yield: 60%
Fishing method: Line and trawl.

Lemon Sole*

Microstomus kitt
French: Limande-sole
Italian: Sogliola limanda
Spanish: Mendo limón
Portuguese: Solha-limão
German: Limande, Echte Rotzunge
Finnish: Paksuhuulinen-kampela

What remarkable consistency we Europeans show in naming the lemon sole – apart, that is, from the wayward Finns! Since Dover sole is considered beyond the pockets of many, the lemon sole has been elevated to the sole that we can just about afford. It is good, not great, and has a slightly less firm texture and duller taste than the Dover sole. In England we have possibly the best lemon sole fishery around, and the smaller Cornish ports, particularly Looe, land large quantities of really first-class fish. During Christmas, when demand from Spain pushes prices into the realms of lunacy, it's best to stay away.

Cooked on the bone, simply grilled, the lemon sole is a reliable and consistent fish whose wide distribution means that supplies are generally easy. Fillets are often tired but the easy bone structure should encourage you to eat it whole.

Season: All year round.
Price: ££
Yield: 60%
Fishing method: Beam trawl, trawl, nets.

Megrim, Whiff®

Lepidorhombus whiffiagonis
French: Cardine franche
Italian: Rombo giallo
Spanish: Gallo, Iliseria
Portuguese: Areiro
German: Scheefschnut, Flügelbutt

I once became quite excited about megrim, until someone let me know that the Spaniards call them 'English cork'. I had imagined that this was a fish that could take over from Dover or lemon sole when supplies were tight, but UK law forbids it to be called sole at

LEMON SOLE

all, and most people remain ignorant as to what a plain megrim really is. They are small to medium flat fish, caught mainly off the south-west coast of England. A related species found in deeper water, *L.boscii*, is distinguished by four black marks on the rear of the dorsal fin. This is considered by the Spanish to be a better fish to eat. They continue to be exported in vast numbers and remain almost uneaten over here.

Best eaten on the bone, megrim can be a little dry and need to be exceptionally fresh. A fish weighing 300–400g (11–14 oz) will feed one, and is a better bet than larger fish which do not fillet well.

Season: All year round.
Price: £/££
Yield: 50%
Fishing method: Mainly trawl.

Plaice®

Pleuronectes platessa
French: Carrelet, Plie
Italian: Passera
Spanish: Solla
Portuguese: Solha
German: Scholle, Goldbutt

Plaice can be deeply boring but some people seem to love them. The finest I have ever eaten came from a small area of southern England where divers swim down to spike the fish in true Japanese style. Some plaice fillets can be worse to eat than blotting paper. This is the supreme example of a fish that fades fast into tastelessness, and great attention should be paid to its freshness.

Whether bought whole or as fillets, check that the orange spots on the skin are really bright (a good indication of freshness), and avoid plaice in the early summer, when they are watery and tasteless. A 350–450g (12–16 oz) fish with its head on, or a 175g (6 oz) fillet will feed one. Any recipe for lemon sole, megrim or even Dover sole will suit the plaice but it is particularly good fried in batter when perfectly fresh.

Season: All year round.
Price: £
Yield: 50%
Fishing method: Day-boat fish and spiked fish best. Trawled fish flabby.

Sole, Dover Sole***

Solea solea
French: Sole
Italian: Sogliola
Spanish: Lenguado
Portuguese: Linguado
German: Seezunge

The much-loved Dover sole was the mainstay of classic English fish cookery in the earlier part of this century. These days it's more lemongrass and mango than cream and butter to accompany your sole but simply grilled is still the very best way to eat it.

The Dover sole is both well known and oversubscribed, and simply too expensive for many. It was once fished in massive quantities in the North Sea.

Many people prefer a sole to be slightly mature – three days old is thought best – but do remember that the process of fishing, packing and transporting can mean that the fish are often six or seven days old before they actually get to the shop. Two or three days from being *caught* is just right.

Dover sole come inshore to spawn in the spring. Their movements and whereabouts are so well known that the controversial practice of beam trawling owes a great debt to them. Beam trawling, which drags a large trawl along the seabed, using a 'beam' to keep the mouth of the net open, was originally developed off the sandbanks of the Belgian and Dutch coasts, and resulted in phenomenally rich landings. What many consider to be one of the blacker arts of fishing was eagerly adopted by the English, who have fished for Dover sole and other flat fish in the North Sea and the south-west for generations. Beam trawling catches virtually everything in its path, and extensively damages the sea bed. The debate between beam trawlers and other fishermen is one of the most heated in the industry.

There is a closely related species, *Pegusa lascaris*, the sand sole, that occasionally finds its way into fish shops. I hope it remains clearly marked, and cheaper too, than *Solea solea*; it lacks the Dover sole's excellence.

The very small sole that some people take to be undersized Dover sole, called *cétaux* or *langue d'avocats* in France, are in fact another separate species, *Dicologoglossa cuneata*, a name I defy anyone to remember. They are a fish to forget, too: fiddly and thoroughly insubstantial. A slip sole is a small Dover sole, which weighs in at about 10–12 oz.

Such is the demand that there is a clear buyers' hierarchy, with 14–16 oz fish (metric sizes seem to have passed the Dover sole by in the UK) being the best portion-sized fish to go for. Larger fish, often called blanket sole, can be filleted, but the grill and the Dover sole are a match made in heaven.

Season: Spring, summer, with a lean period after spawning which varies according to region.
Price: £££
Yield: Large fish, 55%
Fishing method: Beam trawl, trawl or net.

Turbot★★★

Psetta maxima
French: Turbot
Italian: Rombo chiodato
Spanish: Rodaballo
Portuguese: Pregado
German: Steinbutt

A chunk of poached turbot, served with a few new potatoes fresh from the garden, is the nearest thing you will ever get to edible perfection. This wonderful, firm-fleshed, fine-tasting fish is easy to handle and fillet, in almost every way perfect apart from its price. They are ungainly beasts, with a tiny head set around a massive body, but what a body! The turbot has brown skin as knobbly as a toad, and if you are ever in Turkey, look out for the fish they call *kalkan*, the spiny turbot, which has a more fearsome set of knobbles but is just as tasty. They are bottom-dwelling, carnivorous fish and are quite widely distributed, from the far north of Scotland right down to the Mediterranean.

Turbot farming has taken off over the past few years, and both the quality and size of the fish have improved enormously; in the early days, farmed turbot were reared on salmon feed, which made them very bland and fatty. Turbot are lazy, slobbing about on the bottom of the tanks, and fish farmers find it quite difficult to get them to eat at all. But as soon as someone came up with a special turbot feed, the markets noticed how much the quality of the fish had improved, and farming turbot became a more realistic proposition.

Farmed turbot are often killed by being immersed in icy water, and can be sold ungutted. They are not fed for two days to ensure that their guts are empty, which means that they keep well. Some farms can offer 4–5kg (9–11 lb) fish grown in only three and a half years.

Over the last few years, larger wild fish have become rarer, so eating a goodly wad of turbot is a rare treat. The gelatinous bones give the fish taste and finesse so, if at all possible, eat and cook it on the bone, with the skin on. Smaller fish are a disappointment, and I suggest that you never try to fillet a small, 500g (1 lb 2 oz) fish. You will feel as sick as a turbot when you see just how little flesh you get.

If you want to eat turbot fillet, you'd better off buying a larger 1.2–1.5kg (2¾–3¼ lb) fish, which will feed four. Remember not to throw away the bones as they make marvellous stock. Turbot has startlingly pure white flesh, which can be poached in milk or *fumet*, and classically is served with hollandaise sauce (see page 316). One of the finest fish in the sea.

Season: Summer easiest.
Price: £££
Yield: 35%
Fishing method: Day boat, small trawl, beam trawls.

Witch, Torbay Sole

Glyptocephalus cynoglossus
French: Plie cynoglosse, Plie grise
Italian: Passera lingua di cane
Spanish: Mendo
Portuguese: Solhão
German: Rotzunge

A fish which little pleases, witch sole is mostly fished off the south-west of England and is best eaten when extremely fresh. It resembles a megrim in taste and looks but is seldom marketed countrywide. You may have had a tasty Torbay sole on holiday, and this was probably it. Simply grilled, it's better than a pork pie. Cook as megrim.

Season: All year round.
Price: £
Yield: 50%
Fishing method: Various.

DOVER SOLE

Baked Brill with Crème Fraîche, Cherry Tomatoes and Parmesan

Alternatives: John Dory, turbot, bass, sole, hake, pollack, cod

The children had been full of bed-time fun and frolics, and getting them into bed and on the road to sleep took longer than planned. Supper had to be quick; we had to use up the rather choice fillets of brill left in the fridge (we'd been recipe-testing two days before) and whatever else was to be found. This is the 'what-else-is-in-the-fridge' recipe that emerged, and it has become a household favourite. It's absolutely brilliant for dinner parties but easily adapted to a mid-week treat for two.

SERVES 4

700g (1½ lb) brill fillets, skinned
15g (½ oz) butter
150g (5 oz) cherry tomatoes, halved
200ml (7 fl oz) *crème fraîche*
6–8 fresh basil leaves, shredded
110g (4 oz) Parmesan cheese, freshly grated
salt and pepper

Preheat the oven to 220°C/425°F/Gas Mark 7. Season the brill with salt and pepper. Use about half of the butter to grease a baking dish large enough to take the fillets in a single, snug layer. Lay the fillets in it. Dot the cherry tomatoes around and over them. Smear the cream over and around the brill and tomatoes, covering the fish more or less evenly. Scatter over the basil and then sprinkle the Parmesan evenly over the top. Grind a little more pepper over the whole thing and dot with the last of the butter. Bake for 15 minutes, until the fish is just cooked through. Serve bubbling and sizzling.

Brill Cooked in Beer

Alternatives: turbot, any sole, John Dory, bass, halibut

Brill has long been one of my favourite fish, with its sweet, firm-tender flesh and fine flavour. I came across this recipe when I was writing an article on cooking with beer, and at first it seemed to me a somewhat ridiculous pairing of ingredients. Surely the beer, boiled down as it is, would be too strong and coarse? What with juniper in there as well . . . oh heavens, a recipe for disaster! I tried it anyway and was proved utterly wrong on all counts.

The beer, softened by the butter and the brill's own juices, takes on a subtle, delicious flavour, which does nothing to mask the excellence of the brill. On the contrary, it highlights the fish's flavour with gentle aplomb.

SERVES 2

45g (1½ oz) butter
1 small onion, sliced
1 celery stick, thinly sliced
1 fresh parsley sprig
1 bay leaf
1 fresh thyme sprig
280ml (scant ½ pint) dry Pilsner lager or
    Duvel lager
3 juniper berries, bruised
375–400g (13–14 oz) skinned brill fillets
salt and pepper
chopped fresh parsley, to garnish

Melt 30g (1 oz) of the butter in a pan wide enough to take the fillets in a close, single layer. Cube and chill the remaining butter. Cook the onion and celery gently in the butter until tender. Tie the herbs in a bundle with string and add to the pan with the beer, juniper berries, pepper and just a little salt. Bring up to the boil and then lay the brill fillets in the pan. Reduce the heat to a bare simmer and poach the fillets for 3–5 minutes, until barely cooked. Lift out carefully and transfer to a shallow serving dish. Keep warm.

Raise the heat under the pan and boil hard until the liquid is reduced by about three-quarters. Add the remaining butter a few cubes at a time, swirling and tilting the pan to dissolve it in the sauce. Taste and adjust the seasoning, then strain through a sieve over the fish. Sprinkle with a little chopped parsley and serve immediately.

Brill and Scallop Ceviche with Avocado, Cherry Tomatoes and Marinated Red Onion

Alternatives: turbot, bass, grouper, Dover sole, lemon sole

This is a perfect starter for a summer supper party or, indeed, a perfect light lunch dish in its own right. The brill and scallops must be sparklingly fresh, no question about that, but if you can get your seafood in prime condition a *ceviche* will show it off at its best.

The acidity of the lime juice has much the same effect as heat, coagulating the proteins in the fish so that they become opaque. In that sense the fish is 'cooked', even if its temperature never climbs above that of the fridge.

There are all kinds of variations on the basic theme of *ceviche*. This is one I happen to favour at the moment: brill and scallops partnered and softened by avocado, tomatoes, grapefruit and superb marinated red onion rings so good that I could almost eat them by themselves.

SERVES 4

400g (14 oz) skinned brill fillet
8 large scallops
juice of 3 limes
1 fresh red chilli, de-seeded and finely chopped
3 tablespoons roughly chopped fresh coriander
salt

For the Marinated Red Onion:
1 medium red onion, very thinly sliced into rings
juice of 1–2 limes
½ tablespoon salt
½ tablespoon sugar

For the Rest:
1 grapefruit, pink or yellow fleshed as the fancy
   takes you
2 tablespoons light oil, e.g. grapeseed, safflower
   or sunflower
1 avocado
200g (7 oz) cherry tomatoes, cut in half
salt, pepper and sugar

Begin by making the marinated onion. Mix all the ingredients, cover and leave for 2–4 hours. Squeeze them in the marinade and then drain and cover with cling film until needed.

Now the fish. Cut the brill into strips about 1cm (½ inch) wide. Slice the whites of the scallops horizontally into two or three discs, depending on thickness. Mix both brill and scallops, with their corals if you have them, with the lime juice, chilli and salt. Leave for 1 hour before using. Though they will come to no harm if left for up to 24 hours, they will lose some of their immediate freshness. Just before serving, drain and toss with the coriander.

Peel and segment the grapefruit, removing as much of the pith as humanly possible, to reveal the glossy inner flesh. Save as much of the juice as you can and whisk it with the oil. Season with salt, pepper, and a pinch of sugar if it is on the tart side. Peel and slice the avocado into half-moons and turn them in the fruit juice mixture. Toss the tomatoes in a little more, then arrange the avocado, tomatoes, grapefruit and fish on individual plates or one large serving plate and top with the marinated onion. Serve immediately.

Roast Chicken Halibut with Mustard and Sun-dried Tomato Crust

Alternatives: grouper, bass, zander, grey mullet (reducing roasting size to suit size)

Size, of course, is relative, and a 2.5kg (5 lb) halibut counts as small by halibut standards (hence the term chicken halibut, as opposed, I suppose, to turkey-sized), though it looks pretty impressive to your average human. A whole small halibut, roasted speedily in the oven, is a magnificent sight and a brilliant dish to serve for a large dinner party. You can roast it plainly, just brushing the skin with oil or melted butter and maybe stuffing a handful of herbs inside, but a mixture of mustard and sun-dried tomato purée brings an extra layer of pleasure.

SERVES ABOUT 8–10

1 chicken halibut, weighing about 2–2.5kg
   (4½–5 lb)
3 tablespoons coarse-grained mustard
3 tablespoons sun-dried tomato purée
1 tablespoon lemon juice
finely grated zest of 1 lemon
30g (1 oz) butter
salt and pepper

To Serve:
lemon wedges
fresh parsley sprigs
110g (4 oz) butter, melted

Preheat the oven to 200°C/400°F/Gas Mark 6. Season the halibut inside with salt and pepper. Mix all the remaining ingredients, mashing them thoroughly together. Smear thickly over both sides of the halibut. Lay it in an ovenproof dish, if you have one big enough, or on a large baking tray. Roast for about 30–40 minutes, until just cooked through.

Transfer to a serving dish if necessary and tuck the lemon wedges and sprigs of parsley decoratively around it. Serve with the warm melted butter in a jug.

Halibut with Welsh Rarebit Crust

Alternatives: cod, haddock, monkfish, brill, grouper

This recipe is part of my childhood; indeed, it is a regular visitor throughout my entire life. My mother made it from time to time as I grew up, and published the recipe in her book *Fish Cookery* in 1973, as *flétan au fromage* – a very French name for a dish which gilds fine halibut steaks with what is, essentially, a Welsh rarebit mixture. The sizzling, bubbling molten cheese, softened with butter and cream and a touch of mustard, is a marvellous foil to the lovely dryish texture of halibut, though it goes well with other white fish steaks, particularly cod.

In my mother's recipe, she suggested serving the steaks with new potatoes. To that, I'd add a tomato and red onion salad, dressed with good wine vinegar and olive oil.

SERVES 6

6 halibut steaks, weighing about 200g (7 oz) each, or 3 x 2-portion halibut steaks, weighing about 400g (14 oz) each
60g (2 oz) butter, softened
salt and pepper
For the Welsh Rarebit:
225g (8 oz) cheese, preferably Gruyère but Cheddar is fine too, grated
1 tablespoon Dijon mustard
3 tablespoons single or double cream

Preheat the oven to 190°C/375°F/Gas Mark 5. Season the steaks lightly with salt and generously with pepper. Use the butter to grease a baking dish large enough to take all the steaks comfortably. Mix the cheese with the mustard and cream to make a paste and spread it over the upper surface of the steaks. Bake for about 20 minutes, until the halibut is just cooked through. If the cheese mixture becomes too brown, protect it with a butter paper or a piece of buttered foil. Serve immediately.

Fillets of Lemon Sole on a Pea and Pancetta Purée

Alternatives: Dover sole, lemon sole, megrim, brill, plaice

If you grow your own peas, this is a lovely way to make the most of them when the season is in full swing and they are maturing just beyond the perfect miniature size. If you don't, then it is a good way to transform a pack of frozen *petits-pois* into a very fetching accompaniment to a fish which, even if it is not as classy as its cousin Dover, is still a fine eat when good and fresh.

SERVES 4

4 slices of pancetta
butter, for frying
2 lemon sole, weighing about 400g (14 oz)
    each, filleted
plain flour, seasoned, for coating
salt and pepper
lemon wedges, to serve

For the Pea and Pancetta Purée:
1 onion, chopped
60g (2 oz) pancetta, cubed
60g (2 oz) butter
250g (9 oz) shelled fresh peas or thawed
    frozen peas
1 fresh mint sprig
200ml (7 fl oz) light chicken stock
200g (7 oz) peeled potato, diced
1 fresh thyme sprig
3 tablespoons single cream
salt and pepper

To make the pea purée, sauté the onion and pancetta in half the butter until golden. Add the peas, mint, stock, potato, thyme, salt and pepper and bring up to the boil. Simmer gently, half covered, until the potato is tender. Remove the sprigs of mint and thyme. Purée the whole lot together, then stir in the cream. It should be quite runny so, if necessary, add a little extra chicken stock or cream to loosen the mixture. Re-heat when needed, stirring in the remaining butter and adjusting the seasoning.

Shortly before serving, preheat the grill and grill the slices of pancetta until crisp. Melt some butter in a frying pan and heat until it foams. Meanwhile, dust the sole fillets with seasoned flour. Fry in the hot butter for about 1–2 minutes per side, until barely cooked.

Spoon a puddle of pea purée on to each plate (or tip it all into one warmed serving plate) and arrange the sole fillets and pancetta on top. Serve immediately, with the lemon wedges.

Lemon Sole Meunière

Alternatives: Dover sole, megrim, brill, plaice

This is a dish only to be made with the freshest of flat fish. It is, naturally, sensational with sole but also an excellent way to cook the lesser members of this group, even the lowly flounder and dab, as long as they have not been kept lingering on the way from the sea to your kitchen. At first glance, the recipe seems simplicity itself, though it takes a degree of patience (it really is worth clarifying the butter first) since the fish are best cooked one at a time. Unless you eat in the kitchen, it is probably a dish to save for a twosome rather than to feed a crowd.

SERVES 2

100g (3½ oz) unsalted butter
2 whole lemon sole
plain flour, well seasoned, for coating

To Serve:
fresh parsley sprigs
lemon wedges

Clarify 60g (2 oz) of the butter (see page 307).

Heat half the clarified butter in a frying pan large enough to take one of the soles. When it is foaming, coat the first sole in seasoned flour and shake off the excess. Put the sole in the butter and cook for about 1½ minutes on each side, until golden brown and cooked through. Transfer to a warm dish and keep warm. Tip the used butter out of the pan and add the remaining clarified butter. Cook the second fish in the same way.

Tip out the butter in the pan and wipe clean with a piece of kitchen paper. Add the unclarified butter and melt, then let it cook over a moderate heat until it turns a tempting light hazelnut brown. Immediately pour it over your sole, tuck parsley sprigs and lemon wedges round the side and serve immediately.

Megrim with Anchovy, Tomato and Red Pepper Sauce

Alternatives: Dover sole, lemon sole, turbot, brill, plaice, cod, halibut, salmon

Roasting the megrim in foil preserves all of its flavour but it still benefits from a perky sauce like this one. The sauce can be made well in advance and reheated whenever required.

It goes well with all kinds of white fish, as well as with the delicate Quenelles de Brochet (see page 268).

SERVES 4

4 megrim, weighing about 400g (14 oz) each, trimmed and cleaned
butter
salt and pepper

For the Sauce:
1 onion, chopped
2 garlic cloves, chopped
1 carrot, diced
1 large red pepper, de-seeded and chopped
bouquet garni of 1 bay leaf, 1 fresh thyme sprig and 1 fresh parsley stem, tied together with string
45g (1½ oz) unsalted butter
400g (14 oz) tin of chopped tomatoes
1 tablespoon tomato purée
½ teaspoon sugar
150ml (¼ pint) dry white wine
1–2 tablespoons anchovy essence
110ml (4 fl oz) double cream
salt and pepper

To make the sauce, put the onion, garlic, carrot, red pepper, *bouquet garni* and butter into a saucepan, cover and sweat over a low heat for 10–15 minutes, until the onion is tender, stirring occasionally.

Add the tinned tomatoes, tomato purée, sugar and white wine and bring to the boil. Boil until reduced to a moderately thick sauce. Stir in a tablespoon of the anchovy essence and then season with salt and pepper. Cool slightly, then remove the *bouquet garni* and process until smooth. Rub through a sieve, back into the saucepan, and stir in the cream. Taste and adjust the seasoning, adding more anchovy essence if you think it necessary. Re-heat when needed. Preheat the oven to 200°C/400°F/Gas Mark 6.

To cook the megrim, tear off four large rectangles of foil and grease the centre of each one with butter. Place a megrim in the centre of each piece of foil, dot with a little more butter, season with salt and pepper and then wrap in the foil, sealing the edges neatly. Lay the parcels on baking trays and bake for about 15–18 minutes, until just cooked through. Serve the fish in their parcels, passing the sauce around in a jug for everyone to help themselves.

Roast Plaice with Mushroom and Dill Salsa

Alternatives: Dover sole, lemon sole, megrim, brill

Somehow, plaice and heavy cream sauces seem all wrong for each other but a small touch of richness is another thing altogether. In this recipe the plaice is baked with a shake of Noilly Prat and not much more than that, then served with a warm mushroom salsa, bound lightly with cream. Luxury of a modest kind.

SERVES 2

2 whole plaice, weighing about 450g (1 lb) each, cleaned
20g (²/₃ oz) butter
100ml (3½ fl oz) Noilly Prat or dry white wine
salt and pepper
2 fresh dill sprigs, to garnish
lemon wedges, to serve

For the Mushroom and Dill Salsa:
250g (9 oz) mushrooms, wiped and fairly finely diced
45g (1½ oz) butter
1 tablespoon chopped fresh dill
2 tablespoons *crème fraîche* or soured cream
salt and pepper

Preheat the oven to 200°C/400°F/Gas Mark 6. To make the mushroom and dill salsa (it can be re-heated), fry the mushrooms in the butter over a gentle heat. At first the juices will flow out but keep cooking and stirring over a gentle heat until they have evaporated, leaving a moist mixture. Draw off the heat, stir in the dill and cream and season with salt and pepper.

Trim the fins from the plaice with scissors. Make three slashes across the thickest part of the fish on each side. Lay in a lightly greased, shallow baking dish or roasting tin. Dot with the butter and pour over the Noilly Prat or wine. Season with salt and pepper. Bake for about 15 minutes, until just cooked.

Reheat the salsa gently without letting it boil. Put a dollop of the salsa on each plate alongside the plaice, moistened with a little of the pan juices. Add a sprig of dill and a wedge or two of lemon.

Golden Pan-fried Plaice with Roast Tomatoes and Mint

Alternatives: Dover sole, lemon sole, megrim, brill

This is such a pretty, cheerful dish, with the golden brown of the cornmeal on the plaice itself and the dark red of the tomatoes, brushed with brown where they've caramelised in the heat of the oven. It's a dish of contrasting textures and flavours, too, with the softness of the fish against the crunch of the cornmeal and the melting sweetness of the tomatoes redolent of garlic and mint.

SERVES 2

2 whole plaice, weighing about 450g (1 lb) each, cleaned
fine cornmeal (polenta)
30g (1 oz) butter
2 tablespoons olive oil
salt and pepper
2 fresh mint sprigs, to garnish
lemon wedges, to serve

For the Tomatoes:
4 plum tomatoes
1 large or 2 small garlic cloves, cut into slivers
8 fresh mint leaves
3–4 tablespoons olive oil
coarse sea salt and freshly ground pepper

Preheat the oven to 220°C/425°F/Gas Mark 7. Start with the tomatoes. Cut them in half lengthwise and place, cut-side up, in an ovenproof dish. Push the slivers of garlic into the tomato flesh and, with the handle of a teaspoon, wedge a mint leaf into each half as well. Drizzle over the olive oil, sprinkle with sea salt and season with pepper. Roast for about 40–50 minutes, until meltingly tender and browned and charred at the edges. Keep warm or re-heat as needed.

Now for the plaice. Trim off the fins with scissors. Season a few tablespoons of cornmeal with salt and pepper. Coat each fish in cornmeal, shaking off the excess. Heat the butter and olive oil until hot and foaming, in a pan large enough to take the plaice (you may have to cook them separately). Fry the fish for about 2–3 minutes on each side, until just cooked through. Lift on to serving plates, add the roast tomatoes, garnish with mint sprigs and lemon wedges and serve.

Grilled Dover Sole

Alternative: plaice

Just one of the most perfect ways to cook this most delicious of fish. As with many simple recipes, it requires attention to detail – only prime fresh fish, good butter, a little sea salt – and, above all, an attentive cook who doesn't let the fish overcook. This is the kind of thing that I'd choose to cook as a treat for myself all alone, after a long hard day, or to share with one special friend when I wanted something that didn't require enormous amounts of preparation but that showed I cared.

I prefer to cook the fish with nothing more than a protective brush of melted butter but, if you want a touch more definition in the outer layer, you can coat the fish lightly in seasoned flour after brushing it generously with butter. Traditionally, grilled sole is served just as it is, pure and simple, but if you want a sauce with it, why not? A hollandaise or a lemony *beurre blanc* (see pages 309 and 302) would honour such a choice creature very well.

PER PERSON

1 Dover sole, 350–450g (12–14 oz), cleaned and
    skinned
melted butter
coarse sea salt and freshly ground black pepper

To Serve:
fresh parsley sprigs
lemon wedges

Preheat the grill thoroughly. Line the grill rack with kitchen foil. Brush the foil with melted butter. Brush one side of the sole with melted butter and season with salt and pepper. Lay on the grill rack, buttered side towards the heat. Grill about 5–7.5cm (2–3 inches) away from the heat, until just firm and cooked through, having lost that translucent look – some 3–4 minutes. Turn the fish over carefully and brush the other side with butter. Season with salt and pepper and pop back under the grill until the other side is done, too.

Serve immediately with sprigs of parsley and lemon wedges.

Fillets of Sole with Anchovy Butter

Alternatives: lemon sole, brill, plaice

An old favourite of mine, which is based on the main course of an amazing meal I managed to sneak in on years ago, down amongst the vineyards of Bordeaux, in one of the grand châteaux there. Not somewhere I get to visit often, I'm sad to say.

There they made this dish with very small sole; here I find it easier to buy fillets of sole, which actually makes life much simpler in the kitchen.

The anchovy butter can be made several days in advance and stored, covered, in the fridge; it can even be frozen, if that suits better. Leftovers are wonderful on baked potatoes or steamed new potatoes and on other plainly cooked vegetables, too, especially cauliflower.

SERVES 4

2 x 700g (1½ lb) Dover soles, skinned, or lemon
   soles, filleted
plain flour, seasoned
clarified butter (see page 305)
lemon wedges, to serve

For the Anchovy Butter:
110g (4 oz) unsalted butter, softened
6 tinned anchovy fillets
1½ tablespoons double cream
lemon juice

Process all the ingredients for the anchovy butter until smooth and evenly amalgamated. If you don't have a food processor, liquidise the anchovies with the cream and then beat into the butter with the lemon juice. Completely gadget-less? Chop the anchovy fillets finely and then mash with 30g (1 oz) of the butter. Beat with the remaining ingredients. Pile into a bowl and chill.

Dust the sole fillets with seasoned flour. Heat a little clarified butter in a frying pan until foaming. Fry the fillets quickly on either side until golden. You'll probably need to do this in several batches – speed up the process by using two large frying pans. Replace the butter with a fresh knob if it darkens too much. Serve quickly with the lemon wedges, handing round the cool anchovy butter separately.

Sole Véronique

Alternative: brill

When *Sole Véronique* is made carefully, with love and attention, the freshest sole and sweet sharp grapes, and little or nothing in the way of floury thickening for the sauce, it is as palely elegant to view as it is good to eat. It's the more slapdash approach, to mask sole that is too old for grilling, that leads it astray far too often. I've only recently come round to it, thanks to that genial, talented chef Phil Vickery. He cooked his version of *Sole Véronique* for the cameras when we were filming together recently, and showed me the charm of the dish, which I'd failed to register in the past.

SERVES 4

2 x 700g (1½ lb) Dover soles, skinned and
     filleted
30g (1 oz) butter
1 tablespoon sunflower oil
85ml (3 fl oz) Noilly Prat
225ml (8 fl oz) Fish Stock (see page 308)
300ml (½ pint) double cream
40 seedless grapes, halved
lemon juice
salt and pepper

Season the sole fillets with salt and pepper (if you are particularly keen on the pale purity of the dish, use white pepper rather than black). Heat half the butter in a frying pan with half the oil. When it is foaming pat the fillets dry on kitchen paper, then lay as many in the pan as will fit in a single layer (with a generous pan, you should get half of them in). Fry gently for about 1–1½ minutes on each side, then transfer to a serving dish and keep warm. Tip out the fat and repeat with the remaining butter, oil and fillets.

Tip excess fat out of the pan and then deglaze with the Noilly Prat: in other words, pour it in and bring up to the boil, stirring and scraping in the residues from frying the fish. Boil until reduced to a thin film on the bottom of the pan. Add the fish stock and boil until reduced by two-thirds. Now stir in the cream and simmer for 3–5 minutes or so, until reduced to a pleasing consistency. Stir in the grapes, a dash of lemon juice and salt and pepper to taste. Simmer for a minute or so longer, to warm the grapes and allow some of their juice to sweeten the sauce. Tip any juices that have gathered around the sole fillets into the sauce and stir in. Taste and adjust the seasoning and then spoon the sauce over the fillets and serve immediately.

Turbot aux Chicons

Turbot with Chicory

Alternatives: Dover sole, brill, cod

This is a rich, celebratory dish from the north of France but it is also, as are so many good things, remarkably simple. It relies absolutely on the quality of its ingredients. The turbot, finest of all flat fish, must be fresh and pearly, the chicory crisp and pale, its tapering, ivory leaves edged with bands of pale gold (not green, which indicates that it has been left out too long in the light and will be too bitter to enjoy), the cream thick and unctuous. If you can get these three right, then a fine supper is within your grasp.

SERVES 4

1 x 1.5kg (3¼ lb) turbot, filleted
85g (3 oz) unsalted butter
2 heads of chicory, trimmed and sliced 5mm
   (¼ inch) thick
1 teaspoon caster sugar
450ml (¾ pint) *crème fraîche* or double cream
freshly grated nutmeg
lemon juice (if you use double cream)
2 tablespoons chopped fresh chervil or parsley
salt and pepper

Cut the turbot into 4 portions, each weighing around 200g (7 oz). Season the fillets with salt and pepper and set aside. Melt the butter in a deep frying pan and add the sliced chicory. Cover and cook gently until tender, about 5–10 minutes. Now add the sugar and cook for a further 3–4 minutes. Next, stir in the cream and season with salt, pepper and a little nutmeg. Simmer until reduced by about one-third, to a good coating consistency. Taste and adjust the seasoning, stirring in a squeeze of lemon juice if you used double cream.

While the sauce simmers, steam the fillets for about 5 minutes, until just cooked through. Drain thoroughly. Place a portion of turbot on each plate and spoon over some of the sauce. Serve immediately, sprinkled with chervil or parsley.

Seared Turbot with Wild Mushrooms

Alternatives: cod, sea bass

Just when I was pondering on a second recipe for the turbot section I stumbled, almost literally, across a hoard of small *boletus* mushrooms growing beneath trees near our house. They may not have been the finest variety but, taken straight from the field to the kitchen and cooked within hours of picking, they were still way above bought mushrooms. A wild luxury, and just the thing to cook with the king of the flat fish, the turbot. This, then, is the dish that came into being, a rare treat, though now that you can buy wild mushrooms from some supermarkets (*chanterelles, trompettes de la mort* and *girolles* would all be excellent for this dish), not as rare as it might once have been.

If you haven't got any reduced fish stock, you can use straight fish stock (you'll need twice as much) but will have to allow extra time for it to boil right down to a sticky, syrupy glaze, so start the sauce *before* you cook the fish.

SERVES 2

2 pieces of skinned turbot fillet, weighing about
    175g (6 oz) each
oil
salt and pepper

For the Sauce:
30g (1 oz) butter
½ tablespoon sunflower oil
1 shallot, very finely chopped
110g (4 oz) small wild mushrooms (e.g. baby
    ceps, chanterelles or whatever is most easily
    available), cleaned, cut in half or sliced if on
    the large side
150ml (¼ pint) Reduced Fish Stock
    (see page 308)
1 tablespoon chopped fresh chervil
salt and pepper

Wipe a heavy-based pan lightly with oil and then put it over a high heat. When it is intensely hot, brush one side of each turbot fillet with a little more oil and lay it in the pan. Leave for 3 minutes before turning. Reduce the heat a little and cook for a further 1–2 minutes, until just cooked through. Keep warm until needed.

In a separate pan, make the sauce. Heat half the butter with the oil. Fry the shallot gently until tender, then raise the heat and put in the mushrooms. Cook over a good heat, stirring once or twice, until they are soft and cooked through. Add the reduced fish stock, chervil, salt and pepper and bring to the boil. Simmer for 1–3 minutes until syrupy, then reduce the heat slightly and whisk in the last of the butter, cut into small pieces, to thicken the sauce. Taste and adjust the seasoning and spoon the sauce over the turbot. Devour immediately.

Herrings and other Clupeiformes

Do herrings say cheese or do they sneeze? Fish have every right to be vocal when hauled out of the sea but fishermen are divided as to whether it's a sneeze or the sound 'cheese' that passes their lips. Vocal fish then, and fickle too. Herring shoals have an alarming tendency to appear and disappear on a whim, and such whimsy has played a significant part in history. In the latter part of the twelfth century there was a famous herring fair in Skania, southern Sweden, which attracted merchants and traders from all over northern Europe, largely dealing with salted rather than fresh fish. By 1500 the fair had become so big that over 7,500 boats and 100,000 people were involved in the trade of this valuable fish. But suddenly the herring appeared no more, and the fair became irrelevant.

The herring had moved further south, and the Dutch began to exploit the fishery on an even more massive scale, helped by the ingenuity of one Wilhelm Beuckels who, in the fourteenth century, discovered that if herring were barrelled and salted on board rather than on shore, they kept in far better condition. It took us in the UK about 500 years to produce a herring to the same standards as the Dutch. We could invent trains, electricity and Spinning Jennies, we could even dominate half the world, but barrelling herrings seemed to be beyond our capabilities.

The herring family, Clupeiformes, includes the sardine and anchovy. They are all silver, sleek and fairly fatty fish. Like the salmon, they are scientifically quite primitive, as indicated by having pelvic fins situated well back on the underside of the body, a form that more closely resembles the bone structure of their terrestrial ancestors.

Anchovy

Engraulis encrasicolus
French: Anchois
Italian: Acciuga, Alice
Spanish: Boquerón
Portuguese: Biqueirão
German: Sardelle

I think it often escapes us that anchovies can actually be eaten fresh and that they don't live in tins. In fact, you can eat them raw, as I have done in France. One of my best suppliers once treated me to a plate of scintillatingly fresh, filleted uncooked anchovies, sprinkled with a touch of local sea salt – *sel de Guérande* – a little olive oil and a gentle quirt of lemon, nothing more. Wonderful!

Fresh anchovies are fished throughout the Mediterranean, around the Iberian peninsula and up as far as Brittany. When anchovy shoals arrive in the spring there is great excitement among the fishing fleets, who stand to make a great deal of money, but, as always, there is a lot of uncertainty about quite how big these shoals will be. Anchovies themselves are small fish, seldom more than 7.5–10cm (3–4 inches) long.

The majority of the catch is sent to processors, mainly Spanish, to make their beloved *boquerones*. But anchovy love is not just an Iberian weakness. The Turks are also decidedly passionate about their *hamsa*, even though supplies have been hit by the terrible state of the Black Sea, one of the most heavily polluted seas in the world. The anchovies were fished along the Black Sea coast as far as the city of Trabzon for many years, but a lot of work has to be done to bring this sea – and the anchovy fishery – back to its former glory.

Fresh anchovies are at their best in the early summer, and the better fish to buy fresh in the UK are the larger ones from Brittany. Mediterranean fish have a long way to travel, deteriorate rapidly and are often poorly packed. They can be fried or marinated, or eaten raw when impeccably fresh.

To fillet a whole anchovy, run your thumbnail (and if you don't have one you're in trouble here) along the spine from head to tail on both sides and you should have fillets in one hand, guts and skeleton in the other.

See also Preserved Fish (page 277).
Season: Early summer.
Price: £
Yield: About 60%
Fishing method: Net.

Herring®♥

Clupea harengus
French: Hareng
Italian: Aringa
Spanish: Arenque
Portuguese: Arenque
German: Hering

The small port of Etaples in northern France has a herring festival in the autumn, where Miss *Hareng*, and *harengs frites* feature strongly. When I last went there, to show an Australian chef that we *can* get decent fish in Europe, I was amazed to see everyone being so particular about their herrings. Wonderful Art Deco stalls on the water's edge were draped with quivering fish and pile upon pile of exquisite silver herring. Attentive boat owners, their wives and families, manned the stalls until every single fish was sold, which only took until lunchtime, by the way.

People like this type of market, and the boat owners get a much better deal for their money since they and their families are allowed to sell directly to the public. But it was the sight of men and women running their hands along the bellies of the herrings and exchanging knowledgeable words that intrigued me. It even impressed my Australian companion.

The experienced herring eater prefers a fish that's full and fat, just before it has spawned, and touching the belly quickly indicates whether it is a male with soft roe or a female with hard roe. The roe is an intricate part of the herring experience, and both hard (female) and soft (male) roe, or milt, are edible. For once it seems that the males have an edge over the females. Herring milts are quite delicious and easy to use. They are traditionally fried and served with toast and a touch of cayenne. Most people seem to prefer them to hard female roes.

HERRING

Immense shoals of herring are an easy target for the fishing fleets. At spawning time, the fish congregate close to the coast and, conveniently for the fishermen, can even be caught during the day. The Norwegians have perfected the art of large-scale herring fishing. After surrounding the shoals with a huge seine net, they often leave them in the water until their stomachs have emptied, for herrings with full bellies can split and spoil easily.

I've often wondered why it is that some herring on display have bloodshot eyes, and red gill covers. The answer may be that these are drift-netted rather than seined fish, and become damaged when their gills are caught in the nets. If any one knows better, please tell me.

The level of fresh herring consumption in the UK is pathetically low. Restaurant customers seem to feel cheated if offered a herring and, as demand for Dories and turbot lurches out of control, poor old *Clupea harengus* sits neglected on fish counters all over the country. However, we do have a passion here for sweet cured herrings and rollmops in glutinous sauces, although we seem to forget that fresh herring can make an excellent and healthy dish.

An easy way to fillet a herring – which only works if the fish is very fresh – is to lay a gutted fish on a chopping board stomach-side down and press quite hard with the palm of your hand. The backbone is pushed away from the flesh, bringing most of the small bones with it. Herring scales come off easily, by the way. Simply scrape them off under cold running water.

In Scotland herring are often rolled in oatmeal and fried in bacon fat, then served whole with the bacon (best quality, please) and a squeeze of lemon. They are excellent baked whole with a stuffing of apple and beetroot, or grilled with a mustard sauce. Like any fatty fish, they benefit from a sharp sauce. Any mackerel or sardine recipe can be used for herring as well.

See also Preserved Fish (pages 276–83).

Season: Various. Atlanto-Scandian and Thames herring: spring spawning; north Scotland: summer spawning; southern stock: autumn spawning.
Price: £
Yield: 35–45%, depending on season
Fishing method: Seine or drift net.

Sardine, Pilchard

Sardinus pilchardus
French: Sardine
Italian: Sardina
Spanish: Sardina
Portuguese: Sardinha
German: Pilchard, Sardine

It's odd, but many people don't like pilchards, while they love sardines. I don't want to shatter any illusion but they are one and the same. A pilchard is a larger, older and presumably wiser sardine.

In the past, most UK-caught pilchards have been sold to East European factory ships, or klondykers, which arrive each year in the West Country with the shoals of fish. It seems

SARDINE

a little crazy that we pay more money for fresh large sardines from France than we ever do for West Country pilchards. It's quite possible that many of these sardines are caught off the English coast anyway!

Both sardines and pilchards are perfect fish for barbecuing. Their skin crisps nicely over charcoal and smells intoxicating, better outside than in, where it can be quite overwhelming. Maybe this is why so much eating and cooking in Portugal is done on the street. The Portuguese love sardines, and there is a distinct etiquette to observe when eating them. Firstly, never use lemon. And secondly, eat them on a piece of bread, whole and enthusiastically, while somehow managing to discard the bones. This will mark you out as a true sardine *aficionado*.

Fresh sardines are essentially summer food. Scrape off the scales under the tap and gut them. Allow 2–3 large sardines per person, more if they are smaller Mediterranean sardines. They can be filleted by hand. Hold the fish in your left hand if you're right handed, and vice versa if not, twist the head and pull it off towards you, pulling the guts with you. Slide your thumbnail under the tail end of the spine to free it from the flesh then gently pull it away. This can be done in two deft strokes . . . honest!

See also Preserved Fish (pages 276–283).

Season: Summer.
Price: £
Yield: 50%
Fishing method: Net.

Sprat♥

Sprattus sprattus
French: Sprat
Italian: Papalina
Spanish: Espadin
Portuguese: Espadilha
German: Sprotte, Sprott

Sprats are seldom sold fresh these days, being mostly smoked or cured, or sold for fishmeal. Once the sprat was an important fish, swimming up the River Thames, where juvenile fish became part of that curious non-species, whitebait. A sprat looks very like a young herring. The way to tell them apart is to look at the position of the dorsal fin: in the sprat, it begins past the end of the pelvic fin on the other side, whereas with the herring the converse is true, the dorsal sitting above the pelvic fin.

Sprat are quite tolerant of low salinity and are fished extensively in the Baltic. They can be grilled, or cooked like sardines, and are excellent deep-fried in batter. To fillet by hand, run your thumbnail along the spine from the head to the tail on both sides and lift off the fillet.

Season: Autumn, winter, spring.
Price: £
Yield: Eat whole.
Fishing method: Net.

Whitebait♥

Regional equivalents:
French: Poutine (February, mainly small anchovies and sardines)
Italian: Bianchetti
Spanish: Aladroch

Unique in this book, this is a fish that scientifically doesn't exist. It is a truly British oddity. Quite what whitebait are has been a subject of learned discussion for many years. Once they were thought to be a separate species, *Clupea alba* or *Clupea alosa*, but there always seemed to be a nagging uncertainty as to whether they were merely juvenile fish. And if so, of what species? Scientists argued to and fro, while the whitebait fishermen lent their weight to the separate species theory, to avoid accusations that they were catching immature fish. But while the arguments raged, Thames-side taverns were filled to bursting with Londoners eating these sweet, succulent fish fried to a crisp.

These days the debate has fizzled out. Boring old science has solved the mystery, and whitebait dinners are no more. Whitebait are juvenile fish after all: a mix, it seems, of herring, sprat, and sometimes shad. The quantity of each species varies during the season, so there is no standing formula. These days most of the whitebait that we eat are frozen fish caught off Holland and New Zealand.

Season: Summer.
Price: £
Yield: Eat whole.
Fishing method: Net.

Marinated Anchovies

Alternatives: sardine, mackerel

Marinated fresh anchovy fillets, with their silvery backs and soft beige uppers, emerged, like salted anchovies, from the need to preserve the precious shoals of glimmering little fish. When the sun beat down in the hot summers of the Mediterranean, they remained fresh and truer to their original state than their salted brethren, though the longevity of marinated anchovies could not match that of salted ones.

Eaten straight from their marinade, with a hunk of bread and a crimson tomato salad, these marinated anchovies make a delicious first course – through choice, these days, rather than necessity. I can't pretend that boning them is a speedy job but, if you've a little time to spare, it isn't at all onerous.

SERVES 4–6 AS A FIRST COURSE

450g (1 lb) fresh anchovies
110ml (4 fl oz) white wine vinegar or rice vinegar
4 tablespoons olive oil
1 garlic clove, finely chopped
1 tablespoon finely chopped fresh chives or parsley
¼ red pepper, very finely chopped
salt

Using a pair of scissors, snip off the anchovy heads, tails and fins (don't forget the little dorsal fin on the back). Then cut down the belly and clean out the insides. Rinse with cold water.

With a small knife, lengthen the cut down to the tail. Sit each one, cut-side down, splayed out like a butterfly, and press down on the backbone with the heel of your hand, flattening out the fish. Turn over and pick out the backbone. With scissors, cut off the ridge of small bones at the edges. Pat dry on kitchen paper.

Spread the anchovies out, skin-side up, in a shallow dish and sprinkle with a little salt between layers. Mix the vinegar and oil and pour over. Cover and leave for 8–24 hours in the fridge, turning occasionally.

About an hour before serving, sprinkle with the garlic and chives or parsley. Just before serving, scatter over the red pepper.

Marinated Anchovy Dip

At the Italian fish restaurant, Zilli Fish, in Soho, London, they put a small bowl of sharp, salty, fishy dip on each table for diners to smear over their bread. After several dips and mouthfuls, I clicked. This singular goo was made of marinated anchovies. To make it, take marinated anchovies (you could do it with bought ones, if you like) out of their oil, shaking off any little nobbles of flavourings. Process thoroughly with a spoonful or two of their marinade and then spoon into a small dish. Add enough olive oil to cover, then serve with warm bread or bread sticks, or both.

Irish Potted Herring

Alternatives: mackerel, sardine

Essentially, this is a form of roll-mop, but made with unboned herring, cooked long and slow in a bath of spiced vinegar until the bones almost melt away. Serve the herring cold or hot as a first course, or as a main course, with warm soda bread and salted butter.

SERVES 6

6 herring, scaled and cleaned
6 black peppercorns
4 cloves
pinch of cayenne pepper
½ onion, sliced into rings
1 blade of mace
1 bay leaf
150ml (¼ pint) white wine vinegar
150ml (¼ pint) water
30g (1 oz) butter
salt and pepper

Preheat the oven to 200°C/400°F/Gas Mark 6. Clean the fish and remove the heads and tails. Wash them out and pat them dry with kitchen paper. Season the cavities with salt and pepper. Arrange them in an ovenproof dish and scatter the peppercorns, cloves, cayenne and onion rings over them. Tuck the mace and bay leaf down between the fish. Mix the vinegar and water and pour over the herrings. Dot with the butter and cover the dish loosely. Bake for 10 minutes, then lower the heat to 140°C/275°F/Gas Mark 1 and cook for a further 3 hours. Remove from the oven and serve hot or cold.

Herring Roes on Toast

This is one of those lovely, comforting dishes that remind me of childhood and home. There's not much to it but what there is is unbeatable. When you buy herring roes for a dish like this, insist on picking out whole ones. Damaged roes are fine for the 'Seftons' on page 130 but they won't do here.

If you want to spice the roes up a little, season the flour well with cayenne pepper to give you devilled roes on toast.

SERVES 2

15g (½ oz) butter
1 tablespoon sunflower oil
250g (9 oz) whole soft herring roes
plain flour, seasoned
2 thick slices of sturdy bread, toasted
salt
lemon wedges and cayenne pepper, to serve

Heat the butter in a frying pan with the oil until good and hot. Toss the roes in the flour and shake off any excess. Fry briskly in the butter and oil until golden brown. The roes will curl up shyly in the pan, which is as it should be.

Pile the roes on to the toast, sprinkle with a little salt and serve with lemon wedges – and a pot of cayenne pepper for those who want a little more spice against the creaminess of the roes.

A Sefton of Herring Roes and Anchovies

An eighteenth-century way with herring roes, made piquant with salty anchovies and capers. It is, I suppose, a sort of soft herring roe pâté, very rich, which is best served on crisp little biscuits, perhaps decorated with a small sprig of watercress. An excellent *hors d'oeuvre*.

SERVES 8

225g (8 oz) soft herring roes
1 tablespoon lemon juice
30g (1 oz) butter
3 anchovy fillets
4 tablespoons double cream, whipped
1 teaspoon capers, rinsed (soaked if salted) and
    chopped
salt and pepper

To Serve:
Bath Olivers, water biscuits or other suitable
    biscuits
cayenne pepper
watercress sprigs

Season the herring roes with the lemon juice and some salt and pepper. Heat the butter in a wide frying pan until foaming, then add the herring roes, drained of any juices. Fry for a few minutes, until cooked and curled and firmed up. Whizz them in a food processor with the pan juices and the anchovy fillets. Cool until tepid.

Fold the whipped cream into the herring roe purée, with the capers. Chill lightly. Shortly before serving, pipe or dollop on to the biscuits. Decorate each biscuit with a leisurely dusting of cayenne and a sprig of watercress.

Fried Mustard Herring

Alternatives: sardine, shad, mackerel

It's a Scottish tradition to fry herring rolled in oats, and a very good one, too. The mealy softness of oats, crisped in the frying pan, provides a fine contrast to the soft oiliness of the flesh. Even better, I find, is to add a hint of mustard. Most of its fieriness will dissipate in the heat of the pan but the flavour lingers on. Though one should really use finely or medium ground oatmeal, I admit to liking this dish just as much when it is made with rolled oats. On occasion, the fine crumbs of Jewish matzo meal (great for coating all kinds of fish and fritters, fishcakes and the like) have stood in very nicely, too.

SERVES 4

4 herring, scaled and cleaned, with roes
   if available
plain flour
1 egg
1 tablespoon Dijon mustard
150–175g (5–6 oz) fine or medium oatmeal
   (or rolled oats or matzo meal)
sunflower oil, for frying
salt and pepper
1 lemon, cut into wedges, to serve

Snip the fins off the herring – these fish are bony enough as it is, so make life easier by removing what you can before cooking! Season the fish inside and out with salt and pepper.

Tip some flour on to a large plate and season with salt and pepper. Beat the egg with the mustard in a shallow dish. Tip the oatmeal on to a second plate.

Set up a production-line system – first the herrings and roes, second the flour, then the egg and finally the oatmeal. Wipe the herring and roes dry with kitchen paper and then coat in flour. Dip in the egg and then roll in oatmeal.

Unless your frying pan is a roomy affair, or your herring are particularly petite, you'll get the best results from frying them in two batches of two, or having two pans on the go at once. Pour enough oil into your frying pan(s) to give a depth of about 5mm (¼ inch). Heat up thoroughly (if it is not hot enough, your coating risks floating off before browning). Fry the fish briskly until patched with brown, turning carefully so as not to disturb the crust. Fry the other side, then drain briefly on kitchen paper.

Serve with lemon wedges, plenty of salt and freshly ground black pepper, and extra mustard.

Moroccan Fried Sardines in Pitta Bread

Alternatives: scad, anchovies

Not long after we first met, William took me to Morocco, on a fish odyssey down the Atlantic coast from Casablanca to Agadir. Heavenly smells emanated from the tiny cafes of the souk in Safi, wafts of grilling sardines, aromatic spices and warm herbs, olive oil and garlic. We followed our noses to a feast of fried braces of sardines, glued together with *chermoula*, a blend of herbs and spices that is also used as a marinade for larger fish (see page 141). Still piping hot from the oil, they were slipped into half-circles of Arab bread, along with cooling slices of tomato and cucumber and lettuce leaves. It is the best way to serve them, I think, though you could simplify matters for a light first course by serving the fried sardines with nothing more than a few lemon wedges.

SERVES 4

12 small sardines or 8 medium–large sardines,
   scaled, cleaned and boned (see page 127)
plain flour, seasoned
olive oil (or a mixture of sunflower oil and olive
   oil, if you prefer), for frying
salt and pepper

For the Chermoula:
3 garlic cloves, chopped
½ tablespoon salt
1 teaspoon ground cumin
1 tablespoon paprika
¼ teaspoon freshly ground black pepper
3 tablespoons roughly chopped fresh coriander
3 tablespoons roughly chopped fresh parsley
2 tablespoons lemon juice
2 tablespoons olive oil

To Serve:
4 pitta bread, halved and warmed through in
   the oven
2 or 3 tomatoes, de-seeded and diced
diced or sliced cucumber
crisp lettuce leaves, shredded (Cos is always a
   good option)
lemon wedges
harissa or chilli sauce

Season the boned sardines with a little salt and pepper. To make the *chermoula*, place all the ingredients in a food processor and whizz to a hash. Spread the *chermoula* generously over the cut sides of half the sardines. Cover each one with a naked-fleshed sardine, cut side to cut side, to form a sandwich, pressing them together firmly. Cut each sandwich into two if the sardines are large. Secure each sandwich with a couple of wooden cocktail sticks.

One by one, coat the sardine sandwiches in seasoned flour and fry in hot oil until browned and just cooked. Drain briefly on kitchen paper. Pass the sardine sandwiches, warm halved pitta, tomatoes, cucumber, lettuce and lemon wedges around, so that each guest can help themselves as they wish. Offer a dab of fiery harissa or some other chilli sauce for those who like a shot of fire.

Tagliatelle with Sardines and Olives

Alternatives: anchovies, mackerel

Here is a good way to stretch a meagre helping of sardines to fill two hungry stomachs. Fried sardines, sweet, ripe, raw tomatoes, salty olives and peppery basil form the dressing for a plate of pasta. Appetising, quick and easy.

SERVES 2

225g (8 oz) tomatoes
2 medium sardines, scaled, cleaned and boned
   (see page 127)
225g (8 oz) tagliatelle
2 generous tablespoons olive oil
6 black olives, pitted and roughly chopped
6 fresh basil leaves, torn into pieces
salt and pepper
lemon wedges, to serve

Halve the tomatoes and squeeze out the seeds. Sprinkle lightly with salt and turn cut-side down to drain while you prepare the sardines. Cut the sardines into pieces about 2.5cm (1-inch) square, discarding heads, tails and fins. Dice the tomatoes roughly.

Cook the tagliatelle in a large pan of salted boiling water. Drain, toss with half the olive oil and keep warm. Heat the remaining oil in a frying pan and add the sardines. Fry for a few seconds, until they turn opaque, and then add the tomato, olives, basil and some pepper. Fry for a further 30–60 seconds, until hot but not collapsing. Toss with the pasta and serve with lemon wedges.

Devilled Whitebait

There's really only one thing to do with whitebait and that is to deep-fry them and serve piping hot and crisp, straight from the pan. I dare say that, if you insisted, you could come up with other ideas but no one ever does, probably because it would be hard to improve on this standard method. The only embellishment that comes to any good is a shake of cayenne in the flour coating. Hey presto, devilled whitebait!

I like quite a noticeable heat (I can't imagine that the Devil would have it any other way), so I use a full teaspoon of cayenne. For a more subtle version – suitable for purgatory, perhaps – stick with a mere ½ teaspoon.

If you are new to whitebait, do not be too aghast at the thought of eating those little fish whole, lock, stock and barrel. When properly cooked they are tremendously good, and you will swiftly forget any qualms you may have had.

SERVES 4

sunflower or vegetable oil, for deep-frying
60g (2 oz) plain flour
½–1 teaspoon cayenne pepper
1 teaspoon salt
500g (1 lb 2 oz) whitebait

To Serve:
lemon wedges
thinly sliced brown bread and butter

Put a pan or wok of oil on to heat up. Sift the flour with the cayenne and salt into a large bowl. Put the whole whitebait into a sieve and rinse with cold water. Shake off the excess and then tip the whitebait into the bowl of flour. Toss them in the flour until evenly coated, then tip into a dry sieve and shake off excess flour.

By now the oil should be hot enough – 190°C/375°F or when a cube of bread dropped into the oil fizzes energetically and starts to brown quickly. Deep-fry a generous handful of fish at a time, so that the temperature of the oil doesn't drop too low. Stir and separate any that stick together (I find that a pair of chopsticks is very handy for doing this). Fry until perfectly crisp and golden, about 3 minutes. Scoop out and drain on kitchen paper. Pass around the cooked ones while the next batch is cooking.

Serve them piping hot, with the lemon wedges and slices of brown bread and butter.

Warm-water and Reef Fish

The 'exotics', as they are called in fish-buying circles, were greeted with disdain when they first appeared in the early 1980s, but things have changed. It all started with the Seychelles. An enterprising firm in London started flying in fish that most of us had never heard of, let alone seen. The quality was good, and fish such as *bourgeois* and *capitaine* began to catch the eyes of buyers in London. The Seychelles has now been joined by Saudi Arabia, Oman, India, Pakistan, Eritrea, Tanzania and Trinidad in the difficult business of exporting fresh fish, so today snappers and pomfret, jacks and emperors are all quite easy fish to buy.

They tend to be colourful, often caught off coral reefs where trawlers simply cannot work, so many are hand-lined and of excellent quality. It may be true that the finest-tasting fish are from cold waters but these species have been the saviour of the wholesale markets, starved of regular and affordable supplies of fish from Europe.

Supermarkets, for all their conformity, have imposed high standards on their suppliers, and are often the best place to go for these imported species. One great advantage to us all is that they tend to be sold at a set, seasonal price, avoiding the startling price fluctuations from which British fish suffer.

Barracuda ♥

French: Barracuda
Italian: Luccio marino, Barracuda
Spanish: Barracuda, Espetón, Espet
Portuguese: Bicuda
German: Pfeilhecht, Barracuda

Great barracuda
Sphyraena barracuda

Yellowtail barracuda
Sphyraena flavicauda

A relaxing swim over a coral reef, with innocent and glamorous reef fish nibbling serenely underneath, can be ruined by a glance from the malevolent old barracuda. They eye you, sizing you up for meat potential, glinting their teeth impudently. I love swimming off coral reefs but can't help feeling very vulnerable, especially when, in the Red Sea, my Eritrean companions, local Dahlak island fishermen, jump in, shoving their hands down murky crannies looking for lobster and spearing fish left, right and centre. Barracuda and shark tend to relate to this sort of behaviour. But revenge is sweet. For the barracuda is easy to catch, and when it's fresh out of the water tastes surprisingly good. It has a reputation as a 'trash' fish but I've tasted much trashier.

The French used to call this fish *brochet de mer*, pike from the sea, which well describes its look. To distinguish the great barracuda from other species, look for a series of black spots on the underside of the fish above the anal fin. The yellowtail barracuda does indeed have a yellow tail, and no dark bars running along the body. Supplies are good, coming from India, Saudi, Eritrea and Oman.

Small barracuda weighing less than 2kg (4½ lb) are quite widely available and can be filleted. The bones are fairly easy to remove and the skin can be eaten if scaled first. Cajun, Thai and Indian flavours suit it well. Avoid cooking it with buttery sauces, and don't eat it raw.
Season: All year round.
Price: £
Yield: 60%
Fishing method: Various.

Bourgeois, Emperor Snapper *

Lutjanus sebae

One of the Seychelles fish that came into the UK and started the interest in exotics (illustration on page 139). Available from Seychelles and Australia, September to May.
Season: Autumn/winter.
Price: ££
Yield: 45%
Fishing method: Line.

Capitaine, Blue Emperor *

Lethrinus nebulosus

The capitaine comes from Seychelles, Mauritius and the Indian Ocean, and is a type of emperor (see Emperor below).
Season: Autumn/winter.
Price: ££
Yield: 45%
Fishing method: Line, traps.

Emperor*

Lethrinus spp.
French: Capitaine
Portuguese: Bica
German: Schnapper

Yellowtail emperor, Sky emperor

Lethrinus mahsena

Snubnose emperor

Lethrinus borbonicus

Longface emperor

Lethrinus olivaceus

The imperial face can be snub-nosed, long-faced or slender. Emperors are one of those groups of fish of which there are endless variations, which should mean that you can keep menu planners, chefs, fish merchants and everyone happy. If only. For some reason, longface emperors are not well liked, although snubnose emperors are. I've eaten both and find them as good as each other. But what about the thumbprint emperor, or the sky emperor?

To look at they are very much like snappers, with a thin body and sharp spines. They can get quite large, but the market prefers a fish that will feed one (400g/14 oz) or two (600–800g/1¼–1¾ lb) so that's what you'll mostly see. Don't ignore larger fish; it is, ecologically speaking, sound practice to eat larger fish that have had a chance to frolic and spawn, making their contribution to increasing the fish stocks. (You can always freeze a bit of fillet if you have some fish left over.) Emperors are excellent baked whole in salt but remember to leave the scales on the fish if you're going to cook it this way or the salt will draw out moisture and taste.

Emperors live off small prawns and crabs, which always give fish a good flavour. When you buy them make sure they're gutted and cleaned well inside, since all fish from hot climates tend to be even more fragile than usual.

> **Season:** All year round.
> **Price:** ££
> **Yield:** 45%
> **Fishing method:** Line, net, trawl.

Flyingfish

Cheilopogon spp.
French: Exocet
Italian: Pesce volante
Spanish: Pez volador
Portuguese: Peixe-voador
German: Fliegender Fisch

Flyingfish tend to get caught up in nets and are essentially a by-catch, but these exotic-looking *exocets* are frivolous fish, both to look at and to eat. Their occasional appearance at the fishmonger's delights everyone who has ever eaten a flying fish before – on some exotic beach where the sun shines and the sea laps gently around your toes – but they are no great culinary shakes in the UK.

Flyingfish have a highly developed, disproportionately large set of pectoral fins, which have evolved into 'wings'. They don't fly but can glide for an amazing distance in the right conditions. They are attracted by bright lights and were once so caught. Fishermen hung a light over the side of the boat, waiting for the fish to jump into a handily placed basket.

Fry whole fish or fillets dusted in seasoned flour in oil, or use in a 'pie', which is how flyingfish are often served in Barbados: bake with a mixture of courgettes, onions and a little cooked rice, covered with a cheese sauce.

> **Season:** December to March.
> **Price:** ££
> **Yield:** 60%
> **Fishing method:** Lamp fishing, net.

Grouper and Rockcod

Some of the more commonly found species:

Black grouper®

Epinephelus marginatus
French: Mérou noir
Italian: Cernia
Spanish: Mero
Portuguese: Mero
German: Zackenbarsch

Wreckfish★★

Polyprion americanus
French: Cernier atlantique
Italian: Cernia
Spanish: Cherna
Portuguese: Cherne
German: Wrackbarsch

Coney (W. Indies)

Cephalopholis fulva

Coral hind, Coral rockcod

Cephalopholis miniata

Malabar grouper (Red Sea)*

Epinephelus malabaricus

Red grouper, Bluespotted grouper (W. Africa)*

Cephalopolis taeniops

You may have eaten *cernia* in Italy or *mérou* in France and wondered where these fish were from. The answer is possibly from the Mediterranean, or perhaps even from outside Europe altogether. If they look spanking fresh and are being hauled out of the sea in front of your very eyes, then that seems pretty conclusive to me.

Groupers are large – at times very large – carnivorous fish that look permanently grumpy. Solitary hunters, they are found over much of the warm-water areas of the world. The largest species, the giant grouper or jewfish, can reach a hefty 300kg (660 lb) but this monster is unlikely to grace your plate, and it reputedly isn't very good to eat anyway. The groupers that you are more likely to see will come from Africa. On the west coast, the Senegalese *thiof*, a rather dull-looking grouper, is highly esteemed and sells well in France, where many Senegalese live. But in the UK we import more fish from the Red Sea, Oman and the Seychelles. One of the favourite West Indian fish is the coney, *Cephalopholis fulva*, a good-looking, reef-dwelling red grouper. Although local demand and overfishing mean that not a lot of this species gets sent out from the Caribbean, it closely resembles the West African bluespotted grouper, *Cephalopolis taeniops.* All of these fish are good grilled and are fairly interchangeable.

One of the best is the wreckfish, or *cernia* in Italian, which is still landed in Italy and Greece, and can rarely be found as far north as the UK. Like the mahi mahi, the wreckfish is attracted to things floating on the surface – not in an aggressive way, it's more a case of eating the smaller fish that tend to collect there.

It has a fairly firm flesh that holds together well when cooked. As I write this I have just eaten a *hamur* (Malabar grouper) in Massawa, on the Red Sea, baked to death in a *tandur* oven, and smothered in the same spicy mix that every fish you ever eat out here is smothered with, but it tasted absolutely wonderful.

As a rule, the red groupers make better eating than the darker fish, but don't eat the skin, which tends to be tough and unpleasant. Almost all of these fish fillet easily and have no intramuscular bones.

Think of the grouper as a large sea bass and you won't go wrong. Small fish are increasingly available and can be cooked whole. Steaming suits it well.

The market doesn't really distinguish between the different species.

Season: All year round.
Price: ££
Yield: 40%
Fishing method: Line, net.

Parrotfish®

Scarus spp.
French: Perroquet
Italian: Pesci pappagallo
Spanish: Vieja
Portuguese: Papagaiao
German: Papageifisch, Seepapagei

Next time you're sitting on a sandy beach in the tropics, vacating your brain, you may like to say a big thank you to the parrotfish. Their powerful, scrunching jaws are strong enough to eat the coral reef itself, passing it out as

PARROTFISH

a fine dust that goes to form sand.

The thing that sticks in my mind about these fish is that they sleep in a bed of mucus. The thing that *should* stick in my mind is their incredible beauty, but I am not entirely enamoured of this species on the eating front.

Parrotfish have rounded, parrot-like faces and, apart from the humpback, are never very large. On the markets they seem to be getting smaller and smaller, which usually means that they are being overfished. Unlike most reef fish, they feed during the day, and are mainly caught in traps. During the night they hit the mucus.

Male parrotfish generally have blue and green colours, females, reds and browns.

Popular and firm fleshed, the parrotfish is best baked or cooked on the bone. Try and buy a fish of about 700g–1kg (1½–2¼ lb) to feed two to three, although it is getting difficult to buy fish this size. Fillets from small fish are fragile, but fine off larger fish. Cook parrotfish with coconut milk and chilli, or with a fairly strong-tasting sauce.

Season: All year round.
Price: ££
Yield: 45%
Fishing method: Trap, net.

Pomfret★

Stromateus spp., Brama spp.
French: Castagnole du Pacifique
Italian: Pesce castagna
Spanish: Palometa, Castañeta
Portuguese: Capelo, Xaputa
German: Brachsenmakrele

White pomfret★
Stromateus cinereus

Pomfret are quite small, silver fish, similar to the pompano but rounder. Supplies of fish from the Indian Ocean will almost certainly increase over the coming years, as it is deemed to be one of the underexploited species, God help it.

A 400g (14 oz) fish is the easiest to find on the markets and it will feed one either whole or filleted. Pomfret are fine fish to eat, and are virtually scale-less. Fillets from this size are thin, so cooking times should be extremely brief. Fresh pomfret are similar to butterfish, which are more widely eaten in the US.

Season: All year round.
Price: ££
Yield: 40%
Fishing method: Line, trawl.

Snapper and Jobfish

French: Vivaneau
Italian: Lutianido
Spanish: Pargo
Portuguese: Luciano, Goraz
German: Schnapper

African red snapper® (west coast)
Lutjanus agennus

American red snapper★★
Lutjanus campechanus

Humpback red snapper★
Lutjanus gibbus

Humphead red snapper★
Lutjanus sanguineus

Jobfish, job
Aprron vivescens, Aphareus furca

Silk snapper★
Lutjanus vivanus

Two-spot snapper★
Lutjanus bohar

Yellowtail snapper★
Ocyurus chrysurus

BOURGEOIS, EMPEROR
SNAPPER

Everybody likes a snapper. But which snapper do you like? The culinary granddaddy of them all is the American red snapper, an excellent fish that has inspired snappers the world over to flip out of the water demanding to be sold. This is a good fish to bake whole, and the throat and shoulders are considered to be exceptionally fine. The easiest way to see if you have a true red snapper is to look at its eyes: if they are red and you're in America then it is probably the genuine article.

But what of the upstarts? There are over 200 species to choose from, so snapper is a safe bet to put on a restaurant menu. One fish that you may find fairly easily is the silk snapper. A supermarket chain once felt a strong desire to sell these fish, which were cheap and looked good, but the true silk snapper, which came originally from Venezuela, has broadened its identity somewhat, and snapper from all over the place seem to have become very silky of late. The yellowtail snapper doesn't keep as well as the red snapper, and has become a breakfast speciality on the Florida Keys, where the morning cry of 'yallertail-rabirubia!' lightens the dawn of the locals. What on earth does 'rabirubia' mean? The Americans think of this fish as one of their very best. It is indeed good, and remarkably adaptable too. There is some difference between the many species; if the true red snapper isn't available, most of the other species are quite good stand-bys. Job, by the way, are slightly thinner than snapper and are fished primarily in the Indian Ocean and Arabian Sea. Both job and snapper are good grilled, baked, poached, steamed, fried, and can even be eaten raw. To feed two, you will need a fish of about 800g–1kg (1¾–2¼ lb).

Season: All year round.
Price: ££
Yield: 50%
Fishing method: Line, net, trawl.

WARNING: Ciguatera Poisoning

Some coral-reef fish, most typically from the Caribbean and the Pacific, feed on a toxic dinoflagellate called *Gambierdiscus toxicus*, and are toxic if eaten. The toxicity remains in the food chain so that bigger fish feeding off the smaller herbivorous fish can also become toxic. Surgeon fish, barracuda, moray eels and some snappers such as the two-spot snapper and groupers are particularly susceptible. Toxins tend to accumulate in the liver, so never eat the liver of a coral-reef fish. The symptoms are a severe headache, tingling, itchy red rashes on the skin, aches, weakness and vomiting. There is often sensory inversion so that hot objects feel cold and vice versa.

Seek immediate assistance if you fall ill after eating any of these fish. Don't panic. The incidence of ciguatera poisoning is extremely low.

Cape Malay Pickled Fish

Alternatives: grouper, bass, cod

Barracuda is the nearest available substitute for the *snoek* that would be used for this dish of cold pickled fish in South Africa. Like the European and South American *escabeche*, this dish probably originated as a method of preserving fresh fish in a hot climate. Fridges and freezers have dispensed with the need for such recipes but we keep them nonetheless for the simple reason that we love to eat them. This is a marvellous dish for the first course of a summery dinner party, since it can be made in advance. In fact, it's rather a neat dish to make at the beginning of what you hope will be a lazy weekend, out of the heat of the kitchen, since it will keep for three or four days or longer in the fridge, and is just enough, served with salads and good bread, to constitute the backbone of a light lunch.

  The turmeric gives the white flesh a golden glow and the sugar softens the blow of the vinegar.

SERVES 4–6

1kg (2¼ lb) barracuda, skinned and cut into 6
  thick slices
4 tablespoons sunflower oil
2 red onions, thinly sliced
3 garlic cloves, thinly sliced
300ml (½ pint) white wine vinegar
300ml (½ pint) water
1 carrot, cut into fine matchsticks
2 teaspoons ground turmeric
3 bay leaves
2 tablespoons caster sugar
1 level teaspoon fennel seeds
8 allspice berries
2 small dried red chillies
1 teaspoon cumin seeds
8 black peppercorns
freshly grated nutmeg
1 cinnamon stick
salt and pepper

Season the fish with a little salt. Heat the oil in a large frying pan over a moderate heat. Fry the fish in batches in the oil for about 3 minutes on each side, until barely cooked through. Drain briefly on kitchen paper and then transfer to a shallow bowl.

Add the onions to the pan and cook for a few minutes, until beginning to soften, then add the garlic and cook for a minute or so longer. Add all the remaining ingredients and simmer for 15 minutes. Pour straight over the fish. Leave to cool and then cover and chill in the fridge.

Grilled Emperor with Chermoula

Alternatives: grey mullet, snapper, bass, grouper

Chermoula is the aromatic, spicy Moroccan marinade that transforms even the dullest of fish into something delightful. It can be made sloppy and wet or thick and pasty, as the recipe demands, and inevitably there are endless small variations. Coriander, paprika, cumin and chilli in some form seem to be essential. Here, I use the wetter sort of marinade with steaks of emperor, though it would work well with cod steaks, too. On page 132, you will find *chermoula* in a thicker form, almost a spread, to glue together braces of boned sardines.

SERVES 4

1.5kg (3¼ lb) emperor, cut into 4 steaks about
    3cm (1¼ inches) thick
salt
lemon wedges, to serve

For the Chermoula:
2 tablespoons finely chopped fresh coriander
2 tablespoons finely chopped fresh parsley
2 garlic cloves, crushed
1 teaspoon paprika
1 teaspoon ground cumin
generous pinch of cayenne pepper
½ teaspoon powdered saffron (optional)
3 tablespoons lemon juice
6 tablespoons olive oil

Mix the ingredients for the *chermoula* together. Place the fish steaks in a shallow bowl and tip over the *chermoula*. Turn the steaks to coat in the mixture, then cover and leave in the fridge for at least an hour or overnight, turning occasionally.

Preheat the grill. Take the steaks out of the marinade and shake off any loose bits. Grill close to the heat for a couple of minutes on each side to brown, then either rearrange the grill rack so that the fish is about 10cm (4 inches) from the grill or lower the heat slightly and grill for a further 2 minutes or so on each side, until just cooked through to the centre. Season with salt and serve with lemon wedges.

Grace's Fish and Groundnut Stew

Alternatives: halibut, cod, snapper, emperor

When I lived in London I had, for several years, a cleaner of remarkable elegance. She made many of her own clothes and always looked marvellous. Her name was Grace, which suited her perfectly. She came from Nigeria, and one day proffered this African recipe for fish cooked in a peanut sauce. It is excellent and unusual, and always reminds me of her.

SERVES 4

110g (4 oz) raw shelled peanuts
2 tablespoons oil
1 onion, chopped
2 garlic cloves, chopped
1 tomato, weighing about 85g (3 oz), skinned
    and chopped
1 tablespoon tomato purée
1 level teaspoon cayenne pepper
300ml (½ pint) water
freshly grated nutmeg
4 grouper steaks, each about 2.5cm (1 inch) thick
salt

Grind the peanuts to a fine powder. Heat the oil in a wide frying pan and gently cook the onion and garlic, without browning, until tender. Add the tomato, tomato purée and the cayenne and cook for 3 minutes, stirring. Then add the water, the ground peanuts, nutmeg and salt and bring up to the boil, stirring.

Embed the fish steaks in the thick sauce. Cover and simmer for 15 minutes or until the fish is just cooked through. Check occasionally and add a little more water if necessary, to prevent it from burning.

Parrotfish with Curry Butter

Alternatives: emperor, snapper, grouper

The bright blues, yellows and reds of parrotfish are enormously beguiling, though hard to preserve as you cook them. I like the taste enough not to mind too much but, for all that, I like to cook them simply, in foil. The curry brings a touch of warmth and richness without overwhelming the delicate flavour.

SERVES 2–3

1 parrotfish, weighing 700g–1kg (1½–2¼ lb)
oil
salt

For the Curry Butter:
110g (4 oz) butter, softened
1 tablespoon vindaloo curry paste
2 tablespoons lemon juice

Either mash or process the butter with the curry paste and lemon juice until smooth and a uniform orange-brown colour. Pile into a bowl and chill. Alternatively you could form it into a sausage shape, wrapped in greaseproof paper, and chill, then slice into neatish discs to serve.

Preheat the oven to 200°C/400°F/Gas Mark 6. Rub the parrotfish all over with oil, paying special attention to the fins and tail – this will prevent the fish from sticking to the foil. Sprinkle the fish lightly with salt and wrap it completely in foil, sealing the edges well. Bake for 30–40 minutes, until the fish is opaque through to the bone.

Lift the fish carefully on to a warmed serving dish and pour the juices over it at the table, so that everyone can admire the beautiful blue. Serve the cold curry butter separately.

Pomfret with Coconut and Tamarind

Alternatives: snapper, jobfish, emperor, bass, pageot

This is based on the thrillingly spicy but terrifyingly hot fish curries of Goa. One recipe I've come across recently contained twenty dried chillies *and* six fresh ones. Ouch. My version is a little tamer, with an emphasis on the richness of coconut, the tartness of the tamarind, and fragrant spices. Coconut cream is a thick liquid that can be bought in small cartons. It is *not* the same as creamed coconut, which comes in solid waxy blocks.

SERVES 4

2 pomfret, weighing about 450–600g (1–1¼ lb)
   each, filleted
200ml (7 fl oz) hot water
45g (1½ oz) tamarind pulp
6 dried red chillies
1 tablespoon coriander seeds
1 tablespoon cumin seeds
1 clove
good pinch of fennel seeds
½ teaspoon ground turmeric
¼ teaspoon ground cinnamon
8 garlic cloves, chopped
2 onions, roughly chopped
4cm (1½ inches) fresh root ginger, chopped
3 tablespoons sunflower or vegetable oil
4 green chillies, de-seeded and chopped
200ml (7 fl oz) carton of coconut cream
150ml (¼ pint) cold water
salt

Season the pomfret fillets with salt. Set aside. Pour the hot water over the tamarind pulp in a small bowl and set aside for 20 minutes. Then mush it up a bit with a fork. Rub through a sieve, discard the seeds and fibres and reserve the tamarind purée.

Grind the dried chillies, whole spices and ground spices together to a powder in an electric spice or coffee mill. In a food processor, process the garlic, onions and ginger to a paste.

Heat the oil in a frying pan wide enough to take the fillets. Fry the onion paste in the oil over a low to moderate heat, stirring, until lightly coloured. When the oil begins to separate out again, it is about ready. All in all, allow about 20 minutes for this.

Now add the green chillies and the spice mixture and cook for a further 2 minutes. Add the tamarind purée, the coconut cream, the cold water and some salt and bring up to the boil. Simmer for about 3 minutes, then add the fish, pressing the fillets gently down into the sauce. Simmer for another 4 minutes or so, until the fish is just cooked. Serve immediately, with rice.

Snapper with Sweet Garlic

Alternatives: sea bream, bass, emperor

Candying garlic in a sugar syrup is an unusual idea to begin with and to partner it with fish seems even more perverse. And yet this sweet garlic cream is marvellous with quickly pan-fried or griddled fish. The idea, I regret to say, is not mine. It comes from the Provençal chef, Antoine Bouterin, now resident in New York; this dish is lightly adapted from a recipe in his excellent book *Cooking Provence* (Macmillan, USA).

The syrup-soaked garlic can be made a week or more in advance. Store it in its syrup in a sealed jam jar in the fridge. Used in moderation, the syrup makes a delicious flavouring for tomato sauces, meaty stews and even salad dressings (mix with soy sauce, red wine or balsamic vinegar and a light oil or olive oil – great with bitter and peppery leaves).

SERVES 4

4 snapper fillets, weighing about 110–175g
    (4–6 oz) each
sunflower or vegetable oil
plain flour, seasoned
salt and pepper

For the Garlic:
150g (5 oz) caster sugar
225ml (8 fl oz) water
16 unpeeled garlic cloves
2 tablespoons extra virgin olive oil
1 tablespoon chopped fresh parsley
salt and pepper

To Garnish:
lemon wedges
fresh rosemary or parsley sprigs

To start the garlic, put the sugar into a pan with the water. Stir over a moderate heat until the sugar has dissolved. Bring up to the boil. Add the garlic, reduce the heat to low and simmer until the garlic is soft, around 40 minutes. If not using immediately, spoon garlic and syrup into a jar and leave to cool, then seal tightly and store in the fridge. If you are going to use it straight away, just let the mixture cool slightly and take the garlic out with a slotted spoon. If you think you may be able to use the garlicky syrup, save it in the fridge, as it won't be needed for this dish.

Set aside 4 cloves for garnishing. Peel off the skins of the remaining cloves as well as you can. This is sticky work. Discard the skins and put the sweet garlic cloves into a mortar. Pound to a paste and gradually work in the olive oil, then stir in the parsley, some pepper and a hint of salt, to form a glorious, green cream of a sauce. Set aside until needed.

Season the fillets of fish lightly with salt and pepper about half an hour before cooking. Heat enough oil to cover the base of a frying pan thinly, over a moderately high heat. One by one, coat the fillets in flour, tapping off any excess. Fry briskly, turning once, until browned and just cooked through, about 4 minutes in all.

Place the fish on warm serving plates or a single large serving dish. Spoon some of the garlic cream on to each one, garnish with the reserved cloves of garlic, the lemon wedges and the rosemary or parsley sprigs and serve at once.

Blaff

Alternatives: sea bream, emperor, pageot

This soup-stew of red snapper from Martinique is a vivid, lively creation, full of zip and fun, and almost as quick to put together as the name is to say. That name comes simply from the sound that the fish make when they drop into the hot poaching liquid – *blaff!*

Blaff can be made with water but the cooking juices taste all the better for being based on a keen fish stock. Although a small whole fish looks pretty in its bowl it is quite a bony creature to tackle, so for smarter occasions you may be better off with fillets from larger fish, which will need only the briefest cooking. Serve with a bowl of steaming white rice.

SERVES 4

4 small red snappers, weighing 350–400g
    (12–14 oz) each, cleaned and scaled,
    heads off, or 2 larger snappers, weighing
    600–800g (1 lb 5 oz–1 lb 12 oz) each, filleted
2 spring onions, sliced, to garnish

For the Marinade:
4 allspice berries, crushed
1 large garlic clove, crushed
½ Scotch bonnet chilli or hot red Thai chilli,
    de-seeded and halved
juice of 3 limes
salt and pepper

For the Soup:
2 red onions, sliced
3 garlic cloves, sliced
1½ tablespoons sunflower oil
3 allspice berries, crushed
juice of 3 limes
bouquet garni of 2 generous fresh thyme sprigs,
    1 fresh parsley sprig and 1 bay leaf, tied
    with string
1 red pepper, de-seeded and sliced
½ Scotch bonnet chilli or 1 red Thai chilli,
    de-seeded and halved
1.7 litres (3 pints) Fish Stock (see page 308)
    or water
salt and pepper

Mix together the marinade ingredients and pour over the fish. Turn to coat evenly and then cover and leave to marinate for an hour or so.

Take half the red onions and half the garlic for the soup and sweat gently in the oil in a large pan, covered, for 10 minutes. Now add the remaining onion and garlic and all the other soup ingredients. Bring up to a rolling boil and let it bubble for a minute or two. Slide the fish in, together with the marinade (hear that 'blaff' as it hits the water?) Bring back to the boil, by which time the fillets should be perfectly cooked through. Whole fish will take 4–5 minutes.

Lift them out carefully and lay in soup dishes. Spoon some of their cooking liquid over them and then sprinkle with the spring onions.

Tuna, Mackerel and Game Fish

Most of the fish in this section are migratory, sleek creatures, subtly coloured to blend in with the predominant background blues and silvers underwater. They are among the most soughtafter fish in the world.

Cooking them isn't difficult but rich, creamy sauces are *hors de combat*. Overcooked tuna is virtually inedible, so try and keep a light touch, and lock up your butter. These are fish that confirmed carnivores can handle and are almost all particularly rich in Omega-3 fatty acids.

TUNA

All tuna are shoaling fish, although larger, older specimens tend to be more solitary. Tuna have red, myoglobin-rich flesh, which stores the oxygen that fuels the muscles of these immensely powerful, magnificent fish.
Several species of tuna appear on the markets. The bluefin is the most expensive and generally considered the best, with yellowfin a more affordable alternative.
Many tuna, particularly bluefin, are under great pressure from overfishing and unless careful measures are applied it may be put on the endangered species list, a move that will be fiercely resisted by the Japanese.

Albacore, Long-fin Tuna®♥

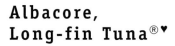

Thunnus alalunga
French: Thon blanc, Germon
Italian: Alalunga
Spanish: Atun blanco, Albacora
Portuguese: Atum-roador
German: Weisser Thun

There is a short season in the summer when a few Cornish fishing boats sail southwards to catch albacore. This fish is particularly sensitive to water temperature, and wayward smaller albacore like to swim where the warm water from the south meets the cold water from the north. Wiser, larger fish stay in the tropics.

Albacore have lighter meat than yellowfin tuna and are often canned. It's not a good tuna to serve raw because the flesh turns an unappetising brown on contact with air.
It is distinguished from the other tunas by having larger eyes and long pectoral fins, which end past the second dorsal fin.

Bigeye®♥

Thunnus obesus
French: Thon obèse
Italian: Tonno obeso
Spanish: Patudo
Portuguese: Atum-patudo
German: Grossaugenthun

The fat one, *Thunnus obesus*, the rollicking cousin of the bluefin, primarily swims in tropical waters. To the Japanese, this fish, the *mebachi*, is becoming increasingly important as the bluefin is moving towards being unaffordable and unobtainable. European-based Japanese are increasingly settling down to platefuls of raw *mebachi*, which is conveniently available when the bluefin is scarce, but the meat has to be carefully selected. There is sometimes a distinctly unpleasant smell from the flesh at the outer edge of the body, and its slightly pale meat has a tendency to stickiness, which isn't conducive to making good *sushi*, especially if you're rolling your own.

Bluefin★★♥

Thunnus thynnus
French: Thon rouge
Italian: Tonno
Spanish: Atún
Portuguese: Atum-rabilho
German: Roter Thun

The lovely, shimmering bluefin *Thunnus thynnus* has a price on its head. At the coronation of Emperor Akahito of Japan a bluefin tuna from New England was sold for nearly $80,000 and flown, practically chauffeur driven I suspect, straight to Tokyo for the occasion. Today, early-season bluefin regularly fetches £20 a kg (2¼ lb), and the Japanese market will pay much more. But why on earth does anyone spend so much money on a fish? The answer is that bluefin tuna is considered to be the finest of all fish that can be served raw as *sashimi* or *sushi*, and demand for top *sashimi*-grade fish is always high, and supply always difficult.

The bluefin tuna is a stubby, thickset fish with fairly short pectoral fins, than can weigh as much as 300kg (660 lb). Migrating bluefin tuna move around relatively select areas of the world. Originally Japan had its own stocks but high demand soon put paid to that. It seems almost unbelievable that tuna was once considered quite unsuitable for *sushi*. Before the days of hand-rolled *nigiri sushi*, rice and fish would be pressed under a weight and left to ferment. The *toro*, the fatty stomach of the tuna which has become so popular and so expensive these days, was originally rejected as inedible. It wasn't even called *toro* – which means 'melt' in Japanese – until about 1918. But habits change, and in the early 1920s the Japanese began to appreciate raw rather than marinated tuna, and the market grew ever larger.

A *sashimi*-grade tuna has three main requirements: the flesh must have a good red colour, a high fat content and a lack of bruising, as well, of course, as a fundamental need to be hyper-fresh. The colour is intricately connected with the fishing method. Netted fish, for instance, can drown, which may seem odd, but tuna need a constant supply of oxygen from water being pushed over their gills by fast forward movement, and nets, by stopping the fish swimming, reduce the oxygen intake so much that the tuna eventually expires. As the oxygen-storing myoglobin is used up, the colour of the flesh turns a muddy, unappetising brown, so a good specimen has to be quickly killed.

Another factor that affects the colour is the fish's body temperature. Unless the tuna are rapidly cooled they tend to cook gently from within, since they have a higher body temperature than the surrounding water. To avoid the dreaded colour change, the fish should be quickly bled and gutted, then gently lowered into an icy slurry, bringing the body temperature right down. This is a lengthy process, however, and one that requires both skill and a high level of equipment.

The fat content is more hit and miss. Experienced buyers can take a piece of tuna, rub it between their fingers and tell how fat it is, which really depends upon the time of year. Fish that are just about to spawn are ideal, rich and fat, and usually *sashimi* buyers disappear as soon as spawning is over to go and trouble another stock elsewhere.

Bruising is easier to check. By running your hands along a tuna's body, you learn to feel for areas of 'give', which indicate a bruise. A bruise is disastrous: the bruised flesh falls apart, so for presenting *sashimi*, which must hold together, it is just not on.

There are three main bluefin tuna areas in the northern hemisphere. In the Western Atlantic, fish swim from the Gulf of Mexico northwards to New England to spawn. Over on our side,

tuna swim off southern Ireland down to the Bay of Biscay, with a few even daring to swim through the North Sea. Some pass through the Straits of Gibraltar into the Mediterranean, where they are fished, trapped and chased by an increasingly high-powered fishing fleet. There tuna spawn off the Balearics, but further to the east, there is yet another group of fish which seems to circulate in the sea between Sicily and Turkey, and here the spawning takes place off Sicily.

Bluefin tuna are available in the Mediterranean from the late winter to summer, but prices drop after spawning. Most *sashimi*-grade fish are sent to Japan, with second-grade fish ending up in Europe, especially in the UK. Most of these are quite good enough for our requirements.

Skipjack♥

Euthynnus pelamis, Katsuwonus pelamis
French: Listao, Bonite à ventre rayé
Italian: Bonita
Spanish: Listado
Portuguese: Gaiado
German: Echter Bonito

The skipjack, a tropical tuna with light-coloured meat, has a rather endearing habit of leaping out of the water and 'skipping' along the surface when chasing shoals of smaller fish. Not so heartening is man's huge appetite for this fish. Skipjack is brined and tinned the world over, providing us with an untold number of tuna sandwiches each year. It is not widely found in the Mediterranean but exists in huge, though diminishing, numbers off the southern Californian coast and in the Pacific. They weigh, on average, about 5kg (11 lb).

Yellowfin★♥

Thunnus albacares
French: Albacore
Italian: Tonno albacora
Spanish: Rabil
Portuguese: Albacora
German: Gelbflossenthun

Although the yellowfin tuna is looked down upon as a *sashimi* fish, it is affordable, available for most of the year, leaner and more to most people's taste than the fatty bluefin. In Europe there is a lot of imported yellowfin available from the Gulf that arrive, come war, sun, or sandstorm, in excellent condition.

The Latin name for yellowfin is, as you can see, *Thunnus albacares*. You may well have assumed that this was the albacore tuna. Well, if you were French it would be, but if you were an English speaker your albacore would be none other than *Thunnus alalunga*, or what the French refer to as *thon blanc* or *germon*.

Yellowfin are widely distributed throughout the warmer waters of the world, and most of the market-size fish weigh between 20 and 25kg (55 lb). Larger specimens above 45kg (100 lb) are rare.

Tuna Cooking and Buying

Tuna is mostly sold off the bone and you should allow about 175g (6 oz) per person. Ask for the portions to be cut for you, and watch out for the following:

Avoid
1. Thawed-out frozen fish.
2. Any fillet with an oily sheen to it.
3. Any brown-looking fillet.
4. Any fillet that appears to be falling apart.

If you want to eat tuna raw, only buy from a specialist dealer who clearly understands the requirements. You need a high fat content, a strong red colour, a firm fillet and extremely fresh fish. If you are eating the fish raw, do not use the dark blood line that is clearly noticeable in the fillet.

Most people prefer to eat tuna underdone, and you can treat it like fillet steak. A tuna steak sandwich takes about a minute to make and is delicious. Split a baguette, sear a tuna steak 2–3cm (1 inch) thick, well seasoned with salt and pepper, in a pan and cook on a high heat for 1 minute each side. Add some tomatoes, mayonnaise, a leaf of lettuce, *et voilà* . . .

Tuna becomes dry when overcooked, so great attention should be paid to cooking times.

Season: Available from different locations throughout the year.
Price: £/££/£££
Yield: Albacore 60%, Bigeye 60%, Bluefin 50%, Skipjack, 65%, Yellowfin 60%
Fishing method: Net, trawl, long line, hand line, live bait (SW France).

BONITO AND LESSER TUNA

These are a sort of halfway fish between mackerel and tuna, which sometimes shoal in great numbers but lack the tuna's delicacy in both looks and eating.

Atlantic Bonito♥

Sarda sarda
French: Bonite à dos rayé, Pélamide
Italian: Palamita
Spanish: Bonito
Portuguese: Sarrajão
German: Bonito, Pelamide

Frigate Mackerel, Bullet Tuna♥

Auxis rochei
French: Auxide, Melva, Bonitou
Italian: Tombarello
Spanish: Melva
Portuguese: Judeu-liso

Kawakawa♥

Euthynnus affinis
French: Thonine
Italian: Tonnetto orientale
Spanish: Bacoreta oriental
Portuguese: Merma-orientale

The bonito has strong-tasting flesh, prone to dryness, and I'm sorry to say it is one of the few fish that I don't like at all. The last one I ate was leapingly fresh, straight out of the Red Sea, and still it failed to captivate my tastebuds. It is, I fear, an unsubtle fish but perhaps subtlety is not what you want. There are a lot of bonito-type fish, good though not great, that can take strong flavours.

In Japan bonito is dried to form *katsuo bushi*, or dried bonito flakes, which are used to make *dashi*, a light and versatile fish stock. For some reason the Ancient Greeks thought highly of this fish, and wrote long discourses on its life-cycle, coming up with the bizarre idea that its eggs were cube shaped and lay in the mud.

Frigate mackerel and kawakawa are mainly fished in the Indian Ocean and the Pacific, and are also fairly cheap but coarse fish.

Cook as tuna.
Season: Summer.
Price: ££
Yield: 50%
Fishing method: Net, line

OTHER FATTY FISH

Bluefish♥

Pomatomus saltatrix
French: Tassergal
Italian: Pesce serra
Spanish: Anjova
Portuguese: Anchova
German: Blaufisch

This is a thoroughly nasty and aggressive little fish that can be found in the Mediterranean and far away in the States, where it is fished for sport. It has a particularly unpleasant habit of regurgitating its stomach contents when hauled on board, which is, I suppose, understandable in the circumstances. In Turkey you may see this fish as the *lüfer*, where it is often cooked over charcoal. Not a brilliant fish but one to shock your friends with. They're fairly small, about 20cm (8 inches) long, and don't keep well. They often chase shoals of fish into harbour mouths, where sports fishermen lie in wait.

Season: Summer.
Price: ££
Yield: 55%
Fishing method: Line.

Horse Mackerel, Scad♥

Trachurus trachurus
French: Chinchard
Italian: Sgombro bastardo
Spanish: Jurel
Portuguese: Carapau
German: Bastardmakrele, Halzmakrele

Scads an' tates, scads an' tates,
scads an' tates an' conger,
An' they who can't eat scads an' tates,
O'they must die of hunger!
Cornish ditty

I have always understood that horse mackerel are so called because they ride along with shoals of mackerel, which sounds good enough to me. The horse mackerel or scad is little used by northern Europeans but greatly loved by the Portuguese, who grill them in the open air along with their beloved sardines, and the Japanese, who eat them raw and cooked.

They don't really look like mackerel, more like a thin jack, and are less fatty to eat. They have a silver body, covered with small tubercles on the lateral line. One of the key tests of proficiency in *sushi* preparation is the removal of this lateral line, the *zengo*. When very fresh, horse mackerel can be simply grilled or fried in tempura batter.

Season: Summer.
Price: £
Yield: 35%
Fishing method: Net, trawl.

Jack and Pompano

African pompano
Alectis ciliaris

Crevalle jack
Caranx hippos
French: Carangue crevalle
Italian: Carango cavallo
Spanish: Caballa
Portuguese: Xareu-macao
German: Bastardmakrele

Bigeye trevally
Caranx sexfasciatus
French: Carangue corace
Italian: Carangidi
Spanish: Caballa
Portuguese: Xareu

Lookdown, Indian threadfish
Alectis indicus

Orange-spotted trevally
Carangoides bajad
French: Carangue lentigine
Italian: Carangidi
Spanish: Caballa
Portuguese: Xareu

These silver-skinned, fatty fish are widely distributed around the warmer seas of the world and look like pumped-up horse mackerel. They tend to shoal off coral reefs, feeding off the smaller reef fish.

The main species sold over here are the African pompano, crevalle jack, and various trevallies and, occasionally, the lookdown, a lugubrious-looking fish with a high sloping forehead and a disdainful mouth. Despite their elegant looks, these fish taste quite ordinary, a 4/10 fish. They are better for having the skin removed. The flesh is dense, strong tasting, and goes well with strong flavours, as in Thai cooking.

> **Season:** All year round.
> **Price:** ££
> **Yield:** 40%
> **Fishing method:** Line, trawl.

Kingfish

Scomberomorus spp.

Narrow-barred Spanish mackerel★♥
Scomberomorus commerson
French: Thazard rayé
Italian: Scombro reale
Spanish: Sierra, Carita
Portuguese: Serra, Cavalho do India
German: Königsmakrele

King mackerel♥
Scomberomorus cavalla
French: Thazard serra
Italian: Scombro reale
Spanish: Sierra
Portuguese: Serra
German: Königsmakrele

Unravelling the complexities of what is and what is not kingfish has taken the now-diminished Holmesian part of my mind a long time. In the UK, kingfish are as above. In the US, kingfish refers to *Menticirrhus littoralis*, or the Gulf kingfish. In Australia and New Zealand, the kingfish, or yellowtail kingfish, refers to *Seriola lalandi*, which is called yellowtail or amberjack in the UK.

Kingfish is becoming increasingly popular. It has excellent firm flesh, tastes good and holds together very well when grilled. They are pelagic fish, furious and fast moving, and are found in the Red Sea, Indian Ocean and the Gulf. As supplies to the UK continue to increase from these areas, we are likely to see more and more kingfish for sale in our markets. The colour of the flesh varies somewhat, but when cooked any greyness tends to disappear. The best fish are from Oman, while Caribbean fish tend to be soft and have greyer flesh.

Any tuna or mackerel recipe will suit the kingfish. It's important not to over-cook the fillet, which has a strong taste and a good texture. Kingfish is excellent grilled, but butter makes it too rich.

> **Season:** All year round.
> **Price:** ££
> **Yield:** 60%
> **Fishing method:** Line, trawl.

Mackerel★♥

Scomber scombrus
French: Maquereau, Lisette (small fish)
Italian: Maccarello, Sgombro
Spanish: Caballa
Portuguese: Sarda
German: Makrele

When people start moaning about the price of fish, whisper one word in their ear: mackerel. Here is an excellent fish, one that almost everyone knows, which is neither too fatty nor bland. It's not a fish to cook in the confines of a bedsit, for it impregnates the air with a mighty strong smell, but it's cheap, widely available, looks good and is good for you. On the down side . . . well, I can't honestly think of anything. The perfect fish? Almost.

Although it's cheap, it's stunningly beautiful when fresh, with an iridescent blue-black back and silver belly. Large fish can weigh 1kg (2¼ lb) or so, but most people in Continental Europe prefer the delicacy of the smaller fish.

Mackerel are pelagic fish, swimming near the surface in shoals of once epic proportions. Together with the pilchard, they were once the backbone of the Cornish fishing industry. Before the railway came along, it was virtually impossible for the local market to absorb the huge amounts of fish, despite the best efforts of 'jowsters' – itinerant fish-sellers who trudged inland with a load of fish on their backs.

Today, the southern English mackerel fishery has been overfished, and is subject to stringent controls. If you happen to be in the Cornish ports of St Ives, Cadgworth or Newlyn, you can still see the remnants of the hand-lining fleet – small licensed fishing boats that look quite out of place among the grubby trawlers nearby – which work the mackerel shoals in the summer months.

Mackerel are widely available and easy to cook. Sear a fillet on either side and serve with a squeeze of lemon or a drop of soy sauce for an incredibly easy and cheap introduction to the joys of mackerel, but once again avoid using any cream or too much butter. They are best with sharp sauces such as the classic gooseberry, or rhubarb. The Japanese prefer to eat autumn mackerel after

MACKEREL

spawning, just as they are fattening up for winter. There is an old Japanese saying that you should never let your daughter-in-law eat mackerel in the autumn or she'll be barren. Unless, that is . . .

Season: Spring/autumn.
Price: £
Yield: 60%
Fishing method: Line, trawl.

Mahi Mahi, Dolphin Fish♥

Coryphaena hippurus
French: Coryphène commune
Italian: Lampuga, Contaluzzo
Spanish: Llampuga, Dorado
Portuguese: Dorado
Maltese: Lampuka
German: Goldmakrele

Alive, this solitary fish is almost impossibly beautiful, the most glorious and sexiest of all the fish in the sea. It has a long, slender, silver body covered in an array of scintillating black, gold and blue spots. Male fish are distinguished by steeply sloping foreheads, which give them a somewhat Mohican appearance. Strong, muscular and fast, the sad thing is that as the fish breathes its last breath, its beauty imperceptibly fades.

Mahi mahi have taken their Hawaiian name rather than the American dolphin, and are widely distributed throughout the warmer waters of the world. They tend to be drawn to objects floating on the water, which is often their undoing. In Malta, the arrival of the *lampuki* in the late summer sees fishermen rushing out to sea to try and get the first of the catch. They lure the *lampuki* using what technicians would call a FAD (Fish Aggregation Device), otherwise known as a piece of wood. The Maltese make *lampuki* into a

delicious pie during the height of the season between September and December. (Never eat lampuki pie out of season – it'll be from frozen fish and the *lampuki* doesn't freeze well.)

Over in Hawaii the mahi mahi is still eaten raw. If you come across dolphin on a menu, as I have done on mainland USA, don't go apoplectic and throw your sandals at the waiter, but enjoy! Its only mahi mahi.

Mackerel and tuna recipes work well with mahi mahi.

Season: Spring to autumn.
Price: ££
Yield: 60%
Fishing method: Line, trawl.

Marlin and Sailfish

Marlin♥
Makaira spp.
French: Makaire
Italian: Pesce lancia
Spanish: Marlin, Pez aguda
Portuguese: Espadim
German: Marlin, Speerfisch

Sailfish♥
Istiophorus spp.
French: Voilier
Italian: Pesce vela
Spanish: Pez vela
Portuguese: Veleiro
German: Segelfisch

Both are warm-water fish that can reach an enormous size; larger fish of 300kg (660 lb) are still occasionally landed but are oddly disappointing to eat. The sailfish is seen more often than the marlin, which is mostly eaten smoked in the UK. It almost seems a shame to eat them, for alive they are both stupendous fish. The 'sail' of the sailfish unravels like

a dinosaur's frill and folds neatly along the fish's back when speeding through the sea. They can swim incredibly fast, reaching speeds of over 100km (60 miles) an hour. But luckily for them they actually taste rather dull, so are mainly pursued by sports fishermen for the thrill of the chase.

The best way by far to eat marlin is Sophie's Hawaiian Poke recipe on page 165. The flesh is tender and marries brilliantly with the seaweed. Otherwise, grill or sear fillets and serve simply with a wedge of lemon.

Marlin can become very large; try to buy freshly cut loins from smaller fish if possible, since all of these large fish – tuna and swordfish included – can accumulate heavy metals in their flesh. Sailfish can be treated in the same way as marlin.

Season: Summer.
Price: ££
Yield: 60%
Fishing method: Line.

Swordfish★♥

Xiphias gladius
French: Espadon
Italian: Pesce spada
Spanish: Pez espada, Emperador
Portuguese: Espadarte
German: Schwertfisch

Slap some swordfish on a barbie, don't overcook it and you'll eat it at its best. There's some reluctance from chefs to take swordfish seriously. Tuna, yes, but swordfish, resoundingly no. The first time I ate it was in an obscure fishing port on the west coast of Sardinia. It was grilled, not overly so, served with a *salmoriglio* of lemon juice, olive oil, salt and fresh oregano, and was so good that I became a swordfish zealot, trying in vain for years to convince chefs that it was indeed a fish worthy of their attention.

The best time to buy swordfish is when the flesh has a nice pink tinge to it, just before spawning in the summer, but the fish have to be a fair size before they get to sexual maturity. Male fish, smaller than females, reach it when they are between two and three years old, and weigh just over 20kg (44 lb). Females take their time; they have to be at least four years old and weigh more than 70kg (155 lb) before they are ready to reproduce. Both males and females are aggressive, solitary fish, and no one seems entirely sure what the sword itself does. There is some doubt as to whether the fish actually kills with the sword – *et tu, pisces?* – or just causes chaos to confuse and stun a shoal of smaller fish.

Off the Calabrian coast, in Italy, swordfish were hunted for hundreds of years by boats with incredibly tall lookouts and sleek, fish-shaped hulls that were thought to fool this easily fooled fish. The boats had an 'antenna', a tall mast about 30m (90 ft) high, where four *speculatores* watched the horizon for the tell-tale ripples that swordfish leave when swimming near the surface. In front of the boat was an even longer *passarella*, or walkway, where the harpoonist lay in wait for the fish. The steering was done from on high, using a long rope connected to the rudder, and two motors gave the boat great speed and manoeuvrability.

Further down the coast, Sicilian fishermen believed that if anyone dared utter a word in Italian the swordfish would immediately plunge to the deeper water below.

I admire this form of combat but these days the Italian fleet uses drift nets, often way beyond the permitted length, to capture the diminishing number of swordfish left in the Mediterranean. With supplies now coming from countries as far apart as Chile and Sri Lanka, the swordfish's wide distribution and high value has cost it dear.

As with the marlin, try and avoid vacuum-packed loins if possible. If you can't, make sure that they are clearly dated and not too old. Remember that larger fish can accumulate heavy metals in their flesh and may not be altogether life-enhancing . . .

Season: All year round.
Price: ££
Yield: 60%
Fishing method: Net, harpoon, line.

Yellowtail, Amberjack

Seriola spp.
French: Sèriole
Italian: Ricciola
Spanish: Serviola, Pez limon
Portuguese: Esmoregal, charuteiro
German: Gelbschwanz, Bernsteinfisch

Greater amberjack**♥
Seriola dumerili

Japanese yellowtail**♥
Seriola guingueradiata

A fatty, elegant fish, greatly appreciated by the Japanese, and a fish I have successfully persuaded many a chef to try. It cooks well and has a fine-tasting flesh, which is well suited to being eaten raw. In Japan they are farmed and called *hamachi*, which technically applies only to juveniles. Bigger wild fish can be found off the Balearic Islands, where they are called *pez limon*, and are caught in the summer. In Europe supplies are irregular but some farmed fish from Japan are imported to be eaten raw. A lot of people ordering yellowtail expect yellowfin tuna and look perplexed when a white-fleshed fish is served.

The yellowtail is widely distributed, a sleek and muscular fish that is almost pink in colour, with a yellow band running the length of the body, clearly distinguishable in very fresh specimens.

Although Japanese shops sometimes sell yellowtail, fishmongers rarely stock it. They are fairly big fish, although larger specimens have coarser flesh than fish less than 50cm (20 inches) long. In fillet form, the yellowtail should be cooked as mackerel or tuna.

Season: Summer.
Price: ££
Yield: 50%
Fishing method: Line, trawl, farmed.

Tuna Tartare

Alternatives: salmon, yellowtail

If your tuna is truly fresh, there are few better ways of serving it than this. Finely diced, its natural, uncooked, sea-salt flavour tempered by the addition of shallots, capers, a touch of crème fraîche and coriander, it makes an elegant, light first course, particularly with its accompanying salad of marinated cucumber.

This is also very good made with salmon.

SERVES 4

450g (1 lb) freshest tuna fillet, finely diced
2 shallots, very finely chopped
2 tablespoons capers, rinsed (soaked if salted), roughly chopped
2 tablespoons chopped fresh coriander, plus a few sprigs to garnish
4 tablespoons *crème fraîche*
1 green chilli, de-seeded and very finely chopped (optional)
2 tablespoons lemon juice
salt and pepper

For the Cucumber Salad:
1 cucumber, peeled and sliced paper thin
2 teaspoons salt
1 tablespoon sugar
2 tablespoons white wine vinegar

Prepare the cucumber salad first. Mix all the ingredients, cover and leave for at least 2 hours.

Mix the tuna with all the other ingredients for the tartare, adding lemon juice and seasoning to taste. Cover and set aside for at least an hour in the fridge.

To serve, drain the tuna thoroughly. Divide the tuna into four portions and pile each portion into a ramekin. Press down to compact the mixture, then run a knife round the edge of each ramekin and turn the moulded tuna out on to a plate. Surround with cucumber salad, add a sprig or two of coriander, and serve.

Tuna Teriyaki with Soba Noodles

Alternatives: salmon, yellowtail, kingfish

These days you can buy very good ready-mixed teriyaki marinades from supermarkets, as well as from shops specialising in oriental foods. You can even buy Japanese soba noodles from some of the big retailers, and they are well worth trying. Made partially or wholly with buckwheat, they have a gentle but distinct flavour that is marvellous with fish. Here I've made them the base for quickly cooked teriyaki tuna. They soak up the salty, sharp, dark sauce so very nicely that they deserve an Oscar for their supporting role.

If you really can't find any soba noodles, this is still an excellent dish made with Chinese medium egg noodles, which are common enough, or even, at a pinch, spaghetti.

SERVES 4

4 portions of tuna steak, cut about 2.5cm
   (1 inch) thick, weighing about 175–225g
   (6–8 oz) each
150ml (¼ pint) teriyaki marinade
juice of 1 lemon
1 tablespoon sunflower oil
salt and pepper

For the Noodles:
250g (9 oz) soba noodles
1 tablespoon sesame oil
butter
salt

To Serve:
small handful of roughly chopped fresh coriander
lime wedges

Marinate the tuna steaks with the teriyaki marinade, lemon juice and some pepper for 30 minutes.

Put a large pan of salted water on to boil for the noodles. When it is at a rolling boil, cook the noodles as per the packet instructions (around 5–6 minutes is usually sufficient). When they are done, drain thoroughly and then toss with the sesame oil, a small knob of butter and a little salt. If you need to re-heat them later (though not too much later, please), I find that the best way is in a tightly covered bowl in the microwave.

Meanwhile, heat the sunflower oil in a heavy cast-iron pan over a high heat until smoking. Take the tuna out of its marinade and lay it in the pan. If the steaks are big, you may have to cook them in two batches. Leave for 1½ minutes without disturbing at all, then turn the tuna over and cook on the other side for a further 1½ minutes. Pour over any juices left from the marinade and then cover and cook for a further 1–2 minutes, depending on how rare you like them done.

Make a pile of noodles on each plate, settle a tuna steak on top, spoon over some of the juice from the pan, add a scattering of coriander and a wedge of lime and serve immediately.

Fresh Tuna with Cracked Pepper and Coriander, with Rocket Salad

Don't throw up your hands in horror when you read the cooking instructions. This strange way of treating tuna – coated in peppercorns and coriander and wrapped in foil – sears the outer layer lightly, sealing the spices in place and leaving the centre pink and raw. It becomes, in effect, a seared tuna carpaccio (the same method works brilliantly with a piece of beef fillet), which is remarkably delicious and meltingly tender. Set the thinly sliced tuna atop a bed of rocket leaves and cherry tomatoes and you have a marvellous combination of flavours and colours. Irresistible.

SERVES 4

450g (1 lb) piece of skinned tuna fillet
olive oil
1 tablespoon black peppercorns, coarsely crushed
1 tablespoon coriander seeds, coarsely crushed

For the Salad:
1 tablespoon balsamic vinegar
4 tablespoons olive oil
about 125g (4½ oz) rocket leaves
12 cherry tomatoes, halved
salt, pepper and sugar
roughly chopped fresh chives, to garnish

Brush the chunk of tuna with olive oil. Mix the pepper and coriander and then roll the tuna in the mixture until thoroughly coated. Wrap up tightly in foil. Heat a heavy cast-iron pan until incredibly hot. Lay the foil-wrapped tuna in it and cook for 10 minutes, turning it methodically every minute or so, making sure that each side gets its turn close to the heat. Take out of the pan and leave to cool.

Whisk the balsamic vinegar with the oil, a pinch of sugar, salt and pepper to make a dressing. Taste and adjust the seasoning.

Shortly before serving, toss the rocket and tomatoes in the dressing and arrange on one large serving plate, or individual plates. Unwrap the tuna, and slice very thinly. Lay the tuna on the salad, scatter with chives and serve immediately.

Tuna with Onions and Lardons

When I first knew William he lived in France, in a pretty but chilly house near Le Touquet. One long, lazy, French weekend, spent largely in front of the fire and in the dining room, apart from the odd invigorating, bracing battle along a windy beach, he cooked me this dish of tuna with sweet onions and salty lardons.

SERVES 2

2 pieces of tuna steak, cut a good 2.5cm (1 inch)
    thick, weighing about 175–225g (6–8 oz) each
60–85g (2–3 oz) *lardons*, or streaky bacon in
    one piece
60g (2 oz) butter
1 onion, sliced
1½ tablespoons red wine vinegar
salt and pepper

Season the tuna with salt and pepper. If you are using bacon you will have to make your own *lardons*: trim off the rind and cut the bacon into tubby little sticks, about 2.5cm (1 inch) long and 5mm (¼ inch) thick.

Melt a third of the butter in a frying pan and add the onion. Cook over a medium heat until it begins to brown, then add the *lardons* and continue cooking until the onion and bacon are well browned. Draw off the heat.

In a separate pan, melt half the remaining butter and fry the tuna steaks over a moderate heat until they are lightly browned on the outside but still pink at heart. When they are nearly done, re-heat the onions and bacon, add the vinegar and sizzle until the liquid has evaporated. Quickly stir in the remaining butter. Transfer the tuna to a warm serving dish and pour over the onions, *lardons* and butter. Serve immediately.

Grilled Bluefish with Cumin and Harissa

Alternative: mackerel

This aromatic way of cooking bluefish with a cumin crust is based on a Tunisian recipe for mackerel, found in the *Time-Life Good Cook* series. I've made the marinade rather stronger than the original and added a generous helping of green coriander for good measure. A brilliant dish for the barbecue but good, too, cooked under the kitchen grill.

SERVES 4

4 bluefish, cleaned
1 teaspoon harissa
5 tablespoons olive oil
4 garlic cloves, crushed
1 tablespoon ground cumin
2 tablespoons chopped fresh coriander
salt
lemon wedges, to serve

Make two diagonal cuts across each side of the fish. Mix all the remaining ingredients except the lemon wedges and smear them over the bluefish. Pour any remaining marinade over them. Set aside for about 1 hour, turning occasionally.

Grill for 5–7 minutes on each side on the barbecue or under a thoroughly preheated grill. Serve immediately, with lemon wedges.

Stir-fried Jack with Mango and Spring Onion

Alternatives: pomfret, mackerel, kingfish

The flesh of the jack is firm enough to be fried in strips, taken out of the pan and returned later to the dish, without collapsing. It has an excellent flavour, with enough presence to stand against the fruitiness of stir-fried semi-ripe mango.

Most of the mangoes we can buy in the UK are sold only half-ripened, the theory being that they will ripen at their own pace in our fruit bowls – a theory that doesn't always work in practice. Still, these semi-ripened mangoes work brilliantly in the wok, being firm enough to hold their shape, not so sweet and soft that they seem like pudding but still with a distinct mango fragrance and a touch of sharpness.

SERVES 4

1 jack weighing about 700–750g (1½–1²⁄₃ lb) filleted, cut into strips about 2 x 7cm (¾ x 2½ inches)
juice of 1 lime
1 large, semi-ripe mango
cornflour, for coating
4 tablespoons sunflower or vegetable oil
2 garlic cloves, chopped
2.5cm (1-inch) piece of fresh root ginger, grated
1 red chilli, de-seeded and cut into thin strips
6 spring onions, cut into 2.5cm (1-inch) lengths
1 tablespoon fish sauce
2 tablespoons roughly chopped fresh coriander
salt and pepper
lime wedges, to serve

Marinate the strips of fish with the lime juice and some salt and pepper for half an hour. Meanwhile, peel the mango and cut into slices about 3mm (⅛ inch) thick. Cut the slices into pieces about 2.5cm (1 inch) across.

Drain any juice from the fish and toss the strips in cornflour, shaking off any excess. Put a wok over a high heat until it's smoking hot. Add 3 tablespoons of the oil, let it warm through for a few seconds and then fry the fish, in several batches, for a couple of minutes each, until barely cooked through. Keep warm. Tip the used oil out of the wok. Return to the heat, leave until smoking and add the last tablespoon of oil. Stir-fry the garlic, ginger and chilli for about 30 seconds, then add the mango and spring onions. Stir-fry until the mango is just tender – about 2–3 minutes, depending on how unripe it was to begin with. Add the fish sauce and about two-thirds of the coriander. Toss to mix well and then taste and adjust the seasoning. Pile the mango up on a serving dish and lay the strips of fish on top. Sprinkle with the remaining coriander, decorate with lime wedges and serve immediately.

Caribbean Fish Curry

Alternatives: tuna, swordfish, cod, halibut

A really good fish stew from the Caribbean, flavoured with a little curry powder, allspice, fennel and a softening scrape of coconut. Everybody loves this one, or at least they do in our household, from my two-year-old son (who demanded seconds and thirds) to granny, and several other visitors into the bargain. Make it with mahi mahi, if you can get it, but don't miss out if such exotic fish have not made it to your neck of the woods. Try it, instead, with halibut or even cod, both of which will be a tad easier to lay your hands on. Serve with rice.

SERVES 4

4 mahi mahi steaks
4 tablespoons sunflower or vegetable oil
6 black peppercorns
1 cardamon pod
4 allspice berries
½ teaspoon fennel seeds
1 tablespoon coriander seeds
pinch of cayenne pepper
½ tablespoon mild curry powder
1 teaspoon grated fresh root ginger
1 onion, chopped
4 garlic cloves, chopped
400g (14 oz) tin of chopped tomatoes
1 tablespoon tomato purée
2 fresh thyme sprigs
1 bay leaf
30g (1 oz) creamed coconut, grated
150ml (¼ pint) water
salt
lime wedges, to serve

Season your fish steaks with salt and set aside.

Heat the oil in a wide, deep frying pan and add all the whole spices and the cayenne and curry powder as well. Fry over a moderate heat for about 3 minutes. Now add the ginger, onion and garlic and continue cooking until the onion is translucent and tender. Add the tomatoes, tomato purée, thyme and bay leaf. Boil vigorously for 15 minutes, until the tomato is well cooked down. Stir in the coconut. When it has melted, add the water and bring back to the boil.

Snuggle the fish steaks into the sauce, spooning it lightly over them, reduce the heat a little and continue simmering for a further 10 minutes or so, until the fish is cooked through. Serve with wedges of lime.

Thai Red Fish Curry

Alternatives: cod, halibut, bream

The advent of ready-made Thai curry pastes, now as much at home on the supermarket shelves as jars of mint sauce and strawberry jam, means that a delicious quick stab at a fragrant South-east Asian curry can be made in a matter of minutes. I say a stab, because although I use the ready-made pastes frequently myself, they can never quite replicate the sensuous, aromatic flavour of freshly fried and ground spices and herbs. Still, it's not always possible, this far away from their native land, to lay one's hands on galangal and lemongrass, tiny bird chillies and the like, and often even less possible to grab the time to grind and prepare them as one should. A jar of red curry paste in the larder is a midweek godsend.

You can also pluck jars of dried kaffir lime leaves, like oriental bay leaves, from the spice rack of larger stores, and tins of coconut milk. Tinned coconut milk has a slippery texture that is not half as nice as fresh (see page 306), though it does well enough as a kitchen-cupboard standby.

SERVES 4

4 kingfish steaks, cut about 3cm (1¼ inches)
   thick (or 1 whole bream)
juice of 1 lime
sunflower or vegetable oil, for frying

For the Sauce:
1–1½ tablespoons red curry paste
5 fresh or dried kaffir lime leaves
300ml (½ pint) coconut milk
1 teaspoon sugar
1 tablespoon fish sauce

To Garnish:
lime wedges
fresh coriander leaves
fine strips of fresh hot red chilli

If using a whole fish, make 2 or 3 diagonal slashes on each side. Sprinkle the lime juice over both sides of the fish or the fish steaks and leave for 15 minutes. Pat dry on kitchen paper.

Pour enough oil into a pan large enough to take the fish to fill it to a depth of about 1cm (½ inch). Heat over a medium heat until pretty hot. Lay the fish or steaks in the oil and fry briskly for about 4 minutes. Turn carefully and cook for another 4 minutes on the other side. The steaks should be verging on done but still a mite away from it, as they will carry on cooking in their own heat while you make the sauce. Cook the whole fish for a minute or two longer on each side. Carefully lift the fish out on to a warm serving plate and keep warm.

Pour all but a tablespoon of the oil out of the pan. Now add the curry paste and lime leaves and fry, stirring constantly, for 2 minutes. Pour in the coconut milk and add the sugar and fish sauce. Stir well and then leave to simmer for 5 minutes. Taste and adjust the seasoning. Pour the sauce over the fish and garnish with lime wedges, a handful of coriander leaves and, if you are feeling daring, strips of hot red chilli.

Maquereau au Vin Blanc

Mackerel in White Wine

A dish that takes me back to my childhood and to long sojourns in France, sitting in the evenings in the little front room lit by a paraffin lamp (electricity and running water were late arrivals in our village). The crumbling texture of mackerel pickled with white wine and aromatics was a favourite of mine, eaten with hunks of baguette and unsalted butter. Sometimes it was home-made but often enough it was tinned. Not quite the same, but eagerly welcomed nevertheless.

When you come across a haul of splendidly fresh mackerel – caught yourself, if you are lucky, or lying on the fishmonger's slab (which still makes you lucky, as they are not expensive fish) – buy some to eat fresh, grilled simply or baked, and some more to cook like this for the next day or the day after. They improve with a few days' sitting in their piquant bath. Serve as a first course or for a light lunch or supper, with good bread and salads.

SERVES 4

4 mackerel, cleaned
1 bay leaf
½ teaspoon fennel seeds or dill seeds
1 dried red chilli, broken in 3 and de-seeded
2 strips of lemon zest
2 garlic cloves
salt
chopped fresh chives or parsley, to garnish

For the *court-bouillon*:
1 bottle of dry white wine
1 carrot, sliced
2 shallots, sliced
1 bay leaf
1 fresh parsley sprig
1 fresh thyme sprig
1 fresh rosemary sprig
8 black peppercorns
150ml (¼ pint) water

First make the *court-bouillon*. Put all the ingredients into a pan, bring up to the boil and boil for 10 minutes. Leave to cool.

Put the mackerel into a shallow, close-fitting pan and add all the remaining ingredients apart from the chives or parsley, salting lightly. Pour over the *court-bouillon* (with all its bits and pieces still in it). Bring gently up to the boil, simmer for a minute and then draw the pan off the heat. Leave the fish to cool in the *court-bouillon*.

Now, skin each fish and carefully lift the fillets away from the bone. Place in a shallow dish and cover with cling film so that they don't dry out. Boil the *court-bouillon* to reduce it by about half, until it has a correspondingly strong and invigorating taste. Cool again and strain over the mackerel fillets. Cover and store in the fridge (where the mackerel will keep for up to a week). Just before serving, pour off most of the *court-bouillon*. Eat at room temperature, scattered with chives or parsley and accompanied by lots of good fresh bread and butter.

Baked Mackerel with Lemon, Thyme and Sun-dried Tomatoes

Alternatives: bonito, bluefish

Here, tart lemon juice softens the oiliness of the mackerel flesh but is relieved by the warmth of thyme and the saltiness of sun-dried tomatoes and black olives. A dish of vivid flavours, which work well hot – perhaps with a tangle of noodles or some new potatoes – and cold, with good bread and a light salad of sweet tomatoes or lively bitter and mild greenery.

SERVES 4

4 mackerel, filleted
juice of 2 lemons
1 teaspoon fresh thyme leaves
5 tablespoons olive oil
6 pieces of sun-dried tomato, cut into thin strips
16 black olives, stoned and sliced
salt and pepper
chopped fresh chervil, to garnish

Lay the mackerel fillets in an oiled, shallow ovenproof dish in a single layer and season with salt and pepper. Pour over the lemon juice, cover and leave to marinate for 4–8 hours, turning the fish occasionally.

Preheat the oven to 190°C/375°F/Gas Mark 5. Uncover the fish, scatter with the thyme and spoon on the olive oil. Bake for 10 minutes. Sprinkle over the sun-dried tomato and olives and bake for a further 5 minutes, until the mackerel is cooked through. Serve hot or cold, sprinkled with the chervil.

Mackerel with Mustard Sauce

Alternatives: bonito, bluefish

As I was flicking through the entry for mackerel in *Larousse Gastronomique*, my eye fell upon a recipe for mackerel with mustard sauce. This is my interpretation of the idea. Although the heat of the mustard is cooked out, its flavour sits well with mackerel. Cooking mackerel in a sharp liquid (here wine provides the acidity) gives it an almost creamy texture.

SERVES 4

4 mackerel, cleaned and filleted
1 onion, finely chopped
2 fresh thyme sprigs
1 bay leaf
1 fresh parsley sprig
150ml (¼ pint) dry white wine
2 tablespoons coarse-grained mustard
45g (1½ oz) unsalted butter, cubed and chilled
salt and pepper
chopped fresh parsley or chervil, to garnish

Preheat the oven to 240°C/475°F/Gas Mark 9. Season the mackerel fillets with salt and pepper. In a lightly greased dish, make a bed of the onion with the thyme, bay leaf and parsley. Place the fillets on top, skin-side up, and pour over the wine. Bake, uncovered, for 7–10 minutes, until the fillets are barely cooked through. Carefully transfer the fillets to a warm serving dish and keep warm.

Strain the cooking juices into a pan (discard the onion and bits) and boil hard for a few minutes to concentrate the flavours and reduce the volume slightly. Add the mustard and butter, whisk until the butter melts and then simmer for 3 minutes. Spoon the sauce over the fish, sprinkle with a little parsley or chervil and serve immediately.

Mackerel with Gooseberry Sauce

Alternatives: bonito, bluefish

A real early-summer classic, for those balmy June days when gooseberries are plentiful and mackerel plump and rich tasting. A bountiful, economical feast. The tartness of gooseberries comes as a welcome touch against the richness of the mackerel flesh. Earlier on in the year, use rhubarb instead of gooseberries to similar effect. For something a little more fancy, try adding half a star anise as the fruit cook, or ½ teaspoon crushed coriander seeds. Chervil also makes a good addition. Serve with some parsleyed new potatoes.

SERVES 4

4 mackerel, cleaned
salt and pepper

For the Sauce:
450g (1 lb) gooseberries
15g (½ oz) butter
1½ tablespoons sugar
finely grated zest and juice of ½ orange
salt and pepper

If you prefer a chunky sauce, top and tail the gooseberries. If it's a smooth sauce you're after, you don't need to bother, as you will sieve the whole lot when it's cooked. Put the gooseberries into a pan with the butter, sugar and orange juice. Cover and stew over a low heat until the juices begin to run. Remove the lid and raise the heat. Simmer until all the fruit have collapsed and most of the liquid has evaporated (in a rainy season, when gooseberries are juicier, you may have to cook it at a rolling boil to evaporate all the liquid they give out).

When the gooseberries are very tender, draw the pan off the heat. For a smooth sauce, sieve or pass through a *mouli-légumes*. Stir in the orange zest and salt and pepper to taste. If the sauce seems terribly sharp, add a touch more sugar but don't overdo it – this isn't pudding. Either keep warm or re-heat when needed.

Make two diagonal slashes on either side of the mackerel and season inside and out with salt and pepper. Grill for 8–10 minutes on each side and then serve with the sauce.

Hawaiian Poke

Alternatives: tuna, salmon

The subject of the 1997 Oxford Food Symposium was fish. Amongst the many papers submitted was one on Hawaiian poke. I'd never heard of it. I asked an ex-pat Hawaiian friend about it and she told me that when she returns to her homeland she always stops to get a portion of poke on her way from the airport to where she's staying. It's the first thing she longs for.

Poke is raw fish – often tuna but sometimes wahoo – cut into cubes and seasoned with sea salt, chillies, spring onions and seaweed. It is usually served raw, though the fish can be seared before mixing. Hawaiian poke counters offer a wide selection of different variations on the theme.

When I was delving further into the realms of poke, I kept tumbling across recipes for marlin poke. Despite William's poor opinion of marlin I decided to give it a go. He tasted it and declared it quite delicious! Mind you, as soon as we tried searing the marlin it became decidedly dull, and that's being kind. This, we decided, is the dish that marlin was made for.

Serve it just as it is in small bowls, with wedges of lime for those, like me, who relish a little sharpness, or pile it up on a bed of lightly dressed mixed lettuce leaves.

SERVES 4–6

450g (1 lb) raw marlin fillet, skinned
2–3 teaspoons soy sauce
6–8 tablespoons finely chopped onion
4 spring onions, chopped
1–2 hot red chillies, de-seeded and finely chopped
60g (2 oz) fresh dulse or other seaweed,
   rinsed thoroughly, dried and cut into strips,
   if necessary
1½ tablespoons sesame oil

Cut the marlin into 1cm (½ inch) cubes. Mix with all the remaining ingredients. Chill lightly before serving.

Grilled Swordfish with Hazelnut Tarator Sauce

Alternatives: cod, halibut

If you prefer, you can fry the swordfish steaks but since the sauce is already fairly rich I think it is nicer to grill or barbecue them. The Middle Eastern tarator sauce, not to be confused with tartare sauce, is a rich cream made of nuts, bread, garlic and olive oil. Lovely with all kinds of fish, it goes particularly well with a meaty white fish like swordfish.

SERVES 4

4 swordfish or cod steaks, about 2.5cm (1 inch) thick
extra virgin olive oil
salt and pepper
lemon wedges, to serve

For the Sauce:
110g (4 oz) shelled hazelnuts
2 thick slices of stale white bread, weighing about 60g (2 oz), crusts cut off
2 garlic cloves, chopped
2 tablespoons roughly chopped fresh parsley
100–150ml (3½–5 fl oz) extra virgin olive oil
juice of 1 lemon
salt and pepper

Preheat the oven to 200°C/400°F/Gas Mark 6. Spread the hazelnuts out on a baking sheet and toast in the hot oven for 5–10 minutes, until beginning to brown. Set aside until cool enough to handle. Rub between the palms of your hands to remove the skins. Grind in a coffee grinder.

Pour cold water over the slices of bread and drain quickly. Squeeze hard to get rid of excess moisture, then add to the ground nuts with the garlic and parsley. If you don't have a food processor, pound together in a pestle and mortar, gradually adding enough oil to give a thick sauce. If you do have a processor, whizz the nuts, bread, garlic, and parsley together, gradually trickling in the oil until you have a thick, creamy sauce. Add salt, pepper and lemon juice to taste – you'll probably need all of the lemon juice as it is quite rich.

Brush the fish steaks with a little oil, season and grill under a high heat, turning once, until just cooked through. Serve immediately, with the tarator sauce and lemon wedges.

Grilled Swordfish with Marinated Cucumber Salsa

Alternatives: sailfish, marlin, tuna

This is an easy, summery dish of grilled swordfish served with a salsa that has echoes of Europe, Asia and Latin America all entwined together within it. One of my favourite warm-weather salads is Danish marinated cucumber, and the same principle of marinating the cucumber with sugar, salt and vinegar forms the basis of this vibrant salsa. I've used oriental rice vinegar instead of white wine vinegar, then enlivened it with marinated onion (a big thing in Ecuador), tomatoes, coriander and chilli. It tastes gloriously fresh when first put together but actually keeps very well in the fridge, covered tightly, for up to three days.

When the weather is suitably clement, cook the swordfish on an outdoor barbecue if you have one.

SERVES 4

4 swordfish steaks
juice of 1 lime
3 tablespoons olive oil
2 garlic cloves, finely chopped
salt and pepper

For the Salsa:
½ cucumber, weighing about 200g (7 oz), peeled
   and very thinly sliced
2 tablespoons caster sugar
2 teaspoons salt
2 tablespoons rice vinegar
½ red onion, very thinly sliced
2 tomatoes, peeled, de-seeded and finely diced
2 tablespoons chopped fresh coriander
½–1 medium fresh red chilli (depending on the
   heat level you crave), de-seeded and cut into
   short, thin strips

For the salsa, cut the rounds of cucumber into quarters. Place in a bowl, with 1 tablespoon of the caster sugar, 1 teaspoon of the salt and 1 tablespoon of the rice vinegar. Stir and then leave for at least 1 hour. Meanwhile, quarter the slices of onion and marinate with the remaining caster sugar, salt and rice vinegar in exactly the same way as the cucumber.

Put the swordfish steaks in a shallow dish. Mix the lime juice, olive oil, garlic, salt and pepper and spoon over the steaks. Turn to coat evenly and leave to marinate for at least half an hour.

Preheat the grill thoroughly (or get the barbie stoked up and ready to roll). Shortly before cooking, drain the cucumber and onion and mix with the tomatoes, coriander and chilli. Taste and adjust the seasoning, adding a splash more vinegar, sugar or salt as needed.

Grill the swordfish close to the heat for about 2 minutes on each side. Don't overcook it or it will be tough and dry. It should be just cooked through and no more. Serve immediately, with the cucumber salsa.

Spanish Fishermen's Swordfish Stew

Alternatives: sailfish, tuna

This recipe for a stew of swordfish cooked with noodles and potatoes and flavoured with saffron belongs to the fishermen of the Murcia. The fishermen's perk, or perhaps the one bit that they might not be able to sell, is the nuggets of meat cut from the swordfish head, the *picos*, which have a strong flavour and are oilier than the flesh from the body. Finding *picos* here is likely to be hard work, and probably downright impossible, so you'll have to settle for a lump of meat from the body, which actually works very nicely even if it might not be quite so authentic.

The recipe comes from a book called *Ranchos de a Bordo*, published by the Spanish Ministry of Agriculture and Fisheries, though I came across it in *Spanish Gourmetour*, a glossy commercial magazine extolling the virtues of Iberian produce. I've adapted it slightly (those fishermen must have had gargantuan appetites) but the basic hearty nature of the stew remains intact.

SERVES 4–6

generous pinch of saffron threads
4 tablespoons extra virgin olive oil
2 large onions, chopped
2 green peppers, de-seeded and diced
1kg (2¼ lb) potatoes, peeled and cut into 2.5cm (1-inch) chunks
900g–1kg (2–2¼ lb) chunk of skinned, boned swordfish, cut into 3cm (1¼-inch) cubes
250g (9 oz) thin vermicelli noodles
salt and pepper

To Serve:
chopped fresh parsley
extra virgin olive oil
wedges of lemon

Dry-fry the saffron threads for a few seconds to crisp them, then cool slightly and pound to a powder.

In a flameproof casserole, heat the oil over a moderate heat. Add the onions and green peppers and sauté, without browning, until soft. Once they are done, add the potatoes, the fish and plenty of salt and pepper (this stew needs generous seasoning to deal with the starchy potatoes and noodles). Sprinkle over the saffron and then add enough water (I used around 750ml /1¼ pints), to cover. Bring up to the boil, reduce the heat and simmer very gently for 15 minutes.

Add the noodles, pushing them down into the stew, and heat for a further 4 minutes or so, until they are cooked. If absolutely necessary, add a little more hot water to prevent the dish from drying out.

Taste and adjust the seasoning. Sprinkle with parsley. Ladle into bowls and drizzle a little olive oil over each one. Serve with a lemon wedge perched merrily on top.

Migrants

Salmon and eel, quintessential migrators, have lives of such mythical complexity that controlling and managing them is, to say the least, challenging.

Salmon and sea trout are anadramous fish, which means that they migrate from the sea up river to spawn in fresh water. Eels, on the other hand, are catadramous, leaving fresh water to spawn in the sea. All migratory fish do one or the other. Other species, such as cod or tuna, move seasonally to different locations and spawning areas, but the true migrant crosses from one environment to another. Physiologically, this transition from salt to fresh water is highly complex, and involves a radical change within a very short space of time.

Eel♥★★

Anguillidae
French: Anguille
Italian: Anguilla
Spanish: Anguila
Portuguese: Enguia, Eiró
German: Aal, Flussaal

European eel
Anguilla anguilla

American eel
Anguilla rostrata

Short-finned eel (Aus/NZ)
Anguilla australis

Long-finned eel
Anguilla dieffenbachii

The serpentine eel has remarkable habits. Not only does it start its life migrating halfway across the world but it ends it by doing pretty much the same sort of thing. European and American eels are born in the Sargasso Sea in the Atlantic and spend three years swimming back to the rivers that their parents once inhabited. And when they reach maturity it's back to the Sargasso again to spawn.

When the Sargasso Sea beckons, freshwater eels begin to change colour subtly, turning from their habitual yellow or brown to silver. Their noses become pointed, their vents close up and they stop eating, preparing themselves for the immense task ahead. Mind and instinct are as one, so off they set on the autumn tides, swimming down from the rivers that have been their home for many years. At this point they are called silver eels and are at their fattest, for it is the fat that gives them the energy to swim such a prodigious distance. These autumnal eels are superb to eat and even finer smoked. The real eel McCoy.

Around the Rivers Severn and Wye, in the west of England, there is an ancient, but still active, eel fishery, one of the few left where glass eels, or elvers, are caught. These are the babies born all those thousands of miles away in the Sargasso, carried by the winds and currents, miraculously arriving at the right place at the right time. They are caught primarily to re-stock other fisheries but once they were fished to be eaten as well. I can remember munching on fried elvers for breakfast in the Forest of Dean but these days, with the cost being so prohibitive, it's back to the cornflakes.

One of the weirdest ways to catch an eel is called 'clotting'. A ball of wool and worms is lowered into the water, along the reed beds at a good eeling spot, and the eels, drawn by the smell, bite into the ball of wool, which becomes stuck in their teeth. All it takes is a quick tug to pull the fish out of the water and a very firm grip to stop it slithering away. A good fisherman can land about 20–30kg (44–66 lb) eels using this method, but more are caught using fyke nets, which funnel the eel into a narrow end, or by hand-held lave nets.

Most eel smokers use farmed eel, which have a consistency that wild eel do not. Female eel are larger than males, so a fat female silver eel is the best of all to eat.

I would seriously suggest that your fish supplier prepares the eel for you. Eels should be bought live, and killing and skinning an eel is not a very mouthwatering business. Allow about 175g (6 oz) per person; eel is rich and filling.

Season: Glass eels, spring.
Silver eels, in the autumn (UK).
Farmed eels, all year round.
Price: £££
Yield: 60%
Fishing method: Various.

Atlantic Salmon (Wild Fish♥★★★)

Salmo salar
French: Saumon
Italian: Salmone
Spanish: Salmón
Portuguese: Salmão
German: Lachs

Salmo salar has lurched from everyday food to luxury and back again with indecent haste over the past few hundred years, but if it is cheap once again, is it cheerful? Or is there trouble down at the old fish farm?

With its natural habitat bashed, battered, polluted and dammed for generations, *Salmo salar*, the Atlantic salmon, has a major problem. Stocks of wild fish have been in steep decline for many years, but as one goes down, the other goes up. Farmed fish are being produced (many would say over produced) on a huge scale. In 1995 245,000 tonnes of salmon were farmed worldwide, and most of us have forgotten that salmon ever were 'wild' at all. But if fish farming, or aquaculture, has solved the supply problem, what exactly is it producing? Answer: a marine couch potato. Aquaculture is big business, where the pressure is on to cut costs and to get salmon to marketable size as soon as possible. Recently the fat level of the feed has been practically doubled, so our salmon are more likely than ever to be Bunteresque and bland.

On fish farms, adult fish are densely packed in cages, often in lochs and bays with little tidal flow, and lead very indolent lives. They eat no wild food and are very prone to disease and gruesome infestations of sea lice, which multiply rapidly when the fish are so close together. Sea lice are a nightmare, eating into the flesh and bodies of the salmon in a most unpleasant way. Their presence on farmed salmon is now thought to lead to an increased infestation of wild fish, and many think that the disappearance of wild salmon trout in Ireland could be due to their attention as well.

Local shellfish producers have expressed great concern about this. Another chemical, Dichlorvos, is not only even more toxic but sea lice appear to be developing a resistance to it. And then there are the antibiotics, the colouring agents, the feed – the list is too long and worrying. Consumers may well be rightfully indignant that once again they are eating a product that has an uncertain bill of health. These issues need to be clarified by the fish-farming fraternity for their sake as well as our own.

Some farms are trying hard to create a more wholesome creature by using feeds and colouring agents from natural products, reducing the density of the fish and putting the cages in sea with a tidal flow, so salmon can actually build up some natural muscle. The quality of fish can be greatly improved but the price, unfortunately, is the price. Such fish cost more to produce, so once again the pressure to supply cheap food is in direct conflict with our quest for quality food.

In 1990 an experiment in the Shetlands tested whether you could deter sea lice by dangling onions in the cages, and it appeared to work quite well. In Norway a small fish – the goldsinny or cleaner wrasse – has been used to eat the lice off live salmon, and industrious

Wild salmon are anadramous fish, feeding and fattening themselves in salt water before swimming up river to spawn in fresh. Like the eel, they use fat as an energy reserve so, just as eel are at their best when they set off in the autumn, salmon are at *their* best when they arrive at the river's mouth.

These days actually getting there deserves a medal. Atlantic salmon were once thought to disperse quite widely, converging on their home rivers when they reached maturity, but the discovery of a substantial feeding ground in the North Atlantic, off the Greenland coast, seemed to indicate that many of them lived closely together. When the news of the discovery seeped out in the 1970s, fishing boats started eating into the stocks before the salmon had got anywhere near their home rivers.

Migratory fish stocks are particularly susceptible to irresponsible fishing. Scottish and Welsh rivers are affected by overfishing in Ireland, just as Canadian stocks are affected by overfishing in the States. It's all very complex, and needs a level of control and co-operation that the fishing industry finds extremely hard to agree to, let alone implement.

It is pollution that has caused one of the greatest threats to the wild salmon's habitat. As long ago as 1896, Cornish rivers were poisoned by tin mining, the Tyne was practically toxic and other rivers around the country flowed thick with human and industrial waste. It is quite possible that the species would have completely disappeared had the prospect of no fish – and no income from fishing – not been all too much for the salmon fishery owners, who introduced strict controls which stopped the decline to some extent.

SALMON

I'm ambivalent about farmed salmon. It's wonderful that fish can be made more affordable, and I know that farmed salmon *can* be good. I also know that the technology and experience is there to make it even better, but what I'm not entirely happy about is what exactly goes into the fish. Let me explain.

Some powerful and extremely toxic substances are permitted in the process of salmon farming. To control sea lice, a toxic chemical called Ivermectin can be used which builds up in the food chain.

Norwegian schoolchildren are paid good money to collect the small fish. Are the days far off when chemical-free salmon will be the norm? I hope not.

Wild salmon in prime condition are exquisite, elegant, sweet smelling and definitely sexy. Not long ago, thousands of rivers throughout Europe and in the Americas – there are no salmon native to the southern hemisphere – had healthy populations of fish which arrived each year at the river mouths to start their epic journey upstream.

But the biggest threat of all comes from the countryside itself. Arable farming along river banks disturbs the soil, which flows into the water as silt, clogging up the very gravel in which salmon build their redds, where they lay their eggs. Quite how this particular conflict of interest will be resolved remains to be seen, but the condition of the land surrounding the salmon rivers is now recognised as being absolutely critical. There are some grounds for optimism. Netting is being strictly controlled and banned in many areas and there are even some conscientious salmon farmers who have started to release young fish into the rivers to increase the population. Salmon have even been caught in the Thames, and the Tyne has its own (small) population of fish once more.

Buying a wild fish isn't always easy. A good fishmonger will distinguish clearly between wild and farmed fish and should know – if not indicate – the river from which the fish came. Wild fish are sleeker. They have clearly defined tail fins and fewer spots on their skin. If you place one against the other the difference is marked. Farmed fish are tubby, round and soft fleshed. A wild fish in prime condition has a glorious sheen to it, is hard to the touch because of its finer muscle tone, and has flesh coloured red from a natural diet of crustaceans.

Tay salmon, Tweed salmon, Wye, Esk or Severn fish all have their own seasons but, as far as the consumer is concerned, wild fish are normally available, at a price, from as early as January through to late-run fish in August/September. Remember that the ideal fish to buy is one that has just entered the estuary on its way upstream. One way of telling this is if your salmon has sea lice on it which, since they fall off in fresh water, will mean that it was caught in sea or estuarine water and should be in good condition.

Monstrous fish of 20kg (44 lb) or more were once caught but have virtually disappeared. Grilse (fish that are returning to their home river for the first time) are good value if there's only one or two of you, and tend to weigh between 1–1.35kg (2¼–3 lb). Larger adult fish can be frozen on the bone for a week or two if they are too large to handle in one go. A 1.8kg (4 lb) fish will feed four to six, a 2.75kg (6 lb) fish six to eight, and so on.

Farmed salmon is a consistent, if mediocre, product that can be very fatty. Avoid using too much butter or cream with these fish, but a wild salmon can be fine with either. Poached whole, served with an hollandaise sauce (see page

SEA TROUT

316), or seared with its skin on, wild salmon is a superb treat that should be enjoyed at least once a year.

Season: Closed seasons apply for wild fish. Farmed fish all year round.
Price: £ farmed; ££ organic, from £ grilse to £££ early season wild.
Yield: 70%
Fishing method: Wild fish, net, rod and line.

Sea Trout, Salmon Trout, Sewin★★★

Salmo trutta
First-run fish: Peal (West Country), Herling, Finnock (north), Whitling
French: Truite de mer
Italian: Trota di mare
Spanish: Trucha marina
Portuguese: Truta-marisca marinha
German: Meerforelle, Bachorelle

Fish *cognoscenti* love this fish. It's wild, as near a salmon as you can get without being one, and calls for some expertise in distinguishing it from its larger cousin. You don't often see it for sale but the sea trout is delicious, both to eat and to look at, and gives you loads of fish brownie points if you can tell the difference. You could say that all trout are sea trout but the story is rather complex.

Although the sea trout is considered to be the same as the brown trout as far as classification is concerned, it migrates to the sea, which the brown trout doesn't, and has a smolt (juvenile) stage, unlike the brown trout. When the sea trout starts to think of the sea, between two to three years old, it develops a characteristic silvery sheen and glands that enable it to live in salt water. So there is something inherent in its genetic make-up that is absent in its stay-at-home relations. When wild sea trout offspring are reared, they always retain that seaward wanderlust, whereas hatchery-bred fish stay put.

Distinguishing between salmon and large sea trout is far harder than telling a brown and sea trout apart. With smaller fish it's easy. Sea trout are spottier and thinner than salmon, but it gets harder the bigger they become. To my eyes, it's the chunkiness of the sea trout that strikes one first. It has a squarer tail, a thicker tail base and a different anal fin from the wild salmon but if you still have doubts, look at the mouth, which in a sea trout is longer and ends past the eye. In the salmon, it doesn't.

The best fish to buy are those that have just entered the estuary, which often have a bronze sheen to their skin.

Like salmon, sea trout eat crustaceans and fish, which gives them a red flesh that tastes as sweet and fine as salmon – to many, even finer. Cook as salmon.

Season: Summer.
Price: ££
Yield: 65%
Fishing method: Rod, line and net.

Matelote d'Anguille

Eel and red wine stew

I once heard an eminent food writer emit a grunt of disgust at the thought of the Touraine dish of eel stewed with prunes. He should have known better. Perhaps he should have tried it before being so dismissive. It is a glorious dish, full of rich, deep flavours. The best *matelote* I know is served in the restaurant of the Hôtel de France on the main square of La Chartre-sur-le-Loir. It's been an annual pleasure to go there ever since I was a tiny girl, first with my parents and now with my own small family. I love their *matelote* and am sorry to say that, good though my version is, it doesn't quite match up to theirs. Maybe one day I'll be honoured with the recipe, if I'm very lucky.

If you can't make it to the Hôtel de France, do try this dish and don't be as silly as that eminent food writer. We enjoy plenty of duets of savoury and sweet in this country. The French think it odd that we serve redcurrant jelly with lamb (we know better), and this is no more unusual a mixture than that.

SERVES 6

1kg (2¼ lb) eel, skinned and cut into 2.5cm
  (1-inch) lengths
30 large prunes, with stones
1 bottle of good red wine (a Cabernet Sauvignon
  will hold its colour well)
1 onion, chopped
white of 1 leek, chopped
1 carrot, finely diced
bouquet garni of 1 fresh thyme sprig, 2 fresh
  parsley sprigs and 1 bay leaf, tied with string
60g (2 oz) butter
1 tablespoon sunflower oil
24 pearl onions, skinned
125g (4½ oz) *lardons*
plain flour
3 tablespoons brandy
300–450ml (½–¾ pint) chicken stock
salt and pepper
6 triangles of fried bread, to serve

Season the eel with salt and pepper. Soak the prunes in one-third of the wine for at least 4 hours. Put the remaining wine into a pan with the onion, leek, carrot and *bouquet garni*. Bring up to the boil, reduce the heat and simmer for 30 minutes. Strain and reserve the wine.

Heat 15g (½ oz) of the butter with the oil in a deep, wide frying pan. Fry the pearl onions over a moderate heat until patched with brown all over. Scoop out and add the *lardons*. Fry until lightly browned, then scoop out and add to the onions. Now tip out the fat if it looks a bit on the brown side and add another 15g (½ oz) of butter to the pan.

Coat the pieces of eel in flour, shaking off any excess, and then fry until lightly browned. Pour the brandy into the pan, warm through for a few seconds and then set alight, either by tilting the pan towards the flame, if you have a gas stove, or with a match, at arm's length, if you cook on an electric hob. When the flames have died down, return the onions and *lardons* to the pan, add the prunes and their wine, the reduced wine, salt and pepper and enough chicken stock to barely cover. Bring up to the boil, reduce the heat and simmer for about 15 minutes, until the eel is very tender and the onions are fully cooked.

Meanwhile, mash the remaining 30g (1 oz) of butter with 30g (1 oz) of flour to form a *beurre manié*. When the stew is about done, add little lumps of this to it, stirring them in to thicken the juices. Just add enough to thicken the stew lightly – you probably won't need it all. Cook very gently for a further 5 minutes to dissipate the taste of raw flour. Taste and adjust the seasoning (if it is a little on the tart side, add a pinch of sugar) and then serve with the triangles of fried bread.

Anguilla allo Spiedo

Eel Kebabs

Alternatives: monkfish

My childhood memories of holidays in France with my parents are punctuated with delicious, simple meals. Our friend Maurice, who knew the land and the river like the back of his hand, would often stroll up the path with an offering – some wild mushrooms, a rabbit, blackberries or wild service berries and, when we were really lucky, a wriggling eel. He skinned and cleaned it, then made a fire of vine cuttings from his little vineyard (in those days the hillside was striped from top to bottom with vines) and grilled the eel over them. A feast virtually for free.

Eating these eel kebabs in Umbria brought the taste of that eel flooding back to me. The Italian version is a little more complicated, the eel sitting shoulder to shoulder with sage or bay leaves and cubes of bread that toast to a crisp lightness, which counterbalances the richness of the eel. Serve them with a salad of rocket leaves or watercress.

SERVES 4

1kg (2¼ lb) eel, cleaned, skinned and cut into
  pieces about 4cm (1½ inches) long
sage leaves or fresh bay leaves, or both
4–6 x 2.5cm (1-inch) thick slices of slightly stale
  white bread, crusts removed, cut into 4cm
  (1½-inch) squares
olive oil
salt and pepper
lemon wedges, to serve

Take eight skewers and divide the eel and bread between them as follows. Start each skewer with a piece of eel, slide on either a bay leaf or a sage leaf, follow with a chunk of bread, and then another bay leaf or sage leaf (settle for one or other and don't mix them on any one skewer). Repeat the ingredients in the same order, finishing each skewerful with a cube of bread, until all the eel has been used up. Brush with oil and season with salt and pepper.

Barbecue moderately close to the embers, turning the skewers frequently, until the eel is cooked through and deliciously tender – around 10 minutes or even a little more, as long as the bread isn't too burnt. Serve immediately, with the lemon wedges.

Koulibiac

Alternative: smoked haddock

Koulibiac is about as sophisticated as a fish pie can get. It's a brilliant party piece, and not so very difficult to construct, though you will need to set aside a little time to lavish on its preparation. It also has the added bonus that it can be served hot or cold with equal success. As long, that is, as cold doesn't mean more than a day after it has been cooked.

Serve it on its own or, for an even more luxurious affair, with a *beurre blanc* (see page 302) or hollandaise sauce (see page 309). To cook the salmon, either wrap in foil, greased with a little butter and moistened with a splash of white wine, and bake, or poach it in a *court-bouillon* (see page 307).

Koulibiac made with smoked haddock is terrific, too. If it's smoked haddock I'm using, I'd usually poach it in milk with a bay leaf, a few peppercorns and a stem or two of parsley. The strained milk can be used, together with the soaking liquid from the dried mushrooms, to make a béchamel sauce to serve alongside.

SERVES 6–8

500g (1 lb 2 oz) puff pastry
1 egg, beaten
30g (1 oz) butter, melted

For the Filling:
15g (½ oz) dried porcini mushrooms
60g (2 oz) basmati rice
¼ teaspoon ground turmeric
1 onion, chopped
60g (2 oz) butter
175g (6 oz) shiitake mushrooms or button
  mushrooms, chopped
700g (1½ lb) cooked salmon, flaked
2 tablespoons chopped fresh parsley
2 tablespoons chopped fresh dill
2 hard-boiled eggs, shelled and chopped
salt and pepper

Begin by making the filling. Soak the dried porcini in hot water for 30 minutes. Pick out the pieces and chop fairly finely. Leave the soaking liquid to settle, then pour off carefully, leaving behind any grit. If you don't want to use it for a sauce to go with the koulibiac, freeze it to use in soups or stews at some other time (don't just throw it out – the flavour is far too good to waste).

Cook the rice with the turmeric in plenty of lightly salted boiling water until just *al dente*. Drain thoroughly. Cook the onion in the butter without browning, until tender. Add the fresh mushrooms and the porcini and continue cooking until all the water thrown out by the mushrooms has evaporated, leaving a nicely moist mush in the pan. Mix with the rice, salmon, herbs and hard-boiled eggs. Season generously with salt and pepper.

Roll out the pastry on a lightly floured board to form a rectangle about 35 x 45cm (14 x 18 inches). Transfer to a lightly greased baking sheet. Mound the filling down the centre of the pastry, patting it in to form a fat sausage. Lift the sides of the pastry up round it, brush the edges with the beaten egg and press together to join. Seal the ends, too, using beaten egg and folding the joints towards the long, central seam. Gently roll the koulibiac over, so that the joins are tucked away underneath. Decorate, if you wish, with pretty pastry shapes. Rest for half an hour before baking. Preheat the oven to 200°C/400°F/Gas Mark 6.

Brush the pastry with beaten egg and make four slashes across the top, so that steam can escape. Bake for 35–40 minutes, until golden brown. Take out of the oven and carefully pour the melted butter into the koulibiac, through the slits in the top. Serve hot or cold.

Salmon Fishcakes

Alternatives: cod, smoked haddock, sea trout

An old favourite, which has found great favour in bistros and restaurants over recent years. So much so, perhaps, that we have forgotten how easy they are to make at home, and how very good they can be, as long as they are made with a high proportion of fish to potato. I usually make them when I have leftover cooked fish – salmon is always a treat but smoked haddock comes a close second and cod is not far behind. In fact, they are so good that you may well want to cook a piece of fish specially for them. In that case, poach your fish gently in a little fish stock or water sharpened with a splash of wine vinegar; or use milk, adding a few aromatics – a sprig of dill, a few slices of onion, bay leaves or sprigs of parsley – for good measure.

I love fishcakes with a good parsley sauce but mayonnaise-based sauces go well with them, too.

SERVES 4

around 300g (11 oz) potatoes
30g (1 oz) butter, softened
225g (8 oz) cooked salmon fillet
1 tablespoon finely chopped fresh dill
2 tablespoons chopped fresh parsley
1 tablespoon lemon juice
finely grated zest of 1 lemon
1 egg, beaten
plain flour
butter and oil, for frying
salt and pepper

To Serve:
4 lemon wedges
Parsley Sauce, Hollandaise Sauce, Tartare Sauce
    or Lemon Mayonnaise (see pages 303, 309,
    312 or 311)

Preheat the oven to about 200°C/400°F/Gas Mark 6 and bake the potatoes in their skins until soft. If you don't have time to bake them, cook in the microwave. Boiling makes the flesh soggy but, if you must, boil them in their skins. Peel and mash with the butter. Weigh out 225g (8 oz) of mashed potato.

Flake the salmon and add to the potatoes with the dill, parsley, lemon juice and zest, salt and pepper. Add enough beaten egg to give a soft but still firm dough. Decide whether you want to make four large, plump fishcakes or eight smaller ones. Divide the mixture into four or eight accordingly. Flour your hands and pat each portion into a plump, round cake. Leave in the fridge to firm up for at least half an hour or until you are almost ready to eat. Coat each one evenly in flour.

Heat a mixture of half butter and half oil in a frying pan and fry the fishcakes on both sides until crisp and well browned. Serve immediately, with the lemon wedges and whatever sauce you've chosen.

Pan-Fried Salmon with Sweet Soy Sauce

Alternatives: mackerel, sea bass, sea trout

The trick to pan-frying pieces of salmon is to use a heavy-bottomed pan and to get it ferociously hot, so that you can crisp the skin without overcooking the inside. Rather like tuna, salmon benefits enormously from being cooked a tad on the rare side, keeping the very heart pink and moist.

Kecap manis is the Indonesian soy sauce, thick, dark and both sweet and salty. It is a superb condiment that deserves to be more widely known. Quite a few of the major supermarkets now sell it, and you are bound to find it in any halfway-decent oriental food store.

SERVES 2

2 pieces of salmon fillet, weighing about 175g
   (6 oz) each
oil
1½ tablespoons *kecap manis*
3 tablespoons dry sherry
4 tablespoons water
1cm (½-inch) piece of fresh root ginger, cut into
   fine matchsticks
1 small garlic clove, sliced
chopped fresh chives or coriander, to garnish

Heat a heavy-based frying pan until searingly hot (and I mean really *seriously* searingly hot). Brush the cut side of the salmon with oil. Plop the salmon, cut-side down, on to the ungreased pan. Cook for about 1 minute, until browned underneath. Brush the skin with oil and turn over. Cook for a further 2–3 minutes, until the skin is browned and crisp. Remove from the pan and keep warm.

Mix the *kecap manis*, sherry and water. Pour into the pan and add the ginger and garlic. Bring up to the boil, stirring, and simmer for a few minutes, until reduced to a sticky glaze. Return the fish to the pan, turn to coat, then serve immediately, with the bits of ginger and garlic. Sprinkle with a few herbs for a hint of colour.

Baked Whole Salmon

Alternative: sea trout

We were ten for lunch the day before I wrote this recipe, a sizeable party for a Sunday, with lots of children running around. In June or July, even when it is not blazing hot, as it wasn't, there is little more enjoyable, luxurious and easy to serve for a special lunch than a whole salmon, gilded with a velvety hollandaise sauce (see page 309), served alongside a mound of new potatoes, scented with a little mint. Add, maybe, some young broad beans or fresh peas, or even just a sprightly green salad, and you have a feast fit for kings.

The timings given below are for serving the salmon hot, or at least warm. If you wish to cook it in advance and serve it cold, with lemony mayonnaise perhaps (see page 311), reduce the cooking time by about 5–10 minutes and take the fish from the oven when it is still slightly undercooked and translucent in the centre; it will continue to cook in its own heat as it cools. Use oil not butter to grease the foil.

SERVES 6-12

1 salmon, weighing about 2–4kg (4½–9 lb)
4 generous fresh parsley, fennel, dill or tarragon
   sprigs
5 lemon slices, halved
melted butter or sunflower oil
1 glass of white wine (about 110ml/4 fl oz)
salt and pepper

First of all, check that the fish will fit into your oven. If it is on the large side, and can't easily be curved to fit, you have two options. The first is to cut off the head and possibly also the tail – if you wish, these can be wrapped in foil and popped into the oven along with the fish, so that you can reassemble the fish on the dish (if that's big enough) and do a passable impression of serving the fish whole, which is far more dramatic and stylish. A fetching ruff of parsley or other greenery, can be used to disguise the joins. Alternatively, cut the fish in half somewhere along the centre of the body and cook the two halves individually wrapped in foil. A parsley belt remains a possibility for disguising the join but it can look rather bizarre, stuck in the middle. Better, I think, just to nestle the two halves firmly together and leave it at that.

Whatever you do, continue as follows. Trim the fish and rub the inner cavity with a little salt. Tuck a herb sprig inside the fish with two of the half lemon slices. Take two large rectangles of foil (each large enough to wrap the fish up in), or four if you've cleaved it in half, in which case distribute seasonings evenly between the two packages. Brush the first piece with melted butter or oil. Lay the salmon on it, pull up the edges to form a loose container and pour over the wine. Lay the remaining herbs and lemon on top and then season. Bring the sides of the foil up over the salmon and seal tightly. Seal the ends, then wrap it in a second, reinforcing layer of foil.

If your fish weighs 2–3kg (4½–6 lb), preheat the oven to 220°C/425°F/Gas Mark 7 and bake for about 25–40 minutes, until just cooked through. If it weighs 3–4kg (6–9 lb), preheat the oven to 190°C/375°F/Gas Mark 5 and bake for 50–60 minutes. Check regularly, re-sealing firmly each time, and take the salmon out of the oven when a skewer or the blade of a knife just slips through to the bone in the thickest part, with only marginal resistance.

Open the foil and lift the salmon on to a serving dish. Remove the skin if you want to. The pink flesh looks pretty but, if you are feeling flustered, don't make extra work for yourself. Serve with hollandaise sauce or simply melted butter, sharpened with generous squeezes of lemon juice, accompanied by the juices from the foil parcel.

Salmon in Pastry with Ginger and Currants

Alternative: sea trout

To the uninitiated, the mixture of salmon, ginger and currants may come as a surprise but it only takes one mouthful to convert the most sceptical. This classic amongst salmon dishes was recreated from a medieval recipe by that inspired restaurateur, George Perry-Smith, when he ran the Hole-in-the-Wall, in Bath, many years ago.

Try to get two pieces of fillet that are roughly the same shape, so that they can be sandwiched together. Otherwise, you'll have to use a little ingenuity when you put the parcel together. You can make the salmon parcel in advance but don't cook it until the last minute.

In the past, I've often adapted the recipe to serve two, by making individual parcels of salmon fillet with the same ginger, currant and butter topping. Once you get the hang of it, you'll find it the most amenable recipe.

SERVES 4

700g (1½ lb) tail piece of salmon, filleted
60g (2 oz) butter
2–3 knobs of preserved stem ginger, finely chopped
30g (1 oz) currants
700g (1½ lb) shortcrust pastry
1 egg yolk
salt and pepper

For the Cream Sauce:
60g (2 oz) butter
300ml (½ pint) double cream
1 teaspoon Dijon mustard
4 tablespoons finely chopped fresh herbs, e.g.
    parsley, chives, tarragon or chervil, marjoram
lemon juice
salt and pepper

Preheat the oven to 230°C/450°F/Gas Mark 8 and put a baking sheet in it. Season the salmon with salt and pepper. Mix the butter with the ginger and currants, then sandwich the two pieces of salmon together with the mixture, cut-sides in, skin-sides out.

Roll out the pastry to form a rectangle large enough to envelop the salmon. Place the salmon in the centre and bring the edges up to form a neat parcel, sealing well with egg yolk. Turn the other way up, so that the joins are hidden away underneath, and place on a baking sheet. Brush the top with egg yolk.

Put the salmon on its baking sheet on top of the hot baking sheet in the oven (which will give the underneath an instant blast of heat). Bake for about 20 minutes. Test with a skewer; it should slip through easily, with no resistance, if it is ready.

To make the sauce, melt the butter and stir in the cream. Let it bubble and thicken for few a minutes and then stir in the mustard and herbs. Draw off the heat and sharpen with a few squeezes of lemon juice. Season with salt and pepper. Serve immediately with the salmon.

Sea Trout in Filo Pastry with Tarragon

Alternative: salmon

French tarragon, with its sweet, green, aniseed flavour, is usually saved for chicken dishes but why should it be so restricted? It works admirably with fish, as long as it is not used with a heavy hand. Here it brings life to a pretty parcel of pink sea trout, wrapped in a crisp jacket of filo pastry.

SERVES 4

500g (1 lb 2 oz) skinned sea trout fillet, divided
    into 4 portions
4 large sheets of filo pastry
30g (1 oz) butter, melted
salt and pepper

For the Tarragon Butter:
30g (1 oz) lightly salted or unsalted butter,
    softened
1 tablespoon chopped fresh tarragon leaves
finely grated zest of ½ lemon
2 teaspoons lemon juice
salt and pepper

Preheat the oven to 230°C/450°F/Gas Mark 8. Season the sea trout with salt and pepper. To make the tarragon butter, beat the butter with all the remaining ingredients, seasoning lightly if needed.

Extract the sheets of filo pastry from their packet. To prevent them from drying out, lay them on a table, cover with a sheet of greaseproof paper, then cover that with a tea towel wrung out in cold water.

Take the first sheet of filo, brush with melted butter and lay a piece of sea trout in the centre. Spread a quarter of the tarragon butter over it. Wrap the sea trout up neatly in the filo, keeping the tarragon-butter side on top but tucking the joins and ends away underneath. Lay on a greased baking sheet. Repeat with the remaining filo, sea trout and tarragon butter. Brush the tops and sides of the parcels with any remaining melted butter. Cover and keep cool for a short while if not cooking straightaway.

Bake the parcels, uncovered, for 5 minutes, then reduce the heat to 190°C/375°F/Gas Mark 5 and cook for a further 10–12 minutes. Serve immediately.

Three-Minute Sewin with Mango, Coriander and Spring Onion Salsa

Alternatives: salmon, cod, halibut

This way of flash-roasting fish, cut into thin slivers, preserves its purest taste, keeping all its freshness. It works with cod or halibut but is best with sea trout (sewin) and salmon. The fish and its cool, fruity salsa can both be prepared ahead of time, then, as long as you remember to preheat the oven well in advance, you can cook the fish in less time than it takes to clear the table.

SERVES 4–6

600–700g (1¼–1½ lb) sea trout fillet, skinned
lemon olive oil or ordinary olive oil
salt and pepper
fresh coriander sprigs, to garnish

For the Salsa:
1 large, ripe mango, peeled, stoned and finely diced
juice of 1 lime
5 spring onions, thinly sliced
½–1 red chilli, de-seeded and finely chopped
2 celery sticks, finely diced
3 tablespoons chopped fresh coriander
salt

To make the salsa, mix all the ingredients and set aside, covered, in the fridge until needed. Taste and adjust the seasoning just before serving.

Wrap the fish in cling film and pop into the freezer for about 1 hour to firm up. You can get away without doing this but it does make it easier to slice thinly. Do be careful, though, not to leave it so long that it freezes solid.

Slice the chilled fish as thinly as you can, cutting it slightly on the diagonal to make larger slices. Find one large or 4–6 individual ovenproof plates, depending on how many are eating. Brush them with oil. Lay the fish on the dish(es), overlapping the slices as little as possible but covering the surface entirely. Brush again with oil.

Preheat the oven to its highest setting. When every-one is gathered at the table, pop the fish into the oven. Take out after 3 minutes (no longer), season quickly with salt and pepper and serve immediately, with the coriander sprigs as a garnish, and the salsa.

Deep and Distant

The majority of sea fish live in plankton-rich waters close to land. Not all, though. There is a range of mysterious creatures that inhabit the deeper waters of the oceans: snapping, large-toothed fish with luminous lures and odd shapes, many of which look quite inedible. The problem with establishing a sustainable level of fishing with these species is that not only is it very hard to assess how many fish there are but their life cycles are extremely complex and difficult to observe. The orange roughy, for instance, doesn't reach sexual maturity for forty years, so any irresponsible overfishing could damage the stocks for a long time.

Due to the great depths at which these fish are found, fishing boats need enormous power to pull in the nets, and often process the catch on board since the ports are so far away. Some of the richest deep-water fisheries are found off the New Zealand, South African and Chilean coasts, although the orange roughy was initially exploited in the North Atlantic, to the south of Iceland.

You rarely see these fish in any form other than a fillet, so don't worry about familiarising yourself with their looks when whole. Yield is not given in this section for this reason.

Grenadier, Rat Tail

Coryphaenoides rupestris
French: Grenadier
Spanish: Granadero
Portuguese: Granadeiro
German: Grenadierfisch

This hideously ugly fish with an enormous head and insubstantial tapering tail is a surprising candidate for any fishery but its fillet – despite having an odd, pointed shape – is good and firm, so the grenadier is considered one of the better deep-sea fish available. It lives at great depths – at times deeper than 5,000m (16,400 ft), but rises towards shallower water at night. Although little can be seen at these depths, its large eyes will pick up anything luminous, and its enlarged head hides an advanced navigation system.

Some species have long barbels with which they rootle around the murky depths. Grenadier are relatively easy to catch because they shoal. The Atlantic stocks have been overfished and the annual landings are well below the 80,000 tonnes of a few years back.

By all accounts this has a firm and tasty fillet, and will benefit from a goodly dose of dairy products to make it interesting.

> **Season:** All year round.
> **Price:** £
> **Fishing method:** Deep-sea trawl.

Hoki

Macruronus novazealandiae
French: Hoki
Italian: Nasello azzurro
Spanish: Merluza azul
Portuguese: Granadeiro-azul
German: Langschwanz-Seehecht

The great white hoki of the fishing industry, this fish, once unknown in the UK, appears in supermarkets everywhere these days. It is fished in large quantities off New Zealand, whose domestic market is quite tiny and fishing fleet disproportionately large. It is said that the New Zealand fishery can support a yield of at least 200,000 tonnes per annum.

The hoki resembles a hake from the front and a tadpole from the back. It is fished in deep water up to 900–5,000m (2,970 ft) below the surface.

Hoki fillet is white, quite bland and relatively bone-free, which the industry constantly tells us is what the public requires. It can be fried, baked or poached with some success, and will take a rich sauce with ease.

> **Season:** All year round.
> **Price:** ££
> **Fishing method:** Deep-sea trawl.

Orange Roughy®

Hoplostethus atlanticus
French: Hoplostète rouge, Empereur, Beryx
Spanish: Reloj
Portuguese: Olho-de-vidro-laranja
German: Granatbarsch

Originally this fish was known as slimehead, but someone wisely thought that slimehead and chips didn't have a particularly attractive ring to it and came up with the rather more palatable 'orange roughy'. The French have also had a nomenclature problem for this excellent deep-sea fish, and it can appear as *empereur* or *hoplostète rouge*, depending on how correct your *poissonnier* is feeling.

Originally, orange roughy were thought to be found only in the deep water to the south of Iceland but in the 1970s stocks were discovered on the opposite side of the world, between

Tasmania and New Zealand. Despite this, the fish has retained its *atlanticus*.

One curious property of this fish is a layer of fat, or waxy ester, under its skin, which provides it with a degree of lift and buoyancy. If eaten it acts as a powerful laxative. This layer is removed in the filleting process but if you do find a whole orange roughy – beware!

Thawed-out fillets are widely available but can be very dull. Use plenty of rich ingredients to make them excel, but fresh fish should be cooked with a lighter touch. I once ate some delicious fresh orange roughy in the wilds of western Iceland, where it was served with a light crab sauce. Cod and hake recipes work with orange roughy.

Season: All year round.
Price: ££
Fishing method: Deep-sea trawl.

Redfish, Norway Haddock, Ocean Perch

French: Sébaste, Dorade sébaste, Rascasse (north)
Italian: Sebaste, Scorfano di Norvegia
Spanish: Gallineta nórdica
Portuguese: Cantarilho
German: Rotbarsch, Goldbarsch

Atlantic species
Sebastes marinus, Sebastes mentella, Sebastes viviparus

Pacific species
Helicolenus maculatus, Helicolenus dactylopterus

The redfish was for years the most important deep-sea fish, landed in vast quantities, especially in northern ports such as Cuxhaven in Germany and Hirtshals in Denmark. Until, that is, New Zealand began to exploit her deep waters, and brought to the market a whole load of new species to try and fill the worldwide demand for fish.

In the Pacific there are some closely related species – many of which are highly esteemed by the Chinese and Japanese – which, when very fresh, are reputed to be excellent eating.

This is a popular fish that can be fried or cooked like cod. It has a flaky flesh and would go well with Sophie's Welsh rarebit recipe (see page 113).

Season: All year round.
Price: ££
Fishing method: Deep-sea trawl.

Scabbard Fish, Cutlass Fish®

Trichiurus lepturus (Atlantic)
French: Sabre
Italian: Pesce coltello, Pesce scabiola
Spanish: Pez sable, Pez cinto
Portuguese: Peixe-espada
German: Degefisch

Frostfish
Lepidopus caudatus (S. hemisphere)

Black scabbard fish
Aphanopus carbo

Long, glamorous but desperately thin and sharp toothed, scabbard may look a meagre catch but they are spectacular. At wholesale markets they are often packed curled up neatly in open wooden boxes, looking distinctly Jurassic.

The Portuguese love this fish, and use it often. They have an even more exotic species, the *Espada preta*, or black scabbard, which is found in the deep waters surrounding the island of Madeira. It is a fearsome beast, with jet-black, shiny skin, and the Madeirans spend a lot of time and energy hunting it. Traditionally, dyed black hand-lines are lowered as far down as 1,000m (3,280 ft) to capture the fish.

Their skin and bellies are fragile, so they must be handled delicately, but a market full of scabbard fish lined up with military correctness is a magnificent sight. I have seen both species available in the UK, which is good news.

The scabbard's strange shape makes it an unlikely candidate for filleting, so be prepared to eat it on the bone. Cut the fish into 5cm (2-inch) sections to cook. The flesh has a unique texture, firm but loosely fibred. Most recipes for scabbard are Portuguese or Madeiran. Try the unlikely combination of bananas and scabbard fish given on page 189.

Season: Summer.
Price: ££
Fishing method: Deep-sea trawl, hand-line.

Toothfish, Patagonian Toothfish, Icefish, Antarctic Sea Bass, Chilean Sea Bass

Dissostichus eleginoides

As you can see, this fish has yet to find its true identity. It has rather dense flesh and is yet another species considered to be the answer to the world's supply problems. Since it has only appeared quite recently on the markets, questions should rightly be asked as to just how extensive the stocks of this fish really are, but answers will, I suspect, come too late. It is fished solely in the southern oceans, off the Falklands, South Georgia, Argentina and round to the Chilean coast.

A good texture and clean white fillet has already made this a popular fish, and although it lacks the delicacy of bass, you can cook it in the same way. It can also be used instead of cod, and is a fairly useful stand-by for many round sea fish.

Season: All year round.
Price: ££
Fishing method: Deep-sea trawl.

SCABBARD FISH

Kebabs of Hoki with Pesto Dressing

Alternatives: monkfish, tuna, scallops, cod

I love barbecued fish but it does have a peevish tendency either to stick to the bars of the grill rack or to start flaking into the coals as you lift it off. A double-sided grill rack helps on the latter count but is not entirely successful when you are using pieces of fish rather than whole swimmers. When it comes to kebabs, the answer is to wrap the fish in a protective jacket. Old-fashioned caul fat (the stuff they used to use to wrap faggots) – if you can get it – works very well, basting the fish as it cooks, but these days it is probably easier to lay your hands on finely sliced pancetta, the Italian answer to our own streaky bacon. It's not great for a bacon butty but it does add an excellent flavour to fish and, being fatty, keeps it moist as it cooks.

Here, I've married my pancetta-wrapped fish with a selection of other ingredients that speak of southern skies – aubergine, tomatoes, olive oil and pesto.

SERVES 6

1 aubergine, cut into 2.5cm (1-inch) cubes
150g (5 oz) thinly sliced pancetta
700g (1½ lb) skinned hoki fillet, cut into 4cm (1½-inch) cubes
350g (12 oz) cherry tomatoes
fresh bay leaves or sage leaves (optional)
extra virgin olive oil
salt and pepper

For the Pesto Dressing:
1 heaped tablespoon pesto (home-made or bought)
juice of ½ lemon
6 tablespoons olive oil
2 medium tomatoes (around 150g/5 oz), peeled, de-seeded and finely diced
salt and pepper

Spread the aubergine cubes out on a plate and sprinkle lightly with salt. Set aside for half an hour to degorge. Make the dressing while you wait. Mix the pesto with the lemon juice and some salt and pepper, then gradually whisk in the olive oil. Stir in the tomatoes and cover until needed.

Rinse the aubergine quickly and pat dry. Cut the pancetta into pieces just long enough to wrap round the cubes of fish, like a deep red cummerbund. Now set up your kebab production line, with aubergine, fish, pancetta, cherry tomatoes and bay or sage leaves spread out in front of you. Thread the kebabs with succeeding trios of cherry tomato, aubergine cube and chunk of fish wrapped in pancetta, interspersing every now and then with a leaf. Brush generously with olive oil and grill over charcoal or under a hot grill, turning every couple of minutes, until the aubergine and fish are just cooked through. Serve with the dressing, gently warmed through or at room temperature.

Orange Roughy with a Roast Courgette and Tomato Sauce

Alternatives: cod, redfish, haddock

My favourite way to make a tomato sauce is also one of the easiest. All the ingredients go into a roasting tin together and they roast slowly in the oven, requiring no attention at all as they cook. That leaves me free to get on with other things. In this recipe, I've added some courgettes to the tin so that they cook along with everything else, and even the fish itself, the orange roughy, ends up in the oven in that very same roasting tin. A one-dish wonder.

SERVES 4

700g (1½ lb) orange roughy fillet, skinned
450g (1 lb) courgettes, cut into chunks
1 onion, cut into 8 wedges
4 whole, unpeeled garlic cloves
700g (1½ lb) tomatoes, halved across the centre
1 large fresh rosemary sprig
2 fresh thyme sprigs
3 tablespoons olive oil
1 tablespoon caster sugar
1 tablespoon red wine vinegar
coarse salt and pepper

Preheat the oven to 240°C/450°F/Gas Mark 8. Season the fish with salt and pepper and set aside.

Find a capacious ovenproof dish or small roasting tin. Put the courgettes, onion, garlic, tomatoes and herbs into the dish and pour over the olive oil. Turn the pieces with your hands so that they are all coated, then sprinkle over the caster sugar and drizzle over the vinegar. Season with salt and pepper. Roast, uncovered, stirring once or twice, for about 35 minutes.

Carefully extract and reserve the chunks of courgette. Brush the fish with a little oil and lay it on top of the other ingredients. Return to the oven for a further 5–10 minutes, until the fish is just barely cooked through. Lift off and keep warm until needed.

Tip the remaining contents of the roasting tin into a food processor, juices, gunky bits stuck to the roasting tin and all. Process. If the result is rather thick, dilute it with a little water. Sieve out all the skins and things, then taste and adjust the seasoning. Re-heat with the courgettes and serve with the orange roughy.

Orange Roughy Chowder

Alternatives: cod, smoked haddock and most white fish

I started to make fish chowders when I was a student and I've carried on ever since. Filling, warming, main-course soups, big bowls of chowder are a wonder for sloughing away the blues on a chilly evening. A relatively small amount of fish is expanded with plenty of vegetables, so it won't break the bank either. Orange roughy turns out to be a good fish for a chowder but, if there's none to be had, cod and its lesser relatives, or smoked haddock, are all first-rate chowder fish.

SERVES 4–6

350g (12 oz) orange roughy fillet, cut into
   2.5 cm (1-inch) cubes
45g (1½ oz) butter
1 tablespoon sunflower or groundnut oil
1 onion, chopped
2 celery sticks, sliced
4 rashers of smoked back bacon, cut into strips
2 carrots, sliced
2 medium potatoes, cut in 2cm (¾-inch) cubes
1 bay leaf
2 fresh thyme sprigs
2 heaped tablespoons plain flour
¼ teaspoon ground turmeric
900ml (1½ pints) milk
110g (4 oz) frozen peas, thawed
lemon juice
salt, pepper and freshly grated nutmeg
chopped fresh parsley, to garnish
grated Cheddar cheese, to serve

Season the orange roughy with salt and pepper. Melt the butter with the oil in a large saucepan. Add the onion, celery and bacon and cook gently without browning until the onion is tender. Add the carrots, potatoes, bay leaf and thyme and stir to coat in fat. Cover tightly and sweat over a very low heat for 5 minutes, stirring once or twice. Uncover and sprinkle over the flour and turmeric. Stir for 30 seconds or so and then gradually stir in the milk. Season lightly with salt and pepper. Bring up to the boil and simmer gently for 15–20 minutes, until the vegetables are tender. If the soup is getting absurdly thick, thin it with a little more milk or a splash of water.

Now stir in the orange roughy and the peas and cook for a final 4–5 minutes, until the fish is just cooked through. Add a dash of lemon juice and a good scraping of fresh nutmeg. Taste and adjust the seasoning and serve sprinkled with parsley. Pass around a bowl of grated Cheddar, for those who want to scatter it over their soup.

Redfish Mornay

Alternatives: cod, halibut and most flaky white fish

William insists that the only way to cook redfish is with a creamy sauce of some kind. After a few experiments, I'm inclined to agree with him. Its firm, dryish flakes need a generous lubricant, and that valiant old war-horse, Mornay sauce, made with a shot of cream to lift it above the ordinary, is just the ticket. 'Retro' cooking is all the rage, and Mornay sauce is poised to make a comeback, which is good news. As long as it is not made with a heavy hand and dull spirit, it is a fine accompaniment to any firm-fleshed fish. I would not, however, use it to drown the spirit of sweet scallops, as has happened all too frequently in the past, and I draw the line at piping curls and frills of *duchesse* potato round the edge of the dish. Far better to serve your redfish (or other fish) Mornay with a big bowlful of mash, enlivened with plenty of finely chopped parsley and a handful of finely chopped spring onion.

SERVES 4–6

600g (1¼ lb) redfish fillets
butter
salt and pepper

For the Sauce:
30g (1 oz) butter
30g (1 oz) plain flour
150ml (¼ pint) Fish Stock (see page 308)
300ml (½ pint) milk
150ml (¼ pint) whipping cream
30g (1 oz) Parmesan cheese, finely grated
30g (1 oz) Gruyère cheese, finely grated
salt and pepper

Preheat the oven to 190°C/375°F/Gas Mark 5. To make the sauce, melt the butter in a pan and stir in the flour. Cook for about a minute, stirring. Draw off the heat and gradually stir in the stock, a splash at a time, and then the milk, by which time the sauce should be thinning out so you can add it with a more carefree hand. Stir in the cream, too, and return to the heat. Simmer for a good 8–10 minutes, stirring frequently, until the sauce is rather thick and the flavour of raw flour has completely gone. Draw off the heat and stir in half the Parmesan and half the Gruyère. Season with salt and pepper. If not using immediately, spear a small knob of butter on a fork and rub it over the surface of the sauce to prevent a skin forming.

Butter two sheets of foil, each one large enough to enclose half the fillets. Place half the redfish fillets in the centre of each one, season with salt and pepper and wrap up snugly. Bake for about 15 minutes, until just cooked, or steam for about 10 minutes if you prefer.

Preheat the grill. Once the fish is done, re-heat the sauce, drain the juice from the foil parcels into it and stir well. Lay the fillets in a heatproof dish and cover with sauce. Don't worry if the fillets fall apart – it won't show at all. In fact, if this is for children or bone-ophobic adults you may well prefer to flake the fish, removing any stray bones and skin, and then stir it into the Mornay sauce and pile into the dish, smoothing the surface down. Mix the remaining Parmesan and Gruyère and sprinkle over the surface. Whisk under the grill and grill until browned and bubbling.

If you wish, the dish can be prepared in advance. Instead of grilling, reheat in the oven, set to 200°C/400°F/Gas Mark 6, for about 25 minutes, until browned and bubbling.

Madeiran Fried Scabbard Fish with Banana

Alternatives: brill fillet, Dover sole fillet, lemon sole fillet

I've never been to Madeira but William returned from a business trip there raving about a dish of fried scabbard fish and bananas that he had eaten frequently in a matter of a few days. It sounded a bizarre combination but he convinced me that I had to try it. Just as well that he did, because it is truly lovely. The tender flesh of the scabbard, with a hint of sharpness from the lemon marinade, marries surprisingly well with sweet fried bananas and coriander.

William thinks that one banana per person is quite enough. I, with the zeal of a new convert, rather fancied a bit more, but then I am particularly partial to fried bananas.

SERVES 4

1–1.2kg (2¼–2¾ lb) scabbard fish, cleaned
3 garlic cloves, crushed
juice of 1 lemon
plain flour, seasoned
4–6 bananas
30g (1 oz) butter
2 tablespoons sunflower oil
salt and pepper
chopped fresh coriander, to garnish
4 lemon wedges, to serve

Cut the scabbard fish into pieces about 7.5–10cm (3–4 inches) long, discarding head and tail. Use a pair of sturdy scissors to trim off the dorsal spines that run all along the back of the fish. Place the pieces in a shallow dish and then sprinkle with the crushed garlic, lemon juice and some salt and pepper. Turn with your hands so that each piece is coated. Leave for half an hour, turning the pieces again once, if you remember.

Spread the seasoned flour out on a plate. Take two frying pans and heat one-third of the butter with about one-third of the oil in one pan. As the butter heats up, quickly peel the bananas and put them into the pan. Fry gently, turning once or twice, until prettily browned and cooked through. Keep warm, if necessary.

Meanwhile, heat the remaining butter and oil in the second pan. One by one, coat the pieces of scabbard in seasoned flour and fry in the butter and oil (you'll probably have to do this in two batches), giving them about 2 minutes on each side until just cooked through. Keep the first lot of fish warm while you cook the second. Arrange fish and bananas on a warm serving dish, sprinkle with a little chopped coriander, and serve with the lemon wedges.

Tod Man

Alternatives: grouper, cod and most flaky white fish

Tod Man were the very first thing I tasted in the very first Thai meal I ever ate, almost twenty years ago when Thai food was still a rarity and the very thought of British pubs dishing up Thai delicacies alongside their steak and kidney pies was laughable. They are, to put it baldly, fishcakes, but being from Thailand they are laden with herbs and spicy ingredients to transform them into something a million miles from our own fishcakes. I love them now just as much as I did that first blissful mouthful, all those years ago.

Their flavour is much improved by marinating the fish with the flavourings overnight, though if you forget you will probably be forgiven by your fellow diners. They should be served with a sweet chilli sauce but I rather like them with the Spicy Tomato Ketchup on page 58 or with the Marinated Cucumber Salsa on page 168. Or, better still, both.

Any white-fleshed, flaky fish will work well in this recipe, but since toothfish, when it is available, is relatively well priced it makes a good option.

MAKES ABOUT 20

1kg/(2½lb) toothfish fillet, diced
oil, for frying
lemon wedges, to serve

For the Marinade:
5 shallots or ½ onion, diced
4 garlic cloves
3 red or green chillies, de-seeded and chopped
4 coriander roots, chopped, or 3 tablespoons chopped fresh coriander leaves
4 dried or fresh kaffir lime leaves, or 2 lemongrass stems, chopped
60g (2 oz) French beans or yardlong beans, cut into thin rounds
2 teaspoons sugar
2 teaspoons soy sauce
½ teaspoon salt
¼ teaspoon pepper
2 tablespoons olive oil

Mix the fish with all the marinade ingredients. Leave for at least 30–40 minutes or overnight in the fridge. Mince or process the whole lot together. Roll tablespoons of the mixture into balls. At this point you can cover them and leave in the fridge for 24 hours. Heat the oil in a wok or deep-fryer to a temperature of 190°C/375°F. Flatten the balls to a thickness of about 2cm (3⁄4 inch) and deep-fry for 2–3 minutes. Drain on kitchen paper. Serve with wedges of lemon or as appetisers with drinks, in which case you may want to make the fishcakes rather smaller.

What-You-Will Fish Stew

This stew can make the centrepiece of a casual lunch, served with warm, crusty bread and a green salad and followed by fruit and cheese, or star in a more formal setting, after a light first course, served with noodles or rice or boiled new potatoes and a green vegetable. One Sunday we dished it up with roast winter squash and chard from the garden. Very good.

On that occasion, we made the stew with cod, snapper and swordfish but it is a good vehicle for almost any fish, particularly for these imported deep-water fish that sell relatively cheaply and are great for bulking out more costly fish. You can use just one type of fish alone, but I think the result is better with a mixture. The flavour is deepened and the contrasting textures make the stew more enjoyable to eat. You could also add some shellfish, which will give a special sweetness – try a handful of raw prawns or a few mussels or clams. In fact, tune it to fit your own requirements, taking it from the simple and homely to the fancy and grand.

If you haven't got any fish stock, the wine becomes essential. In an ideal world, both would be thrown in.

SERVES 6

1kg (2¼ lb) mixed fish fillets, e.g. hoki, orange roughy, swordfish, cod, snapper, etc., cut into pieces about 2.5cm (1 inch) across and 4cm (1½ inches) long
good pinch of saffron strands (optional)
1 white or red onion, chopped
2 celery sticks, thinly sliced
4 tablespoons extra virgin olive oil
4 garlic cloves, chopped
1 tablespoon coriander seeds, roughly crushed
1 teaspoon cumin seeds or ½ teaspoon ground cumin
2 bay leaves
1 sizeable fresh thyme sprig
2 x 400g (14 oz) tins of chopped tomatoes
2 heaped tablespoons tomato purée or sun-dried tomato purée
1 glass (110ml/4 fl oz) red wine (optional)
300ml (½ pint) Fish Stock (see page 308) or water
1–2 tablespoons sugar (optional)
salt and pepper

Season the fish with salt and pepper and set aside. Put the saffron into a small bowl, if using, and add a tablespoon of hot water. Leave to infuse.

Fry the onion and celery in the olive oil over a moderate heat, letting them colour here and there. When they are almost done, add the garlic, coriander, cumin, bay leaves and thyme. Cook for 2 minutes.

Stir in the tomatoes and tomato purée, then leave to boil down until very thick – about 10 minutes – stirring occasionally. Now add the wine, if using, bring back to the boil and cook for a minute or so, then add the stock or water. Season with salt and pepper. Simmer for 5 minutes and then taste. If it is rather sharp tasting, which it probably will be, add sugar, to soften it to a pleasing state. Simmer for another 5–10 minutes. The stew can be prepared to this stage in advance. If you do this, re-heat it thoroughly, about 10 minutes before you wish to serve it.

Add all the fish to the stew, together with the saffron, give it a quick stir and then let it simmer gently for about 5 minutes. Draw off the heat, taste and adjust the seasonings, then serve.

Shellfish

Shellfish can be eaten with nothing more than a squeeze of lemon, and even that can detract from the taste. They are molluscs that have either one shell – univalves – or two – bivalves. Both can deteriorate rapidly as soon as they die, so they are often eaten raw, and must be cooked when alive. Be careful about drinking spirits with shellfish, particularly oysters; alcohol hardens the flesh in your gut and can cause a lot of discomfort. Stick to decent wine!

The quality of the seawater that shellfish come from is critically important. European waters are categorised into A, the cleanest (where shellfish can be eaten directly from the water), and B, where the water has to be purified. Purification is a relatively simple matter of passing water through an ultraviolet lamp which kills any bacteria, so be careful of eating shellfish straight from the sea.

Despite this, some people seem to have a persistent reaction to shellfish – my father was one of them – and if you have had some nasty experiences in the past it may well be better to avoid eating them altogether.

Some French words have become more widely known than their rather unwieldy British equivalents, and where appropriate I have used them.

Preparing Clams

Either hold the clam in a clean towel in your palm or place on a chopping board (depending upon how brave you are) and run a knife between the shells, remembering as always to cut away from you. With practice this is easier to do in your hand. If it's too difficult, put the clams in the oven or grill them for a minute or two and the shells should open up. Retain the juice in a bowl but filter it before use to remove any sediment or broken shell.

Preparing Mussels

These days, most mussels have already been partially cleaned by the time they reach the fishmonger, reducing the amount of work to be done at home, though by no means eliminating it. A mouthful of grit in an otherwise perfectly cooked dish of mussels is seriously unpleasant and ruins the whole thing. Besides, cleaning them gives you a chance to check that they are all in good condition.

Tip the mussels into the sink and cover with plenty of cold water. One by one, scrape away the barnacles and hairy 'beard' (this is the byssus, which attaches the living mussel to the post, rope or rock it grows on) and scrub. Throw away any that refuse to close when tapped firmly, or any that are cracked. Discard, too, any that feel abnormally heavy; they are probably filled with sand. Drain, rinse at least once more, if not twice for good measure. Never leave them sitting in fresh water too long or it will kill them.

Some people claim that the best route to fat little mussels is to feed them overnight on a handful of oatmeal, in a bucket of cold water. But too many mussels drown (yes, honestly, it can happen) and are seen in the morning gaping open and beyond saving. A waste of time, mussels and oatmeal. Save it for porridge.

This is the classic way to open mussels. Pour 1cm (½ inch) of water or other cooking liquid (e.g. white wine) into a wide, large pan. Add chopped onion, garlic, herbs or any other flavourings. Bring up to the boil. Tip in the mussels, cover tightly and shake over a high heat for a couple of minutes. Remove those mussels that have opened. Cover again and shake for a minute or two longer, or until the vast majority have opened. Discard any that remain steadfastly closed.

The cooking liquor will probably be incorporated into the dish you are using but, if not, don't waste it. It makes a marvellous stock for fish sauces and soups. There's always some grit hanging around in it so either strain it through a sieve lined with muslin (or a coffee filter) or tip it into a bowl, leave to settle and then carefully pour off the liquor, leaving the grit behind in the bowl. Freeze, if you are not using it straight away.

If you fancy a change, try steaming the mussels open in several batches, or spread them out on a baking tray and give them a blast of heat in a hot oven or under the grill. Keep dry cooking methods as brief as possible if the mussels are not to dry out.

Preparing Oysters

To open an oyster, lay it on a hard surface wrapped in a clean tea towel, with the cup side down. Wash the shells before opening if they look grubby. Native oysters are usually cleaner.

Rock or Pacific oysters
Take an oyster knife and work the blade into the hinge, making sure you point the knife away from you. Once you've broken the hinge, slide the knife along the inside of the the upper shell to cut the meat free, leaving it to sit in the lower, cup-shaped shell. Try to keep as much juice as possible in the oyster, so arrange them where they won't tip over.

Native oysters
Hold the oyster in your hand wrapped in a cloth, with the hinge sitting next to the thumb side of your palm. Take a long-bladed oyster knife and run the edge from the outside towards the hinge, cutting the meat from the upper shell. Try and retain as much juice as possible.

Oyster knives
Stubby-bladed knives are suitable for rock oysters. Long-bladed knives are better for native oysters. Many are sold with a guard, which is useful since it protects your fingers from the sharp shell.

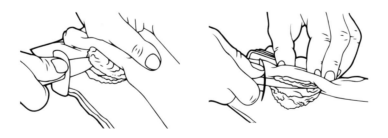

An experienced oyster opener will make it all look desperately simple. I find it one of the most tedious jobs in the world, possibly because I've had to open hundreds for weddings and parties and am not particularly good at it. Rock oysters can be difficult because their shape is so irregular. Try to buy oysters with as flat a top as possible and a straight join between the shells, not one with waves and wobbles. Also, look at the hinge.

Some are bent inaccessibly back upon themselves, and are also difficult to open. Another word of warning: some oysters are brittle. If you see a friable, frilly edge to them, they may not have been hardened up enough. Oysters should be left to be finished on the foreshore, stranded at low tide, which builds up shell strength.

Preparing Scallops

Place the scallop flat side up. Take a long knife and run it along the inside of the inner surface of the flat shell, cutting the meat away from the shell. The edible part is the central adductor muscle, plus the orange coral.

The rest, the accusing eyes and the beard, can be thrown out. Do not soak your scallop in water. If the scallops have been dredged there may be some sand in them, so rinse the scallop meat under water. There is a slightly whiter ligament attached to the muscle which should be removed.

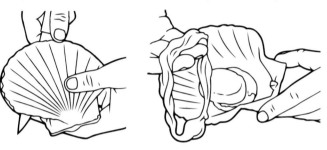

Preparing Sea Urchins

Cut the centre of the top of a sea urchin – the end without the mouth – with a sharp pair of fine-pointed scissors or, if you're really flash, with a *coupe oursin* specifically designed for the job. Cut around as if opening a hard-boiled egg and you will see the orange roe lying along the edge of the shell ready to eat.

UNIVALVES

Abalone, Ormer★

Haliotis tuberculata (Europe)
French: Ormeau
Italian: Orechia marina
Spanish: Oreja de mar
Portuguese: Orelha
German: Seeohr

Sea ear
Haliotis iris (NZ)

It you should happen to be on the island of Guernsey in January, go down to the sea at low tide during the full moon and you're quite likely to see the odd figure bent over a pile of seaweed. For the first four months of the year, on the six days following the full moon, the gathering of ormers is permitted, and people from all over the island hurry to the markets, buying abalone by the score to make their traditional ormer stew.

Guernsey is one of the few places left where the native European abalone, *Haliotis tuberculata*, still exists. Abalone eat seaweed and are extremely sensitive to pollution, so in a sense it is a relief to have any at all. But at wholesale prices of around £15 per kg (2¼ lb), temptation has led a few unscrupulous people to overexploit the stocks, particularly in Brittany. Not long ago, a French lorry was found to have about 5 tonnes of illegally fished abalone hidden in its hold, and I have been offered dodgy abalone in Paris more times than I care to mention (this was in the fish market, not wandering the streets late at night by the way). And yes, of course I said no.

In France abalone are fished by divers, both legally and illegally, but on the Channel Islands the only permitted method of fishing is from the shore.

Abalone cling tenaciously to rocks and are particularly well camouflaged. If left alone they can grow to 20cm (8 inches) or so in length but they seldom reach this size, so valuable a species have they become. The flesh is tough, however you eat it, but tastes very good. The secret is to tenderise the foot, the edible part, by a vigorous bashing. From then on you can go the *sashimi* route (serve it raw), or the long slow cooking route, as in stewed ormers, Guernsey style, where the abalone foot is fried in butter, then stewed for hours with chicken stock, bacon and potatoes.

Season: Closed season.
Price: £££

Conch and Whelk

Conch
Strombus gigas

Whelk, Dog whelk®
Buccinum undatum

French: Bulot, Buccin, Escargot de mer
Italian: Buccina
Spanish: Bocina, Caracola
Portuguese: Búzio

A true conch, pronounced 'konk' by the way, will seldom come our way in the UK. They are native in various forms to Florida, the West Indies and the Pacific coast, and are a glamorous version of our whelk, which isn't exactly highly esteemed in the UK. The first time I ate whelks and realised that there was possibly something to them was in one of Paris's best seafood restaurants, where they were boiled in very salty water for an hour and served warm with home-made mayonnaise. Delicious!

The whelk fishery in Europe is booming. High demand from Japan and Korea has revived what many considered to be a lost cause.

In South America the conch is often used to make an excellent *ceviche* but in the West Indies and Florida the larger conchs are made into a chowder.

You may see a variety of whelk called murex (*Murex brandaris*) for sale, known in the South of France as *escargots de mer*. They usually appear in *plateaux de fruits de mer* and were once used, as were dog whelks, for the remarkably intense purple dye derived from a vein inside their body.
    Season: All year round.
    Price: £

Winkle, Periwinkle

Littorina littorea
French: Bigorneau, Littorine, Vignot
Italian: Chiocciola di mare
Spanish: Bigaro
Portuguese: Borrelho
German: Strandschnecke

It may seem a little ludicrous to eat something so small but do try them, although not, may I suggest, swimming in malt vinegar. Winkles have their place as a nibble, or as a garnish with a piece of fish (taken out of their shell, that is).

Cook only live winkles, which should have a tightly shut operculum. Boil them for 5 minutes in heavily salted water (as near sea water salinity as possible) with a bay leaf and a handful of peppercorns. Serve with a toothpick to pick out the winkle from its shell.
    Season: All year round.
    Price: £

BIVALVES

Amande, Dog Cockle

Glycymeris glycymeris
French: Amande (de mer)
Italian: Pié d'asino
Spanish: Almendra de mar
Portuguese: Castanhola-do-mar

Amandes are imported from France in those dinky little wooden shellfish baskets that make you want to get on the ferry, put on your beret and eat. They have an attractive striated shell but have no real purpose other than making a seafood platter look good. Taste-wise, they are very ordinary.
    Season: Summer.
    Price: ££

Clam, American Hardshell Clam, Quahog®

Mercenaria mercenaria
French: Clam
Italian: Vongola dura, Arsella
Spanish: Almeja, Clame
Portuguese: Cadelinha
German: Sandklaffmuschel

Clams are an American seafood thang. The American hardshell clam, or simply clam to most, is now found over here in good supply. Recently the Solent became the Clam Staten Island when a few clam migrants were either thrown, dropped or jumped into Southampton Water and successfully colonised the

CLAM

Solent, but these days most are raised on shellfish farms throughout the UK.

Dull, thick shells conceal the meat which, once shucked, must be used quickly to avoid any bacterial build-up. Similarly, when buying clams, make sure that the shells are tightly closed and that the clams are alive.

If you are going to eat clams raw – an excellent idea, by the way – then buy smaller clams, called littlenecks and cherrystones in the States. If you're intent on a genuine American clam bake, you should use soft-shell clams (see page 200), with their characteristic long syphon, which are also excellent in chowders. However, hardshell clams do nicely. Clam juice is quite delicious, by the way, and even canned can have its uses, so never throw it away. Allow six small clams or four larger ones per person. Before you use them be sure to scrub the shells clean under running water.

Quahog shells (pronounced co-hogs) were once used as money by some native Americans on the East coast, and called *wampum*.
    Season: All year round.
    Price: ££

Cockle★

Cardium edule
French: Coque
Italian: Cuore edule
Spanish: Berberecho
Portuguese: Berbigão
German: Herzmuschel

Tucked away in an obscure modernist development in the XIV *arrondissement* of Paris is a seafood restaurant, a little past its prime these days, called La Cagouille. There is a genial overweight host, once known as a very particular fish buyer, who even refused to let his fish be tainted by ice. If you ever eat there, a small plate of succulent cockles bathed in butter and white wine might be brought to the table – a clever ruse, for few realise just how tasty the humble cockle can be. It serves as a *leitmotif* for his style of cooking, where underrated fish are sold at inflated prices, but bought and cooked very competently, I must add.

Fresh cockles are difficult to obtain in the UK since they are almost all processed. South Wales and East Anglia are the only areas of England still working the cockle beds, but all is not well. In Essex the fishermen from the River Blackwater are fiercely protective of their cockle beds, and have to wage a virtual war against fishermen from up the coast who, they believe, have fished their own beds to depletion and seem intent on doing the same to theirs. Then there is the spectre of progress. There is a system of suction fishing that hoovers the sea bed and is so powerful that, if used irresponsibly, can wipe out a whole cockle bed in hours.

There is also the small matter of spat fall. Like all shellfish, cockles are susceptible to the vagaries of the weather. In 1996, after a promising start, just about all that year's newly hatched stock, called spat, were killed by an unseasonable cold snap.

Cockles can be sandy. If you're using fresh cockles, purge them by leaving them overnight in a bucket of clean salty water. Avoid cockles that have a dark shell because the meat tends to be dark and unappetising as well. These dark cockles are normally fished from areas that are exposed at low tide.

Season: Spring/summer.
Price: £

Mussel

European mussel,
Blue mussel★

Mytilus edulis
French: Moule
Italian: Cozza
Spanish: Mejillón
Portuguese: Mexhilhão
German: Miesmuschel

New Zealand green-lipped mussel
Perna canaliculus

When I started in the fish business, mussels used to come in huge sacks and were enormous, muddy and smelly. When you got down to eating them they could be quite good, but 0/10 for presentation. It took ages to wash and scrub them clean and get rid of that tacky old beard (the byssus). Then, one day, some neat little 2kg (2¼ lb) bags of Dutch mussels appeared which were, lo and behold, already cleaned. Everybody flocked to them and smelly old mussels became a thing of the past.

Mussels naturally cling to rocks, poles, tiles and oil-rig legs – but many of the mussels you eat are cultivated. In 1235, the story goes, an Irish boat was shipwrecked on the Breton coast and all hands save two (and some sheep) were lost. One of the survivors, an Irishman called Patrick Walton, has become the curious godfather of myticulture (mussel cultivation), for he noticed that mussels had grown on the poles he had placed in the mud to hold a net for capturing sea birds to eat; Mr Walton was an inventive as well as a hungry man.

The locals were so impressed that the practice caught on in a big way, and today you can see thousands upon thousands of wooden poles sticking into the air along much of the Norman and Breton coasts, especially in Mont St Michel Bay where mussels have been successfully grown since Mr Walton's day. The French consume thousands of tonnes of these mussels every year, and call them *moules bouchots*. The word *bouchot* is thought to derive from the Celtic *bout* for post and *choat* for wood.

Don't be too carried away by the idea that all French seafood is marvellous. These mussels can be a bit of a rip-off, thin and insipid, so make sure that you buy them when they are at their fullest, just before spawning, or you could be sorely disappointed. I have tasted some excellent Scottish rope-grown mussels (literally grown on ropes suspended in the water), and Scottish water is far more salubrious than that of Mont St Michel Bay.

Size-wise, the smaller rope-grown mussels are ideal for *moules frites*, *moules marinières* or dishes along those lines, but for bigger, stuffable mussels, you will be better off looking for either Spanish mussels (*moules d'Espagne* in French), or New Zealand green-lipped mussels (which, frankly, I don't like at all). Spanish mussels are farmed on a massive scale in Galicia and can be good to terrible, again depending largely upon the time of year. With all shellfish cultivation the meat content depends upon how much food is available. Where there are too many shellfish in a limited area, or where natural food is deficient, then the meat inside the shell will be thin. Before buying, pick up the mussels if you can, to make sure that they seem full. If you tap a couple together and they sound hollow then they may well be spent, or just plain old – either way don't buy them. I like the way that some fish shops display an open mussel or two to show how meaty their mussels really are.

If you ever feel the need to determine the sex of a mussel for your own personal reasons or to wildly impress your friends, white-fleshed ones are usually male and orange/yellow-fleshed female. Mussels don't have the confused sexuality of an oyster and remain true to one sex for life.

Be careful about collecting mussels from a beach. They filter water and collect bacteria that are normally killed by the purification process. Many remote beaches in Ireland and Scotland are fine but Mediterranean mussels should not be eaten raw.

Older recipes give mussel quantities in pints rather than by weight, so it may be helpful to know that 1 pint of mussels is roughly equivalent to 450g or 1 lb of mussels.

Season: Autumn/winter.
Price: £

Oyster

Native oyster★★★
Ostrea edulis
French: Huître plate, Belon
Italian: Ostrica
Spanish: Ostra plana
Portuguese: Ostra
German: Auster

Pacific oyster, Gigas oyster, Rock oyster★★
Crassostrea gigas
French: Huître creuse
Italian: Ostrica
Spanish: Ostión
Portuguese: Ostra
German: Auster

Portuguese oyster
Crassostrea angulata
French: Huître portugaise

In 1868, during a trip back from the Tagus estuary, the ship Le Morlasien, heavily laden with tons of Portuguese oysters, was holed up in the mouth of the Gironde waiting for a gale to pass. The storm raged for days and eventually, since the shipment seemed doomed, the captain decided to chuck the whole lot overboard. To the surprise of many, the oysters thrived, and became the first generation of Portuguese oysters in France. They satisfied the demand for cheap plain oysters until they were wiped out by disease in the 1970s.

The native oyster (illustration on page 198) was at that time seriously overfished in France, and Emperor Napoleon III had asked the *Inspecteur Général des Pêches*, a Monsieur Coste, to prepare a report to help solve the problem, for there was a very real possibility that France would soon be *sans huîtres*. The wise M. Coste was convinced that the answer lay in oyster cultivation, and spent the rest of his days encouraging French *ostreicultures* to develop a workable system.

In principle, oyster farming is quite simple. At first oysters need something to grow on, a firm substrate or a fine net, to let them reach a marketable size. In France, the spat, or baby oysters, settle on tiles previously soaked in lime and dried in the sun, but in the UK oysters are raised mostly in nets, and are often bought in at a larger size and then grown on. Both the native and the Portuguese oyster reproduce naturally in European waters, so capturing the spat was relatively easy. But since the demise of the Portuguese, another species has come on to the scene, *Crassostrea gigas*, the Pacific oyster, which has proved more resistant to disease. As it doesn't reproduce naturally in our waters, *gigas* spat are raised in hatcheries.

Oysters thrive in plankton-rich, well oxygenated salty water, and the warmer it is, the quicker they grow. The great advantage of *gigas* over the native oyster is the time they take to reach a marketable size. Whereas a native will take anything between five and seven years, a Pacific or rock oyster (illustration on page 198) will be ready in three. But a good oyster farmer will not just sit back and watch. Nets need to be tended and oysters thinned out.

I spent my formative fish years working on an Irish oyster farm, where we raised oysters on an elaborate series of rafts floating in the River Bandon at Kinsale. Our control system was utterly useless, and one day we noticed that a raft had escaped our attention for so long that it was practically sinking under the weight of colossal oysters that nobody wanted.

What we did get right was the salinity. French oysters tend to be raised in the open sea, and are much saltier than the best oysters that are grown in sweeter, estuarine water, which we had in abundance in Ireland. In England we are better at growing the native oyster, *Ostrea edulis*, which at its best is delectable and unbeatable.

One of the more bizarre oysters you may come across is the *huître verte de Marennes*. These oysters are put into shallow *claires*, or pits, which are periodically dried out and left naked to the rain and sun. The soil takes in oxygen which encourages a green algal growth, which in turn not only colours the oysters but gives them a very particular (and pleasant) taste.

The cheapest French oysters, the *fines de claires*, usually have the thinnest meat, while the best are called *spéciales*, infinitely fatter and tastier. The difference here is the density at which the oyster *parcs* are stocked. It's all common sense really. The more oysters there are to eat the food, the less fat they will be. Some French oysters are quite frankly unacceptable. To struggle with a knife, risking life and limb, only to be confronted by a miniscule oyster is not my idea of a joke, so beware.

How to choose an oyster

- Oysters must be bought alive. They deteriorate rapidly once dead and can be quite toxic to the human stomach. By law, they have to come from either grade A water, or B, when they must be passed through a UV (ultraviolet) filtration system to kill any harmful bacteria that might be absorbed.

- A live oyster will be tightly shut. If it is at all open, it should close when touched. They need to be kept cool, as this slows down their metabolism, and stored cup-side down in the refrigerator, where they will keep for a few days. In order to appreciate them at their best, you should eat them straight away, as they tend to lose their liquor after a while.

- They should feel heavy, and sound full if you tap the shell.

- The native oyster is at its best during the winter, and is rounder in shape. It is traditionally eaten when there is an 'R' in the month; during the summer when it reproduces it becomes milky and unpalatable. Oddly, the Pacific oyster is eaten year round, despite becoming milky during the late summer as it nears the spawning season.

Season: Native, September-April; Pacific, all year round.
Price: £££ (Native) ££ (Pacific)

NATIVE OYSTER

ROCK OYSTER

Palourde, Carpet-shell Clam★★

Venerupis decussata
French: Palourde, Clovisse
Italian: Vongola verace
Spanish: Almeja fina
Portuguese: Ameijoa-boa
German: Teppichmuschel

Although strictly speaking they are called carpet-shell clams in English, this is not really current usage and you are better off using the French word *palourde*. These are excellent smallish clams, with attractive striated shells and a meat of great tenderness inside. They are excellent raw but can be cooked in many ways. The attractive Manilla clam, *Tapes philipbinarum*, is now extensively

PALOURDE

farmed and sold as palourdes. They are both excellent grilled with Maître d'Hôtel butter (see page 234).
    Season: All year round.
    Price: ££

Praire, Warty Venus★

Venus verrucosa
French: Praire
Italian: Tartufo di mare
Spanish: Verigueto
Portuguese: Pé de burro
German: Venusmuschel

These, too, have a correct English name, but who on earth is going to go into a fish shop and ask, 'Got any warty venus, mate?'! No, let's carry on irritating the Europhobes among us and call them *praires*. A little like a giant cockle, they are a really excellent species, well worth trying, and are best eaten raw. The Italians have given it due respect by calling it the sea truffle – a little over the top perhaps – and sometimes serve them with linguine.
    Season: Summer
    Price: ££

Queen Scallop★♥

Chlamys opercularis
French: Pétoncle, Vanneau
Italian: Canastrello liscio
Spanish: Volandeira
Portuguese: Vieira
German: Kamm-Muschel

Small and sweet, both to eat and to look at, queen scallops – also known familiarly as queenies – are now farmed in Scotland and are quite widely available in the big cities. Although less substantial than king scallops, they are excellent and more affordable. They are extremely pretty, with their pert little coral and delicate shell, and have the same sweet subtlety as their larger cousins. They are good grilled with Maître d'Hôtel butter (see page 234), which is how they are often served in France.
    Season: All year round.
    Price: ££

PRAIRE

Razorshell, Razor clam, Razors★

Solen marginatus
French: Couteau
Italian: Cappa lunga, Cannolicchio
Spanish: Navaja, Longueirón
Portuguese: Longueirão, Faca
German: Meerscheiden, Scheiden-Muschel

Rude things, razors, and impossible to fish. They used to be found quite frequently on beaches (when I was young, anyway), and look just like an old-style strop razor. The first time I realised they were edible was in Galicia, where eating shellfish seems to be a major occupation. Plates of fabulously fresh clams and langoustines, and even the odd little *percebe* (goose necked barnacle) were often joined by the immodest razor.
    They can be found in the intertidal zone at low tide, but have a habit of shooting deep down into the sand, which makes catching them tricky. If you're going a-razoring, take some carpet slippers to tread softly and a load of fine salt, which you pour down the hole in the sand where you suspect a razor may be. The salt should make the razor surrender but you may still need something to hook it out of the sand.
    Season: All year round.
    Price: ££

Scallop, King or Pilgrim★★♥

Pecten maximus
French: Coquille St Jacques
Italian: Ventaglio-pettine maggiore
Spanish: Viera
Portuguese: Viera
German: Kamm-Muschel, Pilger-Muschel

Scallops are a delight – sweet, tender and pleasingly well designed. When in sea water they have one almost unbearably endearing habit. They dance. By snapping their shells shut, scallops push themselves along, moving quickly through the water with graceful leaps and bounds, escaping the enemy and then settling once again on the sea floor. They have another even more endearing characteristic. They taste divine.

The best scallops are bought live, on the shell, but just how lively they are will depend on how they have been fished. The finest scallops of all are caught by divers, and are positively mollycoddled compared to the dredged fish one often finds. There is a bit of a geographic divide here. The west coast of Scotland has become the source of the nation's finest scallops. There is a network of divers who, winter, spring, summer and autumn, in weather foul and pleasant, continue to try and satisfy the growing demand for these top-quality scallops. Many of them are ex-oil-rig divers seeking a quieter life!

If you can get hold of live scallops, make sure you cook them quickly to savour that perfect sweetness. Inside

VERNI

the shell (see page 194 on how to shell and prepare), a thousand eyes on a frilly edge, and shiny red roe sit around the solid chunk of muscle which is the edible centrepiece of the whole thing.

Scallops tend to get somewhat abused by mankind. If you buy them off the shell, beware. Particularly plump, pure-white scallops have often been soaked in water, whereas a pure, unsoaked fresh scallop looks slightly off-white. Soaking plumps up the flesh and detracts completely from all that is good about it: taste, texture and cookability.

The shell itself is oozing with religious significance and has become closely associated with the legend of St James, Sant Iago, to whom the cathedral in Santiago de Compostela is dedicated. This also explains why the French call scallops *coquilles St Jacques*, St James's shells. The pilgrims, who came from as far away as Britain, would wear scallop-shaped badges as they followed the famous trail to Compostela.

The story goes like this. When the body of St James was being returned to Galicia, borne by a boat with 'neither oars, nor sails', it passed a village called Padron, where a wedding was taking place. While frolicking on the sands with his friends, the bridegroom was suddenly dragged into the sea by his panicky horse. Much to everyone's astonishment, they surfaced beside the ship carrying St James and his followers who proceeded, as Christians so often do, to preach the Gospel, telling Senor X that it was the power of God that had saved him. He then promptly converted to Christianity, was baptised, and returned to the shore where his friends were amazed to see both him and his horse covered in scallop shells. They all promptly became Christians, and this is how the nearby Santiago de Compostela became such an important centre of pilgrimage.

When you come across a scallop, you should try its sweet-tasting flesh cooked in as minimalist a way as possible. Cut the meat through the middle horizontally, season lightly and sear for a mere 30 seconds on each side. Serve with a squeeze of lemon. You might like to do the same with a frozen scallop one day and note the difference. I personally think that scallops are

better for not being cooked in any liquid at all, but many might disagree. Allow 4–6 per person, depending upon size, but at all costs avoid frozen scallops. Also never buy them if they have been cut and soaked in water.
Season: All year round.
Price: £££

Sea Urchin★★♥

Paracentrotus lividus, Echinus esculentus
French: Oursin
Italian: Riccio di mare
Spanish: Erizo de mar
Portuguese: Ouriço-do-mar
German: Seeigel
Japanese: Uni

Walking along the wild clifftops of western Ireland will, I think, turn your thoughts to matters poetic: to Yeats and Synge perhaps, and possibly not to sea urchin gonads. But if the salt and iodine work their magic on your appetite, you would be well advised to seek them out, for here lives the purple sea urchin, *Paracentrotus lividus*, whose gonads are particularly tasty.

Sea urchin roe is, to my mind, one of the most exquisite things to come from the sea and this species, native to the rocky coasts of Ireland and Brittany, is among the best. And to their great cost, too. The fishing of the sea urchin has been poorly regulated and in Ireland the annual yield has dropped from 500 to 10 tonnes per annum. In Chile, too, the situation is just as bleak. Thousands of people have been laid off as sea urchin stocks have collapsed from overfishing.

You can't eat the whole of the inside, but open the shell carefully (see page 194) and drain the juice through a small sieve and you should clearly see the gonads – orange in females and more yellow in males – which can be gently scooped out and eaten. The roe tastes lightly, not overpoweringly, of iodine.

The larger whitish, short-spined sea urchins (*Echinus esculentus*) you sometimes see for sale in the UK taste alarmingly strong, so buy the purple or, if you ever see them, the small, long-spined, green sea urchins that are fished in Brittany and cost a fortune.

I once found an excellent supplier in Ireland who regularly sent out sea urchins so fresh that their spines were still undulating. A famously starred French restaurant decided to offer them as an *amuse-gueule*, served in the shell, with the roe sitting prettily on a bed of scrambled eggs. A very serious-looking customer, ostentatiously placing his *Guide Michelin* on the table, took the plunge and chomped his way through the whole thing, including the shell (spines removed). He didn't stay for long, poor man, and rushed into the loo, appearing some minutes later looking greener but wiser. He wasn't charged for the meal. It may seem a meagre part of the animal but it is, I emphasise, the roe rather than the shell which is to be eaten.

In Sicily it is served simply with spaghetti and olive oil but sea urchin is at its best when eaten raw. At La Tante Claire restaurant in London, Pierre Koffmann's scrambled eggs and roe is wonderful, or you can use the roe to make a sauce, adding it to a hollandaise, for example. It never needs to be more than warmed through. Japanese shops sometimes sell fresh cleaned roe but supplies are becoming difficult. You can keep a sea urchin for three or four days in the fridge.

Sea urchin roe is at its best during a full moon. Females tend to cover themselves up with seaweed, so next time you're diving you'll know which ones to pick.

Season: September to March.
Price: £££

Soft-shell Clam

Various spp.
French: Mye
Italian: Vongola molle
Spanish: Almeja de rio
Portuguese: Clama de areia
German: Sandklaffmuschel

Geoduck
Panopea generosa

Steamer clam
Mya arenaria

Despite their names, soft-shell clams have brittle rather than soft shells. The geoduck – pronounced gooey-duck, by the way – can weigh an enormous 4kg (9 lb) and is an American speciality. The rather lewd and long syphon found inside can be eaten raw, and makes excellent clam chowder, as well as being used traditionally in that all-American spectacle, the clam bake.

Steamer clams, often called soft-shell clams in their own right, can be found in Europe but are native to the east coast of America. They are particularly common in New England and the Chesapeake Bay, but have found their way to the west coast of America where they are greatly appreciated fried, stuffed and grilled as well as steamed.

Season: All year round.
Price: ££

Surf Clam

Spisula solidissima
French: Mactre solide
Spanish: Escupiña
German: Dickschalige Trogmuschel

These are quite similar to hardshell clams, but with a whiter shell and a slightly more elongated body. They are less fine to eat, and are found in small quantities in Scotland.

Season: Winter.
Price: ££

Telline, Wedge Shell, Coquina Clam

Donax trunculus
French: Telline, Olive de mer
Italian: Tellina
Spanish: Coquina, Tallarina
Portuguese: Cadelhina

Tellines are small, smooth-shelled bivalves found mainly in the South of France. They live in sand and are fished by an army of locals using a very simple shellfish rake called a *tellinière*. Over the past few years the supply of *tellines* has increased dramatically, due to the number of fishermen who can no longer make a living from the sea turning to *telline* fishing instead. Along much of the Languedoc coast, licences, complete with photos, are now issued, but *telline* fraud is rife.

Season: All year round.
Price: ££

Venus Clam

Veneridae spp.
French: Venus
Italian: Vongola
Spanish: Almeja
Portuguese: Cadelinha
German: Klaffmuschel

Venus clams are found quite commonly in Europe and come almost exclusively from the French Atlantic coast. They are cheap, adaptable and fairly small shellfish that go well with pasta. But beware, they can be quite sandy inside, so try and filter any sauce made from them. They don't keep well, so eat them straight away.

Season: All year round.
Price: ££

Verni

Callista chione
French: Verni, Pelote
Spanish: Almejón brillante
Portuguese: Concha fina

A beautiful clam with a lascivious red tongue (illustration on page 199) . You sometimes find them in a *plateau de fruits de mer* and they are very French, but not desperately good to eat.

Season: Summer.
Price: ££

Spaghetti alle Vongole

Spaghetti with Clams

Spaghetti alle vongole reminds me of my first trip to the Amalfi coast and the thrill of discovering a place so dramatically beautiful, where good food could be had, as long as one steered clear of the main tourist spots, for a reasonable price – essential to a backpacking student. I lived on plates of *spaghetti alle vongole* and other maritime pastas, followed by sweet peaches or muscat grapes.

SERVES 4

2kg (4½ lb) small clams, such as palourdes or venus clams
1 onion, chopped
2 garlic cloves, chopped
3 tablespoons olive oil, plus a little extra
450g (1 lb) tomatoes, peeled, de-seeded and chopped
1 tablespoon tomato purée
2 tablespoons chopped fresh parsley
½ teaspoon caster sugar
350–450g (12–16 oz) thin spaghetti
salt and pepper

Scrub the clams under running water, discarding any that will not close when firmly rapped against a hard surface. Pour water to a depth of 1cm (½ inch) into a pan large enough to hold the clams. Heat until boiling. Add the clams and cover tightly. Shake over the heat for a few minutes until all the clams have opened. Discard any that refuse to open.

Take the clams out of the pan and boil the cooking liquid down hard, until reduced by half. Strain to remove any grit and then reserve. Set aside 12 clams on their shells and pick the clam meat out of the remaining shells.

Soften the onion and garlic in the olive oil over a medium heat without browning, until translucent. Add the tomatoes, tomato purée, parsley, sugar, pepper and a little salt (not too much, as the clam juices may be rather salty). Pour in the reserved clam-cooking liquid. Boil down until the sauce is thick and pulpy. Taste and adjust the seasoning.

Meanwhile, cook the spaghetti in plenty of lightly salted boiling water until *al dente*. Drain, toss with a splash of olive oil and keep warm. Stir the shelled clams into the sauce and re-heat gently. Pour the sauce over the spaghetti and scatter over the reserved clams in their shells. Serve immediately.

Manhattan Clam Chowder

New England chowders are white, creamy, soothing soup-stews but the Manhattan chowder is red, zesty and invigorating. Quite a different kettle of clams. In America they would probably use the large quahog but here you will have to settle for the largest clams your fishmonger can offer – probably *palourdes*.

SERVES 4

1.35kg (3 lb) large clams, such as palourdes
1–1.15 litres (1¾–2 pints) Fish Stock
    (see page 308)
110g (4 oz) streaky bacon, chopped
1 large onion, chopped
2 celery sticks, chopped
sunflower oil
1 large potato, diced
2 leeks, thickly sliced
2 fresh thyme sprigs
1 bay leaf
400g (14 oz) tin of chopped tomatoes
3 tablespoons chopped fresh parsley
salt and pepper

Scrub the clams under running water, discarding any that refuse to close when sharply rapped. Pour 1cm (½ inch) of water into a pan large enough to take all the clams. Bring to the boil and tip in the clams. Cover tightly and shake over a high heat for a few minutes until they are all opened. Discard any that stay stubbornly shut. Strain the cooking juices to remove any grit, then add enough fish stock to make up to 1.15 litres (2 pints). Remove the clams from their shells.

Fry the bacon over a high heat in a small, non-stick frying pan until crisp and browned. Remove the pan from the heat and lift out the bacon with a slotted spoon. Drain on kitchen paper and set aside.

Pour the bacon fat into a large pan and fry the onion and celery in it until soft and lightly browned, adding a little sunflower oil if necessary. Add the potato, leeks, thyme and bay leaf and stir for a minute. Add the diluted clam liquid, tomatoes, parsley, salt and pepper. Bring to the boil and simmer until the potato is tender. Taste and adjust the seasoning.

Before serving, stir the clams into the soup. Simmer for about a minute to heat through. Serve the bacon scattered over the top.

American Clam Hash

Alternatives: cockles, palourdes

Most people have heard of corned beef hash but, for non-Americans, clam hash is a new treat – soft-fried potatoes seasoned with the salty sea scent of clams, then finished with melting cheese and crumbled crisp bacon. It is wonderful, homely, comfort food, the kind of thing that I find irresistible, especially when the weather is less than clement. For this recipe, buy the biggest clams you can find. The ratio of meat to shell works more in your favour.

Make clam hash for the Sunday brunch to end all Sunday brunches, or take it to the other end of the day, to soothe you after all that hard work. To turn it into a meal that's even more down-home delicious, top each portion with one (or more if you're hungry) fried or poached egg.

SERVES 4 AS A HEFTY FIRST COURSE

1.35kg (3 lb) large clams
60g (2 oz) unsalted butter
3 tablespoons chopped onion
700g (1½ lb) firm main-crop potatoes, e.g. Cara,
    cut into 1cm (½-inch) cubes and cooked until
    just tender
freshly grated nutmeg
cayenne pepper
2 tablespoons double cream
60g (2 oz) Cheddar cheese, grated
4 bacon rashers, crisply grilled and crumbled
salt and pepper

Scrub the clams under running water, discarding any that don't close when sharply rapped. Pour about 2cm (¾ inch) of water into a large pan and bring up to the boil. Add the clams, cover and shake over a high heat for a few minutes, until opened. Discard any that remain stubbornly closed. Scoop the clams out into a colander (you might want to save the cooking liquid to use as a light clam stock – strain and boil down, then freeze for later use). When the clams have cooled a little, extract the clam meat and chop roughly.

Melt half the butter in a wide frying pan over a high heat. Add the onion and a little salt and sauté for 2 minutes, until the onion is beginning to colour. Add the remaining butter and, when melted, add the potatoes and clams and season with black pepper, nutmeg and a pinch of cayenne. Stir, then press the mixture down into the pan smoothly with a spatula. Leave to cook over a moderate heat, without disturbing, for about 8–10 minutes, until browned underneath. Now stir the mixture, scraping up the crusty brown bits from the bottom of the pan. Press down again and then spoon over the cream and scatter over the cheese. Cover and leave for a few minutes until the cheese has melted. Scatter over the bacon and serve immediately.

Moules Marinières

Alternatives: cockles, palourdes

The sight of a big bowl of steaming *moules marinières* is a joy indeed: the gleaming black of the shells, flashes of orange, wisps of steam furling upwards, the scent of the sea and the promise of a messy pleasure to come. Once the mussels are cleaned (since you won't have a chance to strain the liquid, this is doubly essential) and the onion chopped, it takes only a few minutes to put together. Serve with sturdy hunks of bread to mop up the juices.

If you want to upgrade your *moules*, stir a few spoonfuls of crème fraîche into the juices instead of (or as well as!) the butter.

SERVES 4

2kg (4½ lb) mussels
2 onions, chopped
2 garlic cloves, chopped
4 tablespoons chopped fresh parsley
200ml (7 fl oz) dry white wine
150ml (¼ pint) water
30g (1 oz) unsalted butter
salt and pepper

Clean the mussels (see page 192), then rinse them one more time, just to be safe. Put the onions, garlic, 3 tablespoons of the parsley, wine, water and some pepper into a pan large enough to take all the mussels as well. Bring up to the boil, reduce the heat and simmer for about 15 minutes. Raise the heat so that the liquid is boiling, tip in the mussels, clamp on the lid and shake over the heat for a few minutes until all the mussels have opened. Discard any that steadfastly refuse to open.

Scoop the mussels out into a warm tureen or bowl and keep warm. Quickly boil down the liquid left in the pan for 2–3 minutes. Whisk in the butter, then taste and adjust the seasoning. Pour the liquid over the mussels, sprinkle with the remaining parsley and serve.

Mussels with Tomato, Saffron and Coriander

Alternatives: cockles, clams

The natural sweetness of mussels goes spectacularly well with saffron and coriander in this soupy mussel stew. Indeed, our little group of household testers fell on the dish with reckless enthusiasm and copies of the recipe were issued to one and all. Serve it in big bowls, with plenty of napkins for sticky fingers and soup spoons to scoop up the scarlet juices. If you make the tomato sauce and clean the mussels in advance, the final cooking is just a matter of minutes.

SERVES 4 AS A MAIN COURSE,

6 AS A STARTER

1.35kg (3 lb) mussels
generous pinch of saffron strands
2 tablespoons hot water
1 large onion, chopped
3 garlic cloves, chopped
1 teaspoon coriander seeds, crushed
3 tablespoons olive oil
2 x 400g (14 oz) tins of tomatoes
1 tablespoon tomato purée
1 teaspoon sugar
¼ teaspoon dried chilli flakes
3 tablespoons roughly chopped fresh coriander
salt and pepper

Clean the mussels (see page 192). Soak the saffron threads in the hot water.

To make the tomato sauce, gently cook the onion, garlic and coriander seeds in the oil, without browning, until tender. Add the tomatoes, tomato purée, sugar, chilli, salt and pepper and bring to the boil. Simmer, breaking up the tomatoes with a spoon, until very thick. Stir in the saffron and its water and simmer for a further 2 minutes or so. Taste and adjust the seasoning. Reserve until needed.

Put enough water to give a 1cm (½ inch) depth in a large pan and bring to the boil. Add the mussels, cover and cook as usual (see page 193). Keep the opened mussels warm. Quickly strain their cooking liquid to remove grit, then stir it into the tomato sauce. Bring the sauce back to the boil and simmer for a minute or two. Stir in the coriander leaves, pour into a warmed serving bowl or tureen and pile the mussels on top. Serve immediately.

Stuffed Mussels with Ginger, Coriander and Garlic

Alternatives: cockles, clams

An updating of a well-used idea, and a fine example of 'East meets West' cooking. These mussels are stuffed with a mixture of breadcrumbs, butter and garlic (so far, so Frenchish) but the dish is gingered up, literally, with ginger and coriander leaf (over to the East). Not the speediest of recipes to concoct, but your patience will be amply rewarded.

SERVES 4

900g (2 lb) mussels
3 shallots, finely chopped
4 garlic cloves, finely chopped
150g (5 oz) butter, melted
2.5cm (1-inch) piece of fresh root ginger, finely chopped
3 tablespoons finely chopped fresh coriander
3 tablespoons finely chopped fresh parsley
75g (2½ oz) fine dry breadcrumbs
salt and pepper

Clean the mussels (see page 192), and open them by whatever method you prefer (see page 193), taking great care not to overcook them. Once they are cooked, remove and discard the upper half of each shell.

To make the stuffing, gently cook the shallots and garlic in 2 tablespoons of the melted butter until tender, without browning. Mix with the remaining ingredients. Fill the shells with the stuffing, covering the orange flesh of the mussels well. Cover and keep cool until needed.

To cook, whizz under a thoroughly preheated grill until brown and bubbling. Eat instantly.

Mussel Soufflé

Alternatives: clams, oysters

The discreet use of curry powder with mussels is a French fancy, and works very well as long as it is not heavyhanded. Here it adds a mild impact to a light-as-air, hold-your-breath soufflé. A dish to send your guests into ecstasies.

SERVES 4–6

1.35kg (3 lb) mussels
150ml (¼ pint) dry white wine
1 onion, sliced
2 fresh parsley sprigs
juice of ½ lemon
juice of ½ orange
45g (1½ oz) butter
45g (1½ oz) plain flour
1 teaspoon mild or medium curry powder
85ml (3 fl oz) double cream
4 eggs, separated
salt and pepper

Clean the mussels (see page 192). Place the wine, onion, parsley, lemon and orange juice in a wide, deep pan and bring to the boil. Add the mussels and cook in the usual way (see page 193). Once done, remove the meat from the shells and reserve. Strain the cooking liquor and measure out 200ml (7 fl oz).

Melt the butter in a pan and stir in the flour and curry powder. Stir over a gentle heat for about a minute. Off the heat, gradually stir in the measured cooking liquor, a little at a time, to make a smooth sauce. Enrich with the cream, then simmer quietly, stirring every now and then, for 5 minutes, until very thick. Cool slightly. Process two-thirds of the cooked mussels with a couple of tablespoons of sauce, then add the rest of the sauce, along with the egg yolks, salt and pepper.

Preheat the oven to 200°C/400°F/Gas Mark 6. Just before cooking the soufflé, whisk the egg whites until they form soft peaks. Fold into the mussel mixture, with the reserved whole mussels. Spoon into a buttered 18cm (7-inch) soufflé dish, filling it no more than two-thirds full. Rush it into the oven and bake for 25–30 minutes, until well risen and nicely browned. Give the dish a little shake – if the soufflé wobbles alarmingly, it needs another 3–4 minutes.

Baked Oysters with Apples

One of the most memorable feasts of my life took place on the Cotentin peninsula, at the home of an oyster-grower. That morning, we'd piled on to the back of a tractor and splashed our way out to the oyster beds. Ravenous from the sea air and early start, we entered his barn to catch a glimpse of a truly beautiful sight. The oyster-sorting machinery and rusting farm equipment had been pushed back and, in the centre, stood a table covered with red and white checked cloth, bearing a jug of striped tulips, a pitcher of local cider, a plate of gold and red pears from his tree, another of lemon wedges, and a mountain of fresh oysters. There was crusty fresh bread and sweet, home-made butter. After we'd gorged ourselves on fresh oysters, the oyster-grower's wife brought in a succession of cooked oyster dishes, and we finished with goat's cheese from the neighbouring farm, eaten with those perfectly ripe pears.

Amongst the cooked dishes was this one, of lightly baked oysters perched on top of apple rings, kept moist with crème fraîche. Salt and sweet and smooth all in one mouthful. Serve with good bread to mop up the juices.

as many oysters as you can afford, opened and off the shell (see page 193)
eating apples
butter
crème fraîche, **or double cream sharpened with a dash of lemon juice**
salt and pepper

Preheat the oven to 250°C/475°F/Gas Mark 9. Core the apples and slice into discs 5mm (¼ inch) thick – you need one disc per oyster. Butter an ovenproof dish that is just large enough to take the apple slices in a single layer. Alternatively, use individual dishes, again just large enough to take the allotted number of apple slices. Arrange the apples in the dish(es), season lightly and cover with foil. Cook for 7 minutes.

Sit an oyster in the centre of each apple slice and top with a generous teaspoonful of crème fraîche and some salt and pepper. Return to the oven for 4–5 minutes. Serve immediately.

Oyster Po'boy Sandwich

Alternative: scallops

In New Orleans, where oysters are relatively cheap, this is a favourite lunchtime sandwich, particularly when the weather is chilly and you need something sprightly to warm those bones. The oysters are deep-fried in a coat of cornmeal and then popped into a warm baguette and slathered with mayonnaise and Tabasco. Wonderful.

These days you can buy 'half baguettes', short versions of the long ones, which are ideal for these po'boys. Otherwise, cut a whole baguette into thirds.

PER PERSON

1 half baguette or one-third of a full-length
  baguette
6 oysters, opened and off the shell (see page
  193)
fine cornmeal (polenta) or seasoned plain flour
oil, for frying
Mayonnaise (see page 310)
2–3 crisp lettuce leaves, shredded
1 small tomato, sliced
salt
Tabasco sauce

Preheat the oven to 200°C/400°F/Gas Mark 6. Split the baguette in half lengthways. Clamp the halves together, wrap in foil and heat through in the oven for 10–15 minutes. Meanwhile, toss the oysters in the cornmeal or seasoned flour, coating evenly. Fry them in hot oil until golden brown.

Spread each half of the hot loaf generously with mayonnaise. Top one half with lettuce, then the fried oysters and finally the tomato slices. Season with salt and a few shakes of Tabasco and clamp the top on quickly. Eat immediately, while still warm.

Oysters in Champagne Sauce

Alternatives: large mussels, clams

A grand-sounding way of dishing up oysters, in a creamy sauce flavoured with champagne (or a high-quality *méthode champenoise*). They can be served either in the shell, which looks pretty, or in a hollowed-out brioche, which I prefer – the combination is sublime.

SERVES 2–4

12 oysters
150ml (¼ pint) champagne
2 shallots, very finely chopped
150ml (¼ pint) double cream
salt and pepper
coarse sea salt (optional)
chopped fresh chervil, to garnish

For the Brioches (optional):
2–4 individual brioches
butter, melted

Open the oysters (see page 193). Strain and reserve the liquor. Save the lower shells, if using. Put the champagne and shallots into a pan and boil hard until the liquid is reduced by about half. Now add the cream and boil again until reduced by half, to give a thick, rich sauce. Stir in the oyster liquor, taste and season.

To serve in the shell, make a bed of coarse sea salt in an ovenproof dish and nestle the half shells in it (this is just to keep them steady). Return each raw oyster to its shell, pour over the sauce and pop under a preheated grill until the sauce bubbles vigorously – a couple of minutes and no more. Sprinkle with a little chervil and serve.

If serving in brioches, slice a lid from the top of each one and pull out some of the crumb to form a sturdy bowl. Brush inside and out with melted butter and bake for 5–10 minutes at 200°C/400°F/Gas Mark 6, until lightly browned and crisp. When the sauce is just about ready, slip the oysters into it and cook for about a minute. Spoon the sauce and oysters into the brioche cases, scatter with chervil and eat immediately.

Huntingdon Fried Scallops

Alternatives: Queen scallops, oysters

Quite what this recipe has to do with Huntingdon I don't know, for there is little in the way of prose and preamble to the often excellent recipes in *British Cookery*, edited by Lizzie Boyd (Christopher Helm), from which it comes, with a few minor adjustments. However, if I can tell you nothing of its origin, I can still assure you that the scallops, coated in a crisp, savoury crust, are sensationally good.

SERVES 4 AS A FIRST COURSE

1 tablespoon olive oil
juice of 1 lemon
1 tablespoon chopped fresh parsley
8–12 large scallops
75g (2½ oz) ham, very finely chopped
75g (2½ oz) fresh white breadcrumbs
30g (1 oz) Parmesan cheese, freshly grated
plain flour, seasoned
1 egg, lightly beaten
sunflower or vegetable oil, for deep-frying
salt and pepper
lemon wedges, to serve

Mix the olive oil with the lemon juice, parsley and some salt and pepper. Stir in the scallops and leave to marinate for 30 minutes.

Mix the ham with the breadcrumbs and cheese.

Drain the scallops, coat in seasoned flour and then dip them in the egg. Now coat with the ham, cheese and breadcrumb mixture, pressing it on firmly. Leave to set for half an hour in the fridge, if time permits.

Deep-fry in hot oil (about 185°C/360°F or when a cube of bread dropped into the oil fizzes violently and starts to brown immediately) until browned and crisp. Drain briefly on kitchen paper and then serve with lemon wedges.

Warm Seared Scallop and Black Pudding Salad

Alternative: Queen scallops

Scallops and black pudding . . . diametric opposites, it seems. Heaven and earth, light and dark, luxury and cheap fare. And yet, brought together in this quickly made warm salad, they marry well. Try it and see.

SERVES 4

12 scallops
60ml (2 fl oz) olive oil
8 slices of black pudding, weighing about 110g
    (4 oz) in total
1 tablespoon red wine vinegar
½ teaspoon Dijon mustard
125g (4½ oz) pack of mixed baby salad leaves
salt and pepper
lemon wedges, to serve

Separate the scallop corals from the whites. If the whites are thick, cut each one into two discs horizontally.

Brush a heavy-based frying pan or griddle with a little of the olive oil and heat over a high heat until it is ferociously and disconcertingly hot – allow a good 3–5 minutes. Lay the scallop discs and corals on the pan, give them about 20 seconds and then turn them over. Leave for another 20 seconds and that's about it. Take them out and keep warm. Add the remaining oil to the pan, allow it to heat through and then add the black pudding. Cook for a minute or two on each side, to brown, then lift out and keep warm with the scallops. Draw the pan off the heat and let it cool for 2–3 minutes.

Stir in the vinegar (at arm's length, as it may spit back at you), mustard (don't worry if it doesn't mix in easily – do what you can and then you'll find it disappears as you toss the salad) and some salt and pepper. Pour this dressing over the salad greens, toss quickly and then pile on to four plates. Dot the scallops and black pudding over the salad greens and serve immediately, with lemon wedges.

Steamed Scallops with Lemongrass

Alternatives: Queen scallops, small clams

Despite their sweet, delicate flavour and fine reputation, scallops can hold their own with strong oriental flavours such as garlic, chilli and ginger. Indeed, they revel in them. This, then, is a marvellous first course, or light main course if appetite is diminished, which will send a thrill of delight through the tastebuds. Guaranteed to perk up the most jaded of palates.

SERVES 2 AS A FIRST COURSE

4–6 large scallops on the shell or 12 queenies on
   the shell
1 fresh lemongrass stem
½ teaspoon grated fresh root ginger
¼–½ fresh red chilli, de-seeded and chopped
1 garlic clove, finely chopped
1 tablespoon sesame oil
1 tablespoon grapeseed or other bland oil
1 tablespoon sake or dry sherry
1 tablespoon fish sauce

Clean the scallops if necessary (see page 194). Cut the top off the stem of lemongrass, leaving just the lower 10cm (4 inches) or so. Discard the upper portion and bruise the lower part with the end of a rolling pin or a wooden mallet. Trim off the base and remove and discard the outer layer of leaves. Slice the soft inner stem very thinly and mix with the ginger, chilli, garlic, oils, sake or sherry and fish sauce. Set aside for an hour.

Half an hour before you wish to eat, sprinkle each of the scallops with a little of the marinade, being sure to include a few shreds of ginger, chilli, garlic and lemongrass. Arrange the scallops on a steamer basket and steam for 6 minutes if they are large or 4 minutes if they are the small queenies. Lift the shells from the steamer without tipping – you want to lose as little as possible of all those juices – and serve immediately.

Spaghetti con Ricci di Mare

One evening in Palermo, we were whisked out of the city centre and along the shore to a seaside suburb packed with little restaurants specialising in seafood. We were in for one of Sicily's most prized treats. Set back from the main drag, down a small back street, stood a little shabby restaurant that is famed, amongst those *Palermitani* in the know, for its cooking. There our feast began with this dish of spaghetti studded with sea urchin roe and parsley. Marvellous.

You shouldn't really sprinkle grated Parmesan over this – it will be too strong and dominant when you want the iodine salty-sweetness of the roes to take star billing. Still, if it takes your fancy, who is going to know?

SERVES 4

8–12 large sea urchins (or more if you can
   afford it)
400g (14 oz) fine spaghetti
5 tablespoons extra virgin olive oil
3 garlic cloves, finely chopped
3 tablespoons chopped fresh parsley
salt and pepper

Open the sea urchins (see page 194) and scrape out the roes. Bring a large pan of salted water to the boil and add the spaghetti. Cook until *al dente*, then drain thoroughly.

Meanwhile, put the oil and garlic into a frying pan and place over a moderate heat. Fry for 3 or 4 minutes without letting the garlic brown. Draw off the heat but re-heat slightly when needed. Toss the garlic and oil with the pasta, parsley, pepper and a little salt, if needed. Tip into a serving dish and scatter the roes over. Serve immediately.

Crustaceans

Crustaceans have a protective outer layer, the exoskeleton or shell, which, although fine and dandy most of the time, becomes restrictive as the creature grows – for the simple reason that it stays the same size. This is why crustaceans have to shed their outer shells and spend a short time in a vulnerable soft-shell stage.

Most crustaceans are scavengers with foul habits. The esteemed and overly expensive lobster is a waspish creature, which readily eats its brothers, sisters, children even, when confined in tanks. This, by the way, is why you often see them with their claws firmly closed by elastic bands. At the other end of the scale size-wise is the equally vicious freshwater crayfish. Smaller still is the fiddly but delicious common shrimp.

One day it may be completely illegal to sell, eat or fish female 'berried' crustaceans. It should be. These are females with eggs attached to the underside of the tail, without whom there will be no future for crustaceans at all.

When buying, allow 500g (1 lb 2 oz) gross weight per person but remember that the percentage of actual meat can be as low as 15 per cent, so make sure to use the shell – in a sauce, for example – whenever possible.

Preparing Crustaceans

You will know, I suspect, that lobsters, crab and crayfish should be cooked alive. This is because once dead the flesh deteriorates rapidly and can become toxic. Although it is not known for certain if crustaceans feel pain, I think that common sense would suggest that they do. We are in duty bound to make them suffer as little as possible, and to many of you that will involve neither eating nor cooking them. Here are the more humane methods of dealing with a live crustacean as recommended by the RSPCA.

Lobster

Put the lobster(s) firmly into a large freezer, set to at least –18°C, and leave them there for 2 hours, to chill them into unconsciousness. They have a remarkable tolerance to cold but then I suppose they are used to it, down at the bottom of the sea – a thought that makes me feel less uncomfortable about their incarceration. It does take almost the full 2 hours before they become comatose enough to give up all movement.

Meanwhile, make a strong brine. Throw enormous amounts of salt (about 100g/3½ oz to every litre/1¾ pints of water) into a large pan of water and stir over a low heat until the salt has dissolved. Grab an egg (unboiled) and lay it gently in the water. If it floats merrily on the surface, the brine is salty enough. Bring the pan up to a rolling boil, then head off to the freezer and retrieve your lobster(s). Weigh each one quickly, drop them swiftly into the pan, clamp on the lid and bring back to the boil. To calculate cooking times (work it out on a per lobster basis, not collectively), allow 18 minutes for the first 500g (1 lb 2 oz) and an additional 11 minutes for every 500g (1 lb 2 oz) after that. When they are done, transformed to the familiar, beautiful brick-red colour of cooked lobster, lift them out and leave to cool.

Serve them soon after, split in half, with a big bowl of mayonnaise on the side. Or go for something a little more fancy . . .

An Easy Way with Lobster for the Timid

I don't mind freezing lobsters and crabs gently, then plunging them into boiling water, as described above. In the past, before I learnt to mend my ways, I was even brutal enough to plunge them straight into boiling water, but I draw the line at splitting them in half when they are still alive. The RSPCA declares that this is a sure, quick, painless way to dispatch them, but it is beyond me. My aim has never been that good anyway. Still, for some recipes the dastardly deed needs to be done. Halved lobsters that have not been cooked are what is called for and, rather than miss out altogether, I take the middle path by par-cooking them in boiling brine for a few minutes, so that they are well and truly sent on their way to the next world before I grapple with my cleaver.

Begin cooking your lobster(s) in the usual way, freezing them first, then dropping them into boiling brine (see above). Bring back to the boil and let the water bubble merrily for 4 minutes, then lift your lobsters out and drain thoroughly. When cool enough to handle, take a large knife, or better still a cleaver, and cut down right along the centre of the head and body, splitting the lobster into two neat halves. Now proceed with the recipe.

Crab

You can freeze your crabs to render them unconscious in much the same way as you should a lobster (see above).

Now for the cooking. Prepare a brine as for lobster (above), then bob that egg. Bring the pan up to the boil and slide in the crab(s). Bring back to a simmer and cook for 15 minutes for the first 500g (1 lb 2 oz), adding an extra 10 minutes for every extra 500g (1 lb 2 oz). Lift out of the pan when done and leave to cool.

The cold-water method

Some people recommend putting the crab or lobster into cold salted water and bringing it to the boil. This is no longer considered humane.

Crayfish

Smaller crustaceans die quickly in boiling water but placing them in a freezer for an hour or so puts them to sleep. The guts of crayfish can be bitter, so make sure that the fish are left for twenty-four hours or so without food before cooking to help to clear their system. Leave them in a damp box in the cool, covered with fresh herbs or nettles, and they will survive for several days. Don't keep them in tap water. When the crayfish are cooked, carefully remove the intestine using a sharp knife.

CRABS

Blue Crab, Soft-shell Crab**

Callinectes sapidus
French: Crabe bleu
Italian: Moleca (Venice)
Spanish: Cangrejo azul
Portuguese: Caranguejo azul
German: Blaukrabbe

One summer I drove around the suburbs of Maryland wearing a T-shirt with 'Good Humor' written on it selling ice-creams to the kids on the block. It was an odd experience. Most of them seemed to wear dental braces and I assumed that there must be something unpleasant in the local water until I was told about orthodontists. Maryland is soft-shell crab territory and this particular 'Good Humor' man, for that was what I was by day, developed a passion for these tender little crabs, the soft-shell stage of the blue crab, *Callinectes sapidus*.

They are seriously good to eat. At first bite it's a little disconcerting to munch into what clearly looks like a crab; you expect a crunch but there isn't one. What happens is this. Crabs are fished and kept in water tanks or 'floats' until they have moulted. Then, before the new shell begins to harden, they are hastily packed and shipped, still alive, around the country. Originally this was very much a local trade. But these days many are frozen, and can even be bought in the UK.

The blue crab has some endearing habits. Males and females moult about twenty times in their life but females have a final moult before they reach sexual maturity. The male crab, or jimmy, finds a mate and protectively leads her to a sheltered spot for a lengthy crab love session. At this stage they are known as 'doublers', with the male completely covering the female until copulation and the final moult is completed. The degree of protectiveness is quite unusual for a male crustacean (or for a male anything, come to that).

It's a tricky business dealing with soft-shell crabs. They die, they eat each other, they are subject to the vagaries of the climate, and must be carefully looked after in the fish pounds. If you're grabbed by the story, there is a marvellous book called *Beautiful Swimmers* by William Warner, which will tell you everything you need to know – and more – about soft-shell crabs. They are well worth a detour even if it means going to the States in July.

Season: (Fresh) summer, (frozen) all year round.
Price: £££
Fishing method: Pots.

Common or Edible Crab***

Cancer pagurus
French: Tourteau, Crabe dormeur
Italian: Granciporro, Favollo
Spanish: Cambero masero, Buey
Portuguese: Caranguejo moure
German: Taschenkrebs

Proust can stuff his *madeleines*. As a wee fish-loathing thing from the suburbs of London, I used to spend the summer holidays sailing around Torbay in a bright red dinghy my father had built. Sailing with children is a fair-weather thing, so we often spent the days trudging along the coast looking at the sea instead of being soaked by it. One rainy, windy day, we sat in a steamy old Volkswagen, munching and crunching a slightly warm, sweet-scented, perfectly boiled crab. Crabs haven't changed much since then, and if you've never eaten one, or never, God forbid, eaten a *fresh* crab sandwich, then you really haven't lived.

For all its charm, dressing a crab (see page 225) is a time-consuming job. You'll need picks, bowls, patience and restraint. It helps to have copious amounts of wine on hand, someone to talk to, or at least a major problem to sort out, for your hands could be busy for an hour or two.

Many people think that hen crabs (females) are sweeter but I think it wiser – especially if you're going to dress a crab – to go for a male or cock crab, whose claws and body are fuller and easier to clean. Hen crabs go well with *plateaux de fruits de mer* and are always cheaper than cock crabs.

The finest crabs in Britain are considered to come from the south coast and the Channel Islands, and thrive on rocky rather than sandy ground.

Crabs are mainly caught in pots that are laid with bait on the sea floor and pulled in every now and again to be emptied. When buying a live crab, firstly make sure that it actually is alive. Pick it up and it should be lively rather than droopy, and wave its claws around aggressively. Look at its feet and shell. If the toes are well worn or if the shell has signs of barnacles or the odd little wiggles that the Irish call 'German writing', then the crab will not have moulted recently and is likely to be fuller and meatier inside. When buying cooked crabs, be careful. Crabs cooked when well dead will not have their legs and feet tightly drawn in and should be avoided.

If you want to buy crab meat, be warned that frozen or pasteurised crab meat is nothing like the real thing. But, since crab meat deteriorates rapidly it may be the best option.

Allow 500g (1 lb 2 oz) gross weight per person, so a 1kg (2¼ lb) hen crab should feed two and a 2kg (4½ lb) cock crab four.

Season: All year round (apart from soft-shell stage in summer).
Price: ££
Fishing method: Pots, nets.

COMMON CRAB

Shore Crab

Carcinus maenas
French: Crabe vert
Italian: Carcino, Granchio
Spanish: Cangrejo de mar
Portuguese: Caranguejo morraceiro
German: Strandkrabbe

These are the small, dull green crabs that can be seen scuttling around harbours and beaches nationwide. An easy and fun thing to do with kids on a summer holiday is to go crabbing. Get a bit of old gut, fish, meat or something really rotten, tie it to a piece of string, then lean over the harbour wall (Looe in Cornwall is an excellent place for this), drop it in the water and wait for a bite. You're more than likely to catch a shore crab or two, aggressive little critters, that will make a particularly good crab soup (follow the Shrimp Soup recipe on page 244).

> **Season:** All year round.
> **Price:** £
> **Fishing method:** Pots.

Spider Crab★★

Maia squinado
French: Araignée de mer
Italian: Maia, Granseola
Spanish: Centolla
Portuguese: Santola
German: Troldkrabbe

We are a peculiar lot in Britain. We like to moan about foreigners taking *our* fish. But why is it that we so studiously ignore some of the finest species of fish in the sea? Spider crabs (spiders for short) are a case in point (illustration on page 222). We have a thriving export trade to Europe, taking huge quantities of crabs across the water to Spain and France. But look for a spider for sale in a fish shop over here, and you'll be hard pressed to find one.

Is it their taste? Unlikely, as they are sweet and gorgeous. Is it because they are a little fiddly, and fragile to boot? More likely, I think.

In the summer, when the mating season begins, spiders behave in a remarkable way. Mounds of them can be found on the sea floor, where they form an orgiastic pyramid with the soft-shelled, mating crabs shielded from danger by an outer layer of fully moulted crabs. So next time you're diving in the English Channel, cover your eyes when you see pulsating mounds of *Maia squinado*. Spider crabs can be used in the same way as the edible crab, although cleaning them is verging on the tedious.

> **Season:** All year round (except soft-shell stage in summer).
> **Price:** ££
> **Fishing method:** Pots.

CRAYFISH

Another confusing category here. Firstly, you could be talking freshwater or seawater crayfish. And if you're talking sea, then you could also call them crawfish or rock lobster. However, if you're in Louisiana, crawfish are freshwater crayfish. To tell which is which, look at the length: freshwater crayfish are small, often only 7.5–10cm (3–4 inches) long. Rock lobsters, on the other hand, are longer, lobster-sized animals.

Freshwater Crayfish

French: Ecrevisse
Italian: Gambero di fiume
Spanish: Cangrejo de rio
Portuguese: Lagostim-do-rio
German: Flusskrebs

European crayfish★★★
Astacus astacus

Signal crayfish★
Pacifasticus leniusculus

Turkish crayfish★
Astacus leptodactylus

Louisiana swamp crayfish★
Procambarus clarkii

Marron (Aus.)★★★
Cherax tenuimanus

Yabbie (Aus.)★★
Cherax destructor

Astacus astacus has been virtually wiped out from its native European waters by the combined effects of pollution and disease. Although there are over 300 species of freshwater crayfish (illustration on page 222) found worldwide we see but a few, and in Europe crayfish from Turkey and the USA have supplied the markets for many years. I am intrigued by two species from Australia: firstly, *Astacopsis gouldi* for its enormity – it can weigh up to 6kg (13 lb) – and secondly, the marron, so called because of its gentle maroon colour. I have yet to savour this reportedly delicious crustacean, but it is beginning to be farmed outside Australia and will, I suspect, feature more strongly in the years to come.

When I first started working with fish, melba toast was still to be seen in restaurants, and freshwater crayfish were the domain of romantic *auberges* in rural France. It all changed when the Turks started exporting huge quantities of crayfish from Lake Van, and the hungry market could breathe once more. Much of the demand comes from Scandinavia, where eating crayfish is a venerable and much loved summer pastime. The idea is to watch the sun set, gulp some vodka and eat cold crayfish scented with dill, followed by some beer, and so on until you can neither eat, drink nor stand any longer. These days, most of the crayfish sold are frozen, pre-cooked and ready to go, so you miss out on all that boiling, picking and socialising (but leglessness is still as popular as ever).

A few adventurous souls have started farming crayfish in the UK and have produced a small quantity of magnificent but expensive crayfish. There are even some being caught in Hyde Park, by Royal Command. However, the story isn't an entirely happy one. One of the species chosen, the signal crayfish, grows quickly to maturity but has infected the native fish with a destructive disease, pushing them towards virtual extinction.

Crayfish should be cooked alive, but you have the added complication of removing the gut which, if eaten, can taste bitter. Twisting the tail of a live crayfish to remove the intestine is, I think, no longer acceptable practice, and if it bothers you, you may like to remove the gut after cooking instead, by cutting the top side of the body with a sharp knife and pulling out the intestinal tract. However, an easier option is simply to leave the crayfish in a cool damp place for 24 hours and their guts will empty naturally.

With a yield of only 15 per cent crayfish can be expensive, so it is always worth using the shells to make a sauce or soup.

Season: Winter/spring.
Price: £££
Fishing method: Aquaculture, traps, net.

Seawater Crayfish

(European) Spiny lobster, Crawfish, Langouste, Rock lobster★★★

Palinurus vulgaris
French: Langouste
Italian: Aragosta
Spanish: Langosta
Portuguese: Lagosta
German: Languste

Pink spiny lobster★★

Palinurus mauretanicus
French: Langouste du Cap
Italian: Aragosta
Spanish: Langosta
Portuguese: Lagosta
German: Languste

Crayfish, spiny lobster, crawfish, *langouste* and rock lobster are basically one and the same – clawless and definitely spiny to touch (illustration on page 223). They are a valuable species, and the sweetest of them all lives in European waters, off the rocky coasts of Ireland, Cornwall, Brittany and Galicia. European *langoustes* have become monstrously expensive, especially around Christmas when they are part and parcel of the festivities in France and Spain. When they appear on the markets in the UK they always seem to be unfeasibly

large, and although I can't complain about that I have always assumed that the smaller fish over the legal minimum size are sent where the demand is greatest, and that certainly isn't Britain.

The meat is rich so, as with lobster, avoid any of those complicated creamy dishes that tend to give you indigestion.

Rock lobster fisheries can be disastrously lax affairs. A recent study in Yemen highlighted the problem. Out of a sample 350 lobsters caught, only 40 were sold, 60 used locally, and a staggering 200 used as 'teasers', or live bait. Most of the world's rock lobster fisheries are, may I reassure you, more tightly controlled.

Generally, red rock lobster are the best; many warm-water species are green when alive but turn red when cooked. There is some confusion as to which of the bewildering variety of imported fish are any good. Answer: all, so long as they are fresh.

Cook rock lobsters in heavily salted sea water, or water as salty as the sea, using the same timing as for lobster (see pages 217–218).

Season: All year round.
Price: £££
Fishing method: Pots, divers.

LOBSTERS

European lobster★★★

Homarus gammarus
French: Homard européen
Italian: Astice
Spanish: Bogavante
Portuguese: Lavagante
German: Hummer

Canadian or American lobster★★

Homarus americanus
French: Homard américain

It is odd that these creatures - brutes and scavengers by nature - are so sweet

to eat. Is this Nature's revenge? The lobster is aggressive, carnivorous, cannibalistic even, but is considered by many to be the seafood to beat them all. Personally, I would rather eat a crab, but once in a while eating lobster can make you feel flash, flush and happy. It's hard to believe that the early settlers of New England thought them to be a nuisance and preferred the more solemn joys of salt fish to fresh lobster.

Lobsters live in cold water, and prefer rocky ground. Like most crustaceans, as soon as the water warms up they move into shallower, warmer water, so landings are higher in the summer. In their early years they moult quite frequently as they grow, so smaller lobsters, especially those that have just moulted, are less likely to be full of meat. When they are older, moulting occurs every two years, so the shell has a longer to fill out. Buy lobsters with old shells, barnacles and well-worn feet if at all possible. Males tend to have larger claws than females but females have a reputation for being tastier.

Since demand is high and supplies limited, these days a lot of lobsters regularly wing their way into Europe from Halifax, Canada. The main lobster fisheries over this side of the pond are off Scotland, Ireland, Brittany and, to a lesser extent, the south coast of England. The Scottish lobster is generally considered the hardier, and the Breton the most expensive, but demand almost always outstrips supply, so restaurant groups, supermarkets and all the big buyers import Canadian lobsters almost as a matter of course, except during those rare summer months when the European lobster becomes affordable or, as in 1997, cheap.

For much of the winter, lobster fishermen on both sides of the Atlantic struggle to catch anything at all. When it's cold, the lobster's metabolism slows down and it is difficult to tempt one into a pot. In Canada this period involves much bluff and double bluff among dealers and fishermen, as the suppliers try to get the highest price possible from 'pounded' lobsters, fished earlier in the season and stored in tanks. The dealers have to make some inspired guesses at times as to who has got what, and need to pitch the price just right.

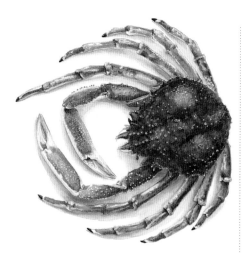

SPIDER CRAB

North American lobsters are quite different in appearance from European lobsters. They have a more uniform colour and are generally greener, whereas the 'Scottish' lobster has a brilliant speckled blue-black body. The flavour of the European lobster is rightly considered to be finer than the American.

Sophie and I diverge about how best to cook lobster. I don't like rich lobster dishes but I know that many do. Indeed some people seem to feel cheated if their lobster isn't served with a heart-stopping amount of butter and cream. Each to his/her own, but simply grilled lobster suits me fine!

Season: All year round. Expensive in winter.
Price: £££
Fishing method: Pots.

Slipper Lobster★★

Scyllaridae latus
French: Cigale
Italian: Cicala di mare
Spanish: Cigarra
Portuguese: Lagosta da pedra
German: Barenkrebs

Imagine a rock lobster flattened and cross-bred with a shrimp and you'll get the idea. Slipper lobsters were once quite frequently seen in the Mediterranean, but have been overfished and supplies are now limited. Some new fisheries have recently been opened up, especially along the east coast of Africa, so we may begin to see them available once more. Slipper lobsters lack claws, are much more docile and lethargic than European lobsters, and have an odd, paddle-shaped front end that burrows into sand to look for food. There are quite a few species, and most are caught in traps or by divers.

Supplies mainly come from Africa, and species you may see include *Scyllarides haanii* and *Scyllarides squammosus*. In the Mediterranean the Grande Cigale (*Scyllaridae latus*) is much sought after, but now rare. Cook as lobster or crayfish.

Season: Summer.
Price: £££
Fishing method: Traps, divers.

PRAWNS

Prawns live in both cold and warm water, and in Britain the name correctly refers to members of the families *Pandalidae*, *Penaeidae* and *Palaemonidae*. Larger prawns tend to come from warmer waters and in Europe are mostly sold frozen. Buy prawns with their shell on wherever possible, for they retain the taste and succulence that shelled prawns lack.
It is quite difficult to tell whether a fresh prawn is truly fresh or thawed-out frozen. The best way is to look at the eyes. Frozen prawns have crumpled rather than spherical eyes, the difference being like that between a deflated or inflated football.

Common Prawn★★

Palaemon serratus
French: Crevette rose, Bouquet
Italian: Gambero
Spanish: Camarón, Quisquilla
Portuguese: Camarão
German: Sägegarnele

One of the most ridiculously expensive things that I ever used to buy from the Paris fish market was boxes of *bouquets royales*, freshly cooked luscious little prawns of the species *Palaemon serratus*. A thin ply box lined with wax paper was filled with a generous mound of these lovely red prawns. But this wasn't a case of pile 'em high, sell 'em cheap. Chefs blanched when I told them how much they cost, and I probably ate more than I ever sold. But, if you happen to see genuine fresh *bouquets* for sale in France, eat them with nothing more than bread and butter, sloshed down with some cool white wine.

Season: All year round, *bouquets* in early summer.
Price: ££
Fishing method: Trawl.

Deep-water Prawn, Pink Shrimp★

Pandalus borealis
French: Crevette
Italian: Gambero
Spanish: Camarón
Portuguese: Camarão
German: Tiefseegarnele

The prawn cocktail, that loving marriage of green and pink, can actually taste quite good with a little effort and first-class ingredients, although it has yet to be widely saved from mediocrity. This species of prawn, *Pandalus borealis*,

FRESHWATER CRAYFISH

swims in the far north and is the one largely condemned to sit in those sundae dishes covered in pinkness.

They don't have a lot of versatility, since they are almost always sold cooked, but the shells can be used in a sauce or to flavour a shrimp or fish soup. They are at their best when eaten as they are, messily, with the shell on. You can get a lot of flavour by sucking on a prawn's front half, so don't just chuck it away, suck!

At present, this fishery is extremely wasteful, with far too many immature prawns being caught.

Season: All year round.
Price: £
Fishing method: Trawl.

Langoustine, Dublin Bay prawn, Prawn (Scotland), Scampi, Norway lobster★★★

Nephrops norvegicus
French: Langoustine
Italian: Scampi
Spanish: Cigala, Langostina
Portuguese: Lagostim
German: Kaisergranat, Norwegischer Schlankhummer, Tiefseehummer

Gone are the days when scampi were only eaten in baskets. This wonderful crustacean, so grossly abused over the years, now has a definite niche in the restaurant world, where the great, the good and the mad wrestle among themselves to get some of the limited supplies of possibly the finest crustacean of all. To call them 'scampi' is almost pejorative, so 'langoustine' has won through. There just isn't a snappy English word to use. 'Dublin Bay prawn' is ridiculous, and 'prawn' too vague.

Scotland has developed a particularly successful way of fishing langoustines using creels, or pots. However, most of the fish you see are trawled in deep water, then quickly frozen and processed. Although

langoustines benefit from being cooked alive, they simply don't have the resilience of a lobster or crab and will often die in a matter of hours.

Long dead 'fresh' langoustines can taste like cotton wool. The industrial solution to keeping them fresh involves treating them to a chemical bath which acts as an emetic. With guts emptied, they duly last longer. You can tell if they have been treated from their pale pink colour and generally faded demeanour. A live langoustine is an elegant fiery red, but nothing like as mobile out of water as a lobster. A vague twitch is as much of a sign of freshness as you'll generally get, so don't expect them to be hopping around.

Langoustines need to be cooked very briefly. A particularly good way to eat them is to roast them whole in a very hot oven for no more than 5 minutes (see page 243). They are mostly sold graded, with the greatest demand being for the larger sizes. However, smaller fish are good value and are excellent eaten whole in that messy, slurping way that brings out the flavour so well.

Season: Winter/spring.
Price: £££
Fishing method: Trawl, creel.

Mediterranean Prawn★★★

Aristeus antennatus
French: Crevette rose
Italian: Gambero di fondale
Spanish: Carabinero
Portuguese: Gamba rosada
German: Krabbe, Garnele

A lot of prawns eaten in the Mediterranean are exactly the same species as we buy in the UK, but there are still a few areas, in Spain, Italy and Portugal in particular, where real Mediterranean prawns are caught. One of the tastiest of all the Mediterranean species is this one, which has a Spanish sobriquet, *chorizo*, on account of the

ROCK LOBSTER
(LANGOUSTE)

blood-red juices that spill out from its body when cooked.

Another species that you might just come across in Spain or Morocco is *Aristeomorpha foliacea*, a gorgeous beetroot-red prawn of great tenderness. A Moroccan supplier I worked with for many years used to send a box over as a Ramadan treat every year, together with Casablancan pancakes and honey. We feasted while they fasted. He called these prawns *crevettes impériales*, and I take the Latin name from Alan Davidson's lovely little book (his best in my opinion) *The Tio Pepe Guide to the Seafood of Spain and Portugal*. At the end of one Ramadan my supplier and his wife completely and utterly disappeared, and to this day I know not what happened to them . . .

Season: Summer.
Price: £££
Fishing method: Net, trawl.

Warm-water Prawns

French: Crevette
Italian: Gambero
Spanish: Camarón
Portuguese: Camarão

Black tiger prawn, Giant tiger prawn, King prawn★★
Penaeus monodon

Banana prawn, Cat prawn★
Penaeus merguiensis

Common tiger prawn★
Penaeus esculentus

Kuruma prawn★
Penaeus japonicus

Indian White prawn★
Penaeus indicus

One of the most ravishing smells in the world is sizzling prawns. You may have salivated under a coconut palm or sat in a tropical restaurant, tempted by the aroma, but cook them over here and you could well be a little disappointed. Sadly we simply don't have those giant mega-prawns swimming near by, so the ones we see are almost all frozen, and frozen prawns, though good, never rival a fresh one for taste and texture. It is worth trying to buy them uncooked and, whenever possible, fresh, although supplies in this country are limited. Fresh prawns that have sat on an aeroplane must be eaten virtually as soon as Customs let them through.

In Australia utterly delicious fresh prawns are quite widely available. They are trawled and quickly placed in an ice-cold seawater slurry to keep them fresh – a technique that if adopted elsewhere might mean that we too could have access to better-quality fresh prawns soon. At present, small quantities of Red Sea prawns, known as whites, appear on the markets in the autumn but they have an extremely short shelf-life.

Some freshwater prawns are farmed in India and the Far East, mainly of the genus *Macrobranchium*, but they are less classy than a wild sea prawn. Prawn farming can be an ecological disaster area. Huge tracts of land have been taken over – particularly in Ecuador, India and Thailand – and put to prawn farming, but without extremely careful management disease can often make the whole farm unworkable, and the land quickly becomes sterile, and wasted.

As you might expect, the market is large and complex, and full of some terrible aberrations. The very worst are prawns glazed to the point of ridiculousness, silly little tails that taste of nothing. A glaze can serve a purpose, to protect the prawn from drying out in the freezer, but it can also push up the weight of third-rate produce making it seem much cheaper than it really is. Some cooked prawns are fine, but go for a good brand, and buy whole prawns if possible.

Allow 3 large prawns per person, or 4–6 medium ones. There is high demand for large prawns (graded as under 10 per kg/2¼ lb), so smaller ones may be easier to find. There's about 50 per cent meat to shell, so bear that in mind when buying for any recipe that calls for prawn tails only.

When cooking larger prawns, you may prefer to take out the intestines that run along the length of the tail. Simply cut the tail along the back down to the level of the gut and remove with the point of a sharp knife.

Season: All year round.
Price: ££
Fishing method: Aquaculture, net, trawl.

SHRIMPS

Brown Shrimp, Common Shrimp★

Crangon crangon
French: Crevette grise
Italian: Gamberetto grigio
Spanish: Quisquilla
Portuguese: Camarão negro
German: Garnele, Granat, Speisekrabbe

In the UK we call members of the Crangonidae family the shrimp or, more commonly, brown shrimp. In French this species is known as *crevette grise*. In the States 'shrimp' refers to what we would call prawns, and are fished mainly in warm waters.

Those delicious, spicy pots of potted shrimps from Morecambe Bay are about the only form of British brown shrimp we see these days. The Dutch have cornered the market and provide much of Europe with excellent frozen and vacuum-packed peeled, whole shrimps.

You can still see the odd fisherman walking through the surf, especially around Le Touquet in northern France, netting the shrimps that swim in with the tide, while further up the coast, around Dunkirk, stocky Flemish horses stomp through the sea, pulling shrimp nets – the last known horse-drawn fishery in Europe.

If you buy live shrimps, make sure that the water you boil them in is very salty. There is an astonishingly simple Belgian dish, *Tomates aux crevettes*, which even the least adventurous should be able to handle: take a large tomato, scoop out the flesh and seeds and fill with some peeled shrimps. Serve. That's it.

Season: All year round.
Price: ££
Fishing method: Net.

Dressed Crab

Whether you've cooked your own or bought whole crab ready cooked, your next task is to dig out all the meat. With patience, you should get 225g (8 oz) mixed white and brown meat from an average-sized crab. Begin by twisting off the legs and claws and then crack them open and extract the sweet white flesh. Now turn the main body on its back and twist off the bony, pointed flap. Push the tip of a knife between the main shell and the bit to which the legs and claws were attached. Wiggle to loosen and then twist the blade to push it up and remove. Scrape out the well of brown meat in the main shell (quite the nicest bit, I think).

Go back to the upper-body section and snap off the mouth. Pull away the greyish, soft gills (the 'dead man's fingers') and discard. Split the body in half. Now you need all the patience you can muster. With a darning needle, skewer or whatever thin, pointed implement you can rustle up (my mother favoured a fine crochet hook), work your way through the cavities of the body, pulling out every last shred of white meat.

To enjoy the meat at its purest, I think it quite good enough to serve up two bowls of white and brown meat and place a bowl of lemony mayonnaise on the table with them, as well as plenty of good brown bread and butter. A tomato salad and/or green salad go down well, too. However, if you want to be a bit more fancy, you can go the whole hog and dress your crab in time-honoured fashion. Here's how.

1 crab per person, cooked (see page 218),
    crabmeat extracted, shell retained
lemon juice
soft white breadcrumbs
hard-boiled eggs, shelled
chopped fresh parsley
salt and pepper

To Serve:
Lemon Mayonnaise (see page 311)
brown bread and butter

First, deal with the shell. Look at the opened side and you will notice a fine line all around the outer rim. Crack and tap along this line to knock away the inner, upper layer, making a neat crab-shell bowl to carry the dressed crab.

Beat the brown meat with a few dashes of lemon juice, a few breadcrumbs to stop the mixture being too sloppy and slippy, and salt and pepper to taste. Spoon this in a band down the centre of the shell, and fill the remaining space on either side with white crabmeat. Chop the egg yolks and whites, keeping them separate, and decorate the meats with neat lines of egg yolk, egg white and parsley.

Serve with a bowl of mayonnaise and some bread and butter.

Crab Cocktail

Alternatives: lobster, rock lobster

Crab cocktail has been out of fashion for a decade or more but I'm delighted that it has now come back with a vengeance. I've always loved it: when made with fresh crab and good mayonnaise, spiked with a hint of tarragon, it is one of the most sublime first courses. The quantities below could be stretched to feed around six people if there was a substantial main course to follow, though I suspect that most people would prefer to major on the cocktail.

SERVES 4–6

400–450g (14–16 oz) crabmeat (white and brown)
225ml (8 fl oz) Mayonnaise (see page 310)
1 shallot, very finely chopped
2 teaspoons Dijon mustard
1 tablespoon tomato purée
2 teaspoons chopped fresh tarragon
Tabasco sauce
4–6 crisp lettuce leaves, e.g. Cos or Webb's
1 tablespoon vinaigrette dressing
salt and pepper

To Serve:
lemon wedges
brown bread and butter or toast

Flake any large bits of white crabmeat. Mix the mayonnaise with the shallot, mustard, tomato purée, tarragon, a few shakes of Tabasco to taste and salt and pepper. Stir about three-quarters into the crab. Taste, and add the rest if you think it needs it (the mixture should be very rich and quite sloppy), then balance the seasoning.

Just before serving, shred the lettuce leaves and toss with the vinaigrette. Divide between individual plates and top with the crab mayonnaise. Serve with lemon wedges and brown bread and butter, or toast.

Maryland Crabcakes

Crabcakes are not made like fishcakes, or at least they should not be. Potato is too heavy a binder. Crabcakes need lighter dry breadcrumbs or cracker crumbs, and only enough to hold them together. Too much and you lose the delicate taste of the crab itself, which renders the whole exercise pretty pointless.

These American crabcakes are sheer bliss, and easy enough to make. The exact quantity of crumbs depends a little on the balance of white meat to brown. Aim for slightly more white meat, if possible.

Serve the crabcakes hot from the pan, with coleslaw (as long as it is of good quality), a tomato salad, maybe, and lemon wedges, and have a bottle of Tabasco standing at the ready on the table.

SERVES 4

225g (8 oz) fresh crabmeat, brown and white
1 egg
1 tablespoon Mayonnaise (see page 310)
2 teaspoons Dijon mustard
1 tablespoon finely chopped fresh parsley
4 spring onions, finely chopped
60–85g (2–3 oz) dried breadcrumbs
oil, for grilling or frying
salt and pepper

Place the crab in a bowl and season with salt and pepper. Add all the remaining ingredients except for the crumbs and oil. Mix and add enough crumbs to bind. Quarter the mixture and pat each portion into a flat, round cake, about 2cm (3/4 inch) thick.

Fry the cakes in a little oil until browned on both sides. Alternatively, brush the grill rack and crabcakes with oil and grill until well browned on both sides, turning once. Serve immediately.

Thai Crab Curry

Alternatives are: lobster, rock lobster

This is an aromatic curry, perfectly suited to the natural sweetness of crab. Be warned, however, that it makes for messy eating – you have to use your fingers and pick and suck at the crab to get the full pleasure of the dish. Slurpy, sticky and delicious.

If you can't get lime leaves, substitute two strips of lemon or lime zest. Serve with rice.

SERVES 4

2 hen crabs, cooked (see page 218)
8 fresh coriander sprigs, with stalks
2 lemongrass stems
2–3 fresh chillies, de-seeded and roughly chopped
3 garlic cloves, roughly chopped
3 shallots, chopped
3 tablespoons sunflower or vegetable oil
2 kaffir lime leaves
400ml (14 fl oz) coconut milk (see page 306)
2 tablespoons fish sauce
salt and pepper

Break the crabs into pieces: pull off the legs and claws and crack them so that they are easy to break open when the curry is made. Now turn the main body on its back and twist off the bony, pointed flap. Push the tip of a knife between the main shell and the bit to which the legs and claws were attached. Wiggle to loosen, then twist the blade to push it up and remove. Snap the mouth off this upper-body section and pull away the 'dead man's fingers' (the greyish, soft gills) and discard. Cut the remainder in half. Break or cut the main shell in half.

Cut the leaves off the coriander stalks and set aside. Chop the stalks roughly. Use just the lower, fatter 7.5–10cm (3–4 inches) of the lemongrass. Save the tough tips for flavouring stock or soup, or discard. Bruise the lower part with a wooden spoon, then strip off the outer layer of stalk. Chop the inner layers.

Mix the coriander stalks, lemongrass, chillies, garlic and shallots, and pound to a rough paste, with a little salt, in a mortar (or, if you have a food processor that can handle small amounts, process to a rough paste, adding a little water if needed).

Heat the oil in a wide, heavy frying pan (it should be large enough to accommodate all the bits of crab) and add the paste. Fry for about 3 minutes. Add the crab pieces and the lime leaves and stir-fry for a further 2 minutes, so that the pieces get nicely coated. Add the coconut milk and bring up to the boil. Reduce the heat and simmer for 10 minutes. Add the fish sauce and reserved coriander leaves. Taste and adjust the seasoning.

Soft-shell Crabs

I love soft-shell crabs (as long as they are not so big that they are beginning to toughen), but they are very rich and, even with smaller ones, two is usually quite enough per person as a first course; three is verging on overdoing it, particularly when they are fried.

They can simply be brushed with oil and grilled but I think frying is the best bet, with a crisp coating of flour to set off the rich, powerful flavour. Serve them just as they are, with salt and lemon wedges, or, even better, with a spicy dipping sauce like Vietnamese Dipping Sauce (see page 55).

To deep-fry soft-shell crabs, put a pan of sunflower or vegetable oil to heat up. Prepare a bowl of plain flour, seasoned with pepper alone, and beat one or two eggs together lightly in a bowl.

When the oil is good and hot – about 180°C/350°F, or when a cube of bread dropped into the oil fizzes very vigorously – start preparing the first crab. Since most soft-shell crabs have been frozen, you will have to dry each one (I'm assuming you've remembered to thaw them before you put the oil on to heat)

assiduously with kitchen paper. Once the crab is dry, dip it first into the flour (don't worry if the odd limb falls off – just cook it separately), coating well, and then into the beaten egg. Pick it out, shake off excess and then dunk it back in the flour again, coating well. Slide into the hot oil and repeat with the remaining crabs, but don't overcrowd the pan.

Deep-fry until golden brown and crisp, turning occasionally. Drain briefly on kitchen paper, then serve.

Steamed Crab Dumplings

These Chinese-style crab dumplings, cosseted in silky white jackets, are a reminder of the finest Chinese-restaurant Sunday lunches, when little *dim sum* become the mainstay of the meal. I love making them and adore eating them. My patience is limited, however, so I reserve them for a first course.

SERVES 4 AS A FIRST COURSE

For the Filling:
110g (4 oz) crabmeat, white and brown
60g (2 oz) radishes or white radish, finely chopped
½ teaspoon soy sauce
½ teaspoon sesame oil
½ teaspoon grated fresh root ginger
¼ teaspoon sugar
pepper

For the Dough:
60g (2 oz) plain flour
¼ teaspoon salt
60–85ml (2–3 fl oz) boiling water

To Serve:
soy sauce
sesame oil

Mix all the filling ingredients together. Set aside for half an hour, then taste and adjust the seasonings.

For the dough: sift the flour with the salt. Add enough boiling water to form a soft dough. Knead, dusting with flour as you work, until you have a smooth, elastic dough. Divide into 16 pieces and roll each into a ball. Roll out thinly on a lightly floured board to form circles 7.5–10cm (3–4 inches) in diameter.

Place a teaspoon of the filling in the centre of each. Fold to form a half circle and pinch the edges together to seal them. Arrange the dumplings in a well oiled steamer basket and steam for 5 minutes. Serve with extra soy sauce and sesame oil to sprinkle over the dumplings.

Ecrevisses à la Nage

Poached Crayfish

. . . Or, in other words, what to do when you are blessed with an abundance of live crayfish! Once, when I was a child, we were taken as a special treat to a tiny restaurant out, I think, on the Beauce, the big fertile plain to the west of Paris. That morning, the restaurateur's son had returned from a midnight escapade with baskets full of crayfish. The whole restaurant dined royally on *écrevisses à la nage*, napkins tucked into collars, melted butter and juices running unheeded down chins. The rest of the meal seemed immaterial.

You will need at least six crayfish per person, more if possible. Multiply up the quantity of *court-bouillon* as needed, and serve the freshly boiled crayfish with bowls of melted butter, sharpened with lemon juice for dipping.

live crayfish
court-bouillon (see page 307)
dry white wine
star anise
coriander seeds
salt and pepper

To Serve:
melted butter
lemon juice

Rinse the crayfish thoroughly and then freeze them until they give in and stop moving – 1–1½ hours. Of course, if you are the tough sort, you can skip the freezing and cook them live. The RSPCA seems to think this is OK but it makes me feel like a complete heel.

Put the *court-bouillon* into a wide pan with the wine and a few star anise petals and coriander seeds. Boil until reduced by a third. Season with salt and pepper. Tip in the crayfish, clamp on the lid and simmer for about 6–8 minutes.

Pile the crayfish up in a shallow platter, spooning some of the boiling liquor around them, and serve with melted butter sharpened with lemon juice, plenty of napkins, bowls for the debris, and fingerbowls filled with warm water. Tuck in and have a ball.

Sauce Nantua

Alternatives: langoustines, prawns

This is absolutely the classic thing to do with freshwater crayfish, a hedonistically sensational sauce coloured a beautiful coral orange, with a powerful, deep shellfish flavour. It may not be a five-minute job but it is surprisingly easy to make successfully, and it extracts the maximum flavour out of the shells of the little darlings, which might otherwise be lost. Serve the *sauce Nantua* and the little crayfish tails with *Quenelles de Brochet* (see page 268) or steamed or poached fish of the classiest nature – turbot is an obvious choice but it would be just as fitting with brill or sole.

SERVES 6–8

20 live crayfish
45g (1½ oz) butter
1 tablespoon sunflower oil
1 carrot, finely diced
3 shallots, chopped
½ fennel bulb, diced
1 garlic clove, chopped
bouquet garni made with 2 fresh parsley sprigs, 1 fresh thyme sprig and 1 bay leaf, tied together
3 tablespoons Cognac or Armagnac
225g (8 oz) tomatoes, peeled, de-seeded and chopped
1 tablespoon tomato purée
300ml (½ pint) dry white wine
300ml (½ pint) *crème fraîche*
½ tablespoon chopped fresh chervil or fennel
salt and pepper

For the Beurre Manié:
15g (½ oz) butter
15g (½ oz) plain flour

Rinse the crayfish thoroughly, then drain and freeze rapidly for 1–1½ hours (see page 218).

Melt 30g (1 oz) of the butter with the oil in a deep, wide frying pan. When it is good and hot, add the crayfish, cover swiftly and cook over a moderate heat for 8 minutes, shaking the pan occasionally. Draw off the heat, take the crayfish out of the pan and leave to cool. Don't wash the pan up!

Peel and de-vein the crayfish. Put the shells and heads into the food processor and process bravely, until pulverised into small pieces. Put the pan back on the heat and melt the remaining butter in it, then add the carrot, shallots, fennel, garlic and *bouquet garni*. Cook gently for 5 minutes. Scrape in the pulverised crayfish shells and heads. Continue cooking over a moderate heat for a further 10 minutes, stirring frequently. Now add the Cognac or Armagnac and simmer for a couple of minutes longer. Add the tomatoes, tomato purée, white wine and some salt and pepper. Simmer until reduced by two-thirds (around 10 minutes). Next, stir in the cream and chervil or fennel and leave to simmer over a very low heat for a further 10 minutes.

Rub the sauce through a fine sieve, pressing to extract the very last little drops of flavour. Return to the heat and bring up to very near simmering point. As it reheats, make the *beurre manié* by mashing the butter and flour together thoroughly. Drop little knobs of this into the hot sauce, whisking them in, until it is thickened to your taste. Continue to cook for 5 minutes or so, without letting it boil, to eliminate the taste of raw flour. Taste and adjust the seasoning.

When you need the sauce, re-heat and it's ready to use. Don't forget the crayfish themselves, which should be used as an added royal garnish to whatever you are serving the sauce with.

Grilled Lobster

Alternative: rock lobster

This is one of my favourite ways to eat lobster, sizzling hot from the grill with a good dunking sauce on the side. My favourite is the Fennel Seed, Shallot and Lemongrass Vinaigrette opposite (note that you need to prepare the lemongrass oil at least two days in advance), but I'm partial to the more conventional drawn butter or garlicky Maître d'Hôtel butter, too. Take your pick.

SERVES 4

2 lobsters weighing about 450–600g (1–1¼ lb)
    par-cooked and split in half (see page 218)
sunflower oil or melted butter
salt and pepper

To serve:
Fennel seed, Shallot and Lemongrass Vinaigrette
    (page 235), or Drawn Butter or Maître d'Hôtel
    Butter (see below)

Brush the lobster meat with a little oil or melted butter and season with salt and pepper. Grill under a moderate grill: put the shell side to the heat first and then turn to cook the cut side, for a total of about 15 minutes. Drizzle a little of your chosen sauce over the flesh and serve with the remainder in a small bowl.

Drawn Butter

Nothing more fancy than melted butter, sharpened with a few squeezes of lemon juice and seasoned with plenty of black pepper. Serve in a small jug. Brush the lobster with melted butter rather than oil before grilling.

Maître d'Hôtel Butter

As the lobster sizzles under the grill (again, brush with melted butter rather than oil), chop 2 garlic cloves finely. Melt 125g (4½ oz) of butter (if it is unsalted, remember to add a little salt at the end) and add the garlic. Cook over a very gentle heat for about 4–5 minutes, without browning the garlic. Stir in 2 tablespoons of finely chopped fresh parsley, the finely grated zest of ½ lemon and 1 tablespoon of freshly squeezed lemon juice. Serve warm, with the grilled lobster.

Fennel Seed, Shallot and Lemongrass Vinaigrette

This fragrant, zesty vinaigrette is marvellous with all kinds of crustaceans and shellfish. You won't need all the lemongrass oil, so save the rest to drizzle over plainly cooked flat fish (very nice with brill or sole), or to whisk with balsamic vinegar to make a classy dressing for a mixed green salad or a tomato salad.

SERVES 4–6

4 lemongrass stems
150ml (¼ pint) grapeseed or safflower oil
1 teaspoon fennel seeds
15g (½ oz) shallot, very finely chopped
½ fresh red chilli, de-seeded and finely chopped
1 tablespoon balsamic vinegar
4 fresh basil leaves, very finely shredded
salt and pepper

Begin by making the lemongrass oil at least two days in advance; a week is better. Trim the lemongrass and then bash with a rolling pin to break down the fibres. Slice thinly and place in a jar with the oil. Leave in the light for at least 48 hours.

To make the vinaigrette proper, bruise the fennel seeds in a mortar with a pestle, or with the end of a rolling pin in a sturdy bowl. Mix with the shallot, chilli, vinegar and 3 tablespoons of lemongrass oil. Season with salt and pepper. Shortly before serving, mix in the basil shreds, then taste and adjust the seasoning, adding a little more oil if it seems on the sharp side.

Homard en Chemise

Alternative: rock lobster

Another simple but effective way of cooking lobster, or *langouste* (we use excellent frozen tails of rock lobster, sold as 'Caribbean lobster', which are extremely meaty), enclosed in greaseproof paper – the *chemise* or 'shirt' of the title – which means that no juices are lost to the heat of the oven. Serve them still in their little paper shirts, with any of the sauces I suggest for grilled lobster (see opposite) or a *vinaigrette aux fines herbes* – in other words an ordinary vinaigrette enlivened with plenty of chopped fresh chives, parsley, chervil and a little tarragon.

SERVES 4

4 lobster or *langouste* tails, weighing about 175g
   (6 oz) each
about 30–45g (1–1½ oz) butter, softened
coarse salt and freshly ground black pepper

Preheat the oven to 220°C/425°F/Gas Mark 7. Smear each lobster tail generously with butter. Lay each one in the centre of a capacious square of greaseproof paper and season with salt and pepper. Fold up like a parcel, tuck the joins neatly underneath and lay on a baking tray. Bake for 15 minutes, until just cooked through. Serve with whatever sauce takes your fancy.

Lobster Thermidor

Alternative: rock lobster

William was rather snooty when I said I liked lobster thermidor. He thinks the old-fashioned thermidor sauce too rich for lobster but I disagree, and so did the three other people who were hanging around the kitchen when the sizzling, sauced lobsters emerged from the oven.

This is a dish for special occasions, when you want to take a little trouble in the kitchen and when you want a spot of serious indulgence. It is rich and heavenly. Don't take any notice of William in this one instance, but take my word for it.

SERVES 4

1 large lobster, weighing around 1kg (2¼ lb),
    or 2 lobsters weighing about 450–600g
    (1–1¼ lb) each
45g (1½ oz) butter

For the Sauce:
30g (1 oz) butter
30g (1 oz) plain flour
350ml (12 fl oz) milk
3 tablespoons dry sherry
5 tablespoons *crème fraîche* or double cream
1 tablespoon Dijon mustard
60g (2 oz) Parmesan cheese, freshly grated
salt and pepper

Boil the lobsters until about half cooked (see page 218), then drain and cool. Split the bodies in half lengthways and ease the lobster meat out of the shells without damaging them. Cut the flesh into bite-sized pieces. Reserve.

For the sauce, melt the butter in a pan and stir in the flour. Stir over a moderate heat for about a minute. Draw off the heat and gradually stir in the milk to form a white sauce. Bring up to the boil, stirring, and then simmer gently for 10 minutes, stirring frequently to prevent catching and deter lumps. Stir in the sherry and simmer for another 3 minutes or so, before stirring in the cream, mustard and 2 tablespoons of the Parmesan. Taste and adjust the seasoning. Curiously enough, I wasn't so deeply taken with the sauce at this stage – it needs the balance of sweet lobster flesh and melting grilled cheese to make it sing. If not using immediately, rub a knob of butter over the surface of the sauce to prevent a skin forming.

Shortly before serving, preheat the grill. Re-heat the sauce. While it is re-heating, warm the lobster flesh through in the butter over a moderate heat. Spoon about a third of the sauce into the shells, add the lobster flesh and then spoon over the remaining sauce. Sprinkle over the remaining Parmesan and dot with a little butter. Whizz under the grill for a few minutes until browned and sizzling. Serve immediately.

Lobster, Avocado and Mango Salad

Alternative: rock lobster

William was dubious about putting mango with lobster, too, but when he got a chance to taste it, this salad won him round fairly and squarely. It is as light and refreshing as lobster thermidor is rich and indulgent. The total opposite, in fact, and the perfect dish for a summer party, when the temperature is soaring outside. It also happens to be incredibly healthy and low in calories, without sacrificing one iota in terms of flavour.

SERVES 4

1 lobster, weighing about 1kg (2¼ lb), cooked
  (see page 218)
2 avocados
1 lime, halved
2 ripe mangoes
125g (4½ oz) pack of mixed baby lettuce leaves,
  or lamb's lettuce

For the Dressing:
1 teaspoon cumin seeds
1 teaspoon coriander seeds
½ dried red chilli, de-seeded
1 level teaspoon black poppy seeds
juice of ½ lime

To make the dressing, dry-fry the cumin and coriander seeds until they give off a delicious, toasty, perfumed scent. Tip into a bowl and cool. Dry-fry the chilli for a few seconds, until it turns a shade darker. Add to the cumin and coriander and grind to a fine powder. Dry-fry the poppy seeds for about a minute and tip into a separate bowl.

Split the lobster in half and take the meat out of the body. Cut into bite-sized pieces. Crack open the claws and extract the meat from them as well. Peel the avocados and slice thinly, turning them in lime juice as you work to prevent them browning. Peel the mangoes and slice them too.

Make a bed of lettuce on a large plate. Mound up the lobster in the centre and then surround with slices of avocado and mango in a decorative fashion. Sprinkle over the ground spices (you'll only need about half) and the poppy seeds, then squeeze over the lime juice. Serve immediately, before the mango and avocado start to brown.

Insalata di Mare

Seafood salad

The very essence of the Italian seaside in summer, this salad of mixed seafood tossed in lemon juice and olive oil is one of life's great pleasures when eaten freshly made. It's a far cry from the commercial packs of mixed seafood salad sozzled in crude vinegar. Make it at home, open a bottle of iced dry Italian white wine, and dream yourself down to the Amalfi coast.

Make it in the morning for that evening, or even the day before, and allow plenty of time for preparation. Don't throw out the cooking juices either: they make a first-rate seafood stock for soups and other dishes – freeze it if you can't use it within the next 24 hours. *Insalata di mare* is one of the easiest of seafood dishes to make but demands a little patience. I promise you that, in the end, you'll be delighted that you took the trouble.

SERVES 8–10 AS A STARTER, 6–8 AS A LIGHT LUNCH

3 strips of lemon zest
1kg (2¼ lb) live palourdes or other small clams, scrubbed clean
1kg (2¼ lb) live mussels, cleaned (see page 192)
600g (1¼ lb) squid, cleaned (see page 247)
500g (1 lb 2 oz) large raw prawns
1 medium sole (lemon or Dover), filleted and cut into 2cm (¾-inch) wide strips
bunch of fresh flat-leaved parsley, chopped
juice of 2 lemons
150ml (¼ pint) extra virgin olive oil
1 garlic clove, finely chopped
125g (4½ oz) pack of mixed baby salad leaves
175g (6 oz) small cherry tomatoes, halved
6 fresh basil leaves, shredded
salt and pepper

Pour enough water into a large saucepan to cover the base by about 5mm (¼ inch). Add the lemon zest to the pan and set over a high heat. Add the clams, cover tightly and shake over a high heat until the shells have opened – about 6 minutes, give or take. Scoop out the clams with a slotted spoon and transfer to a bowl. Discard any that refuse to open.

Now tip the mussels into the pan, cover and shake again over a high heat until they have all opened – around 5 minutes. Scoop the mussels into the bowl

with the clams, again discarding any that refuse to open. Let the liquid in the saucepan settle, then strain it through a fine sieve lined with muslin and return to the pan.

Pick the mussel and clam meat out of the shells. Strain the juices left in the bowl into the cooking juices in the saucepan.

Cut the bodies of the squid into rings about 1cm (½ inch) wide. Leave the tentacles clumped together in bunches. Bring the saucepan of juice back to the boil and add the squid. Simmer for about 1–2 minutes, until just white and opaque. Quickly lift out with a slotted spoon and add to the mussels and clams.

Next, drop the prawns into the juices (if they've boiled down too much, add a splash of hot water) and simmer for about 3 minutes, until they are pink and opaque. Scoop them out and allow to cool. Nearly there now!

Next, lay the strips of sole in the last of the simmering juice and cook for 30–60 seconds, until just opaque. Quickly and carefully lift out and allow to cool.

Peel the prawns and de-vein them (see page 224). Mix all the seafood, bar the sole, with the parsley, the juice of 1½ lemons, 8 tablespoons of the olive oil and the garlic, salt and pepper. Very carefully stir in the sole, trying not to break it up too much. Chill lightly in the fridge.

Whisk the remaining lemon juice with the remaining olive oil, 2 tablespoons of the cooking liquid and some salt and pepper. Toss the baby lettuce in two-thirds of the dressing and the halved tomatoes and shredded basil in the remainder. Make a bed of lettuce on each plate, or on one large platter. Mound the seafood salad on top. Arrange the tomatoes and basil around the edge and serve.

Tom Yam Goong

Thai Hot and Sour Prawn Soup

This chilli-hot sour soup is virtually ubiquitous in Thai restaurants around the world. No wonder, for it is heavenly: refreshing and invigorating, and just the way to zap tastebuds and appetite into full attention. The other big plus is that it takes no time at all to make, a characteristic that is every bit as welcome in domestic kitchens as professional ones.

For something this pure and simple you must use good-quality ingredients. Classy chicken stock, not a stock cube, is essential (the ready-made stocks aren't all bad but a home-made one will be vastly superior). It is worth searching out raw prawns, even if they have been frozen, rather than plumping for tasteless, woolly cooked ones.

SERVES 4

3 lemongrass stems
900ml (generous 1½ pints) light chicken stock
2 kaffir lime leaves, roughly torn up, or 4 wide
    strips of lime zest
2–3 small fresh red chillies, de-seeded and sliced
8 coriander stems, with leaves, roughly chopped up
2cm (¾ inch) piece of fresh galangal or fresh
    root ginger, thinly sliced
350g (12 oz) raw peeled prawns, thawed if
    frozen, and de-veined (see page 224)
3–4 tablespoons freshly squeezed lime juice
3 tablespoons fish sauce

Cut the top thin end of the lemongrass stems off and discard, leaving about 10cm (4 inches) of the plumper end. Hit the stems with a mallet or the back of a wooden spoon, crushing them to release their flavour, yet keeping them more or less in one piece.

Bring the stock to the boil and add the lemongrass, lime leaves (or zest), chillies, coriander and galangal (or ginger), then bring back to the boil. Simmer for a minute, then add the prawns, lime juice and fish sauce. Bring back to the boil and simmer for 2–3 minutes, until the prawns are just cooked through. Taste and adjust the seasoning – it should be quite noticeably sharp from the lime juice. If you are patient, fish out and discard the lemongrass stems. Serve immediately.

Gambas al Pil Pil

Prawns with Chilli and Garlic

The first time I tasted *gambas al pil pil* was in a small flat looking down over the Freemason's Hall in Drury Lane. I remember the prawns sizzling from the kitchen to the table, streaming wafts of garlic behind and before them. We pulled them apart, sucking the delicious juices from their shells and then dunking bread into the garlicky oil. That was a long time ago, but *gambas al pil pil* remains a favourite quick first course.

Try your hardest to get raw prawns (frozen ones are better than fresh cooked ones, as long as you remember to let them thaw out in time). I like to use big tiger prawns or king prawns, heads and all, but any type of prawn will work well. Change the parsley to coriander and you move the dish geographically from Spain to Portugal. Both versions are excellent.

They should really be cooked in individual earthenware *cazuelas* but, since the ones I brought back from Spain have all broken, I have to resort to an ordinary frying pan. It works well, as long as you don't mind displaying it on the table with the prawns still sizzling merrily within its confines. Peeling the prawns is a happily messy business, so be thoughtful and provide fingerbowls full of warm water, perhaps with a slice of lemon floating in each one, and, of course, plenty of napkins.

SERVES 4

110ml (4 fl oz) extra virgin olive oil
3 garlic cloves, chopped
2 small hot dried red chillies, snapped in two
12 large prawns (tiger or king prawns)
1 tablespoon finely chopped fresh parsley
coarse sea salt

Heat the oil in a frying pan and add the garlic and chillies. Stir around for a minute or so and then tip in the prawns. Fry over a sizzling heat until pink and cooked through – about 3 minutes. Sprinkle over the parsley and salt and serve immediately, straight from the pan, with plenty of good bread.

Roast Langoustines with Pernod Mayonnaise

Alternatives: large prawns, such as tiger or king prawns

The best way to serve langoustines? No doubt about it. Just as they are, with a large bowl of mayonnaise, big white linen napkins and warm fingerbowls with a slice of lemon floating in them. Slices of good bread and butter and a bottle of chilled dry white wine, the condensation gathering on the glass, are the only other additions to be considered. Share the langoustines with people you care about; don't waste them on people you are merely trying to impress – they'll probably turn out to be allergic to shellfish anyway.

Unless you are mixing them with other shellfish and crustaceans to make a grand *plateau de fruits de mer*, you will need at least three langoustines per person, more if possible. Roasting them in the oven ensures that you lose none of their sweet savour to the cooking water.

SERVES 4

at least 12 langoustines
oil

For the Mayonnaise:
2 egg yolks
1 level teaspoon Dijon mustard
300ml (½ pint) light oil, e.g. sunflower,
    safflower or grapeseed oil, or one-third olive
    oil and two-thirds sunflower, grapeseed or
    safflower oil
1 tablespoon lemon juice
½ tablespoon Pernod
salt and pepper

To make the mayonnaise, beat the egg yolks with the mustard. Keep beating and add the oil, a drop at a time at first. Once you've worked your way through one-third of the oil, beat in half the lemon juice. Go back to the oil, always beating the mayonnaise continuously, and pour it in in a slow, steady trickle until all is incorporated. Beat in the Pernod, salt and pepper. Taste and add more lemon juice, Pernod or salt and pepper, if needed.

To roast the langoustines, preheat the oven to 240°C/450°F/Gas Mark 8. Pour a little oil (match it to the oil used in the mayonnaise) into a baking tray (or baking trays) large enough to house all the langoustines. Put them in the tray and turn with your hands, wiping oil over them. A greasy job but there's no better way to do it, and your hands will probably end up a mite softer and smoother for it. Roast the langoustines for 5 minutes, then leave to cool. Serve soon after, with the mayonnaise.

Shrimp Soup

Alternative: prawns

I've always loved sitting and nibbling away at tiny brown shrimps with a drink before dinner. Small, briny and full of the taste of the sea, they are one of nature's perfect, ready-made pre-meal *amuse-gueules*. Here, that incredible flavour is transformed into a strong, briny soup, softened by cream to a remarkable liquid. If you can't be bothered to shell any of the shrimps (and I don't blame you – it's a tedious, lengthy task), or don't have time, don't worry. Those denuded commas are a welcome garnish, but not essential.

SERVES 8

1.1kg (2½ lb) cooked whole brown shrimps in
   their shells
110g (4 oz) butter
1 celery stick, diced
3 carrots, diced
1 onion, chopped
3 garlic cloves, chopped
bouquet garni of 2 fresh parsley sprigs, 1 fresh
   thyme sprig and 1 bay leaf, tied together with
   string
45g (1½ oz) tomato purée
500ml (18 fl oz) dry white wine
1.5 litres (2½ pints) Fish Stock (see page 308)
225ml (8 fl oz) *crème fraîche*
salt and pepper
snipped fresh chives, to garnish

Weigh out 100g (3½ oz) of shrimps, turn the radio on and settle down to shell them, saving the shells as well as the meat. Set aside the shelled shrimps to use as a garnish.

Melt the butter in a roomy saucepan and add the vegetables, garlic and *bouquet garni*. Stir, cover and sweat for 10 minutes over a low heat. Next, add the tomato purée and the whole shrimps in their shells, as well as the empty shells. Stir for a minute or so, then cover again and leave to sweat over a low heat for a further 5 minutes.

Add the wine and bring to the boil. As soon as it is boiling, pour in the fish stock, season with lots of pepper but no salt (the shrimps may well be quite salty enough to season the entire soup) and bring back to the boil. Leave to simmer gently for 30 minutes.

Cool slightly. Locate and discard the *bouquet garni*, then liquidise or process the soup, shells and all. Rub through a fine sieve, pressing down on the debris to extract the last drops of liquid.

Rinse the pan out and return the soup to it. Over a gentle heat, whisk in the cream and bring back to the boil. Taste and adjust the seasoning, then serve piping hot, scattering the reserved shelled shrimps and snipped chives over the surface of each bowl of soup as you pass them round.

Potted Shrimps

Alternative: small prawns

I once prepared potted shrimps for a party of French friends. I presented my British speciality proudly, and they were quite delighted with it. Now, every time I cook for them, they demand British food, even if I'm far more inclined to go native (this is in France), or travel even further afield for recipes. Never mind. It's good to feel that I've dispelled, to some degree, the belief that we don't know how to cook at all.

Potted shrimps are one of our finest creations. Though you can buy them ready-potted, they will taste twice as good when freshly prepared at home. Try them.

SERVES 4

85g (3 oz) butter
225g (8 oz) shelled cooked shrimps
1 large or 2 small blades of mace
¼ teaspoon cayenne pepper
pinch of ground ginger

To Serve:
thin brown bread or warm toast
lemon wedges

Melt the butter over a low heat in a small pan. Add the remaining ingredients and heat slowly, without boiling. When hot, take out the mace and divide the prawns between four small ramekins, or pour them into a larger bowl.

Leave to cool and set. Serve with thin brown bread or toast and lemon wedges.

If you wish to keep the shrimps for a couple of days, seal the ramekins with 110g (4 oz) clarified butter (see page 305). Melt and pour a thick layer over each pot, covering the shrimps completely.

Norwegian Shrimp Sauce

Alternative: small prawns

This is a lovely sauce to serve with all manner of plainly cooked fish, poached, baked, or steamed. It is full of the vigour of little shrimps and goes particularly well with the Norwegian fishcakes on page 46.

SERVES 4–6

450g (1 lb) cooked shrimps or small prawns in
  their shells
300ml (½ pint) Fish Stock (see page 308)
30g (1 oz) butter
30g (1 oz) plain flour
150ml (¼ pint) double cream
lemon juice
1 tablespoon chopped fresh dill
salt and pepper

Shell the shrimps or prawns. Process the shells and heads roughly and put into a pan with the fish stock. Bring to the boil and simmer for 10 minutes. Strain and reserve the stock. Chop the shrimps or prawns roughly.

Melt the butter and stir in the flour. Stir over a low heat for a minute, then draw off the heat. Gradually mix in the stock, a little at a time, to form a smooth sauce. Then stir in the cream. Bring back to the boil and simmer for 5 minutes. Stir in the shrimps or prawns and simmer for a further minute or so. Add a generous squeeze of lemon juice, the dill and salt and pepper to taste.

If not serving immediately, spear a small knob of butter on a fork and rub over the surface of the sauce to prevent a skin from forming.

Squid, Octopus and Cuttlefish

These cephalopods have a certain fascination for monster-spotters but seem to be just too much for many of us ever to contemplate eating, let alone buying. Despite their appearance they are among the most intelligent creatures in the sea, and include the squid, the cuttlefish and the octopus among their number. Cephalopod is from the Greek meaning 'head on their feet'. The inference is clear.

Squid and cuttle need to be cooked either very briefly or for a very long time. Anything in between won't do. Frozen squid can be a little rubbery but frozen octopus, on the other hand, is excellent; in this case the freezing tenderises what can be a tough and chewy tentacle.

There are about 700 species of cephalopods throughout the world, so it's quite easy to cook one wherever you live. Technically they are molluscs, but to the non-scientist they don't seem to fit easily into the same group as shellfish, so in this book they have their own section.

To Clean Squid

This is fun.

Step 1

Lay the squid on a chopping board and, holding the mantle (body) with one hand, grasp the tentacles at their base and gently pull with the other. The whole lot will come away from the body. Remove the quill, and wonder at its beauty. Throw away the guts but retain the ink sac if you want to. It is small and silvery dark, and is usually quite clearly visible. Cut it carefully out of the innards, trying not to pierce it. You can use it in black risotto, or to make an ink sauce. To use, place in a cup, pierce, dilute the contents with a little water, then pass it through a sieve. The ink freezes well.

Step 2

Wash the body and remove the thin membrane on the outside by hand. It comes off easily, but isn't always present. Also remove the 'wings', which can clearly be seen attached to the body, and keep them to one side.

Step 3

Cut away the tentacles just in front of the eyes and squeeze out the small beak, or mouth, in the middle, which you throw away. Give everything a quick rinse and pat dry on kitchen paper. If you want to have squid rings, chop the body straight through. Otherwise, cut the body open, and prepare as required. The tentacles and wings are quite as edible as the rest of the body of squid. Don't throw them away.

To Clean Cuttlefish

As above, except that you will find a cuttle inside the body, and you usually cook the body of the cuttle whole rather than in rings. Cut the body on the cuttle side, open it and then remove the guts. The ink sac will be attached to the other side. Wash the body well and retain the ink sac, if required.

To Prepare Octopus

Large octopus have mostly been frozen ready-prepared. The best octopi have two rows of suckers; single-rowed octopi aren't really worth the effort. This is what you can do with a whole fresh octopus if you come across one. First you must tenderise it.

1) The Greek way
Take the octopus and make a small cut on the head, then turn the hood inside out. Discard everything apart from the highly prized ink sac and the dark stomach, or *loló*, which can be cooked separately. Remove the beak. Beat the octopus 100 times against a rock, rubbing it into the surface with a circular motion. Hang it up to dry, then serve grilled over a charcoal fire. They can be frozen at this stage, or dried in the hot sun for three days. The skin can be left on.

2) The Japanese way
Keep head and tentacles together, using the same method as above. Discard everything else. Place in a bowl with a whole grated daikon and knead vigorously for ten minutes, making sure that every last tentacle gets the same treatment. Plunge the octopus into boiling water, with a dash of soy sauce, but no salt should be added since it toughens the octopus. Remove from the water and leave to cool, then repeat five or six times, leaving it under the water for thirty seconds each time. Then boil for five minutes, and hang to dry slowly. The octopus is now ready to use. The tentacles are considered the best part.

3) The long slow method
Simmer a cleaned octopus in unsalted water for at least an hour.

Cuttlefish®

Sepia officinalis
French: Seiche (large/medium), Casseron (small)
Italian: Seppia
Spanish: Sepia, Jibia (large)
Portuguese: Choco
German: Sepia, Gemeiner Tintenfisch

Little Cuttlefish**
Sepiola rondeleti
French: Supion, Scippion
Italian: Seppiette, Seppioline

Spanish: Chipirón
Portuguese: Chopo, Choquinho
German: Zwergsepia

I really don't know why we don't eat more cuttlefish. Perhaps we think that what's fit for budgie isn't fit for master, but all poor old budgie gets is the cuttle, the inner piece, so what happens to the rest of the fish? Perhaps it's the horrific mess cuttlefish can create – they are particularly liberal with their ink – or their generally alien look that puts people off. What is infinitely more

CUTTLEFISH

attractive is the cleaned-up white body, which in France and Spain is quite freely available, sold ready to use.

Large cuttlefish can get a little coarse, so it's always best to eat them when they're young and tender. Don't let your conscience get the better of you if you are in the Mediterranean and confronted by the impossibly tiny little cuttlefish the French call *supion*. These are in fact a separate, smaller species rather than immature fish and, fried quickly in olive oil and garlic, are one of the most delectable things to eat. You'll need an army of willing helpers to clean them, for the cuttle has to be removed from each tiny fish. Ideally they should be eaten in the South of France – *garrigue*, sea, sun, barbecue, wine, you know the sort of thing. Oh, and cicadas.

Cuttle are aggressive creatures: when fish move to shallower water to spawn they are often followed by a whole army of hungry cuttle. As a result, markets are sometimes flooded with dark and inky boxes of not just cuttle but mauled fish, stained to such an extent that they fetch next to nothing at auction. A canny buyer can often make a fast (well, quite slow, actually) buck by filleting the fish and washing off the ink.

The cuttle, the bit that budgies eat, has a spongy interior which can be pumped up with air by the cuttlefish to give it extra buoyancy. During the day, the cuttle is mainly filled with liquid, and the fish stays on the sea floor. Live cuttle are particularly impressive; they can threaten and cajole through a vivid change of skin colour, a sight of astonishing beauty whatever the intended message.

Season: Summer to autumn.
Price: ££
Yield: 80%
Fishing method: Nets, traps.

Octopus

French: Poulpe, Pieuvre (live)
Italian: Polpo, Moscardino
Spanish: Pulpo
Portuguese: Polvo
Catalan: Pop
Greek: Octapódi
German: Krake, Tintenfisch

Common octopus★
Octopus vulgaris

Lesser octopus★
Eledone cirrhosa

One of Greece's main attractions as a holiday destination is to watch swarthy fishermen beating the hell out of dead octopi. An ignominious end for this marine brainbox but necessary to make it tender, for those eight slippery legs can be tough. Tradition has it that 99 damned good thrashings suffice.

Octopi have astonished scientists by their ability to learn to distinguish between coloured balls under a controlled experiment. This 'observational learning' is apparently OK for rats and mice, but invertebrates? No. You may well ask of what practical use is ball distinction under the sea. The answer is that the cephalopods are thinking hunters. They assess their prey and react accordingly. And the octopus's intelligence is all the more remarkable because, unlike squid and cuttle, they are distinctly unsociable, and only really ever get together to copulate.

Greece and octopi go arm in arm. I particularly like the story of Cretan fishermen who used octopi to retrieve coal lost overboard in the war. They tied an octopus to a rope and dangled it over a pile of coal on the sea bed. As soon as it touched the ground, or in this case a nugget of coal, the octopus would curl itself around it, only to be promptly hauled back up again with coal in hand. The myth of Sisyphus, cephalopod style.

One of the classic ways to catch an octopus is to wave a white rag outside its nest and wait for the bite. And if you want to stay in Classical mode, then a bite behind the octopus's eyes, severing the main nerve, is an effective way to dispatch them.

Season: All year round.
Price: ££
Yield: 90%
Fishing method: Traps, line.

Squid, Inkfish
Loligo spp.

European squid★★
Loligo vulgaris
French: Encornet, Calmar
Italian: Calamaro
Spanish: Calamar, Puntilla
Portuguese: Lula
German: Kalmar, Tintenfisch

California squid★
Loligo opalescens

Flying squid★
Illex coindetii
French: Calmar
Italian: Calamaro
Spanish: Volador
Portuguese: Pota

Squid are remarkable molluscs. To amuse your children, or yourself for that matter, go and buy a squid or two, make sure they're very fresh, and don't wear anything white. Take the tentacles, gently pull them away from the body and you'll see what looks like a clear piece of plastic. No, they haven't ingested industrial detritus, but this wonderful thing, the quill, is 100 per cent natural.

The squid you'll see for sale in the UK are most likely to be *Loligo vulgaris*, the common European squid, if they're fresh rather than frozen. One species you won't see is *Architeuthis dux*, the mysterious giant squid that can reach a length of nearly 20m (66 ft). Calamari rings from this would be Brobdingnagian.

After years of neglect, the UK government has reassessed the fish stocks that surround the Falkland Islands, starting a great international squid bonanza. Huge stocks of the oceanic short-finned squid, *Illex illecebrosus*, have been fished under licence, and the islands have grown rich from their exploitation. The fishery is being quite carefully controlled, and quotas have been reduced as the fishery has inevitably begun to suffer. The squid is frozen on board and sold all over the world.

Season: All year round.
Price: ££
Yield: 80%
Fishing method: Various.

EUROPEAN SQUID

Kiwi-marinated Grilled Squid with Garlic, Chilli and Coriander

Alternative: cuttlefish

A recipe that comes, I believe, from Down Under. I first came across the unlikely combination of kiwi fruit and squid when I was judging a cookery competition. It doesn't sound too promising, does it? I ignored it. But then it reappeared in an Australian cookbook and I finally clicked that the point of the kiwi fruit is to tenderise the squid. It is texture, more than flavour, that it changes, and the effect is quite remarkable. Even frozen squid, which tends to be tougher than fresh, is softened by its contact with the juice of the kiwi fruit, giving it a unique, almost velvety, feel in the mouth.

Once the kiwi fruit has done its work, the real flavour-bearers, the powerful chilli, garlic and coriander, have a field day. Accompany the squid with a rocket or mixed green salad, and perhaps a tomato and orange or tomato and black olive salad, and lots of crusty bread.

SERVES 2

350g (12 oz) fresh squid (or frozen, if you have
no choice), prepared (see page 247)
1 ripe kiwi fruit
1 or 2 hot Thai chillies, de-seeded and thinly sliced
juice of ½ lime
3 tablespoons roughly chopped fresh coriander
2 tablespoons olive oil
2 garlic cloves, crushed
salt and pepper
½ lime, cut into wedges, to serve

You should end up with about 225g (8 oz) of squid, once prepared. Put the squid into a shallow bowl. Peel the kiwi fruit and chop roughly, then mash with a fork and add to the squid, along with 1 de-seeded, sliced chilli and the lime juice. Cover and leave somewhere cool for at least 2 hours; better still, leave in the fridge overnight, turning occasionally.

About 20–30 minutes before cooking, pick the squid out and mix with all the remaining ingredients. If you like your food chilli-hot, add a second de-seeded sliced chilli, but if a mild tingle is quite enough for your taste, leave it out. Leave in a cool place (not in the fridge, unless the day or your kitchen is very hot), until ready to cook.

To grill or, better still, barbecue, make sure the grill or barbecue is thoroughly preheated. Lay the pieces of squid on it one by one. If they are small, turn them over as soon as you have got them all on the grill. Larger ones should be left for about 20–30 seconds before turning. Give them 10–20 seconds on the other side and then lift off and serve immediately, with lime wedges to squeeze over.

To griddle the squid, heat a ridged cast-iron griddle or heavy cast-iron frying pan over a high heat for 3–5 minutes. Lay the pieces on the griddle and cook and serve as above.

Squid in Tomato and Wine Sauce

Alternative: cuttlefish

This is a straightforward, richly flavoured squid stew in the Mediterranean style. It can take being made in advance and re-heated, if needs be. Serve it with rice or noodles.

SERVES 4

700g (1½ lb) squid, cleaned (see page 247)

For the Sauce:
1 onion, chopped
4 garlic cloves, chopped
2 tablespoons olive oil
400g (14 oz) tin of chopped tomatoes
110ml (4 fl oz) red wine
1 tablespoon sun-dried tomato purée
1 tablespoon capers, rinsed (soaked if salted)
12 black olives, pitted and sliced
½ teaspoon sugar
salt and pepper

Cut the body sacs of the squid into rings. Save the ink sacs, if you can find them, and beat with a tablespoon of water in a small bowl to release the ink. This is not mandatory but will give an even better flavour in the end. Cut the tentacles in half.

In a wide saucepan or deep frying pan, fry the onion and garlic gently in the olive oil until tender. Add all the remaining sauce ingredients, bring up to the boil and add the squid and their strained ink. Reduce to a gentle simmer and cook for 40–60 minutes, until the squid are tender. Taste and adjust the seasoning, then serve.

Chorizo-stuffed Squid

Alternative: cuttlefish

The body sac, or mantle, of the squid is a natural container for a stuffing. It just begs to be filled and stewed gently until tender, around its precious cargo. With a lively stuffing and a bit of patience (you can't rush a stewing squid), the final dish is one to be savoured.

The spiciness of good *chorizo* (from proper delicatessens, not the terrible 'Spanish-style' stuff they pass off as *chorizo* in too many supermarkets) packs vigour into this stuffing. You can use either the softer cooking *chorizo*, which looks rather like an ordinary sausage, or would do if it weren't orangey-brown, or the slightly firmer *chorizo* that is meant to be eaten like salami. The latter is likely to be easier to locate, though a good Spanish, Portuguese or Italian deli should stock both. I like the simplicity of cooking the stuffed squid gently in olive oil but, if you prefer, they can be stewed in a tomato sauce.

SERVES 6

6 medium squid (with bodies about 15cm/6 inches long)
4 tablespoons olive oil
6 tablespoons water
salt and pepper

For the Stuffing:
1 small onion, chopped
2 garlic cloves, chopped
2 tablespoons olive oil
175g (6 oz) spicy *chorizo*, skinned and diced
1 tablespoon lemon juice
finely grated zest of ½ lemon
60g (2 oz) cooked rice
2 tablespoons finely chopped fresh parsley
1 egg, beaten
salt and pepper

Clean the squid (see page 247), leaving the body sac whole and the wings *in situ*. Chop the tentacles into small bits.

To make the stuffing, cook the onion, garlic and squid tentacles gently in the olive oil until tender. Add the *chorizo* and cook for a few minutes longer. Mix with all the remaining stuffing ingredients, adding enough egg to bind. Season to taste.

Carefully stuff each sac with this mixture, filling it only about two-thirds full. Either sew up, or secure the ends with a wooden cocktail stick. Warm the 4 tablespoons of olive oil in a pan large enough to take all the squid. Lay them in it carefully, add the water and some salt and pepper, then cover and cook gently, turning occasionally, for about 40 minutes, until tender. Serve as they are or leave to cool for a few minutes and then slice into thick rings.

Thai Squid Salad

Alternative: cuttlefish

I love the taste of this cool, herb-laden Thai salad. It makes a brilliant summer lunch dish or a starter for a summery dinner party. Though you can get away with using fresh ginger instead of the similar-looking, but more aromatic, galangal, there's no point in trying to substitute anything for the fish sauce and lemongrass. No need, either, these days, as so many supermarkets and good food shops sell both.

SERVES 6 GENEROUSLY AS A FIRST COURSE,

4 AS A MAIN COURSE

900g (2 lb) squid, cleaned (see page 247)
2 lemongrass stems
4 crisp lettuce leaves, such as Webb's or Cos,
    shredded
1 red pepper, de-seeded and thinly sliced
3 tablespoons lime juice
2 tablespoons fish sauce
2–3 dried chillies, crushed
1 tablespoon finely chopped garlic
1 tablespoon finely chopped galangal or fresh
    root ginger
4 shallots, thinly sliced
about 20 fresh coriander leaves, roughly chopped
10 fresh mint leaves, torn up
8 fresh holy basil or ordinary basil leaves, torn up
1 fresh red chilli, de-seeded and shredded
    (optional)

Chop the squid tentacles roughly. Slit open the body sacs and score criss-cross lines, about 5mm (¼ inch) apart, all across the inside. Cut into strips 1cm (½ inch) wide and 5cm (2 inches) long. Cut off the upper, narrow part of the lemongrass stems, leaving the plumper, lower 10cm (4 inches) to use. Remove the outer layer, then bruise the stems to release the flavour. Slice very thinly.

Drop the squid strips and tentacles into boiling water and simmer for a minute or so, until they turn white and opaque. Drain immediately. Mix the squid with the lemongrass and all the remaining ingredients, except the coriander, mint, basil and fresh chilli, tip into a serving bowl and leave to cool.

Taste and adjust the seasoning, adding more lime juice or fish sauce if needed. Scatter over the coriander, basil and mint, adding, if you wish, a few shreds of fresh red chilli for colour. Toss in the herbs as you serve.

Octopus Stewed in its Own Juices

This is the most wonderful and elemental of all ways to cook octopus. If you only ever try cooking octopus once, try this pure Greek method. The octopus cooks in its own juices alone – no need for water, nor salt, nor even pepper. Serve it warm, as an hors d'oeuvre, with cocktail sticks to skewer the chunks and wedges of lemon or even lime for those who want a touch of acidity. Bliss.

SERVES 6

1–1.5kg (2¼–3¼ lb) octopus, cleaned

Cut the octopus up into 2.5cm (1-inch) pieces. Put them in a pan, cover and place over a very low heat (a diffuser mat is a great help here). Leave to cook gently. Raise the lid after a few minutes for a quick peek; you will be surprised to see the octopus simmering gently in a pool of its own purple-red juice. Cover it again quickly and leave it alone. Check again after about 20 minutes and give it a stir, then stir every 5–10 minutes. Very gradually, the octopus' juices will begin to diminish and become quite dense and syrupy.

When the juices are well reduced, try a knob of octopus. If it is still too tough for your liking, add a small splash of water to the pan and continue cooking until the sauce is reduced again. Try a piece of octopus. Repeat until you are happy. Serve warm.

Greek Octopus and Red Wine Stew

This rich, dark red wine and octopus stew begins with the slow cooking of octopus in its own juices, progressing on to simmer it with tomatoes and wine. The end result is marvellously tender octopus in a voluptuous sauce. An ideal dish for anyone who is a little nervous about eating octopus. I bet you they will end up asking for more.

SERVES 6 GENEROUSLY

1kg (2¼ lb) octopus, cleaned
1 onion, chopped
4 tablespoons olive oil
2 garlic cloves, chopped
400g (14 oz) tin of chopped tomatoes
1 tablespoon tomato purée
½–1 tablespoon caster sugar
1 bay leaf
250ml (9 fl oz) red wine
salt and pepper

Prepare the octopus and cook in its own juice, as described in the recipe on page 254.

In a clean pan, cook the onion gently in the olive oil until tender. Add the garlic and cook for a further 2–3 minutes. Add the tomatoes, tomato purée, ½ tablespoon of sugar, bay leaf, salt and pepper and the cooked octopus. Set over a moderate heat.

Pour the wine into the pan you cooked the octopus in and bring up to the boil, stirring to make sure that not one little drop of the sticky residue from cooking the octopus is wasted. Tip into the pan of other ingredients. Bring back to the boil, cover and simmer very gently for about 50 minutes, until the sauce is voluptuously thick.

Taste and stir in the remaining sugar if it is on the tart side. Adjust the seasoning. Serve warm, with rice or small pasta shapes.

Octopus Salad

Another very simple octopus dish, this time made of plain boiled octopus dressed with lemon juice and olive oil. Serve it as a first course, with warm pitta bread.

SERVES 4–6

1kg (2¼ lb) octopus, cleaned
juice of 1 lemon
6–8 tablespoons extra virgin olive oil
3 tablespoons chopped fresh parsley
1 shallot, very finely chopped
salt and pepper

Boil the octopus in unsalted water for about 40–60 minutes, until very tender.

Drain the octopus and scrape off the skin and the suckers while still warm. Cut into neat little bite-sized pieces. Dress with half the lemon juice, the olive oil, parsley, shallot, salt and pepper. Taste and add a little more lemon if needed. Serve at room temperature.

Sepia a la Plancha

Alternative: squid

This Spanish recipe for grilled cuttlefish is uncommonly good. The cuttlefish itself is hardly fussed about with at all before cooking, leaving its flavour strikingly pure and true. It is served with two sauces, a hot one of pounded almonds, garlic and parsley and a cool *alioli* (garlicky mayonnaise). Both sauces, incidentally, go well with all manner of shellfish and grilled fish.

The recipe comes from the Casa Salvador Restaurant near Valencia, via Penelope Casas' excellent book *Delicioso* (Alfred A. Knopf).

SERVES 4 AS A FIRST COURSE,

2 AS A MAIN COURSE

500g (1 lb 2 oz) cuttlefish, cleaned
olive oil
salt and pepper

For the Almond and Parsley Sauce:
10 unpeeled almonds, roughly chopped
3 tablespoons chopped fresh parsley
3 garlic cloves, chopped
4 tablespoons extra virgin olive oil
4 tablespoons white wine vinegar
salt

For the Alioli:
6 garlic cloves, roughly chopped
¼ teaspoon salt
2 egg yolks
1–2 tablespoons lemon juice
150ml (¼ pint) sunflower or grapeseed oil
150ml (¼ pint) extra virgin olive oil
salt and pepper

Clean the cuttlefish (see page 247), taking care not to burst the ink sacs or you will end up with black stains left, right and centre. Cut off the fins. Reserve, along with the tentacles. Slit the body sac open and then cut in half. Score the inside of the cuttlefish with criss-cross lines. Season with salt and pepper and set aside until needed.

To make the almond and parsley sauce, pound the almonds with 2 tablespoons of the parsley and a couple of pinches of salt to form a paste. Put the garlic and the oil into a small pan and heat gently. When the garlic begins to sizzle (don't let it brown), add the vinegar and simmer slowly for 5 minutes. Now add the almond and parsley paste, stir well and simmer for a further 5 minutes. Set aside.

To make the *alioli*, pound the garlic with the salt to form a paste. Work in the egg yolks and 1 tablespoon of the lemon juice. Mix the two oils. Whisking constantly, start adding the oils, drop by drop at first, gradually increasing to a slow, timorous trickle. When about one-third of the oil has been incorporated you can speed the trickle up to a thin, slow stream, but don't get too cocky or your mayonnaise risks curdling. When all the oil is incorporated, taste and adjust the seasoning with lemon juice, salt and pepper.

To cook the cuttlefish, brush a griddle or heavy cast-iron frying pan lightly with oil, then heat over a high flame until smoking. Lay the cuttlefish pieces on the pan (don't try to overcrowd it or they will stew rather than sear) and cook for about 4 minutes on each side. Arrange on a serving dish or individual dishes. Re-heat the almond and garlic sauce quickly and spoon it over the cuttlefish. Sprinkle with the last of the parsley and serve with *alioli* on the side.

Freshwater Fish

When sea fish were difficult to come by and Friday came along, poor Christians – if they ate fish at all – might have chewed on a piece of salt fish, while the rich leant corpulently over the fish pond to haul out a bream or two. Kings and queens and many of their richer subjects regularly feasted on sturgeon and salmon, as well as some of the smaller freshwater fish, but by looking at the remains of fishbones, historians think that by the thirteenth century the aristocracy was beginning to eat sea fish more often, and freshwater fish began its long slide into obscurity. Except, that is, for three key species – salmon and eel, both of which are migratory fish, spending only part of their lives in fresh water (see pages 169–171), and that good old standby, the trout.

Freshwater fish have a salt level greater than that of the surrounding water so they have to deal with the constant inward osmotic pressure; this they do by having a thick layer of slime, particularly noticeable on the mirror carp (which has few scales), and by passing out great quantities of dilute urine.

The state of most inland waters in Europe is poor, so it's not surprising that supplies are largely dependent on farmed fish.

Bream

Abramis brama
French: Brème
Italian: Brama
Portuguese: Brema
German: Brachse

The bream's natural habitat is muddy water, which has never made it a popular fish. In the Middle Ages, before the carp appeared in Europe in the fifteenth century, it was better known, and was often the most important fish to be found in the fish-ponds that were scattered around the country.

The bream has quite bony flesh. Whole fish are difficult to fillet when fresh and need to be scaled before cooking.

    Season: Summer.
    Price: £
    Yield: 35%
    Fishing method: Farmed.

Carp ♥

Cyprinus carpio
French: Carpe
Italian: Carpa
Spanish: Carpa
Portuguese: Carpa
German: Weissfische, Karpfen

We have had marine sheep; now meet the aquatic rabbit. Prodigious, hardy and fast growing, the carp family are giant minnows that have moved far and wide from their original home waters in China. Carp were once food fit for Chinese emperors, and so impressed early travellers by their fortitude that they were brought back to Europe by the traders who used the Silk Road. Many of them were Jewish, and the carp became and has remained one of their favourite fish. Jewish communities often lived far away from the sea, and the carp could easily be stored and farmed in fresh water, which in those days was relatively unpolluted.

Carp have an amazing ability to stay alive out of water. I used to load them (alive) in France, spend hours on a ferry, spend even more hours dealing with Customs (remember those days?) and then sleep briefly. Most of the carp would still be gently opening and closing their mouths, with infinite patience, by the time I offloaded them the following day.

The species you are most likely to come across are the grass carp and the mirror carp. The former is longer and more classically fish-shaped than its slightly hump-backed relation, with a regular network of scales. The mirror carp, on the other hand, is remarkable for its irregular pattern of large scales. The key to good carp is to rear them in clear, rather than muddy, water.

Farmed carp are often sold alive and kicking, and are highly rated in Chinese cooking. Fillets can occasionally be bought and are a good bet, since the carp is a difficult fish to fillet when very fresh. Carp are also good in a freshwater fish soup, particularly the Burgundian *Pochouse*.

    Season: All year round.
    Price: ££
    Yield: 35%
    Fishing method: Farmed, pond reared.

Catfish ®

French: Wels, Silure
German: Welse, Katfisch

Danube catfish
Silurus glanis

American catfish
Ictalurus spp.

African catfish
Clarias gariepinus

I predict a bright future for the catfish. It is a solid chunky fish, well suited to strong Southern American cooking, and since it is being farmed it is likely to become more widely available soon.

Catfish can be monstrous and are distinguished, as one would suspect, by fishy whiskers that serve as feelers in muddy water. Most species have four – two up, two down – and almost all are carnivorous. Recently a species of blind, cave-dwelling catfish has been discovered. It appears to live off baboon droppings, which gives you some idea of how tough these fish can be.

In the 1980s some Danube catfish escaped into the River Loire, and there are tales of French codgers, berets askew, tackling enormous catfish in the quiet backwaters of the region. They have no natural predator apart from man, so life is relatively easy. Fish weighing 50kg (111 lb) or more are now routinely seen, but seldom caught to eat, since the flesh of these larger fish is notoriously coarse, as is that of the fast-growing African catfish which has red flesh but is even coarser. The best of all the species are considered to be the various American catfish, but whichever you see they are best bought in fillet form – around 175g (6 oz) per person.

Season: All year round.
Price: ££
Yield: 40%
Fishing method: Farmed, net.

Char,
Arctic Char,
Char⋆

Salvelinus alpinus
French: Omble chevalier
Italian: Salmerino
Spanish: Salvelino
Portuguese: Salvelino-ártico
German: Saiblinge

Char are attractive, delicate fish, troutlike but more colourful, most closely resembling the brook trout, *Salvinus fontinalis*, or *saumon de fontaine* in French. Char were once found quite widely in Britain, and there are some excellent recipes for potted char from Lake Windermere. The char is

now farmed, and Arctic char from Iceland seem to have cornered the market. Any variation on the trout is a welcome relief, and these fish can be steamed, baked or fried, combining well with a rich or robust sauce, say a *beurre blanc* or hollandaise. They are mostly sold portion sized or filleted, which is convenient.

Season: Farmed fish. All year round. Wild fish available early summer.
Price: ££
Yield: 65%
Fishing method: Farmed, net for wild fish.

Lamprey,
Sea Lamprey⋆♥

Petromyzon marinus
French: Lamproie
Italian: Lampreda
Spanish: Lamprea
Portuguese: Lampreia
German: Neunauge, Flussneunauge

Of all the creatures that live in the water, surely the lamprey must be among the most repulsive. It is a parasitical fish and its mouth consists of a round set of sucking barbs rather than jaws. Early accounts suggest that it was always a popular food; the Romans were known to have treated lampreys to an elaborate death, suffocating them with cloves in their breathing holes and a nutmeg in their mouth.

It is an eel-like fish, mottled green to brown, but is possibly outgunned in the repulsiveness stakes by its cousin the hagfish, *Myxine glutinosa*, which burrows into the gut cavity of larger fish and eats them from the inside out. Charming!

Unhappily for the lamprey, one should always cook and prepare them alive, being careful to retain the blood which is an integral part of the classic Bordelaise lamprey stew.

There are sea lampreys and river lampreys. The marine species are still fished in the mouth of the Gironde and some are caught along the northern Portuguese coast, where a

great Christmas favourite is a sweet version, *Lampreia de ovos*, a cake made in the shape of a lamprey which, of course, contains no lamprey at all but an enormous amount of sugar.

Season: Spring.
Price: £££
Yield: 60%
Fishing method: Net, trap.

Nile Perch

Latus niloticus
French: Perche du Nil
Italian: Persico di Nil
Spanish: Perca del Nilo
Portuguese: Perca
German: Victoriabarsch

No one knows quite how it happened but in the 1950s a large fish called the Nile perch somehow appeared in Lake Victoria, in Africa, and began to gobble up vast quantities of the local fish ecosystem. It spread so rapidly that the countries bordering the lakes – Kenya, Tanzania and Uganda – decided to start exploiting the fishery, and small quantities of fillets began appearing in Europe. Meanwhile, the Cichlid population of the lakes, a vital fish resource for the local people, rapidly declined; in Lake Malawi alone, where the Nile perch also appeared, 200 Cichlid species have been pushed to extinction. It is with some relish that I encourage everyone to go and eat a Nile perch fillet or two.

However, a recent salmonella outbreak has been traced to Nile perch, and all shipments from Africa now have to be rigorously inspected.

These enormous fish grow rapidly. Specimens between 20 and 30kg (44–66 lb) are often landed but the fillets are coarse. Smaller fillets are cheap, so it's a fish gaining in popularity, especially in Germany where cheap, bland freshwater fish are very popular.

Season: All year round.
Price: £
Yield: Sold as fillets, 50%.
Fishing method: Net.

Perch®♥

Perca fluviatilis
French: Perche
Italian: Percha, Pesce persico
Spanish: Perca
Portuguese: Perca
German: Barsch, Flussbarsch

'Tis a pretty fish, orange-finned, green-skinned and good to eat, but seen rarely in Britain. Although they can weigh about 3kg (7 lb) or so, they are more usually found at about 400–500g (about 1 lb), a size that will feed two at a pinch.

Perch eat insects and fish larvae, so aren't among the muddier-tasting freshwater fish. They keep well, and their colours don't fade when they die, so all in all they are one of the better freshwater fish.

Perch fillets are good, firm and don't fall apart when cooked, and go well with a *beurre blanc* sauce (see page 305).
Season: All year round.
Price: ££
Yield: 40%
Fishing method: Net.

Pike*

Esox lucius
French: Brochet
Italian: Luccio
Spanish: Lucio
Portuguese: Lúcio
German: Hecht, Flusshecht

The brooding pike brings drama to any stream or pond where it lurks, for it is, as Isaac Walton once told us, the 'tyrant' of fresh water. Ducklings beware, this carnivore has razor-sharp teeth, a hearty appetite, and is a skilful hunter. It has a strange appearance, being unusually long and thin, and has a soft flesh too full of bones to appeal to many. Smaller fish are finer eating and go well with a simple sorrel sauce; larger fish can get quite weighty and their drier flesh is often made into quenelles (see page 268). These delicate forcemeat lozenges were once very popular, and can be a ravishing and extravagant dish if accompanied by a *Sauce Nantua* made from the finest

freshwater crayfish and loads of cream. A dish for the jaded or toothless.
Season: Autumn.
Price: ££
Yield: 50%
Fishing method: Net, line.

Roach

Rutilus rutilus
French: Gardon
Italian: Triotto
Spanish: Bermejuela
Portuguese: Ruivaca
German: Plötze

You occasionally see small roach available in the late summer in England but their boniness may be off-putting. I once used to buy a wonderful mix of tiny and totally ecologically unsound roach from Burgundy that were quickly fried to make a *friture*, and frying seems to be the best option.
Season: Summer.
Price: £
Yield: Eaten whole, 40%
Fishing method: Net.

Smelt

Osmerus eperlanus
French: Eperlan
Italian: Eperlano
Spanish: Eperlános
Portuguese: Eperlano
German: Stint

Smelt are supposed to smell of cucumber, and it has always intrigued me quite why some do and others don't. It's not just a matter of freshness – some perfectly fresh fish just don't have that smell – but still the essence of smelt is smallness, winter and cucumbers. In 1630 the Mayor of London ruled, in an unusually sensible way, that during the spawning season the smelt fishery must stop to the west of London from 10th March to 14th September to protect the stock. Later accounts tell of barrels of fresh smelt being sold for prices as low as sprats, so it must have worked. Frying small fish, be they sprats, whitebait or smelt, was a very London thing in those

days, but when the old London Bridge was built across the Thames many species – smelt included – could never pass the shallow water underneath.

Smelts were still found in the Medway right up to the 1950s, but these days they are fished mainly in Holland and tend to be too big, smelling only vaguely of cucumbers.
Season: Traditionally winter.
Price: £
Yield: Eaten whole.
Fishing method: Net.

Sturgeon

French: Esturgeon
Italian: Storeone
Spanish: Esturión
Portuguese: Esturjão
German: Stor, Sterlet

European sturgeon
Acipenser sturio

Beluga
Huso huso

Sevruga
Acipenser stellatus

Oscietra
Acipenser gueldanstaedtii

Long gone are the days when the European sturgeon, *Acipenser sturio*, swam freely up our rivers. They are solid, meaty fish and were deemed to be good food for the medieval stomach. Sturgeon is better known for its roe, caviar, a far tastier option than the meat (see pages 280–81).

For some years now sturgeon have been farmed quite successfully in south-west France, producing both meat and caviar. The flesh has always proved more difficult to sell than the roe – surprise, surprise! The flesh tends towards dryness so avoid overcooking it. It can be barded with anchovy fillets and garlic then roasted, but is perhaps at its best smoked.
Season: Farmed all year round.
Price: £££
Yield: 50%
Fishing method: Net, farmed.

Tilapia, St Peter's Fish

Tilapia nilotica

Tilapia are a venerable species of freshwater Cichlids native to the Nile, which grow rapidly but are not among the classiest fish to eat. They look after their young in an odd way – by keeping them in the female's mouths, with the result that females tend to be smaller and leaner than the males, presumably because having a mouth full of babies doesn't improve your ability to eat. Scientists have now engineered an almost entirely male range of fish.

It is sometimes sold as St Peter's fish, which is farmed in some quantity in Israel.

They are very adaptable fish and are widely available. I recently ate a cherry tilapia, a brilliant red fish farmed in Jamaica, and was pleasantly surprised by its taste. Size-wise, a 600–800g (1¼–1¾ lb) fish will feed two, and smaller 300–400g (11–14 oz) fish can be eaten whole or filleted to serve one.

Season: All year round.
Price: ££
Yield: 40%
Fishing method: Farmed.

Trout, Rainbow Trout♥★

Salmo gairdnerii
French: Truite
Italian: Trota
Spanish: Truta
Portuguese: Truta
German: Forelle

I have a terrible admission to make. When I wrote the first of many drafts of this book I completely forgot to mention the trout. It's not that I dislike it but it's just too obvious. Long gone are the days when trout were fished from rippling brooks countrywide. Today they are farmed to such an extent that almost everyone could buy one with ease from any town in the land. This rural fish has become deeply urbanised but, since cheap, easy fish are rare, hats off to the trout for being so omnipresent. Trout is an excellent everyday fish – affordable and adaptable, if perhaps a little unexciting. On the plus side, you seldom see trout that are anything but fresh.

Often smothered in almonds, the trout is, I think, best eaten whole, freshly killed and *au bleu*, but being grilled or baked in foil suits it equally well. I like the idea – although I have never tasted it – of the northern Italian dish of *trota al tartufo*, trout stuffed with white truffles.

Season: All year round.
Price: £
Yield: 55%
Fishing method: Farmed.

Zander, Pike-Perch★★

Stizostedion lucioperca
French: Sandre
Italian: Lucioperca
Portuguese: Lucioperca
German: Zander

Last year a little birdy (or should it have been fishy?) told me that the British Waterways Board had a zander problem. It seemed that zander were beginning to overrun several Midland canals. This was an opportunity not to miss, for this wonderful fish is rarely caught domestically. The problem for British Waterways was clear – the canals needed to be rid of the carnivorous zander, which was eating all the other species and overwhelming the ecosystem – but the problem for me was somewhat different. It was all so unpredictable. A cull was announced but no one quite knew when it was taking place; the quantity and size of the fish could only be guessed at. Zander are not, in fact, native to this country but since their introduction in the 1950s they have spread throughout much of Britain's waterways, although they are not systematically fished. In the end I opted out of the bidding, but if you ever come across this fish, definitely try it.

Zander can become quite large, weighing over 5kg (11 lb) at times, and are more popular abroad than in the UK. The fillet is, for a freshwater fish, exceptionally firm and fine tasting. The best fish are caught in Holland, where there is a strictly controlled closed season. When they're not available, fish are often bought in from Poland or Hungary and even Canada, although the quality of some of the Great Lakes fish is inevitably poor to toxic, given the state of the water.

The Hungarians cannot restrain themselves from plastering the zander, or *fogas*, with paprika and frying it to a crisp, but it has a chameleon-like ability to taste delicate when required, and withstand powerful flavours. The Swedes have an excellent way of cooking it, with beetroot, horseradish and capers, which has an earthiness that well suits this wonderful fish (see page 274).

Supplies are not as easy as they were a few years back when there was a vogue for serving zander in restaurants, for surprisingly it's a difficult fish to sell.

Season: Winter/summer.
Price: ££
Yield: 50%
Fishing method: Net, line.

Carp with Black Sauce

Alternatives: tilapia, zander

This is one of the classic ways of cooking carp, much favoured in Eastern Europe and in Germany, where it is often served at the festive Christmas Eve meal. The carp is cooked in a sweet, sharp, slightly bitter sauce, flavoured – curiously enough – with honey cake (the French *pain d'épices* is ideal but our own gingerbread works well, too). I've adapted the recipe for fillets of carp, which makes it slightly easier to handle, but do take care not to overcook the fillets or they will collapse as you lift them out of the pan.

If this all sounds just too strange to work, let me tell you that my two-year-old thought that the sauce was quite divine, eating it with carrots as well as fish, and the rest of the family was more than inclined to agree with him.

SERVES 6

1.5–1.8kg (3¼–4 lb) carp, scaled and filleted

For the Cooking Broth:
1 onion, sliced
½ celeriac, sliced (optional)
1 large carrot, sliced
2 celery sticks, sliced
¼ lemon, sliced
bouquet garni of 1 bay leaf, 2 fresh thyme sprigs,
    2 fresh parsley stalks, tied together with string
2 cloves
5 black peppercorns
300ml (½ pint) water
750ml (1¼ pints) brown ale
salt

To Finish the Sauce:
60g (2 oz) *pain d'épices*, spiced honeycake or
    gingerbread, crumbled
60g (2 oz) blanched almonds, cut into strips
60g (2 oz) raisins
30g (1 oz) butter, chilled and cubed
salt and pepper

Put all the cooking broth ingredients into a pan large enough to hold the carp fillets. Bring up to the boil and simmer for 30 minutes.

Now lower the fillets gently into the liquid, making sure that they are completely covered (add a little extra water if needed). Simmer gently for about 5–10 minutes, until just cooked. Lift the fish out carefully and keep warm on a serving dish while you finish the sauce.

Pass the broth through a sieve, rubbing through as much of the vegetables as will pass through easily. Return to the pan and add the cake crumbs, almonds and raisins. Simmer until reduced by half. Taste – it should be intensely flavoured. If it seems at all watery, boil it down a little more. Whisk in the butter, bit by bit, to thicken and give the sauce a good gloss. Season to taste with salt and plenty of pepper. Pour over the carp and serve immediately, with boiled potatoes.

Ken Hom's Red-cooked Carp with Tangerine Peel

Alternatives: bream, tilapia, zander, perch

This is a wonderful recipe for carp, dressed with an intense, sweetish sauce, distinguished with the aromatic scent of dried tangerine (or orange) zest. Don't be tempted to replace it with fresh orange zest, which doesn't have quite the same magic. I reckon you need the zest of about 3 or 4 tangerines or 2 large oranges. Either thread the pieces of zest on to a length of cotton with a needle and hang up to dry, or leave it on a rack in a warm kitchen, or very low oven, until completely dried out and brittle.

I've made a few very small alterations to this recipe, which comes originally from one of Ken Hom's best cookery books, *The Taste of China* (Pavilion).

SERVES 2–4

5g (¹/₅ oz) dried tangerine or orange zest (see above)

1.1–1.35kg (2½–3 lb) whole carp, cleaned and scaled

2 teaspoons salt

3–4 tablespoons cornflour

450ml (¾ pint) groundnut or sunflower oil

2 tablespoons finely chopped garlic

3 tablespoons finely chopped peeled fresh root ginger

4 tablespoons finely chopped spring onion

3 tablespoons rice wine or dry sherry

2 tablespoons yellow bean sauce

2 tablespoons dark soy sauce

1 tablespoon sugar

6 tablespoons chicken stock or water

Soak the tangerine or orange zest in warm water for 20 minutes or until it is soft. Rinse under running water, squeeze out any excess liquid, then chop it finely and reserve.

Cut three or four diagonal slashes across the fattest part on each side of the fish to help it cook more evenly. Rub the fish on both sides with the salt. Coat the fish thickly and evenly with the cornflour on both sides, spreading it down into the cuts and over the head. Shake off any excess. Heat the oil in a wok or deep frying pan until hot. Test with a cube of bread – the oil should start fizzing as soon as it is dropped in. Deep-fry the fish for about 3–4 minutes on each side, turning it carefully once, until it is brown and crisp. Lift carefully out of the oil and drain on kitchen paper.

Taking great care, pour most of the oil out of the wok or frying pan into a heatproof bowl (you can strain it for re-use, when cool, but use only for cooking other fish). Leave just 2 tablespoons behind in the wok. Re-heat over a high heat. Add the tangerine zest, garlic, ginger and spring onion and stir-fry for 30 seconds. Add the rest of the ingredients and then return the fish to the pan. Spoon the contents of the pan over the fish. Cover and cook over a low heat for 8 minutes. As soon as the fish is cooked, carefully transfer it to a serving plate and serve immediately.

Southern Fried Catfish with Hush Puppies

Alternatives: zander, tilapia

Fried catfish, coated in a crisp layer of cornmeal, is one of the great down-home dishes of the Middle West and Southern states of America. Hush puppies – cornmeal fritters – are the essential accompaniment, no doubt about that; after that, individual family preferences rule. The cookery writer James Beard suggested serving them with tartare sauce, while another book points you towards a Creole mayonnaise (flavoured with mustard, cayenne, white pepper and ground coriander). In her fascinating book *Soul Food* (Weidenfeld Paperbacks), Sheila Ferguson, best known as the former lead singer of the Three Degrees but obviously a fine cook too, writes that her family make a gigantic meal of the fried catfish, eating it with hush puppies, coleslaw, mustard greens, ham hocks and fried apples (particularly good) or onion rings.

SERVES 4

1kg (2¼ lb) skinned catfish fillets
300ml (½ pint) buttermilk
150g (5 oz) cornmeal
85g (3 oz) plain flour
dripping or equal quantities of butter and
   sunflower oil, for frying
salt and pepper

To Serve:
lemon wedges
Hush Puppies (see opposite)
coleslaw
Tartare Sauce (see page 312)

Soak the catfish fillets in the buttermilk, turning them to coat well and, if necessary, adding a little more buttermilk or a dash of milk. Leave for 15 minutes or so.

Mix the cornmeal with the flour and some salt and pepper and spread out on a wide plate. In a wide frying pan, melt enough dripping, or equal quantities of butter and oil, to give a depth of about 2cm (¾ inch).

When the fat is good and hot, take the fillets out of the buttermilk one by one, sloughing off the excess with your fingers, and then roll in the cornmeal mixture to coat evenly. Lay the fillet in the hot fat and then repeat with the other pieces, taking care not to overcrowd the pan, which would lower the heat of the fat; two to three pieces at a time is quite enough. Fry each fillet for about 3 minutes on each side until browned and crisp, then drain on kitchen paper and keep warm while you fry the rest. Serve steaming hot, with lemon wedges, Hush Puppies, coleslaw and tartare sauce.

Hush Puppies

Hush puppies are crisp little puffs of cornmeal batter: they make a great alternative to chips with all kind of fried foods but especially with fried fish. Eat them warm from the pan, sprinkled with salt.

There are, incidentally, several explanations for the name, all based on similar stories peopled with different characters. The one I like best is that these scraps of corn batter were thrown to the dogs by Confederate soldiers during the Civil War – 'Hush, puppies' – to keep the dogs quiet when they suspected that Yankee soldiers were creeping around nearby.

SERVES 4–6

175g (6 oz) cornmeal, preferably white but
    yellow will do fine
60g (2 oz) plain flour
½ teaspoon salt
1 teaspoon sugar
1 teaspoon baking powder
1 garlic clove, very finely chopped
4 spring onions, very finely chopped
1 egg
Tabasco sauce (optional)
200–250ml (7–9 fl oz) buttermilk or ordinary milk
dripping, lard or sunflower oil, for deep-frying

Mix the cornmeal with the flour, salt, sugar and baking powder and then stir in the garlic and spring onions. Make a well in the centre and add the egg and a shake or two of Tabasco, if using. Gradually mix the egg into the dry ingredients, adding enough buttermilk or milk to make a mixture that will drop 'slow but easy' from a spoon.

Heat the fat to about 185°C/370°F (when a cube of bread fizzes mightily as it is dropped in, and quickly starts to brown). Drop teaspoonfuls of the hush-puppy mixture into the hot oil and deep-fry until golden brown. Don't overcrowd the pan or the temperature of the fat will drop too low. Lift out the hush puppies as they are cooked and drain them briefly on kitchen paper. Keep warm while you cook the rest. Season with salt and serve with fried catfish (or other fried fish).

Char with Kohlrabi and Cider

Alternatives: trout, perch

This is a simple dish that works surprisingly well. Kohlrabi, now fairly widely available in good supermarkets, has a sweet crispness offset with a hint of the characteristic sulphur of the cabbage family, of which it is a member. If you can't get kohlrabi, substitute their cousins, turnips, as long as they are young and still sweet.

SERVES 4

2 tablespoons olive oil
2 kohlrabi, peeled and cut into 5mm (¼-inch) cubes
1 onion, finely chopped
1 garlic clove, chopped
bouquet garni of 1 fresh thyme sprig, 2 fresh parsley sprigs and 1 bay leaf, tied together with string
350ml (12 fl oz) dry cider
2 Arctic char or trout, filleted
300g (11 oz) tomatoes, peeled, de-seeded and chopped
1 tablespoon each of finely chopped fresh parsley and marjoram
1 tablespoon plain flour
lemon juice
salt and pepper

Put 1 tablespoon of the oil in a heavy frying pan and add the kohlrabi, onion, garlic and some salt and pepper. Turn to coat lightly in oil. Add the *bouquet garni* and one-third of the cider. Cover with foil and cook over a very low heat, stirring occasionally, until the kohlrabi is tender and the liquid has been absorbed, 20–30 minutes.

Lay the fish fillets on top of the kohlrabi and scatter with the tomatoes and chopped herbs. Pour over the remaining cider, cover again with foil, and continue cooking over a low heat for 8–10 minutes, until the fillets are just cooked. Carefully pour off the liquid. Keep the fish and vegetables warm.

Quickly make the sauce. Heat the remaining oil gently in a small pan and stir in the flour. Off the heat, add the liquid from the fish, a little at a time, to make a sauce. Bring back to the boil, stirring, and simmer for about 5 minutes. Taste and adjust the seasonings, adding a dash of lemon juice. Serve with the fish and vegetables.

Pike with a Sorrel Sauce

Alternatives: zander, perch, char

The easiest way to cook and eat pike has to be in fillets, making away with the worst of those little bones and savouring the fine flavour of the flesh, untrammelled. I love it with a sharp but creamy sorrel sauce, lengthened by a shot of fish stock.

SERVES 4

4 pieces of pike fillet, weighing about 110–175g
   (4–6 oz) each
court-bouillon (see page 307), for poaching
salt and pepper

For the Sorrel Sauce:
2 good handfuls of sorrel leaves
30g (1 oz) butter
150ml (¼ pint) double cream
4 tablespoons well-flavoured fish stock
salt and pepper

Make the sauce first. Snip the stems off the sorrel leaves and discard. Make little piles of leaves, roll them up like cigars, and then slice thinly, to make fine shreds or, in more technical terms, a *chiffonade*. Reserve a few shreds to use as a garnish. Heat the butter in a small pan and add the sorrel. Stir over a moderate heat until the sorrel dissolves to a rough purée. Stir in the cream and stock. Simmer for a few minutes, then season to taste. Re-heat when needed.

Put the fillets into a pan and add just enough *court-bouillon* to cover. Bring gently up to a simmer, then reduce the heat until the surface of the water just trembles. Poach for 2–3 minutes, until the fillets are barely cooked through. Lift out with a slotted spoon and drain thoroughly. Lay the fillets on warm serving plates and spoon the sauce around them, drizzling a little decoratively over the fillets. Scatter over the reserved raw sorrel and serve.

Quenelles de Brochet

Alternatives: carp and most flaky white fish

William loves *quenelles de brochet*, or at least he loves to eat them with *Sauce Nantua*, the marvellous coral-coloured crayfish sauce on page 233. *Brochet*, pike, is the classic fish to use for these pale, delicate poached fish mousses but since the flavour of the fish is fleeting, comparatively speaking, by the time they are made, many other fish with the right kind of texture can be substituted, with only minimal difference in flavour.

Quenelles de brochet are an essential part of the classic French restaurant repertoire, and it has to be said that there are good reasons for this. The main ones are that pin-boning the pike fillet and then sieving the puréed pike are both tedious jobs. You can just about get away with skipping one or the other but, either way, you are likely to end up with bones in your trembling pale *quenelles*. In a restaurant, of course, this would be a heinous crime. At home, I don't think it matters enormously, as long as everyone eating them is aware that they may come across a bone or two here and there.

Don't attempt to make *quenelles* on a boiling hot day – the mixture is more likely to curdle. I like to cook them in a *court-bouillon*, which gives a mite more flavour, but if you don't have time to make one use plain salted water with a branch or two of dill or fennel in it. If you can get the crayfish, then serve the *quenelles* with *Sauce Nantua* (see page 233), made in advance, for a regal feast; otherwise, choose the Anchovy Tomato and Red Pepper Sauce on page 117.

SERVES 4

500g (1 lb 2 oz) pike, skinned and filleted
2 eggs
325ml (11 fl oz) double cream
court-bouillon, for poaching (page 307)
salt, pepper and freshly grated nutmeg

After skinning and filleting you should be left with about 250g (9 oz) of pike flesh. Pin-bone the fillets, then put the flesh into a food processor and process to a paste. Season well with salt, pepper and plenty of grated nutmeg (the cream will soften the flavour considerably). Rub the purée through a fine sieve into a bowl and then beat the eggs into the mixture. Stand the bowl in a bowl of iced water and gradually whisk in the cream. Don't take it too slowly or you risk overbeating the mixture and making it curdle (remember, butter is made by beating double cream).

Pour the *court-bouillon* into a shallow pan and heat to just below simmering point. Have a mug of iced water standing by, with two tablespoons in it. Before you get going properly, make a quick test run to see whether the texture of the mixture and the temperature of the water are about right.

Use one cold, wet tablespoon to take a scoop of the *quenelle* mixture and then shape the upper part neatly with the bowl of the second damp spoon (you are aiming for something that looks vaguely rugby-ball-shaped). Slide the second spoon under the *quenelle* as it sits in the first spoon, to loosen it, and slide the *quenelle* gently into the barely simmering liquid. Poach for about 4–5 minutes, until it bobs up to the surface and feels fairly firm. Lift out with a slotted spoon, drain briefly and give it a try. If it seems heavy, beat a little more cream into the mixture. If it is still undercooked in the centre, maybe your *court-bouillon* could be a little hotter. Sort yourself out and then poach the rest of the mixture in the same way. As you poach the *quenelles*, keep them warm while the rest are cooking.

Grilled Tilapia
with Tomato and Cucumber Relish

Alternatives: trout, parrotfish, mackerel, sardine

Leaving the scales on a fish as it is grilled is rather like protecting it in its own, perfectly fitting suit of armour. The heat penetrates, fusing the scales together as it blasts in and cooks the flesh, but no moisture is lost in the process: the fish's own natural jacket keeps it all locked in, including every last drop of flavour. Pure and remarkable, the fish needs only a simple, fresh accompaniment, such as this finely diced relish-cum-salsa.

SERVES 4

4 tilapia fish, gutted, not scaled
oil

For the Relish:
½ cucumber, peeled and finely diced
350g (12 oz) tomatoes, peeled, de-seeded and
    finely diced
2 tablespoons lemon or lime juice
4–5 tablespoons olive oil
1 teaspoon sugar
2 tablespoons finely chopped fresh basil
½ tablespoon finely chopped fresh mint
salt and pepper

To make the relish, spread the cucumber out in a sieve, sprinkle lightly with salt and leave to drain over a bowl for a good half hour.

Rinse the cucumber, pat dry and mix with the remaining relish ingredients. Leave in the fridge for an hour or two so that the flavours can develop and the relish is chilled. Just before grilling the fish, taste and adjust the seasonings.

Preheat the grill thoroughly. Brush both sides of the fish with oil and place in a foil-lined grill pan so that the upper side is about 7.5cm (3 inches) away from the grill. Grill until both sides are well browned – about 10 minutes on each side.

Test one fish only with a skewer. Bring the almost charred fish to the table. Cut along the central line and lift off the skin, with its jacket of fused scales, to reveal moist, firm flesh. Serve the hot fish with the chilled relish.

Trout en Escabeche

Alternatives: char, mackerel, tilapia

Summertime, and the cooking is easy . . . Or at least it should be, and the lunches and supper parties undemanding and enjoyable, almost as relaxing for the hosts as for the guests. Here's one dish that can be, needs to be, prepared in advance, and that is served cold with little need for fiddling or flapping. Offer good bread, with a chewy crust and soft crumb, and a few leaves of watercress or rocket, if it is to be a first course; for a main course, serve some boiled new potatoes and a more substantial salad. Then sit back and bask in the warmth.

SERVES 4 AS A MAIN COURSE,

8 AS A STARTER

4 trout, cleaned
juice of 1 lemon
olive oil, for frying
salt and pepper

For the Marinade:
½ cucumber, peeled and thinly sliced
1 red or ordinary onion, sliced paper thin
1 red or yellow pepper, de-seeded and sliced into rings
1 green or red chilli, de-seeded and sliced
1 bay leaf
1 teaspoon allspice berries, crushed
1 garlic clove, chopped
150ml (¼ pint) white wine vinegar
85ml (3 fl oz) olive oil

Rub the lemon juice on the outside and inside of the fish. Season and leave for half an hour. Pat dry and fry in very hot oil until browned on both sides. Place in a shallow dish.

Place the marinade ingredients in a pan and bring up to the boil. Simmer for 3 minutes, then pour over the fish. Cool, cover and leave in the fridge overnight.

Fried Trout with Tomato and Black Bean Sauce

Alternatives: perch, tilapia, mackerel

A quickly made, 'East meets Middle East', vibrant dish of fried trout dressed with a little tomato sauce and kicked into high gear by the addition of Chinese fermented black beans (the whole beans, mind, not the ready-made sauce – any you don't use for this recipe will keep for months in a screw-top jar in the fridge) and a gasp of chilli-hot harissa. These days, you can find this Moroccan chilli and spice paste in good supermarkets but, failing that, you will have to search out a Middle Eastern delicatessen. It's well worth laying in a small supply of harissa (it lasts for ages, too) and, more often than not, it comes in particularly decorative cans. What you don't use of the harissa can also be stored in a small screw-top jar in the fridge; cover with a layer of olive oil before screwing on the lid.

SERVES 2

2 trout, cleaned
30g (1 oz) clarified butter (see page 305) or 15g (½ oz) butter and 1 tablespoon sunflower oil
2 teaspoons fermented black beans, rinsed and chopped
1 garlic clove, chopped
225g (8 oz) tomatoes, peeled, de-seeded and chopped
½ teaspoon fresh thyme leaves
¼ teaspoon harissa or chilli sauce, or a few drops of Tabasco sauce

Slash the trout twice diagonally across the thickest part on each side so that the heat and the sauce can penetrate through to the bone.

Melt the butter or butter and oil in a pan large enough to hold both fish. When it starts to sizzle, add the fish. Fry over a moderate heat until the skin is browned on both sides and the fish is just cooked.

Transfer the fish to a warmed serving plate and keep warm. Add the beans and garlic to the pan and fry for about a minute. Add the remaining ingredients and cook hard for a further 5 minutes or so, until the tomatoes have collapsed and all the wateriness has evaporated to leave a thick sauce. Spoon the sauce over the trout and serve.

Trout Façon William

Alternatives: tilapia, salmon fillet, cod fillet

Or in other words, with a butter, tomato and chive sauce, and very delicious it is too. The sauce also goes extremely well with salmon (fry the salmon in the pan before making the sauce and then deglaze with the Noilly Prat), and chunks of fillet from most firm-fleshed white fish. This sauce is one of William's signature dishes and the one he brings out regularly when he is doing fish demonstrations. Funnily enough, he doesn't cook it that often – or at least not often enough – for us at home. Now that I've wheedled the recipe, with quantities, out of him, I might get a chance to cook it, too.

SERVES 4

4 trout, cleaned
fresh chives
butter
salt and pepper

For the Sauce:
110ml (4 fl oz) Noilly Prat
500g (1 lb 2 oz) ripe, full-flavoured tomatoes, peeled, de-seeded and finely chopped
125g (4½ oz) butter, cubed and chilled
4 tablespoons snipped fresh chives
lemon juice
salt and pepper

Preheat the oven to 220°C/425°F/Gas Mark 7. Season the trout inside and out with salt and pepper. Stuff a few stems of chives into the stomach cavity of each fish. Lay in a buttered dish and cover with foil. Bake for 15–20 minutes, until just cooked through.

Meanwhile, make the sauce. Pour the Noilly Prat into a frying pan and bring to the boil. Boil hard until reduced by about two-thirds. Tip in the tomatoes and cook for 2–3 minutes. Now whisk in the butter in two batches, until fully incorporated. Stir in the chives and lemon juice, salt and pepper to taste. Draw off the heat and keep warm.

When the trout are cooked, uncover and pour the sauce over them. Serve immediately.

Zander, Loir-Style

Alternatives: perch, char, bass, John Dory, grey mullet, turbot, monkfish, brill, Dover sole, barracuda

Around the little part of France that I know best, in the valley of Le Loir (without an 'e' – it's a tributary of the great Loire river of *châteaux* fame), they like to serve zander with a lemony *beurre blanc* sauce. In our own village, the little café serves a dish of zander with *beurre citronée* that is as good as many I've eaten in far smarter restaurants. Maryvonne steams the zander, naps it in the buttery golden sauce and serves it sprinkled with chives, with a lettuce leaf for garnish and a few boiled potatoes for substance. I love it.

SERVES 4

4 portions of zander fillet, weighing about
    110–175g (4–6 oz) each
salt and pepper
4 lettuce leaves, to serve
1 heaped tablespoon chopped fresh chives, to
    garnish

For the Lemon Butter Sauce:
1 shallot, finely chopped
160g (5½ oz) butter, diced
60ml (2 fl oz) dry white wine
150ml (¼ pint) Fish Stock (see page 308)
juice of 1 lemon
finely grated zest of ½ lemon
pinch or two of sugar
4–5 tablespoons double cream
salt

Season the zander fillets with salt and pepper and set aside.

For the lemon butter sauce, soften the shallot in 15g (½ oz) of the butter over a gentle heat, without browning. Put the remaining butter back in the fridge to chill. Add the wine, fish stock and lemon juice to the pan. Boil gently, until reduced to about 3 tablespoons, with a sticky, syrupy consistency. Set aside if not serving the sauce immediately.

When you are ready to complete the sauce, re-heat the reduction. Reduce the heat to a thread (or if it won't turn down sufficiently low, pull the pan back from the heat every now and then so that the sauce doesn't overheat). A few cubes at a time, whisk the butter into the sauce until all is incorporated. Add the lemon zest, sugar and cream; 4 tablespoons at first, adding the last one only if the sauce seems a little on the tart side. A little more sugar can go some way towards rectifying this, too, as long as the sauce doesn't start to enter the realms of sweet custard, but keep it fairly lemony to balance the soft, subtle flavour of the steamed fish. Season with salt to taste and keep warm over a very low heat while the fillets finish cooking.

Should your sauce dare to teeter on the edge of curdling, you are probably overheating it. Plunge the pan into a bowl of very cold water and keep whisking. With any luck, and fast action, it will be saved.

Meanwhile, steam the zander fillets for about 5–7 minutes, depending on thickness, until just cooked through. Lay on serving plates, with a lettuce leaf nestled on one side. Spoon over a generous helping of the sauce, sprinkle with the chives and serve at once.

Zander with Beetroot, Capers and Horseradish

Alternatives: perch, carp, catfish, brill, Dover sole, barracuda

William found this recipe for zander in a Swedish cookery book and asked me to try it. The rub was that the book had not been translated and neither of us understand anything but the odd word of Swedish. Luckily, our minimal combined tally of the language is almost entirely food-orientated and, with a large degree of hilarity and guesswork, we came up with a working version in English. Even if we have missed the finer details, we still finished up with a marvellous dish, bringing together delicate zander fillets with sweet roast beetroot, sharp, salty capers and a sting of horseradish.

SERVES 4

2 raw beetroot, weighing about 110g (4 oz) each
75g (2½ oz) unsalted butter
4 zander fillets, skinned
plain flour, seasoned
3 tablespoons capers, rinsed (soaked if salted)
3 tablespoons chopped fresh parsley
½–1 tablespoon creamed horseradish
salt and pepper
lemon wedges, to serve

Preheat the oven to 170°C/325°F/Gas Mark 3. Wash the beetroot but leave the root and about 2.5cm (1 inch) of stalks in place. Wrap each one in foil and bake for about 1½–2 hours, until the skin scrapes away easily. If you want to speed things up, boil them instead until tender, but you lose some of the flavour to the cooking water. When cooked, leave until cool enough to handle and then pull off the skin and cut the beetroot into 1cm (½-inch) cubes.

Melt 30g (1 oz) of the butter in a wide frying pan. When it is foaming, coat the zander fillets one by one in the seasoned flour and lay them in the pan. Cook for about 1 minute on each side and then transfer to a warm serving dish and keep warm in the oven.

Melt the remaining butter in a second pan and add the capers and beetroot. Fry for about 2 minutes to heat through, then stir in the parsley and horseradish, adding only ½ tablespoon of horseradish for a subtle hint of it, the full tablespoon for a stronger presence. Season to taste. Spoon over the fish and serve immediately, with lemon wedges.

Preserved Fish

We can rummage in freezer cabinets and fridges until we're blue in the face but in days gone by, when neither ice nor refrigeration were being used, other ways had to be found to keep fish from spoiling. The Scandinavians used the dehydrating effect of cold and wind to dry fish, and developed a fascinating trade in both wind-dried and salt cod with southern Europe.

The principles of salting fish have been well known for thousands of years, and were used to preserve fish by the early Greeks and Romans. To this day, anchovies and sardines from the south, as well as cod and herring from the north, are still salted. Tuna, sardines and anchovies are canned, and increasingly every house seems to have a bottle of Thai fish sauce – as it should – stashed away beside the balsamic vinegar, a sauce that comes from fermenting fish of various dimensions.

At the other end of the scale are those horribly expensive and deeply delicious things such as caviar, that you would like to nibble at but such nibbling could seriously damage your bank balance. Smoked salmon, indeed all smoked fish, is much more approachable, and smoking was originally another highly effective way to prevent fish from spoiling.

I provide here a little guidance and direction into the confusing world of preserved fish.

CANNED FISH

Mammas, mamans, mémés and mums have bottled and preserved food at home for aeons, and before you accuse me of being sexist and un-pc, I myself have just chopped, bottled and put aside a whole Cornish tuna. Salmon, tuna and sardines are the canned fish we are all fairly familiar with, salmon less so than in years gone by, when it was sandwiched and fishcaked by the ton. Canned tuna is a valuable product for the fishing world, and has become a very modern one, accommodating the sensibilities of consumers everywhere indignant over the deaths of dolphins (not tuna) in the long nets that are sometimes used to trap them. It's heartening also to see one supermarket chain marketing tuna from the Solomon Islands that has been fished in a responsible, possibly sustainable way, pre-empting a movement in labelling that will undoubtedly be of greater importance in the coming years. Tuna, mainly skipjack, is brined and canned all over the world.

Canned sardines are a more esoteric, and once purely European, speciality. The tradition of preserving sardines in butter and oil in great earthen jars called *oules* was largely Breton. In 1824 Joseph Colin, a *confiseur* of Nantes, opened the first sardine canning factory, producing what by all accounts must have been an excellent can of sardines, for within a few years there were factories springing up all over Brittany and sardine canning had a hero. In fact so central was the name Colin, that a rival Nantes company had the brilliant idea of looking for another Joseph Colin, who they duly found and employed, so that they too could jump on the Colin bandwagon and sell their sardines under the same name. A lawsuit followed, and the upstart Colin company had to back down. Meanwhile, the citizens of Lorient claimed that the invention was that of a local magistrate who had instructed a woman, a *Demoiselle Le Guillon*, to preserve some sardines, once again apparently successfully. While producers squabbled among themselves, the market took off, and the large local fish that shoaled off the Breton coast found an important new market.

There are, as always, secrets and techniques to respect in sardine canning. As soon as the sardines were landed, the processors cleaned, beheaded and soaked the fish in brine for half an hour.

After that, they were dried, then quickly fried in oil and laid in a can, finally being covered with good-quality olive oil – and this was the key, the quality of the oil. Sardines mature in their cans, and indeed a good can should be at least two or three years old so that the bones and spine become soft and edible. Maturing the fish in second-rate vegetable oil is obviously not going to give the same results.

Today, canners have a problem. Supplies of sardines are not what they were, and frozen or brined sardines from Morocco are not considered good enough for canning. Mediterranean sardines are too small, so the industry has had to contract, and our sardines on toast are none the better for it. The habit, incidentally, of cooking canned sardines is somewhat looked down upon by the French, who think that they should always be savoured cold, though Sophie remembers a recipe in a French children's book for souffléed sardines which was, she swears, *les genoux des abeilles*.

When buying canned tuna, you'll find some cans with olive oil and some with less fine vegetable oil. The species canned are light-coloured albacore or skipjack, as a rule. They make excellent sandwiches and, of course, salads such as the classic *Salade Niçoise*. Tuna preserved in brine is also good and less fattening. Canned salmon can be used to make fishcakes or, once again, to fill a sandwich, which is greatly improved by a slice or two of cucumber.

SALTED FISH

One day when you're at a loose end, take a fillet of cod and lie it on a bed of salt – good-quality Ibizan salt if you happen to have some available. Cover it generously so that it's completely surrounded by salt. Leave it for at least two weeks in a cool place, then take a look and see what's happened. Firstly, it shouldn't be off, but notice how much it has shrunk. Salt draws out water, and since bacteria mostly need water to function, salted fish lasts longer. If you put it back in the salt, or even dry it, and then salt it again, you've got the basis of a technique that has been used for generations.

Salt fish certainly isn't indestructible, as some bacteria can thrive even in salty conditions. Remember that salt attracts moisture, so always store salt fish in a dry place. Cod and ling are the ideal fish to be dried and salted, but the fat in fish such as mackerel, herring and tuna can go rancid, so they are mostly salted in barrels or tins to keep the air out.

Anchovies

Collioure is a small, indecently attractive fishing port tucked into the bottom right-hand corner of France. It is part of the French Catalan coast, much loved by artists and artistes, and is the home of a once-thriving anchovy industry ('once-thriving', since imports and nasty old competition have taken much of the market from under their noses). You might have assumed that anchovies were simple to produce, but the story is complex.

As with many pelagic fish, there is an air of predictability about when the shoals arrive. The processors in Collioure are well prepared with stocks of salt, while an army of Catalan women, strong of hand and thick of skin, sit filleting and packing anchovies hour-by-hour, week-by-week in the pungent workshops – I really can't call them factories – that can be found in many of the local fishing ports.

When a boat surrounds a shoal, speed is very much of the essence, for anchovies spoil incredibly quickly. The sooner they die, the sooner the boats steam home towards the auctions and markets of Catalonia, Galicia and around much of the Mediterranean.

Some fish are headed and gutted, others left whole, and they are then placed gently – anchovies are immensely fragile – into large wooden barrels, where they lie heavily salted, for at least three months. There they begin to mature, still gently pressed down by a weight at the top of the barrel, until they are ready for the next stage – filleting. The anchovies are taken out of the barrel and washed and cleaned of the surface salt – ideally in cold water, although some dastardly swine use warm – then dried before being filleted by hand. And so to the tin or jar, where even here fillets are laid one by one, by hand, labelled, stacked and sold until someone like you opens it up and wonders about the intricacies of anchovy fillets. Now you know. This is what is called artisanal production, and long may it survive.

You can still buy some fabulous tins of whole salted anchovies, which even when opened will carry on maturing in a kitchen cupboard. The idea is to take out a fish or two and use them as and when. If you do, be warned. The salt and anchovies mature to make a reddish gunge which may look unappetising but is actually a good sign. Note also that the type of oil in tinned anchovy fillets affects the taste. Olive oil is much better than a bland vegetable oil, so take a look at the label.

In Greece, the heads are removed, the anchovies are placed in brine, then left to dry out in the sun. But what gives Greek anchovies their particular taste is the salt, which is used on several batches of anchovies, adding considerably to their piquancy.

To make a real *Janssons Frestelse* (Jansson's Temptation), you should use Swedish *ansjovis*, which aren't anchovies at all but sprats, lightly cured, and less pungent than anchovies. But don't panic, anchovies – genuine ones – will do instead, since the Swedish fish aren't readily available over here yet.

Herrings

Herrings fat and full, virgin herrings, red herrings – a thousand types of cured herrings exist, and many are little known over here. Let's start in Holland, where the *groene haring* (green herring) and *maatjes* (maiden or virgin herring) make the Dutch go weak at the knees.

Correctly, *groene haring* should be caught and gutted, leaving the gall bladder in, then lightly salted, although this attention to detail may well, I suspect, be on the way out. The gall bladder is said to contain an enzyme that hastens the process of maturation, and all the fish needs is a very light brining overnight. Eaten on street corners in Holland, dipped in onions and gobbled messily, they are, you may be surprised to hear, amazingly delicate. The attraction of both green herring (it doesn't somehow sound so edible in English) and *maatjes* is that the herring are young fish, caught before their gonads have properly developed, which gives them a virginal delicacy. Every year about 1,200 million fillets are sold in Holland alone. *Maatjes* and *groene haring* are not the sort of thing you come across every day, though *maatjes* are now widely frozen and available all year round. They should be eaten with chopped, raw, sweet onion.

Recent Dutch legislation has added a bizarre twist. In order to ensure that herring are parasite-free, all Dutch cured herring have to be made from frozen rather than fresh fish, so for the purist the place to go for real fresh *maatjes* is now Belgium, where the traditional methods are still used.

Further north, in Sweden, *maatjes* become *matjes* – a cured, strong-tasting herring traditionally eaten on midsummer's day with a glob of soured cream, potatoes, chopped hard-boiled egg and copious amounts of aquavit. I love Swedish *matjes*. The key to their taste lies in the well-guarded secret combination of spices used to create the reddish brine, and I was somewhat surprised to learn that mixed in with the allspice, bay, cloves and salt is sandalwood.

France also has its own herring specialities. The pungent zone that surrounds the harbour of Boulogne is home to a few remaining *saurisseries*, or curing houses, where herring have been cured for generations. These days, they seldom process local fish, since there aren't too many around, but use frozen herring from Iceland or Norway instead, which do the job admirably. When I worked in Boulogne, I loved wandering among the hideous old warehouses that dripped tar and made your whole body reek of smoke – and herring, delicious herring.

The *filet d'hareng doux*, a cold-smoked and lightly brined fillet that is traditionally eaten cold, on a bed of potatoes and shallots, is very much a northern French speciality. The *filet saur* is stronger tasting, hot smoked and more heavily brined, but both have their adherents. Stronger-tasting, overly salty foods are not as popular as they once were, and may well die out, but the *filet doux* will, I hope, live on.

The coast of northern France was once surrounded by forests of oak and beech, ideal wood for smoking fish. As tastes changed in the last century, the Boulonnais started to produce a less intensive smoked herring, the *bouffi*, which was brined for twenty-four hours and smoked for only eight, guts and all. Despite being a more fragile product, this is still made, and is none other than the East Anglian bloater.

Our bloater, 'one-third fresh, one-third slightly salt, one-third lightly smoked' is above all a Yarmouth speciality, now sadly fallen by the wayside. Was it those bottles of bloater paste that put us off? Or have our tastes changed? I needn't add that those of you fortunate enough to come across a fresh bloater should snap it up unashamedly, but remember to eat it within a week.

A word about the word. Bloater is said to come from the Swedish *blöta*, meaning to steep or soak, and not from its look of bloatedness, although a bloater is indeed a bloated thing. Its predecessor, the red herring, lacked the bloater's delicacy, and was smoked hard and long to become virtually indestructible. Red herrings gave the East Anglian fishing ports a major boost and were found in the farthest corners of the world – or rather empire for, like custard, they marched hand in hand with the Union Jack.

The English were always out-manoeuvred in the herring trade by the Dutch and the French, but the red herring was one of the few things they couldn't mess up. Herrings need to be taken as quickly as possible to the shore to be smoked, and the Dutch ports were simply too far away from the shoals that often swam within sight of the East Anglian coast. Wood was to be had aplenty, and the British Empire provided a huge market for a food that was so pre-eminently indestructible. Red herring were used in the West Indies to feed the slaves and workers on the plantations, and the legacy of salt and smoked fish is very much apparent in the West Indies to this day.

Although hard cured herring have no market these days, the more delicate kipper is most definitely not out of favour. These days a kipper is a split, mildly cured smoked herring.

Originally, kippered fish were smoked because they had spawned and were therefore not particularly good to eat. The word itself is derived from the Dutch *kippen*, meaning to hatch, and kippers were originally smoked and brined salmon rather than herring. In 1848 a Mr John Woodger started kippering herring in his shop in Seahouses, Northumberland, and immensely popular they proved to be. Kippers soon became indisputably herrings rather than salmon, and have remained so ever since.

The kipper has managed to survive being dyed and generally abused to become one of this country's greatest culinary specialities and, like the bloater, in my opinion, is best eaten grilled.

There are alternative cooking methods, though, which avoid the tendency for the grilling smell to linger on after its welcome has expired. One way to minimise this is to clamp the kippers together in pairs, skin outwards, dabbing butter between them like a sandwich, then wrap in foil and heat thoroughly in a moderate to hot oven for 10 minutes or so. Of course, if you don't mind the smell, or you are off to work as soon as they've been downed, then you may prefer just to grill them, skin side to the heat, with no added fat.

To jug kippers, put them in a tall jug and cover with boiling water. Leave for about 5–10 minutes, then drain and eat.

The easiest way to eat a kipper is to put it on your plate, skin-side up, and work downwards from there. That way you reach the bones last.

Salt Cod

French: Morue
Italian: Baccalà
Spanish: Bacalao
Portuguese: Bacalhau
German: Gesalzener Kabeljau

For every detractor, salt cod has a thousand fans. Often known by its Spanish (*bacalao*) or Portuguese (*bacalhau*) name, salt cod needs strong flavours, and a smidgeon of skill to avoid it becoming completely inedible. There are two absolutely golden rules about salt cod: firstly, it has to be soaked in clear, clean, fresh water before cooking to get rid of the salt and secondly, if you're cooking it in liquid don't let it boil, since this toughens the cod.

In Norway, where the salt cod industry has its spiritual home, fish are selected and split in time-honoured fashion right down the middle, leaving the backbone in place. Gut linings were also left in or taken out before salting, resulting in what is called black wing (lining in) and white wing (lining out). Portugal, the most important market for salt cod, prefers black wing to white wing. But order *bacalao* in Spain, *baccalà* in Italy, or even *bacalhau* in Brazil, and it's almost certainly white wing you'll be eating.

Many words, wise and foolish, have been written about how best to prepare salt cod. Much of it depends upon what type of salt cod it is. Dry salt cod, the type you see mostly in Spain and Portugal, needs to be soaked for a minimum of twenty-four hours, with at least three changes of water. However, this depends upon the thickness of the fillet and the temperature of the water, as well as the number of times you change it; you'll need to check it every now and then by tasting a bit of the fish. If it tastes excessively salty, leave it in for longer.

There are some who say that the last soaking should be in warm water, and others who recommend using running water, but before you get to that stage, concentrate instead on seeking out a really first-class piece of cod: dry, white, thick, and if possible with both bones and skin intact – important because they give the dish a gelatinous twang, essential for a successful dish of *bacalhau*.

Buying salt cod in Britain is vexing, for it seems that much of the market is intent on supplying the cheapest rather than the best. I know that surplus cod stocks that can't find a home as fresh fish are routinely sent up north to be salted, but there are still artisans in this business, people who seek out the best fish and the best salt, and who use the true force of nature to dry their fish. Salt cod connoisseurs tend to prefer Icelandic or Faroese salt cod to Norwegian but there is, of course, good and bad fish from all three.

In Lisbon there is a whole street devoted to *bacalhau*, where you can learn a thing or two. You may notice that the fish are expertly cut, with middles, tongues and tails all fetching different prices. To most, a good thick chunk from the shoulder end is best but the experienced cook can use a middle or end to good effect.

In France the traditional salt cod is what's called wet salt cod, or *morue verte*, green as in natural rather than rotten. The difference here is that there is no drying involved, merely the dehydrating effect of the salt on the fish. This, I suspect, has something to do with the position of the ports involved in the French salt cod trade: Fécamp, Dieppe, Douarnanez and Concarneau are Norman or Breton ports, where sunshine is not as sure a commodity as it is in Spain and Portugal. *Morue verte* is less intense, and lends itself to different cooking techniques. De-salting is also less time-consuming, although twelve hours' minimum soaking is still recommended. Note that, depending on the degree of salt cure, it

can be a more fragile product with a finite shelf-life. *Brandade de morue*, that arduous, rich dish beloved of the Nîmois, is made with *morue verte* or, for the real hard-core purists, with *stoccafisso*, wind-dried cod.

There are, as any Portuguese cook will tell you, enough salt cod recipes to eat a different dish every day of the year, but we in Britain don't seem to share their enthusiasm for *bacalhau*, and use it rarely. It is robust, hearty food, somehow marrying a delicate fish with sun, salt and strong flavours to create a culinary *Gestalt* of epic proportions. I have vivid memories of eating fried *bolhas de bacalhau* in a bar in Ipanema in Brazil, while getting drunk on *caipirinha*. I remember also eating *bacalhau à Gomes dá Sa* in Portugal, cooked with little fuss and great speed, a sumptuous mix of salt cod, egg, onions and a lake of olive oil.

Buy the best, thickest pieces from a Spanish or Portuguese shop for preference and don't treat salt cod as a second-rate dish. Treat it with care and you may be as surprised as I have been.

Salt Ling

If you find yourself in Cork City at Christmas time, go to the market, where you'll see piles of ling, neatly rolled up, salted rather than fresh. Salt ling is a great Irish tradition, to be eaten poached and flaked with buttery mashed potatoes. This is another fish with a glorious past, and ling were once landed, dried and salted, giving not just flesh, but oil for lamps, and livers and sounds (swimbladders) to be eaten.

FISH SAUCE

Thai: Nam pla
Vietnamese: Nuoc-mam
Malay: Budu
Cambodian: Tuk trey
Burma: Ngan-pya-ye
Japanese: Shottsuru
Filipino: Patis
Indonesian: Ketjap-ikan

Every home worth its salt should have a

bottle of Thai fish sauce (*nam pla*). Every Roman household did, centuries ago – not from Thailand, of course, but from their own backyard. The process of fish sauce making has a long history but is essentially one that has changed little over the years. Small fish such as anchovies were piled high in large containers and left to rot in the sun. The end result was a fermented liquid, of varying strength, that in Roman times was used to flavour fish, meat and even vegetables. As well as whole fish, fish livers or just fish guts alone were sometimes used; one of the very best Greek fish sauces, *haimation*, was made solely from the innards of tuna fish. The odd thing about this type of sauce is just how unfishy it tastes. It is not a sauce in the smothering sense of the term, rather a flavouring, to be used with discretion.

There is still a tiny amount of fish sauce being produced on the Côte d'Azur called *pissala*. This is made using a mix of small fish such as anchovies and sardines. A modern Greek version is called *garos*, and is made from the livers of mackerel and bonito.

DRIED FISH

Bombay Duck, Bumalo, Bummalow

It seems a fairly innocuous thing, a dried thin fillet of fish, but why call it duck? Simply put, it is a dried version of a small transparent fish, *Harpodon nehereus*, that swims off the Indian subcontinent. Linguistically the connection is somewhat obscure. The Bombay comes from the Marathi name for the fish, *bombila*, but as far as the duck goes, I can find no adequate reason for it, other than the fact that the fish are said to skim along the water, in duck-like fashion.

Bombay duck are dried extensively in many parts of India and Bangladesh, and often have asafoetida added to them. The taste verges on the unpleasant and they should be used with discretion. At all costs avoid deep-frying Bombay duck: it gives off deeply noxious fumes.

To use them, grill or shallow-fry the fish whole, in dried form, for a couple of minutes and then allow to cool. They can then be crumbled over curries.

Dried Cod, Stockfish

French: Stockfish
Italian: Stoccafisso
Portuguese: Peixe seco
German: Stockfisch
Norwegian: Stokkfisk, Klippfisk

Stand out in a dry, cold, rasping wind and you'll be surprised by just how cold, dry and rasped you may feel. This dehydrating effect of wind has been used for hundreds of years to dry cod. These days, demand is limited. Italy is the great stockfish buyer, and the Lofoten Islands in northern Norway the last remaining producer.

The word itself is derived from the Dutch *stoc* meaning stick, and *vis* meaning fish, an odd linguistic touch perhaps, but at one stage the Dutch were intricately involved in the trade of stockfish. This hard, almost totally dried cod is particularly popular in Liguria and the Veneto, where you will often see it for sale, blisteringly white and ready to use. But beware, in the Veneto *stoccafisso* (Italian for stockfish) is also called *baccalà* – there has to be a confusion somewhere along the line! Elsewhere in Italy, *baccalà* is salt cod.

Stockfish needs to be reconstituted in fresh water, a process that will take at least two days, but to make things even more difficult you need to beat the fish with a rolling pin, hammer or something solid to tenderise it. Stockfish are found whole rather than split, which makes the bashing a little easier. If they are to be cut you will probably need a saw. Change the water every 12 hours or so depending on the temperature and the thickness of the cod. Although dried cod and salt cod recipes are similar, the two are not always interchangeable. *Brandade* can be made with either, but

Italian recipes are generally more suitable for stockfish.

The Norwegians have created a spectacularly peculiar way of dealing with it. The fish is reconstituted, then soaked in a lye (strongly alkaline) solution made originally from the ashes of birch or beech but these days produced artificially by using caustic soda. The whole process takes a minimum of ten days, so this is not exactly fast food. *Lutefisk* is mainly eaten at Christmas time, and seems to be loathed by the young and revered by those who are young no longer. Not to be missed for those keen on a genuine cultural experience on a plate. The Swedes often make it with dried ling.

Mojama, Mosciame

A while back, sitting on a Sardinian waterfront eating *mosciame*, sipping wine and soaking up the sun, thoughts might have turned seawards to try and identify the salty fish between your teeth. It might not in fact have been fish, for much Italian *mosciame* was once made from *delfino*, or dolphin. But suppress your moral outrage, picket not the Italian embassy, the practice is now strictly illegal. Alongside the dolphin swam bluefin and bigeye tuna, which were also used to make this impeccably Mediterranean speciality.

Both tuna and dolphin have long loins of dense red meat that lend themselves well to drying in the strong summer heat. These days, *mojama* is mostly made in Spain, and known by its Spanish rather than its Italian name, although it is the Italians who are the great *mojama* eaters. Tuna are filleted with great skill, with a single straight cut along the loin. Soaked in salt, washed, and then dried for twenty days, the loin dries down dramatically to less than 2kg (4½ lb) from one loin from such a fish, so it can hardly be a profitable business. To eat *mojama*, slice it thinly, nibble, and sip at a glass of good *fino* in the sun, or lay it on a slice of good bread rubbed with garlic and moistened with olive oil topped, perhaps, with a slice of red tomato. Don't think of dolphins.

FISH ROE

Bottarga, Poutargue and Tarama

A wasteful fishery chucks out the heads, and a wasteful cook chucks out the roe. With many fish, wisely so, but there are some species that should be snapped up if in roe. Firstly grey mullet. There is a great Mediterranean speciality called *bottarga*, which is made entirely from the dried and salted roe of either bluefin tuna or grey mullet. It may seem an oddity today, but once *bottarga* was widely known, even mentioned by Pepys himself. Use *bottarga* grated over pasta, or just gently nibbled, thinly sliced. It is strong tasting, and goes well with a glass of *fino*.

You will, I suspect, have trouble locating tuna roe but a good fishmonger could well find some fat grey mullet for you, full to bursting with roe, as they come in to spawn in the early summer. If the complexities of drying, pressing and waxing fish roe are too remote, you could easily make your own *taramasaláta*. I have a real weakness for this kind of thing, as do our children, who like to call anything pink, sludgy and edible, 'dippy'. If you fancy a change from those ominous pink pots, then making your own taramasaláta is easy (see page 73).

Serve *bottarga* grated onto pasta with olive oil and garlic, or tomato sauce.

Caviar♥

Caviar oozes luxury but is it a culinary sham? The basics first: caviar is made from sturgeon roe and comes primarily from the Caspian Sea. In pre-Gorbachev days, when Iran and the Soviet Union were the regional control freaks, the supply was fairly well ordered, but with the demise of the USSR, the centre did not hold and the caviar trade nearly fell apart. Today it's controlled by Iranian theocrats, regional *mafiosi*, and Russian, Turkmen, Azerbaijani and Kazakh politicians. Sturgeon stocks are increasingly threatened by overfishing and the destruction of the habitat, as well as by a general lack of control.

Back in 1952, something big happened to the world of caviar. It was then that the Iranians pulled out of an agreement to sell all of their production to the Russians and began to market it for themselves. Today the Iranians have a highly efficient state body called Shilat, and a lot of effort has been put into getting things right, which they have largely done. Iranian caviar is now without doubt the best, but why?

Firstly, the Iranians fish their sturgeon earlier in the season, when the water is cooler and the eggs firmer – and firmness is important when it comes to caviar. Secondly, they don't mix and match their roe. Every tin has eggs from one fish alone, be it a 30g (1 oz) or 1kg (2¼ lb) tin, whereas the Russians tend to match colour and size and bundle them all together. Thirdly, the fishing method is different. The Iranians leave a net in place, capturing fish at different stages of their cycle, but on the Russian side the technique is more specific: nets are placed across the deltas, catching the fish as they try to swim up river to spawn, when the roe can be almost over-ripe, and too soft to make good caviar.

One thing that holds true wherever your caviar comes from: to get the best, buy from a reliable dealer. I have seen Russian tourists bargaining with Indian fishermen over jars of caviar, and heard tales of dodgy Russian wide boys offering great deals for cash in some of the country's finest restaurants. For years, Polish lorry drivers did an excellent side line in (actually quite good) caviar, but today the centre of dodgy caviar is Baku in Azerbaijan, where lives are lost and fortunes made in this lucrative, dangerous business. Much of the nastiest caviar around gets sold in Dubai, so don't buy in Dubai.

The actual curing process is relatively simple. The eggs are removed and cleaned of all the surrounding membrane and that, apart from the addition of salt and borax, is basically it. Salt, as we have seen, preserves fish, and it is added to caviar too, but there is also the small matter of borax. Borax takes away some of the saltiness and is

an essential ingredient in making good caviar. Caviar buyers do at times specify the amount, usually about 4 per cent salt to 0.5 per cent borax, but taste caviar without borax and you may be surprised by its corkiness.

In France, a sturgeon farm in Bordeaux has begun to produce its own caviar but initially had trouble adding borax under EU law. I understand that the problem has now been solved, but the taste of the caviar *sans borax* was not to the critics' approval. In the US the use of borax is forbidden by law.

The other thing to look out for when buying caviar is whether the eggs have been pasteurised. Although this may well prolong the shelf life, it also hardens the eggs and alters their taste. In any case it all seems quite unnecessary to me. Fresh caviar keeps for months in sealed tins and can perfectly well be frozen – so go for the tins of fresh caviar rather than the jars, which have been pasteurised.

With the lack of control in the Caspian in recent years, stories of doom and gloom have surfaced and dealers are beginning to look elsewhere for caviar supplies. Chinese caviar, launched in the UK a few years back, was initially badly marketed, but it seems likely that their own types of caviar, from Kaluga and Amur fish, could be developed again soon. The second big caviar option is in the hands of aquaculture. The sturgeon farm in Bordeaux is expected to produce nearly 3 tonnes of caviar, and there was even one in Derbyshire until it went bust in 1996.

One encouraging fact: the Iranians have for a long time been releasing hatchling sturgeon into the Caspian in an attempt to boost the natural stocks. In 1996 about 24 million fish were released.

As to whether caviar is a sham or not, the jury's out. Although conspicuous consumption is thankfully distinctly *passé* these days, I have to admit that I love caviar and will carry on eating it even if I have to withdraw to the closet.

Caviar is usually eaten with toast or *blini*, but I have eaten it with spaghetti and it was wonderful. If you do cook with caviar, try to use Sevruga since the eggs are strong enough to withstand being cooked. Another excellent way is to

serve caviar with baked or new potatoes, spooned over a dollop of crème fraîche. I have read that the Russian Tsar's children were in the habit of eating caviar with mashed banana for breakfast, but this I have never tried.

Beluga

The most ostentatious caviar eater will go for Beluga, from the sturgeon of the same name (*Huso huso*). Beluga caviar is characteristically grey to black, the greyer the better, and the fish itself is the one species that is exclusively carnivorous. Only 2 per cent of the catch is from Beluga, so you won't often see it anyway. Some accounts suggest that this species will soon become extinct, so eating Beluga should not be encouraged.

To tell if you've got the genuine article, squeeze an egg and you should see a clear white oil come out.

Beluga should always be sold in blue tins.

Oscietra

The caviar dealer's caviar and one that you would be well advised to try. The Oscietra (*Acipenser guldenstadtii*) can weigh in at 80kg (177-8 lb) maximum, and gives eggs with a delicate but variable taste, which take on a lovely golden colour in older fish. Very old Oscietra can have roe so markedly golden that it is sometimes sold as Golden Caviar. You can tell if your Golden Caviar is genuine by squashing an egg or two on a sheet of white paper. If the liquid that runs out is yellowish, then it is Oscietra. A useful way to remember this is that Oscietra is traditionally sold in yellow tins.

Sevruga

Smaller than the Beluga, the Sevruga (*Acipenser stellatus*) weighs a maximum 25kg (55-6 lb), and has eggs that are smaller, blacker and saltier than the other types.

Pressed caviar

A block of hardened Sevruga that can be used in cooking.

Caviar tips

- Never eat caviar with a silver spoon. It reacts and tastes metallic. Always use bone or, if the worst comes to the worst, plastic spoons, although one wouldn't want to be seen to be encouraging this sort of thing.

- Spring-run Iranian caviar is considered to be the best of all caviar. It is usually available from June.

- Caviar should smell lightly of the sea, and the eggs should be whole and separate rather than a condensed mass. Hard eggs are out.

- Caviar can be stored for two months at 3°C, or can be frozen. When you want to use it, thaw it out slowly in the fridge.

Other Fish Eggs

Although there is nothing quite so fine as caviar, other fish have eggs that are cured in roughly the same way. Salmon eggs, or roe, are often sold as Keta (from the Russian for chum salmon, which have particularly good roe). As you would expect, caviar dealers often do a nice line in Keta, but it can be clumsy and indelicate. Make sure that the eggs, if you can see them, aren't broken. They go well with soured cream. Trout eggs can be treated in the same way.

Swedes swear by their own speciality, *löjrom*, or bleak roe, light golden eggs from the freshwater fish, but I must say I don't.

In the States you might come across paddle fish caviar from the lakes of Tennessee, which I have neither seen nor tasted. I am assured it is good but doesn't keep well. The paddlefish is related to the sturgeon, by the way.

The nastiest of them all comes from a fish with skin as thick as a rhinoceros, the lumpfish, or lumpsucker. The roe from these fish appears to be coloured with Grecian 2000 and tastes very unsubtle. Use with care!

SMOKED FISH

Smoked Salmon, Smoked Eel *et al*

Much of the variation in the taste of smoked fish depends upon the details. Firstly, there are two smoking methods, hot and cold smoking. The first is a little like cooking in a smoky oven at a low temperature but cold smoking, which takes longer, requires all sorts of skills to get the product just right. Just right, of course, is highly subjective, and even within Europe there is a marked difference between what smoke is preferred by whom. I once tried to get a number of chefs to agree on a particular combination of smoke, salt and sugar for their cure. Predictably, there was absolutely no agreement, so the best advice is to go and taste as many varieties as possible and there's sure to be something you like.

In Britain we tend to go for a stronger smoke and a smaller fish. The French amaze me when they seem to prefer bland pink slabs of smoked salmon from Norway. Over here we know better, and the finest smoked salmon of all comes from Scotland and Ireland.

This is the ideal smoked salmon scenario: take a salmon, fresh not frozen, split and fillet it, and dry cure for sixteen hours with a mixture of salt and brown sugar; then get an old whisky barrel, chip it, burn it and smoke your salmon for eight hours. Alternatively, find a trustworthy supplier who will do all this for you.

Some people are lucky enough to have smoked their own wild salmon, but it is a difficult fish to market for the very good reason that the fat content in wild fish can vary enormously. So don't be fooled into thinking wild fish are always best. They can be, but there again they can be infinitely dull.

Eel is generally smoked without sugar, using oak or beech wood for preference. It is rich, almost overwhelmingly so, for eel is an exceedingly fatty fish. To make it sit more lightly in the stomach, serve it with horseradish, with which it has a special affinity. It needs little else than a slice of brown bread and a squeeze of lemon.

Smoked trout, smoked mackerel, smoked cod and even smoked char are easily found these days. They are almost all good to eat.

Smoked Haddock

There is no other country that eats smoked haddock to the degree that we do. And there is no other country that can make it as badly as we do. Or as well. I'm thinking particularly about those luminous yellow pieces of fish sold in fishmongers and supermarkets across the land. Avoid them! They are a travesty.

After the Second World War, it became the habit to dye smoked haddock, and the kipper too, with a hideously synthetic colour. To save costs, the smoking process was reduced, but the end product was considered too pale for the consumer, so a splash of dye was routinely added. It turns out that many of the colouring agents used may well have been carcinogenic, so the public is now being encouraged to eat a more natural, less brash, smoked product which is definitely preferable. Naturally smoked haddock takes on the gentle colour of a field of ripe barley, so buy undyed haddock if you can.

Scotland, the home of haddock smoking, has created a range of specialities that even the French are beginning to *adorent*.

Arbroath smokie, Pinwiddies
Small haddock, headed and gutted, dry salted, tied in pairs and hot smoked over a hardwood fire.

Finnan haddock
Named after the village of Findon, near Aberdeen, where they were once made, Finnan haddies were originally heavily smoked in peat smoke but are now cold smoked in wood. Correctly, they are split and smoked, with the central bone left in. They can be used to make the Scottish soup Cullen Skink.

Glasgow pales

Very lightly smoked haddock. Best served grilled, with a knob of butter and black pepper.

PICKLED FISH

Another way of preserving fish is pickling it by adding a liquid such as vinegar, wine or soured cream to stop the growth of bacteria. These days the pickling tends to be lighter, and imaginative food technologists have come up with some pretty odious variations on this theme. Madeira, whisky and sherry sauces can be some of the foulest things in the fishy repertoire, obliterating the natural taste and texture of the fish within. Other cures are quite wonderful. As you would expect, much of it depends on the quality of the ingredients. Take the vinegar, for instance. Rollmops (rolled herrings in vinegar) can range from the subtle to the inedibly loud, but can be improved by using white wine rather than malt vinegar. In Scandinavia you may come across *krydsill*, herring marinated in allspice; here a relatively strong-tasting spice works well with the herring. (The heavy use of allspice in Scandinavia is intriguing; evidence no doubt of a distant trade in this spice that suited northern tastes.)

It's quite easy to marinate your own herring. Buy them when young and fat, not when they're red eyed and spent, and always use good-quality vinegar. Professionals usually look for a fat level of about 15–18 per cent but you'll have absolutely no way of telling when that is, so ask your fishmonger to look out for some herring just before they are ready to spawn.

BURIED, ROTTEN AND FERMENTED FISH

I suspect you may all have had a nibble at some stage of the famous *gravlax* or *gravad lax*, which translates as 'buried salmon'. (*Gravad* means buried; *lax* is salmon in Swedish.) The Scandinavians, the masters of peculiar fish products, developed some odd ways to store fish through the winter when food was difficult to find. *Gravad lax* was originally buried fermented salmon stored in barrels, but has become a more approachable and mundane form of pressed, cured salmon, strongly flavoured with dill.

The logic behind burying fish seems quite clear to me. Fishing trip, loads of fish, what do we do with it all? Let's dig a pit! Cover it with bark and wood, then a few months later see what has happened. You had two options: firstly, short-term burying, which gave a lightly fermented fish and secondly long-term burying, which created what most of us would call a nauseating mess.

From the latter, we get the Swedes' favourite, *surströmming*, fermented Baltic herring, and the Norwegian *rakefisk*, fermented freshwater trout, as well as *gravad lax*. But the Icelanders have developed something even worse, *hákarl*. Off the coast of Iceland swims the Greenland shark, *Somniosus microcephalus*, a dopey fish that is toxic when eaten fresh. The local people learned from the Inuit (Eskimo) that if the shark was left buried over winter, the poison appeared to seep away. Somehow the process became refined so that the shark meat was buried and then hung up to dry, to make the only food I have ever known that neither Sophie nor myself could bring ourselves to eat.

On the serious side, the conditions for fermenting fish have to be below 6°C to avoid the growth of the deadly microbe, *Clostridium botulinum*. Being an aerobic bacterium this needs oxygen, which is in short supply both underground and in barrels.

Whey was also once used, and still is in Iceland, to preserve fish. Both sugar and whey promote the growth of lactobacilli which change the carbohydrates into acids, thus lowering the pH and creating conditions in which bacteria cannot survive.

Salted Anchovies

The flavour of salt-only anchovies (or sardines) is extra good but they will usually need some work, as they are salted whole. Take what you need from the tin and rinse them thoroughly before beheading and filleting. If you have time, soak the fillets in milk for half an hour or so to soften the salt (or rinse in wine vinegar). The remains of the tin can be kept as is, covered with some coarse salt and a stretch of cling film, or you could go on and fillet the whole lot and then store them in glass jars, with a sprig or two of thyme, maybe a dried chilli, a clove of garlic or a few fennel seeds and olive oil to cover.

Anchovy Fingers

Alternatives: salted sardine fillets

I shan't be making these flaky anchovy bites very often because I eat too many of them. Piled on a plate in the kitchen, they are too tempting to resist. Fennel seeds go remarkably well with salty anchovies but so, too, do sesame seeds. A difficult choice. Maybe you should try half and half.

MAKES 24

250g (9 oz) puff pastry
tin of anchovy fillets, drained and cut in half
    lengthways
1 egg yolk, beaten with 1 tablespoon water
fennel seeds or sesame seeds

Preheat the oven to 220°C/425°F/Gas Mark 7. Roll the pastry out very thinly to form a rectangle. Cut into two equal rectangles. Lay the anchovy strips out in lines over half the pastry, leaving about 1cm (½-inch) gap around each one. Brush between the anchovies with a little water. Lay the second rectangle of pastry over the first and press down gently between the anchovies.

Now, take up your rolling pin again and roll this anchovy and pastry sandwich out to form a rectangle about 3mm (⅛ inch) thick. You should be able to see where the anchovy fillets are. If you can't, roll the pastry out a little more thinly. Brush the egg yolk over the surface of the pastry. Scatter lightly with fennel seeds or sesame seeds. Using a sharp knife, cut the pastry into thin fingers.

Lay on lightly dampened baking sheets and bake for 10–15 minutes, until puffed and browned. Eat warm, or cool and store in an airtight container. Re-heat in a hot oven briefly to crisp up and warm through before serving.

Insalata di Rinforzo

Alternative: salted sardine fillets

This Neapolitan salad is traditionally served over the Christmas and New Year period, but it is too good to confine to those few wintry weeks of the year. Make it whenever you come across a fine specimen of a cauliflower that deserves special treatment. Serve it as a first course, or with salami, ham, cheeses and good bread for a simple lunch.

SERVES 6

1 cauliflower, broken into florets
60g (2 oz) green olives, pitted and halved
60g (2 oz) black olives, pitted and halved
60g (2 oz) *cornichons* or pickled gherkins, thinly sliced
1 red pepper, grilled and skinned (see page 49) and cut into long, thin strips
8 tinned or salted anchovy fillets, halved lengthways
1 tablespoon capers, rinsed (and thoroughly soaked if salted)
3 tablespoons extra virgin olive oil
½ tablespoon white wine vinegar
salt and pepper

Steam or boil the cauliflower until *al dente*. Take great care not to overcook it, as there's nothing worse than overcooked, watery cauliflower and it is quite impossible to disguise. Drain, rinse under the cold tap and then drain again thoroughly. Put into a shallow dish. Scatter over the olives and cornichons or gherkins. Lay strips of red pepper and anchovy decoratively over the top (you might, for instance, make a lattice of them, or lay them in alternating parallel lines). Scatter over the capers.

Whisk the olive oil gradually into the vinegar and season with a little salt and plenty of black pepper. Taste and adjust the seasoning and balance, remembering that a good number of ingredients are already quite salty or sharp tasting. Drizzle the dressing over the whole salad.

Anchovy and Tomato Risotto

Alternative: salted sardine fillets

I love risotto and this one has become something of a favourite. The salty anchovies and the sweetness of good tomatoes are lovely with the buttery rice. I don't think this risotto needs Parmesan but you may well disagree with me. Be sure to use proper risotto rice, and be prepared to stand over the stove and stir for some 15 to 20 minutes as the risotto cooks.

SERVES 4 AS A MAIN COURSE,

6 AS A SUBSTANTIAL STARTER

1 onion, finely chopped
2 garlic cloves, chopped
1 tablespoon olive oil
45g (1½ oz) unsalted butter
285g (10 oz) risotto rice, e.g. arborio or
    vialone nano
6 anchovy fillets, drained and chopped
150ml (¼ pint) dry white wine
1 litre (1¾ pints) chicken stock
1 teaspoon dried oregano
2 tablespoons chopped fresh parsley
450g (1 lb) sweet tomatoes, peeled, de-seeded
    and diced
2 fresh basil sprigs
salt and pepper
freshly grated Parmesan cheese, to serve (optional)

In a large, heavy-based pan, sauté the onion and garlic in the oil and 15g (½ oz) of the butter until tender, without browning. Add the rice and anchovies and cook for a further minute or so, until the rice is translucent. Pour in the wine and simmer, stirring constantly, until all is absorbed. Meanwhile, bring the stock up to the boil in a separate pan, then reduce the heat to a thread to keep it warm.

Stir the oregano, parsley and some pepper into the rice. Now add a ladleful of the hot stock to the risotto and let it simmer very gently, stirring constantly, until the stock is almost all absorbed. Repeat until the rice is tender and creamy. Add the diced tomatoes and the basil leaves, torn up into small pieces. Stir, then add the remaining butter and stir again. Taste and adjust the seasonings and serve immediately, with or without Parmesan cheese.

Marinated Kippers

This recipe comes from *Leith's Cookery Bible* (Bloomsbury), by Prue Leith and Caroline Waldegrave. It needs to be prepared at least a couple of days in advance, though a week will give it even more time to develop. It harks back to traditional recipes for pickled kippers, but this one is softened by the addition of a little brown sugar, which makes it particularly pleasant.

SERVES 4

8 kipper fillets
1 onion, sliced
2 bay leaves
1 teaspoon mustard powder
150ml (¼ pint) olive oil
1 teaspoon light muscovado sugar
2 tablespoons lemon juice
pepper

To Serve:
lemon wedges
thin brown bread and butter

Skin the kipper fillets and cut into wide strips on the diagonal. In a small dish, layer the fillets with the onion and bay leaves, grinding black pepper between the layers.

Place the mustard, olive oil, sugar and lemon juice in a jam jar, screw the lid on firmly and shake vigorously to mix. Pour over the fillets. Cover the dish well with a lid or cling film and leave in the fridge for at least two days, or a week if possible.

Just before serving, drain off most of the oil and discard the onion and bay leaves. Serve the marinated kippers with lemon wedges, and pass around brown bread and butter separately.

Kipper Paste

The easiest of fish pâtés (together with Smoked Mackerel Pâté, see page 297) and, if your kippers are good to start with, you can serve the pâté with pride and a flourish, whatever the company. Jug your kipper(s) (see page 278) or lay them in a shallow dish and cover with boiling water. Leave for 5 minutes. Drain thoroughly, pat dry, then remove and discard the skin and bones. For a fairly coarse pâté, which is nicer, use a couple of forks to shred the flesh, then mash with an equal quantity of unsalted butter. Add lemon juice and cayenne pepper to taste. If you are in a rush, pop everything into a food processor and whizz to a paste, which will be smoother. Pile into a bowl and chill, covered, until needed. Serve with a jaunty sprig of parsley on top, and pass round warm toast and extra lemon wedges.

Brandade de Morue

Brandade de morue is a garlicky, creamy purée of salt cod that comes from the South of France. It is eaten, by those lucky enough to encounter it, as an hors d'oeuvre, with triangles of toast, or smeared on good bread, or perhaps as a filling for small tomatoes, something I am particularly partial to.

Occasionally, *brandade de morue* can separate as you make it, though this is less likely in a food processor. If it does, you can save the day by beating it into a little mashed potato. Leftover *brandade* will keep for several days and is extremely good with poached eggs.

SERVES 8

450g (1 lb) salt cod, soaked and drained
  (see page 279)
2–3 garlic cloves, chopped
450ml (16 fl oz) extra virgin olive oil
150ml (¼ pint) milk
salt
toast triangles, to serve

Poach the salt cod in fresh water for about 10 minutes until it just flakes, but don't overdo it. Drain and discard the skin and bones. Flake the fish and place in a food processor with the garlic. Put the oil and the milk into separate pans. Bring the milk up to the boil, then turn the heat down so that it remains hot. Heat the olive oil. Now set the processor running and alternately dribble in a little oil and a little milk, continuing until both are used up and you have a light, fluffy purée. Taste and add salt, if necessary. Serve warm or cold, with triangles of toast.

Sevillano Salad of Salt Cod and Roast Peppers

During a recent trip to Seville, I encountered two most unexpected and delicious salads made with salt cod. One, which I shall save for another book, was made with olives, oranges and fried salt cod. The second, this one, is a simple but sensational mixture of raw salt cod (soaked first, of course), roasted peppers, garlic, olive oil and vinegar. You must use really good-quality salt cod for this – scrappy tough ends or yellowing and old bits are no good. Similarly, your olive oil must be extra virgin, and the vinegar of the first standing.

SERVES 6

3 red peppers, grilled and skinned (see page 49)
1 or 2 garlic cloves, very finely chopped
150g (5 oz) salt cod, thoroughly soaked and
  drained (see page 279)
1½ tablespoons sherry vinegar or red wine
  vinegar
8 tablespoons extra virgin olive oil
salt and pepper

Cut the peppers into squares or short strips, as the fancy takes you. Put them into a bowl with any juices that have oozed out. Add the garlic. Skin and bone the cod and cut into cubes about 1.5cm (a generous ½ inch) across. Put those in the bowl, too. Add the vinegar and oil, a small touch of salt (you can add more later) and plenty of pepper. Stir with a light hand and then leave to marinate for at least 4 hours before serving.

Stir again, then taste and adjust seasoning just before serving.

Good Friday's Salt Cod

In Catholic countries, particularly the hot ones and particularly inland, well away from the coast, salt cod was the fish to serve on Fridays, when meat was forbidden. On Good Friday it was absolutely essential. This Portuguese dish of salt cod baked between layers of potato, tomato and olives raises penitential abstinence from meat to pleasurable heights. I'd have thought that negated the whole point of the exercise, but then I'm not given to abstinence in any form.

It's important to make sure that the salt is thoroughly soaked away, as some of the cooking water from the salt cod is used in the gratin.

SERVES 4

250g (9 oz) salt cod, well soaked and drained
   (see page 279)
1 bay leaf
1 fresh parsley sprig
450g (1 lb) tomatoes, peeled and chopped
60g (2 oz) black olives, pitted and sliced
5 tablespoons extra virgin olive oil
2 large garlic cloves, finely chopped
700g (1½ lb) floury potatoes, boiled and sliced
3 hard-boiled eggs, shelled and chopped
2 tablespoons chopped fresh parsley
salt and pepper

Preheat the oven to 180°C/350°F/Gas Mark 4. Put the salt cod in a pan. Just cover with water, add the bay leaf and the sprig of parsley and heat gently until the surface of the water trembles. Do not boil. Poach at this temperature for about 10 minutes, until the fish is just cooked. Drain, reserving the stock.

Flake the fish, discarding any bones. Unless you hate the thought of it, keep the skin. Mix the tomatoes with the olives. Mix the oil with the garlic. Brush a little of the garlicky oil around a large ovenproof dish. Lay a layer of potato slices on the base of the dish. Season and cover with half the hard-boiled eggs. Drizzle a tablespoon of olive oil over them. Sprinkle with half the tomatoes and olives, some pepper and half the chopped parsley. Season and spoon over a tablespoon of the olive oil.

Lay all the salt cod on this, then cover with the remaining eggs, season and again drizzle a tablespoon of olive oil over this. Add a final layer of tomato and olive, parsley and pepper and a further tablespoon of olive oil. Finally, finish with the remaining potato and pour over 4 tablespoons of the reserved fish stock. Season with a little salt and pepper. Drizzle the remaining olive oil over the surface. Bake for 30 minutes or until the potato is very tender. If necessary, whip under the grill to brown the upper crust of potatoes. Serve at once.

Poached Eggs with Hollandaise and Caviar

Pure, unabashed luxury, that is what this is. Serve it for a special brunch – maybe a birthday celebration or on Boxing Day, or whenever you fancy a spot of indulgence.

SERVES 4

4 eggs
4 rounds of toast, cut into neat circles
cayenne pepper
4 teaspoons caviar

For the Hollandaise Sauce:
175g (6 oz) unsalted butter
3 egg yolks
2 tablespoons water
lemon juice or white wine vinegar or tarragon
    vinegar
salt and freshly ground black pepper

Poach the eggs in a shallow pan of water. Lift out and drain, then trim off the raggedy bits.

To make the hollandaise, heat the butter in a small pan with a lip, until it has melted and is fairly hot but not beginning to colour. Whizz the egg yolks, water, salt, pepper and a small slug of lemon juice or vinegar in a food processor, until smooth. Keep the blades whirring and start adding the butter in a slow trickle. When you have incorporated about half, add a little more lemon or vinegar, then carry on adding the butter, increasing the flow slightly. Stop pouring when you get down to the cloudy sediment at the bottom of the pan. Taste and adjust the seasoning.

Immediately pop the circles of hot toast on individual plates, perch an egg on each piece, coat generously with hollandaise, then dust lightly with cayenne. Finish with a crowning dollop of caviar and serve instantly.

Corncakes with Caviar

These golden corncakes are every bit as good as, if not rather better than, the more traditional Russian *blini* with soured cream and caviar; with the bonus that they are less trouble to make and look very pretty into the bargain. The recipe comes from the American chef, Anne Rosenzweig.

SERVES 6 AS A FIRST COURSE

350g (12 oz) sweetcorn kernels, thawed if frozen
70ml (2½ fl oz) milk
60g (2 oz) plain flour
110g (4 oz) butter, melted
75g (2½ oz) cornmeal or polenta
2 eggs
1 egg yolk
2 tablespoons chopped fresh chives
salt and pepper

To Serve:
250ml (9 fl oz) *crème fraîche*
lots of caviar
1 tablespoon chopped fresh chives

Process the sweetcorn kernels with a little of the milk. Aim to get a slightly knobbly mush rather than a perfectly smooth cream. Scrape out and mix with the remaining milk, the flour, half the melted butter and the cornmeal or polenta. Beat to mix evenly, then beat in the eggs and yolk, chives and salt and pepper.

Spoon a little of the remaining butter into a heavy frying pan and heat over a moderate heat. Spoon about 2 tablespoons of the batter into the pan at a time to make small corncakes, pressing them down with a spatula and frying them until nicely golden on each side. Keep warm. Serve four per person, topped with the crème fraîche, as much caviar as you can muster and a scattering of chives.

Baked Potatoes with Caviar

Roast little new potatoes (or waxy salad potatoes such as Charlottes or Belles de Fontenay) in their skins, lubricated with olive oil and butter, then split them open neatly and top with a small spoonful of soured cream or crème fraîche and a decorous dollop of caviar. Hand around immediately.

Penne alla Vodka con Caviale

For a while, back in the late Seventies and early Eighties, this pasta dish enjoyed a brief fashionable status, then it disappeared into nowhere. I first ate it in Rome, in a student flat, and adored it instantly. Whenever I can afford the caviar I turn back to it with renewed enthusiasm, even if it isn't considered modern or stylish any more.

SERVES 2 AS A MAIN COURSE,

4 AS A STARTER

225g (8 oz) penne
4 tablespoons passata or peeled, de-seeded and
   liquidised fresh tomatoes
6 tablespoons double cream
1 tablespoon vodka
salt and pepper

To Garnish:
2–4 teaspoons caviar, preferably Sevruga
2 teaspoons chopped fresh chives

Bring a large pan of lightly salted water to the boil and tip in the penne. Cook according to packet instructions until *al dente*. Drain well and transfer to a warm serving dish.

While the pasta cooks, place the passata or liquidised fresh tomatoes and cream in a small pan. Simmer for 5 minutes to thicken slightly, stirring occasionally. Draw off the heat, let the bubbles subside, then stir in the vodka and season.

When the pasta is ready, bring the tomato mixture back to the boil and pour it over the pasta. Spoon the caviar on top and sprinkle with the chives. Toss at the table and serve.

Kedgeree

Alternative: cooked salmon (with a light fish stock for the rice)

For a recipe that started out as an Indian dish of beans and rice, kedgeree has travelled a long way, and it has changed almost beyond recognition on its journey. Not surprisingly, there are now many variations on the Anglo-Indian theme, most of them excellent in their own way, as long as it is not considered a dustbin dish for yesterday's leftovers. I like to use smoked haddock in my kedgeree but others prefer salmon in its place. I also like to introduce a note of sweetness with peas (harking back to those original beans), but you could well replace them, or combine them with raisins. You could even add some flaked almonds for an extra note of texture. If you want to make a richer version, stir in a slug or two of double cream at the end. One thing that is essential is the mango chutney that goes with the finished kedgeree.

Whatever variations you make, kedgeree is the brunch dish *par excellence*, but it also makes a very good lunch or supper dish, served with a green salad on the side.

SERVES 4–6

450–600g (1–1¼ lb) smoked haddock fillet
85g (3 oz) butter
1 tablespoon sunflower or vegetable oil
1 onion, chopped
175g (6 oz) basmati rice, rinsed
½ tablespoon mild curry paste
150g (5 oz) frozen peas, thawed (or fresh at the
    right time of the year)
3 hard-boiled eggs, chopped
2 tablespoons chopped fresh parsley
salt and pepper

To Serve:
lemon or lime wedges
mango chutney

Cover the haddock with boiling water and leave to stand for 5 minutes. Drain, reserving the soaking liquid. Measure and add enough water to make up to 900ml (1½ pints). Skin and flake the haddock, removing any stray bones you come across, and set aside.

Melt 30g (1 oz) of the butter with the oil in a large saucepan. Add the onion and cook gently without browning until tender. Now add the rice and the curry paste and stir for 1–2 minutes. Pour in the measured cooking liquid, bring up to the boil and then reduce the heat to as low as possible and cover tightly.

Let it cook on its own, with no disturbance, for 8 minutes, and then stir in the flaked haddock and the peas. Cover again and leave until the rice is quite tender (another 4–5 minutes), having absorbed virtually all the liquid. If absolutely necessary, add a splash more hot water to prevent it burning.

Draw off the heat, dot with the remaining butter, cover and let it stand for 4 minutes or so. Then add the eggs and parsley and stir in lightly with a fork, fluffing up the grains of rice. Taste and adjust the seasoning, adding salt only if needed. Pile up in a mound on a serving dish and serve steaming hot, with lemon or lime wedges and plenty of mango chutney.

Curried Smoked Haddock Balls

Alternative: smoked cod

If you didn't know that haddock had balls, read on. These particular balls, made in the comfort of your own kitchen, are no joke at all. Made with poached haddock, bound in a thick, thick white sauce, flavoured with a dash of curry, they emerge from the hot oil with a crisp, brown crust and a melting, almost liquid interior. Your guests will love you all the more for having made them yourself. A fabulous first course.

MAKES ABOUT 20 BALLS

350g (12 oz) smoked haddock fillet
450ml (16 fl oz) milk
1 bay leaf
2 fresh parsley sprigs
60g (2 oz) butter
½ small onion, very finely chopped
1 teaspoon curry powder
60g (2 oz) plain flour
1 tablespoon chopped fresh parsley
lemon juice
oil for deep-frying
black pepper
lemon wedges, to serve

To Coat:
plain flour
1–2 eggs, lightly beaten
fine dry breadcrumbs

First cut the haddock into four pieces and poach gently in the milk, with the bay leaf and sprigs of parsley, until just cooked. Strain off the milk and reserve. Skin, bone and flake the haddock. Tear into small shreds, using a pair of forks.

Melt the butter in a saucepan and cook the onion gently in it without browning until tender. Add the curry powder and the flour and stir for a minute. Now gradually add the reserved milk, stirring well to smooth out lumps. Bring up to the boil and simmer for 5–10 minutes, stirring frequently, until very, very thick. Draw off the heat and stir in the haddock, chopped parsley, a dash of lemon juice and some black pepper. Taste and add salt only if absolutely necessary. Turn out into a bowl, cool and chill for at least an hour, until firm. (If, by some mischance, it won't set, you can always boil it down a little more, though this is not the best way to go about things).

Scoop out walnut-sized lumps of the mixture. Flour your hands lightly and roll the mixture into balls; then coat in flour, dip into egg and, finally, coat thoroughly in breadcrumbs. You must take great care to coat the balls all over and leave no gaps for the filling to seep out. Chill again, for half an hour or so.

Just before serving, deep-fry in oil heated to 185°C/360°F, until well browned. Drain briefly on kitchen paper and serve piping hot, with lemon wedges.

Warm Smoked Haddock and Ciabatta Sandwich

Alternative: smoked cod

This is an impressively quick, and impressively more-ish, sort of a lunchtime sandwich, made with that lovely, holey, chewy Italian bread, ciabatta, and packed to overflowing with salad and warm smoked haddock in a gingery dressing. Tuck a napkin into your shirt, open your mouth wide and get ready to feast.

SERVES 2–3

1 ciabatta loaf, split in half lengthways
3 tablespoons olive oil
1 dried red chilli, snapped in two
1 garlic clove, sliced
1cm (½-inch) piece of root ginger, finely
    chopped
175g (6 oz) smoked haddock fillet, cut into strips
1 tablespoon white wine vinegar
about 110g (4 oz) mixed salad leaves
2 tomatoes, sliced
freshly ground black pepper

Preheat the oven to 180°C/350°F/Gas Mark 4. Wrap the ciabatta in foil and put in the oven to warm through. Heat the oil in a frying pan over a low heat and add the chilli, garlic and ginger. Cook gently for 3–4 minutes. Then scoop out the chilli, which should by now have bequeathed a tolerable amount of heat to the oil. Raise the heat and add the smoked haddock. Fry briskly for a few minutes until just cooked through. Draw off the heat and stir in the vinegar and some black pepper.

Quickly unwrap the ciabatta, spread out the salad leaves and tomato slices along its length and then spoon over the haddock, garlic, ginger and dressing. Clamp the 'lid' on top and cut in half or thirds. Eat straight away.

Smoked Mackerel Pâté

On the whole, I tend to save smoked mackerel to serve with salads, with maybe a few warm new potatoes on the side. Our children love the rich, tender flesh and gobble it down avariciously. The one simple recipe I make with it is this, a pâté of smoked mackerel and cream cheese.

Skin and break up the mackerel fillets. Either mash with a fork or process, adding a roughly equal quantity of cream cheese and a few generous squirts of lemon juice. For adults, cayenne pepper livens the whole deal up. A small spoonful of creamed horseradish may work better for company of mixed ages. Alternatively, you might like to stir in a little chopped fresh dill, or add some parsley too.

Serve with warm toast and lemon wedges, or use as a sandwich spread.

Salmon Rillettes on Pumpernickel Circles

Salmon *rillettes* is the smart name for a quickly made pâté of smoked salmon, poached fresh salmon and cream cheese. Funny, really, because in France *rillettes* are a type of meat paste, quite delicious if you happen to like that kind of thing, which I do, but not remotely chic, and certainly in the part of the country that I know, as common as muck.

Be that as it may, these salmon *rillettes* are rather good, rather rich, and rather the thing for little *amuse-gueules* at parties, or a first course for a dinner party, or even for Christmas lunch before the gargantuan turkey. In fact, they are (*rillettes* are properly referred to in the plural) particularly good for large, celebratory family meals, since children of all ages seem to love them. My two genuine small things can't get enough of them, though they prefer them on plainer bread.

SERVES 8

225g (8 oz) fresh salmon fillet
sunflower oil
2 fresh fennel or chervil sprigs
110g (4 oz) smoked salmon
110g (4 oz) cream cheese
lemon juice
1½ tablespoons finely snipped fresh chives
salt and pepper

To Serve:
250g (9 oz) sliced pumpernickel (about 5 slices)
75g (2½ oz) salmon caviar
fresh fennel, chervil or chives, to garnish
lemon wedges

Preheat the oven to 180°C/350°F/Gas Mark 4. Oil a large square of foil and lay the salmon fillet in the centre. Top with sprigs of fennel or chervil and season with salt and pepper. Enclose in the foil and bake for 20–25 minutes, until just cooked through. Cut the salmon up into rough chunks, discarding the herbs, skin and any bones.

Cut up the smoked salmon roughly. Put fresh salmon, smoked salmon, cream cheese and a couple of squeezes of lemon juice into the food processor bowl and pulse in brief bursts, scraping down the sides in between, until evenly mixed but still with a little texture. Stir in the chives and then taste and adjust the seasoning. Chill for at least an hour. The mixture can be made up to 24 hours in advance and stored, covered, in the fridge.

Cut the pumpernickel into 4cm (1½-inch) circles. Roll heaped teaspoons of the salmon mixture into balls. Press on to the pumpernickel. These canapés can be prepared up to this stage 2 or 3 hours in advance. Top with a few eggs of salmon caviar and a small sprig of fennel or chervil or a scattering of chopped chives. Place a few lemon wedges on each platter, to squeeze over as guests desire.

Smoked Salmon and Shallot Quiche

Alternative: cold smoked trout

Quite the grandest of the quiches this, with its burden of smoked salmon, lemon and shallots. I always bake it in a deep pastry case, so that you get a plunging depth of the tender, smooth, velvety filling.

Don't try to cut corners – crème fraîche is the thing to use here, though, if you really can't get it, mix double cream with an equal quantity of soured cream. Anything less drags the quiche right down and is not worth bothering with.

SERVES 6

285g (10 oz) shortcrust pastry

For the Filling:
110g (4 oz) shallots, sliced
60g (2 oz) butter
3 egg yolks
225ml (8 fl oz) *crème fraîche*, or double cream
   mixed with soured cream
1 tablespoon chopped fresh dill
finely grated zest of 1 lemon
110g (4 oz) smoked salmon, cut into thin strips
salt and pepper

Roll the pastry out and line a deep 20–23cm (8–9 inch) tart tin. Rest in the fridge for 30 minutes. Preheat the oven to 200°C/400°F/Gas Mark 6.

Prick the base of the pastry with a fork, line with greaseproof paper or foil and fill with baking beans. Bake blind for 10 minutes. Remove the beans and paper and return the pastry case to the oven for 5 minutes or so to dry out. Cool (at least until tepid) before filling. Reduce the oven temperature to 180°C/350°F/Gas Mark 4.

To make the filling, cook the shallots gently in the butter until translucent, without browning. Beat the egg yolks with the cream, dill, lemon zest, salt and pepper.

Distribute the shallots and salmon strips evenly over the base of the pastry case. Pour in the cream mixture. Bake for about 30 minutes, until just set. Serve warm or cold.

Gravad Lax

Alternatives: sea trout, mackerel

When my mother first published a recipe for *gravad lax*, back in the Seventies, it was almost unknown in this country – a bizarre Scandinavian quirk, this marinating of raw salmon, and no more than that. Twenty-something years on, you can buy *gravad lax* ready marinated and sliced in supermarkets. What a change! Why bother to buy it, though, when it is so easy to make yourself (and a mite cheaper, too)? All you need is a generous piece of sparklingly fresh salmon (order it from a good fishmonger, telling him what you want to do with it so that he can get it in prime condition), and then it is just a question of a bit of mixing, a bit of sprinkling and a bit of patience.

Gravad lax needs at least two days in the fridge before it can be eaten, but is at its best after about four days and will keep quite contentedly for a week or more. In other words, make plenty and enjoy it at your leisure, either as a starter, with its mustardy sauce, or in sandwiches or even hot (see page 304).

SERVES 8–10 AS A FIRST COURSE

1–1.5kg (2¼–3¼ lb) very fresh salmon fillet, with skin
1 tablespoon coarse sea salt
2 tablespoons sugar
1 tablespoon dried dill weed or 2 tablespoons chopped fresh dill
½ tablespoon coarsely crushed black peppercorns

For the Sauce:
2 tablespoons Dijon mustard
1 egg yolk (optional)
1 level tablespoon caster sugar
150ml (¼ pint) sunflower or groundnut oil
1 tablespoon white wine vinegar
3 tablespoons chopped fresh dill or 1½ tablespoons dried dill weed
salt and pepper

Start on the salmon at least two days before you want to eat it but leave the sauce until the day you want to serve. Ideally, you will have two pieces of salmon fillet about the same size and shape, which can be neatly sandwiched together. If not, cut the fillet into large pieces which do fit, more or less, together.

Mix the salt, sugar, dill and peppercorns. Sprinkle an even, thin layer of this curing mix over the base of a shallow dish that will take the sandwiched pairs of salmon fillet snugly. Lay half the salmon, skin-side down, on top. Now sprinkle over a generous helping of the curing mix and cover with the rest of the salmon, skin-side up. Sprinkle over more of the curing mix, but don't feel that you have to use it all up. Cover with cling film or foil, weight the fish down with a board or plate, perch a few tins or weights on top and leave in the fridge for at least two days, turning the sandwiched fillets over once or twice during that time. As the salt draws out the water in the salmon, the curing mix will dissolve to a liquid.

The egg yolk for the sauce is not entirely necessary, though it does make for a nicer, more velvety texture. However, it remains entirely uncooked, so if you are serving this to young children, pregnant women, invalids or elderly people, leave it out to eliminate the minuscule risk of salmonella poisoning. To make the sauce, mix the mustard, egg yolk, if using, and sugar. Gradually whisk in the oil as if you were making a mayonnaise (though it is by no means such a temperamental business). Stir in the vinegar, dill, salt and pepper. Taste and adjust the seasoning.

To serve the *gravad lax*, wipe the pieces of salmon clean and slice them a little thicker than you would smoked salmon, cutting on the diagonal, down towards the skin, in the direction of the thinner, tail end. Serve straight away, with the sauce.

Hot Gravad Lax

Though *gravad lax* is usually served as a starter, thinly sliced with its dill and mustard sauce, the possibilities don't stop there. In Norway I was offered *gravad lax* as a main course, cut a little thicker and served in a generous quantity, either raw or briefly fried, accompanied by hot buttered boiled potatoes and salad. It can also be grilled which, to my mind, is nicest of all. Serve it with the dill and mustard sauce on the previous page, if you like (I do).

Brush the curing mixture lightly from the *gravad lax* but don't be too fussy about this. Odd bits of dill left *in situ* will all add to the deliciousness. Cut the marinated salmon into portions of about 200g (7 oz) each, cutting it into chunks, with the skin left on. Preheat the grill thoroughly and line the grill pan with foil. Grill the *gravad lax*, skin side to the heat, for 8–10 minutes, until the skin is crisply browned. Serve straight away, the flesh half cooked, giving you the best of both raw and cooked salmon.

Feroce de Morue Fumé

Alternatives: fresh cod

Ferocious smoked cod. I loved the name of this dish as soon as I read it. The ferocious part comes from the chilli but it is soothed by a smooth avocado sauce. I like it made with smoked cod, but it is not bad at all with fresh cod, as well.

SERVES 4

700g (1½ lb) smoked cod fillet
2 garlic cloves, crushed
2 teaspoons chilli flakes
6 tablespoons olive oil
2 tablespoons lime juice
lime or lemon wedges, to serve

For the Sauce:
¼ cucumber, finely diced
1 ripe avocado
2 tablespoons lime juice
2 garlic cloves, crushed
150ml (¼ pint) Greek-style yoghurt
110g (4 oz) tomatoes, peeled, de-seeded and
    finely diced
1 shallot, finely chopped
salt and pepper

Cut the cod into four roughly equal portions. Rub the garlic and then the chilli flakes over the surface and place in a shallow dish. Lightly whisk the olive oil with the lime juice and pour it over the cod. Leave for about 8 hours, covered, in a cool place.

To make the sauce, spread the cucumber out in a colander and sprinkle lightly with salt. Leave to drain for 30 minutes to 1 hour. Rinse and pat dry. Peel the avocado, remove the stone, then mash or process the flesh with the lime juice, garlic and yoghurt, until smooth. Fold in the cucumber, tomatoes, shallot and salt and pepper. Taste and adjust the seasoning and keep covered in the fridge until needed.

Take the cod out of its marinade and grill, skin side to the heat first, until browned, then turn over and finish grilling on the other side, until just cooked through. Serve hot, with the cool avocado sauce.

SAUCES, STOCKS etc.

Beurre Blanc

This has become my favourite butter sauce for fish, ever since I discovered that it is not half as difficult to make as reputation would have it. It goes down particularly well in our household, as my small son is allergic to eggs but very partial to fish with a good sauce. It is said to have originated as a hastily cooked béarnaise sauce, made by a flustered cook in the household of the Marquis of Goulaine. So busy was she that she forgot the egg yolks. Luckily, the sauce turned out so well that everyone was delighted. In his grand château near Nantes, the Marquis requested the sauce frequently, and these days it has become a speciality of the Loire region. Serve it with river fish in particular – salmon and pike, or even shad if you should come across it – though it is excellent, too, with the fine sea fish, such as turbot or sole. Needless to say, it raises more lowly fish a cut above the ordinary, too – it's lovely, scented with orange juice, with whiting (see page 59).

The key to making *beurre blanc* is getting the temperature right when the butter is being whisked in. The temperature should be kept low, but not so low that the butter won't melt in. I usually find that drawing the pan off the heat frequently, so that it has a chance to sit for a few seconds without heat, keeps it from curdling.

SERVES 6

2 shallots, very finely chopped
2 tablespoons white wine vinegar
2 tablespoons white wine or Reduced Fish Stock
    (see page 308), or 85ml (3 fl oz) good Fish
    Stock (see page 308)
250g (9 oz) unsalted butter, cubed and chilled
salt and pepper

Put the shallots into a pan with the vinegar and wine or reduced fish stock or fish stock. Boil hard until reduced to about 2 tablespoons, with a good, syrupy consistency. You can do this in advance and then heat it through gently again when you want to finish the sauce.

Whisking continuously with a wire whisk, gradually add the butter a few cubes at a time, whisking each batch in before adding the next. As the butter is incorporated, the sauce becomes thick, pale and creamy. When all the butter is mixed in, draw off the heat and season with salt and pepper. If it is a little on the sharp side, you can soften it with a little more butter, or a pinch of sugar or a tablespoonful or two of cream.

Disaster strikes! If, as you are busy whisking, you notice that your sauce is beginning to look oily rather than thick and creamy, take the pan straight off the heat and plunge it into a bowl of icy-cold water (it's not a bad idea to have one standing by before you start on the sauce, just in case) to cool it down. As it cools off, the sauce should thicken to a cream. Take it back to the stove and start whisking in the remaining butter, taking enormous care not to overheat it again. With any luck, it should turn out all right.

Parsley Sauce

My childhood experience of parsley sauce in the school canteen was nearly enough to put me off for life. But not quite, thank heavens. When the taste of raw flour is properly simmered out and the sauce is enriched with a little cream and butter and flecked with oodles of parsley, it becomes an excellent all-rounder sauce for white-fleshed fish, particularly suitable when you want something that tastes good but has a peaceful, soothing, yet satisfying quality to it.

Of course, a good sauce begs for good fish. Although my school glopped it over grey, overcooked, stringy poached cod, I actually think it nicer with fish that has been seared, or baked with a dab of butter and even, maybe, a splash of white wine.

SERVES 4

15g (½ oz) butter
15g (½ oz) plain flour
300ml (½ pint) milk
60ml (2 fl oz) double cream
lemon juice
4–5 tablespoons chopped fresh parsley
butter
salt and pepper

Melt the butter in a pan and stir in the flour. Stir over a low heat for a minute. Draw off the heat and gradually stir in the milk. Add a small splash first, stir in thoroughly, then another splash, and stir, and carry on like this until you have a thick cream. Then you can add the milk more generously, again stirring it in well until smoothly amalgamated. If you do end up with a few lumps, don't panic. Sieve the sauce when it's finished simmering (but before you add the parsley) and no one will ever know.

Bring the sauce up to the boil, reduce the heat and simmer gently for 5–10 minutes, stirring occasionally to prevent it from catching. By now, the taste of raw flour should have disappeared but, if not, cook it a little longer, possibly raising the heat a touch. Stir in the cream and simmer for a few more minutes, until the sauce is of a pleasing pouring consistency. Stir in a good dash of lemon, the parsley, an extra knob of butter (the size is entirely up to you!) and salt and pepper. Taste and adjust the seasoning then serve.

Béchamel or White Sauce

For some time now, the household white sauce, made with flour, butter and milk (and cream, if you are lucky) has been denigrated by *haute cuisine*. It can be a dreadful affair but, when it is properly cooked (which means at least long enough for the taste of flour to disappear) and well flavoured, it is one of the most useful sauces around, and takes to all sorts of variation.

Though some would argue that béchamel and white sauce are synonymous, I always think of a béchamel as a white sauce made with milk that has been infused with onion, a bay leaf and a clove. Indeed, if you are going to serve the sauce plain and unadorned this extra touch will make it sing. When the white sauce is to be lifted with other flavourings at the end, this business of infusing is not so important.

The biggest worry people have about making these very easy sauces is that they will end up lumpy. They shouldn't, if you pay a little attention to them, but small lumps can usually be whisked out and, if that doesn't work, you can always sieve the sauce when it is made, and no one will be any the wiser.

Otherwise, they are very relaxed and untemperamental beings. A sauce that ends up a bit too thick can be restored simply by whisking in a little more milk. A sauce that is too thin can just be left to simmer down to a creamy thickness and, incidentally, will taste all the better for it. In fact, if you want to make a truly delicious béchamel or white sauce, adding more liquid deliberately and building in plenty of time for it to reduce to the desired consistency is exactly what you should do.

SERVES 4

300ml (½ pint) full-cream milk, plus a little
   extra if necessary
30g (1 oz) butter
20g (⅔ oz) plain flour
salt and pepper (white, if you have it)
freshly grated nutmeg

For a Béchamel Sauce:
1 thick onion slice
1 bay leaf
2 fresh parsley sprigs
2–3 carrot slices
5 black peppercorns

If you are making a béchamel, put the milk into a pan with the onion, bay leaf, parsley, carrot and peppercorns. Bring very slowly up to the boil and then reduce the heat radically, to a mere thread, and leave to infuse very gently for about 10 minutes. Strain and discard the flavourings.

Melt the butter in a heavy-based saucepan. Stir in the flour and stir over a gentle heat for about a minute. Draw off the heat and gradually mix in the milk, a spoonful at a time at first, until the sauce is runny. Now tip in the rest of the milk and stir again. Return to the heat and bring gently up to the boil, stirring. Simmer for at least 10 minutes, stirring frequently to prevent it from catching, until the consistency is to your liking (see above). Season with salt, pepper and freshly grated nutmeg and there it is, ready to use.

Variations

Cream Béchamel: When the sauce is done, stir in anything from 1–6 tablespoons double cream or, nicer still, crème fraîche. Return to the heat and simmer for a few more minutes, then taste and adjust the seasoning.

Caper Sauce: Stir 2 tablespoons of rinsed capers (if they are salted capers, soak out the salt before using, and add a dash of white wine vinegar or lemon juice to the sauce, too) and 2 tablespoons of finely chopped fresh parsley into the sauce, when cooked. The finely grated zest of a lemon would not go amiss, either.

Mrs Beeton's Anchovy Sauce: Add 1–2 teaspoons of anchovy essence – 'Average Cost, about 5d [about 2p]'. Those were the days.

Mrs Beeton's Crab Sauce: Add the meat of 1 medium crab (about 175g/6 oz mixed white and brown meat), 1 teaspoon of anchovy essence, a few drops of lemon juice and a shake of cayenne pepper to the sauce. This is an excellent way of dressing up rather plain fish, giving them a touch of luxury.

Mustard Sauce (for Herring): Stir in about 2 tablespoons Dijon or coarse-grained mustard. If you want to keep the heat of the mustard, serve it as it is. If you just want the flavour, without the heat, simmer for a few minutes.

My Mother's Anise Sauce: Infuse the milk with a whole star anise for 5–10 minutes before making the sauce. Or stir ¼ teaspoon or a little more of Chinese five-spice powder into the butter before adding the flour. Or stir a slug of Pernod into the finished sauce and then simmer for another minute or two.

Clarified Butter

My mother nearly always kept a stock of clarified butter in the fridge, for frying and for sealing little pots of pâté or potted fish. These days, most of us use less butter for cooking than we used to, now that good olive oils are so readily available and we are a touch more aware of the health issues. Frying is no longer the most frequent cooking method and I know that I often choose grilling, searing or baking in preference.

For all that, clarified butter is exceedingly useful, and there is nothing to beat the flavour of pure butter once in a while. The process of clarifying removes all the milk solids that burn so easily in the pan, which makes it ideal for frying. It also gives the butter an almost limitless longevity, which can be most useful.

Concentrated butter, which you can buy in most large supermarkets, can be used instead of clarified butter, although the flavour is not so good. Besides, it is easy enough to clarify butter at home.

Put the butter into a small pan and melt gently. Heat it up calmly and slowly, until you see a white scum on the surface. Strain it through a sieve lined with a double layer of muslin which catches all the milk solids; then store, covered, in the fridge.

Coconut Milk

No doubt about it, the best coconut milk is made from the white flesh of a fresh coconut. The semi-transparent liquid that sloshes around inside the coconut, incidentally, is the coconut juice, a very refreshing drink on a hot day but not at all the same as coconut milk. The second-best option is to make it from desiccated coconut. Tinned coconut milk is a third possibility, a very useful storecupboard standby, but it does have an odd, slimy feel to it when boiled down, which I don't care for a great deal.

To Make Coconut Milk from a Fresh Coconut

You will first need to crack the coconut open. Raid the tool kit and rope in a helper. Clamp the coconut in a vice, or get some brave soul to hold it straight for you. Pierce a hole through two of the eyes, using a drill, a bradawl, or something similar. Drain out the juice and pop it in the fridge to refresh you after all your effort. Tap the coconut all over with a hammer to loosen the flesh inside. Then get heavy with it. Bash your hammer down hard and repeatedly at the centre of the 'ribs' that run from top to bottom of the coconut, until eventually it cracks open. Prise the flesh from the shell and don't worry about the brown inner skin. Break up the bits and pop them into a food processor. Process until finely chopped.

Now add 600ml (1 pint) of hot water and process again. Tip into a fine sieve set over a bowl. When cool enough to handle, knead the flesh with your hands, then strain off the milk, squeezing it out with your hands. This is thick coconut milk. If you repeat this last process with the squeezed coconut and a new batch of water you will get thin coconut milk. Mix thick and thin and you have medium coconut milk (which is usually just referred to as coconut milk, plain and simple).

To Make Coconut Milk from Desiccated Coconut

First of all, make sure that what you have got in your packet has not been sweetened. Then tip 250g (9 oz) of desiccated coconut into a food processor and add 600ml (1 pint) of hot water. Process and strain, squeezing out the coconut milk. This is thick coconut milk. Repeat for thin coconut milk. Mix the two, as above, for medium milk.

Whether you start with fresh coconut or desiccated, the milk should be stored in the fridge if not using immediately, where it will keep for up to 48 hours. In the chill of the fridge, the thick coconut cream will rise to the top, setting in a dense, waxy layer. Once it warms up to room temperature it mixes back in easily. You can also freeze coconut milk.

Court-bouillon

A *court-bouillon* is a flavoured cooking liquid, used primarily for poaching fish but also, in some instances, for cooking shellfish. Plain water alone does nothing for a delicate piece of fish (though it may be fine for something like salt cod). The juices of the fish simmer out and, in exchange, the flesh gets nothing but water. Osmosis of the saddest sort. The point of a *court-bouillon* is to add to the flavour of the fish in a subtle way, replacing what is lost with something even better. There are endless variations on the basic idea, and this is just one. You might want to add a gentle aniseed note with a sliced fennel bulb or a few sprigs of fennel herb or dill. Leek or celeriac could be added, or could replace the onion or celery. For something even more unusual, try coriander (seed or leaf), a small shake of cumin seeds or a star anise, but be careful not to go overboard. The success of a *court-bouillon* is partly that it reveals the subtleties of the fish at their best. It should not mask them.

Note that a *court-bouillon* needs to be made well in advance, so that it has time to cool down before use. Poaching nearly always begins with the fish in a bath of cold water.

110ml (4 fl oz) dry white wine
1 bay leaf
2 fresh thyme branches
1 carrot, thinly sliced
1 onion, sliced
1 celery stick
8 black peppercorns
1.15 litres (2 pints) water
salt

Put all the ingredients into a pan, season with a little salt and bring up to the boil. Simmer for 30 minutes, then cool and strain.

Fish Stock

Of all stocks, fish stock is the easiest and quickest to make. It takes no more than about 30 minutes – indeed, you should never cook it for any longer or it may turn bitter. A good stock makes an enormous difference to fish soups, sauces and stews, giving them an intensity and depth that is hard to match any other way.

Once made, fish stock can be stored in the fridge for two to three days. Any more than that and you must boil it hard for 5 minutes, then let it cool and return it to the fridge. If you are an organised cook with a good memory, this will be no hassle. I, on the other hand, find it far more convenient to reduce the stock and freeze it in cubes, which I use just like any other stock cube (see Reduced Fish Stock below).

Whenever you are cooking fillets of fish, ask your fishmonger for the bones, skin and head as well. Even if you don't have time to make stock that day, you can pop them in a bag in the freezer and, when you've accumulated plenty of bones and the time to spare, thaw them out and make stock at your leisure.

Most sorts of fish bones and debris (but not the innards, I hasten to say) are fine for stock, though you should avoid those of oily fish, such as mackerel or herring. With a good haul of turbot or Dover sole bones, you're really winning.

MAKES ABOUT 1.5 LITRES (2½ PINTS)

700g–1kg (1½–2¼ lb) fish bones, heads and skin
1 generous glass of white wine (around
    110–150ml/4–5 fl oz)
1 large carrot, thickly sliced
1 onion, thickly sliced
2 celery sticks, thickly sliced
6 black peppercorns
1 fresh thyme sprig
1 bay leaf
2 fresh parsley stems

Put the bones and bits into a large pan, breaking or cutting them up to fit easily. Add all the remaining ingredients. Place over a moderate heat and let the wine bubble for about 3 minutes. Now add enough water to cover generously. Bring up to the boil and then simmer, uncovered, for 20–25 minutes, skimming off the scum.

Draw off the heat and strain.

Reduced Fish Stock

In some recipes I list 'reduced fish stock' amongst the ingredients. This is a magic way to make a sauce, giving instant body and flavour. You hardly need anything else. To make it, pour your fish stock into a wide, deep frying pan and boil it down hard until reduced by about two-thirds to three-quarters. Judge by tasting a little of it: the flavour should be marvellously intense and it should feel sticky, syrupy and rich in the mouth. Draw off the heat, and pour into a bowl before it cools down completely. It can be stored, covered, in the fridge for about four days. Better still, freeze it.

To Freeze Fish Stock

To save space in the freezer, I usually reduce my stock as above, taking it down even stronger if possible, without burning it. Before I begin, I make a note of the quantity of unreduced stock. After it has cooled slightly, I pour it into an ice-cube tray, leave it to finish cooling, and then freeze. Finally, I turn out the frozen cubes and pop them into a plastic bag, with a note of how much stock I had originally and how many cubes it made, so that I can work out how much water to add when they are thawed out, to transform them back into stock.

Quick Hollandaise

This is the processor version, almost, if not absolutely, as good as the traditional hand-made version, and a good deal quicker and less temperamental. Since the egg yolks are not cooked, there is the most minute chance that they might be tainted with salmonella. For most of us I would say that the risk is so minimal that we shouldn't worry, but don't offer it to the very young, the very old, pregnant women or invalids, who would suffer far more than people in rude health in the rare event of infection. If you are at all worried, make a *Beurre Blanc* (see page 302) instead.

SERVES 4

110g (4 oz) unsalted butter
2 egg yolks
1½ tablespoons water
lemon juice or tarragon vinegar
salt and pepper

Heat the butter until melted and hot, but draw off the heat before it begins to colour. Put the egg yolks, water, salt, pepper and a small slug of lemon juice or vinegar in a food processor and process until smoothly amalgamated. Keep the motor running and start trickling the butter in, very lazily and slowly. When you have incorporated about half of it, add a dash more lemon or vinegar and then carry on with the butter, increasing the flow slightly. Stop pouring when you get down to the cloudy sediment at the bottom of the pan. Taste and adjust the seasoning and then pour into a warm bowl. If not serving absolutely immediately, set the bowl over a pan of hot, but not simmering, water to keep it warm, making sure that the base does not come into contact with the water. Serve as soon as possible.

Variations

Sauce Maltaise: Stir in the finely grated zest and juice of ½ blood orange.

Sauce Paloise: Stir in finely chopped fresh mint to taste.

Simplified Sauce Béarnaise: Use tarragon vinegar and stir in about 2 teaspoons of chopped fresh tarragon leaves.

Mayonnaise

Mayonnaise is about the most important cold mother sauce. Lovely served just as it is (assuming it has been made with good-quality oils), it is also the base for countless flavoured sauces, from the garlicky *aïoli* of France or its Spanish counterpart, *alioli* (see page 257), to our own favourite Tartare Sauce (see page 312). These days, ready-made mayonnaise at its best can be delicious, and I see no shame in using one of the better brands for everyday purposes. Though mayonnaise is not as difficult to make as many people imagine, it is not such a quick number to conjure up either, particularly when children, friends, family, the washing, the dog, the cat, and the rest of a meal are all clamouring for your attention.

Still, it is worth making the real McCoy from time to time because, however good bottled mayonnaises may be, they can never quite match a freshly whisked mayonnaise, with its lovely eggy taste and heavenly, light richness. Though you can add all sorts of things to a bought mayonnaise, you cannot change its basic substance. When you make your own, you can choose between vinegar or lemon or lime juice for sharpness, you can make it neutral with sunflower oil, add just the right amount of olive oil to suit your taste (I never use more than half, since I find that too much renders a peculiar, unwelcome bitterness), or go wild with lemon olive oil, sesame oil or even a little nut oil. Thin it down, or leave it thick as jelly, wobbling and glistening with a come-hither look about it.

When you have splashed out on a feast of perfect, sea-scented, sweet, juicy shellfish, there are few finer ways to enjoy them than settling down with napkins aplenty, finger bowls for sticky fingers and big bowls of buttercup-yellow, lemony mayonnaise, made by your own hand. It would be a shame to downgrade such a glorious occasion with second best.

However, one word of warning. Mayonnaise is made with raw egg yolks and, though the chances of them being infected with salmonella are, these days, verging on negligible, it is still possible. The very elderly, the very young, pregnant women and invalids should all steer clear of home-made mayonnaise and stick to the bought stuff, which will have been rendered completely safe.

MAKES ABOUT 300ML (½ PINT)

2 egg yolks
1 tablespoon lemon juice or white wine vinegar
1 teaspoon Dijon mustard
300ml (½ pint) oil (I usually go for about
    110–150ml/4–5 fl oz extra virgin olive oil
    mixed with 150–200ml/5–7 fl oz sunflower,
    groundnut, grapeseed or safflower oil)
salt

Before you begin, make sure that all the ingredients are at room temperature. Whisk the egg yolks with the lemon juice or vinegar, mustard and a little salt. Pour the oil(s) into a jug. Whisking continuously, add the oils drip by drip, at a slow, measured pace. Be patient. Be strong. If your bowl starts skittering all over the table, wrap a tea towel round the base to steady it a little. When about one-third of the oil is incorporated, you can increase the flow of oil to a slow, steady trickle, still whisking, whisking, whisking. When it is all incorporated, taste and adjust the seasonings, adding a splash more lemon or vinegar if it needs it.

Help! If the worst comes to the worst and your sauce splits and curdles, all is not lost. Get a new egg yolk, put it in a clean bowl and start adding the curdled mayonnaise, again drop by drop, whisking constantly. Carry on as if making uncurdled mayonnaise.

Variations

Lemon Mayonnaise: This is far and away my favourite mayonnaise for serving with shellfish. Make your mayonnaise as above, using lemon juice for sharpness, and 200ml (7 fl oz) of sunflower or other neutral oil, mixed with 110ml (4 fl oz) lemon olive oil. Lemon olive oil is available from delicatessens and some larger supermarkets and is made by pressing the olives and lemons together, so that the citrus oil from the zest of the lemons is naturally blended with the oil. It is miraculous stuff, and brilliant with all kinds of fish, just lightly drizzled over. You can also buy orange and mandarin olive oils, made in the same fashion.

Orange Mayonnaise (Maltese Mayonnaise): Make a mayonnaise in the usual fashion, flavouring it with lemon juice and treading lightly with the olive oil. If you can find orange olive oil, incorporate a generous splash of that, too. When it is done, stir in the finely grated zest of 1 orange and enough freshly squeezed orange juice to flavour it to your taste. Blood orange juice, in winter, gives it a particularly dramatic hue. Seville orange juice adds the most exquisite flavour of all. With that extra liquid in it, this mayonnaise will have a sloppier consistency than normal.

Saffron Mayonnaise: Before you begin whisking, put a generous pinch of saffron strands into a small bowl and add a tablespoon of hot water. Leave to infuse while you whisk up your mayonnaise. Stir it in when the mayonnaise is done.

Tarragon Mayonnaise: Put about 2–3 teaspoons of roughly chopped fresh tarragon leaves in a bowl. Cover with boiling water and leave for 1 minute. Drain well and pound to a rough paste with a pinch of salt in a bowl large enough to make the mayonnaise in. Then add the egg yolk, high-quality tarragon vinegar and a hint of mustard. Mix thoroughly and proceed as usual. When the mayonnaise is made, taste and add a little more tarragon vinegar or some chopped fresh tarragon, if you think it needs it.

Sauce Marie Rose: The prawn cocktail sauce! Pretty and pink and, when it is made with home-made mayonnaise, really rather good with all kinds of shellfish and cold fish. It was, I believe, invented by chef Filippo Ferraro of the Berkeley Hotel. Mix 300ml (½ pint) of mayonnaise with 2 tablespoons of tomato ketchup, a few drops of Tabasco sauce, 1–2 teaspoonfuls of Worcestershire sauce and a dash of lemon juice. Taste and adjust the balance of seasoning and Bob's your uncle.

Tartare Sauce

Common as muck it may have become but when it is made freshly, with good mayonnaise (brilliant if it is home-made, but high-quality bought mayo is absolutely fine), tartare sauce is fabulous. Serve it with fish and chips, *goujons*, fried catfish (see page 264), in fact any fried fish, or indeed with grilled fish steaks or even steamed fish.

If you use salted capers, rinse them and then soak in cold water for about 20 minutes to soften their saltiness. Taste the sauce before adding any more salt.

SERVES 4

200ml (7 fl oz) mayonnaise
20g (2/3 oz) shallots, very finely chopped
1/2 tablespoon chopped fresh chives
1 tablespoon chopped fresh parsley
1/2 tablespoon chopped fresh chervil (if you can get it)
1 teaspoon chopped fresh tarragon
1 1/2 tablespoons capers, rinsed and roughly chopped
1 tablespoon chopped pickled *cornichons* or 2/3 tablespoon chopped pickled gherkins
salt and pepper

Mix all the ingredients together. Taste and adjust the seasoning.

Apricot and Chilli Blatjang

Don't ignore this sauce just because it is made in seconds with a jar of apricot jam. It is a superb dipping sauce for all kinds of food, especially fried or grilled fish. Serve it with meat and poultry as well, or even use it as a sticky marinade, brushing it on to chicken drumsticks or pork or lamb chops before grilling or baking.

SERVES 6–8

6 medium-hot fresh red chillies, de-seeded and roughly chopped
4 garlic cloves, chopped
225g (8 oz) apricot jam
6 tablespoons white wine vinegar
1/2 teaspoon salt

Put all the ingredients into a food processor or liquidiser and blend until smooth. This sweet, hot and sharp sauce will keep for up to two weeks in a covered container in the fridge.

FISH
CHART
AND
INDEX

International Fish Chart

The following chart provides a list of alternative fish, where available.
The yield indicates the approximate proportion of meat to the whole fish.

FLAKY FISH	YIELD: IN %	USA/CANADA	AUSTRALIA
COD	50	COD	NEW ZEALAND COD
COLEY	60	POLLOCK, COD	ROCK COD, CORAL TROUT, BARRACOUTA
HADDOCK	50	BLUE COD, HOKI	ROCK COD, CORAL TROUT, BARRACOUTA
HAKE	60	HAKE, SILVER HAKE	HAKE, GEMFISH
LING	55	CUSK, LING COBIA	ROCK LING
POLLACK	55	POLLOCK	NEW ZEALAND COD
POUT	50	COD, WHITING	ROCK COD, CORAL TROUT, BARRACOUTA
WHITING	50	WHITING	KING GEORGE WHITING
INSHORE			
CONGER EEL	60	CONGER EEL	CONGER, BLUE GRENADIER
JOHN DORY	35	JOHN DORY, OREO JOHN DORY	JOHN DORY
GREY MULLET	55	MULLET, STRIPED BASS	SEA MULLET, FLAT-TAIL MULLET, GROPER, CORAL TROUT
GURNARD	40	SEA ROBIN	RED GURNARD, CORAL TROUT
MONKFISH	65	MONKFISH, ANGLERFISH	STARGAZER, MONKFISH
RASCASSE	35	SCORPION FISH, ROCKFISH	SCORPION FISH, MONK, STARGAZER
RED MULLET	50	GOATFISH	RED MULLET, BARBOUNIA, BLACKSPOT GOATFISH
SEA BASS	50	SEA BASS	GROPER, DHU FISH, SEA & PEARL PERCH
SEA BREAM	50	SNAPPER	EMPEROR, SNAPPER, SEA BREAM
GILT-HEAD BREAM	50	SNAPPER	EMPEROR, SNAPPER, SEA BREAM
WEEVER	40		STARGAZER, MONK
WRASSE	40	WRASSE, TAUTOG, HOGFISH	LUDERICK
CARTILAGINOUS			
SKATES AND RAYS	50	SKATE	SKATE
DOGFISH	75	SHARK	SHARK, FLAKE, ELEPHANT FISH
BLUE SHARK	40	SHARK	SHARK, FLAKE, ELEPHANT FISH
MAKO SHARK	40	SHARK	SHARK, FLAKE, ELEPHANT FISH
PORBEAGLE	40	SHARK	SHARK, FLAKE, ELEPHANT FISH
TOPE	40	SHARK	SHARK, FLAKE, ELEPHANT FISH
FLAT			
BRILL	50	PETRALE SOLE, BRILL	FLOUNDER, SOLE
DAB	50	FLOUNDER, SOLE	FLOUNDER, SOLE
FLOUNDER	50	FLOUNDER, SOLE	FLOUNDER, SOLE
HALIBUT	60	HALIBUT	GEMFISH, GROPER, WAREHOU
LEMON SOLE	60	ENGLISH SOLE, FLOUNDER	FLOUNDER, SOLE
MEGRIM	50	FLOUNDER, SOLE	FLOUNDER, SOLE
PLAICE	50	FLOUNDER, SOLE	FLOUNDER, SOLE
DOVER SOLE	55	ENGLISH SOLE, GRAY SOLE	FLOUNDER, SOLE
TURBOT	35	FLOUNDER, SOLE	FLOUNDER, SOLE
WITCH	50	FLOUNDER, SOLE	FLOUNDER, SOLE
HERRINGS ETC			
ANCHOVY	60	ANCHOVY	ANCHOVY
HERRING	50	HERRING	HERRING
SARDINE	50	SARDINE	SARDINE, PILCHARD
SPRAT		SMELT	SPRAT
WHITEBAIT		SMELT, WHITEBAIT	WHITEBAIT
WARM-WATER AND REEF			
BARRACUDA	60	BARRACUDA	BARRACOUTA, GEMFISH
BOURGEOIS	45	SNAPPER, PORGY	EMPEROR, SNAPPER, SEA BREAM
CAPITAINE	45	SNAPPER, PORGY	EMPEROR, SNAPPER, SEA BREAM
EMPEROR	45	SNAPPER, PORGY	EMPEROR, SNAPPER, SEA BREAM
FLYINGFISH	60	FLYING FISH	
GROUPER	40	GROUPER, BLACK SEA BASS	GROPER, DHU FISH, PEARL PERCH
JOBFISH	50	SNAPPER, PORGY	EMPEROR, SNAPPER, SEA BREAM
PARROTFISH	45	TAUTOG	TUSKFISH
POMFRET	40	POMPANOS, BUTTERFISH	TREVALLY
SNAPPER	50	SNAPPER, PORGY	EMPEROR, SNAPPER, SEA BREAM
TUNA ETC			
ALBACORE	60	ALBACORE TUNA	ALBACORE
BIGEYE	60	BIGEYE TUNA	BIGEYE
BLUEFIN	50	BLUEFIN TUNA	SOUTHERN BLUEFIN, LONGTAIL TUNA
SKIPJACK	65	SKIPJACK TUNA	SKIPJACK
YELLOWFIN	60	YELLOWFIN, AHI	YELLOWFIN
BONITO	50	BONITO	BONITO
BLUEFISH	55	BLUEFISH	BLUEFISH, TAILOR, SKIPJACK

NZ	SOUTH AFRICA (ENG)	AFRIKAANS
BLUE COD, BARRACOUTA, HOKI, DEEP SEA COD	ROCKCOD	KLIPKABELJOU
BLUE COD, BARRACOUTA, HOKI, DEEP SEA COD	ROCKCOD	KLIPKABELJOU
BLUE COD, BARRACOUTA, HOKI, DEEP SEA COD	ROCKCOD	KLIPKABELJOU
HAKE	CAPE HAKE	STOKVISSE
LING	KINGCLIP, KOB	KONINGKLIPVIS
BLUE COD, BARRACOUTA, HOKI, DEEP SEA COD	ROCKCOD	KLIPKABELJOU
BLUE COD, BARRACOUTA, HOKI, DEEP SEA COD	ROCKCOD	KLIPKABELJOU
SOUTHERN BLUE WHITING	ROCKCOD	KLIPKABELJOU
CONGER, BLUE GRENADIER	CAPE CONGER EEL	KAAPSE SEEPALING
JOHN DORY	JOHN JOH DORY	JANDORIE
GREY MULLET, GROPER, CORAL TROUT	MULLET	HARDER
RED GURNARD	GURNARD	KNOORHAAN
MONKFISH	MONK	MONNIK
SEA PERCH	SCORPION FISH	SKERPJOENVIS
	RED MULLET, GOATFISH	BOKVIS
GROPER	SEA BASS, ROCKCOD	SEEBAARSE, KLIPKABELJOU
SEA BREAM, SNAPPER, TARAKIHI	SEA BREAM, SNAPPER	SEA BRASSE, SNAPPER
SEA BREAM, SNAPPER, TARAKIHI	SEA BREAM, SNAPPER	SEA BRASSE, SNAPPER
MONK	STARGAZER	OPKYKER
KAHAWAI	WRASSE	LIPVIS
SKATE	SKATE	ROG
RIG, ELEPHANT FISH, SHARK	DOGFISH	PENHAAI
RIG, ELEPHANT FISH, SHARK	BLUE SHARK	BLOUHAAI
RIG, ELEPHANT FISH, SHARK	MAKO	MAKO
RIG, ELEPHANT FISH, SHARK	SHARK	HAAI
RIG, ELEPHANT FISH, SHARK	SHARK	HAAI
SOLE, TURBOT	SOLE	TONGVIS
FLOUNDER, BRILL, SOLE	FLOUNDER	BOTVIS
FLOUNDER, BRILL, SOLE	FLOUNDER	BOTVIS
GROPER	SOLE	TONGVIS
LEMON SOLE	SOLE	TONGVIS
FLOUNDER, BRILL, SOLE	FLOUNDER	BOTVIS
FLOUNDER, BRILL, SOLE	FLOUNDER	BOTVIS
NEW ZEALAND SOLE	SOLE	TONGVIS
TURBOT, SOLE	SOLE	TONGVIS
FLOUNDER, BRILL, SOLE	FLOUNDER	BOTVIS
ANCHOVY	ANCHOVY	ANSJOVIS
PILCHARD, SPRAT	HERRING	HARING
SARDINE, PILCHARD	SARDINE, PILCHARD	PELSER, SARDYN
SPRAT	SARDINE, PILCHARD	PELSER, SARDYN
WHITEBAIT	WHITEBAIT	VLEISARDIENTJIE
BARRACOUTA, GEMFISH	BARRACUDA, SNOEK	BARRACUDA, SNOEK
SEA BREAM, SNAPPER, TARAKIHI	SEA BREAM, SNAPPER	SEEBAARSE, SNAPPER
SEA BREAM, SNAPPER, TARAKIHI	SEA BREAM, SNAPPER	SEEBAARSE, SNAPPER
SEA BREAM, SNAPPER, TARAKIHI	BLUE EMPEROR	BLOUKEISER
	FLYING FISH	VLIEËNDE VIS
GROPER	ROCKCOD, WRECKFISH, JACOPEVER	KLIPKABELJOU, WRAKVIS, JAKOPEWER
SNAPPER	GREEN JOBFISH	GROEN JOBVIS
PARROTFISH	PARROTFISH	PAPEGAAOVOSSE
TREVALLY, WAREHOU	POMFRET, ANGEL FISH	POMFRET, ENGELVIS
SNAPPER	SEA BREAM, SNAPPER	SEEBAARSE, SNAPPER
ALBACORE TUNA	ALBACORE	ALBAKOOR
BIGEYE TUNA	BIGEYE TUNA	GROOTOOGTUNA
SOUTHERN BLUEFIN	BLUEFIN TUNA	BLOOVINTUNA
SKIPJACK	SKIPJACK TUNA	PENSSTREEPTUNA
YELLOWFIN TUNA	YELLOWFIN TUNA	GEELVINTUNA
SKIPJACK	ATLANTIC BONITO	ATLANTIESE BONITO
WAREHOU	SHAD, ELF	ELF

TUNA ETC	YIELD: IN %	USA/CANADA	AUSTRALIA
HORSE MACKEREL, SCAD	35	JACKMACKEREL, JACK	YELLOWTAIL SCAD
JACK	40	JACK, POMPANO	TREVALLY, BLUE EYE, TREVALLA
KINGFISH	60	SPANISH MACKEREL	BARRACOUTA
MACKEREL	60	MACKEREL	MACKEREL
MAHI MAHI	60	MAHI MAHI, DOLPHIN	YELLOWTAIL KINGFISH
MARLIN	60	MARLIN	MARLIN
SWORDFISH	60	SWORDFISH	SWORDFISH
YELLOWTAIL	50	AMBERJACK	KINGFISH, YELLOWTAIL
MIGRANTS			
EEL	60	EEL	EEL
SALMON	70	SALMON	ATLANTIC SALMON, OCEAN TROUT (FARMED)
SEA TROUT	65	STEELHEAD TROUT	ATLANTIC SALMON, OCEAN TROUT (FARMED)
DEEP AND DISTANT			
GRENADIER		HOKI, RATTAIL	WAREHOU, GROPER, ROCK COD, GEMFISH
HOKI		HOKI	WAREHOU, GROPER, ROCK COD, GEMFISH
ORANGE ROUGHY		ORANGE ROUGHY	ORANGE ROUGHY, RUFFY
REDFISH	35	OCEAN PERCH	REDFISH, NANNYGAI
SCABBARD			
TOOTHFISH		TOOTHFISH	WAREHOU, GROPER, ROCK COD, GEMFISH
SHELLFISH			
ABALONE		ABALONE, PAUA	PAUA
CONCH			
WINKLE		PERIWINKLE	PERIWINKLE
AMANDE		PIPI	PIPI
CLAM		CLAM	PIPI
COCKLE		COCKLE	COCKLE
MUSSEL		BLUE MUSSEL	MUSSEL, GREEN MUSSEL
OYSTER		OYSTER	ROCK OYSTER
PALOURDE		PIPI	PIPI, TUATUA
PRAIRE		PIPI	PIPI, TUATUA
RAZORSHELL		RAZOR CLAM	RAZOR CLAM
SCALLOP		SEA SCALLOP, BAY SCALLOP	SCALLOP
SEA URCHIN		SEA URCHIN	SEA URCHIN
SURF CLAM		PIPI	PIPI, TUATUA
TELLINE		PIPI	PIPI, TUATUA
VENUS CLAM		SURF CLAM	PIPI
VERNI		PIPI	PIPI, TUATUA
QUEEN SCALLOP		BAY SCALLOP	SCALLOP
CRUSTACEANS			
COMMON CRAB		DUNGENESS CRAB, STONE CRAB	BLUE SWIMMER CRAB, RED SPOT CRAB
SOFT SHELL CRAB		SOFT SHELL CRAB	
SPIDER CRAB		SPIDER, SNOW CRAB	SOUTHERN SPIDER CRAB
SHORE CRAB		BLUE CRAB	BLUE SWIMMER CRAB, RED SPOT CRAB
FRESHWATER CRAYFISH	15	CRAYFISH, CRAWFISH	YABBIES, MARRON
CRAYFISH, CRAWFISH	30	SPINY LOBSTER	ROCK LOBSTER
LANGOUSTINE	20	NORWAY LOBSTER	SCAMPI, YABBIES, MARRON
LOBSTER	30	LOBSTER	ROCK LOBSTER, BUGS
SLIPPER LOBSTER		SLIPPER LOBSTER	BUGS
COMMON PRAWN		PRAWN	PRAWN
DEEP-WATER PRAWN		PRAWN	PRAWN
MEDITERRANEAN PRAWN		PRAWN	PRAWN
BROWN SHRIMP		SHRIMP	SMALL PRAWN
SQUID ETC			
CUTTLEFISH	80	CUTTLE, SQUID	CUTTLEFISH
OCTOPUS	90	OCTOPUS	OCTOPUS
SQUID	80	SQUID, CALAMARI	SQUID
FRESHWATER			
BREAM	35	BREAM	BREAM
CARP	35	CARP	CARP
CATFISH	40	CATFISH	CATFISH, COBBLER
CHAR	65	CHAR	OCEAN TROUT, MURRAY COD, CORAL TROUT
LAMPREY	60	LAMPREY	
NILE PERCH	50	NILE PERCH	BARRAMUNDI, BARRACOUTA
PERCH	40	PERCH	EUROPEAN PERCH, GOLDEN PERCH
PIKE	50	PIKE	BARRAMUNDI
SMELT		SMELT	WHITEBAIT
STURGEON	50	STURGEON, PADDLEFISH	
TILAPIA	40	TILAPIA	MURRAY COD, CORAL TROUT
TROUT	55	TROUT	BROOK TROUT
ZANDER	50	ZANDER, WALLEY	BARRAMUNDI, AUSTRALIAN BASS, MURRAY COD

NZ	SOUTH AFRICA (ENG)	AFRIKAANS
JACK MACKEREL	SCAD, CAPE HORSE MACKEREL.	SKAD, MAASBANKER
TREVALLY	KINGFISH	KONINGVIS
BARRACOUTA	BARRACUDA, SNOEK	BARRAKUDA, SNOEK
MACKEREL	CHUB MACKEREL	MACKRIEL
YELLOWTAIL KINGFISH	DOLPHIN FISH	DORADE
MARLIN	MARLIN	MARLYN
SWORDFISH	SWORDFISH	SWAARDVIS
YELLOWTAIL KINGFISH, NORTHERN KINGFISH	YELLOWTAIL	GEELSTERT
EEL	EEL	PALING
QUINNAT SALMON	SALMON	SALMON
QUINNAT SALMON	ATLANTIC SALMON	SALMON
GRENADIER, BLUE GRENADIER	RATTAIL	ROTSTERTVIS
HOKI	RATTAIL	ROTSTERTVIS
ORANGE ROUGHY	ORANGE ROUGHY	SLYMKOP
KAHAWAI	JACOPEVER	JAKOPEWER
FROSTFISH	CUTLASS	HAARSTERT
WAREHOU, GROPER, ROCK COD, GEMFISH	PATAGONIAN TOOTHFISH	PATAGONIAN TOOTHFISH
ABALONE	PERLEMOEN	
	PERIWINKLE	ALIKREUKELTJIE
PIPI, TUATUA		
COCKLE		
BLUE MUSSEL, GREENSHELL MUSSEL	MUSSEL	MOSSEL
ROCK OYSTER	OYSTER	OESTER
RAZOR CLAM		
SCALLOP		
SEA EGG		
PIPI		
SCALLOP		
COMMON SWIMMING CRAB	CRAB	KRAP
	CRAB	KRAP
SOUTHERN SPIDER CRAB		
COMMON SWIMMING CRAB		
ROCK LOBSTER		
SCAMPI		
ROCK LOBSTER	ROCK LOBSTER	
ROCK LOBSTER		
PRAWN	PRAWN	
PRAWN	PRAWN	
PRAWN	PRAWN	
PRAWN	SHRIMP	
BROAD SQUID	CUTTLEFISH	INKVIS
OCTOPUS	OCTOPUS	SEEKAT
SQUID	SQUID	TJOKKA
BREAM	BREAM	
CARP		
CATFISH		
BARRAMUNDI		

Index